THE WORLD ALMANAC®
InfoPedia

THE WORLD ALMANAC®
InfoPedia
A Visual
Encyclopedia for
Students

Compiled by
Theodore Rowland-Entwistle and Jean Cooke
Other Contributors
David Lambert and Jill Thomas

WORLD ALMANAC
AN IMPRINT OF PHAROS BOOKS • A SCRIPPS HOWARD COMPANY
NEW YORK

Compiled by Theodore Rowland-Entwhistle
and Jean Cooke
Other Contributors: David Lambert and Jill Thomas
Editor: Rachel Pilcher

Library of Congress Cataloging-in-Publication Data

The World almanac's infopedia : a visual encyclopedia
    for students / editors of the World almanac
        p.   cm.
    Summary: An illustrated encyclopedia of concise
articles for students of all ages, covering such major
areas as the universe, history, the human body,
animals, plants, art and entertainment, and sports.
    ISBN 0-88687-500-5 : $17.95. —
    ISBN 0-88687-476-9 (pbk.) : $8.95
    1. Children's encyclopedias and dictionaries. [1.
Encyclopedias and dictionaries.] I. Title: World almanac.
AG5.W835   1990
031 — dc20   90-30435
                                                        CIP
                                                        AC

Cover Design: Bea Jackson
Interior Design: Michele Arron and Clare Finlaison

World Almanac
An Imprint of Pharos Books
A Scripps Howard Company
200 Park Avenue
New York, New York 10166

Printed in the United States of America

10 9 8 7 6 5 4 3 2 1

Contents

The Universe 6

Planet Earth 28

Countries of the World 46

History 110

Human Body 150

Animals 170

Plants 207

Science and Technology 222

Transport 254

Communications 280

Arts and Entertainment 296

Sport 333

Miscellany 357

Index 372

The Universe

The universe is still a mystery to people. Was it really formed 15 billion years ago in one gigantic "Big Bang"? Is the explosion still continuing as planets, asteroids, comets, moons, and billions upon billions of stars hurtle farther into deepest space?

Stars are vast spheres of gas that burn with different colored light. Our Sun is a star and planet Earth spins around it, kept in orbit by gravity. Other stars give off no light: these are the "black holes." Their gravitational force is so strong that even light waves are sucked into them.

All the stars, planets, and other bodies we see in the heavens are known as the universe. Stars are huge spheres of gas that give off light and heat. Our Sun is a typical medium-sized star. It looks so much larger than other stars because it is close to the Earth.

The distances between stars are so vast that the easiest way to measure them is in terms of the time it takes their light to reach us. The Sun's light takes 8 minutes 20 seconds to travel to the Earth. The light from the next nearest star, called Proxima Centauri, takes 4 years 15½ weeks, or 4.3 light-years. The most distant stars are billions of light-years away.

The countless stars?
Nobody knows for certain, but astronomers think there are at least 200 billion billion stars – that is 2 with twenty zeros after it. Some stars are much smaller than the Sun, and are known as dwarf stars. Others are between 100 and 1,000 times bigger, and are known as supergiants. Stars between 10 and 100 times the size of the Sun are called giants.

All stars have one thing in common: the force known as gravitation. Every object has this force, and pulls other objects toward it.

△ Quasars are the most distant objects we know. Each is about 100 times brighter than the brightest galaxies in our local star clusters. Quasar 3C 273, about 600 million light-years away, is one of the closest and brightest quasars known.

The power of gravity depends on the mass of the object – that is, how much material it contains. On Earth, the effect of gravity is that if you let go of something, such as a ball, it falls to the ground, because the Earth's gravitational force is much stronger than that of the ball. A large star that is mostly gas may have less gravitational force than a small, more solid star.

△ How the Milky Way might appear from Earth if the solar system were a few hundred light-years above the Galaxy's arms. In fact, the fierce energy waves from the blazing center would have prevented life from developing on Earth.

Black holes, quasars, and pulsars

There are many different kinds of star. They shine with different-colored light, ranging from white through blue and yellow to red. Some white stars are called white dwarfs. Their gravitational force has shrunk them, making them small and dense. Some stars that give off no light at all are believed to exist. They are called black holes. Their gravitational force is so strong that even light waves cannot escape from them.

There are numbers of star-like bodies in the heavens which are still a mystery. Quasars – short for quasi (almost) star-like objects – give off strong radio waves. Pulsars are similar, but send out their radio waves in regular pulses. There are also stars that give off X-rays, and others that emit heat rather than light.

▽ A pulsar, like this one in the Crab Nebula, is the spinning remains of a supernova, an exploding star. The beam of light and radio waves makes a pulse, like the circling beam of a lighthouse.

△ Astronomers use radio telescopes to collect signals from objects too far away to be seen through ordinary telescopes. This radio telescope at Parkes Observatory in Australia has a collecting dish 210 feet (64 meters) across.

Star clusters

Many stars are grouped in clusters called constellations. A major group of stars, containing many millions, is called a galaxy. We are part of a galaxy called the Milky Way. It has that name because some of its stars form a vast, milky-looking band of light across the night sky. It is a huge, spinning disk made of stars, about 100,000 light-years across. Our Sun is about 30,000 light-years from the center of the disk. There are millions of galaxies – we just do not know how many.

Planets, asteroids, and comets

A planet is a heavenly body that revolves around a star. Our Sun has nine major planets revolving around it, forming the solar system. The Earth is one of the planets. A planet does not give off its own light, like a star, but shines with light reflected from the Sun.

There is also a group of small bodies, called the minor planets, or asteroids. They are found between the orbits of the major planets Mars and Jupiter. All but three of the major planets – Mercury, Venus, and Pluto – have small, planet-like satellites revolving around them. They are called moons. The Earth has just one satellite, called the Moon, but other planets have several.

▽ The diagram below shows the orbits of the main asteroids. These minor planets are small and, though much closer to the Earth than the stars, are difficult to detect in the night sky.

Finally, the solar system contains some wandering bodies called comets. They have very long, elliptical orbits, and shoot away into space after looping around the Sun. Some return after a few years, others not for thousands of years. Comets have been described as "dirty snowballs," consisting of a mixture of dust, gas, and particles of ice.

How old is the universe?

The universe is thought to be at least 15 billion years old. Many scientists think that before that time all matter was collected together in one large ball, a sort of super black hole. Then there was an explosion, called the "Big Bang." Matter was scattered in all directions.

From that matter all the stars were formed. According to one theory, the effects of the Big Bang are still going on, and stars and galaxies are still spreading out from the center of the explosion. Certainly, the galaxies are moving away from each other at high speed.

However, other astronomers believe there never was a Big Bang, and that the universe has always been roughly like it is today.

△ People have always been excited, and often alarmed, by the sight of a visiting comet. Halley's comet was seen over Jerusalem in the year A.D. 66.

△ Halley's comet photographed from South Africa in 1910. It returns close to the Earth every 76 years.

The Constellations

A constellation is a group of conspicuous stars that are found in a particular portion of the night sky. Altogether there are 88 constellations. Of these, 48 can be seen from the northern half of the Earth or from the lands around the Equator.

Astronomers use the constellations as sky landmarks for fixing the position, not only of their own stars, but of any others that are detected with powerful telescopes.

The ancient Greeks gave the constellations the names of real and mythical beasts and their gods and heroes, because they imagined they saw patterns of stars that fitted these names. The patterns have changed since then.

When the constellations of the southern hemisphere were discovered later, astronomers gave them similar names. The names are in Latin, because for centuries all scholarly books were written in that language.

CONSTELLATIONS

Latin name	English name	Latin name	English name
Andromeda	Andromeda	Lacerta	Lizard
Antlia	Air Pump	Leo	Lion
Apus	Bird of Paradise	Leo Minor	Little Lion
Aquarius	Water Bearer	Lepus	Hare
Aquila	Eagle	Libra	Scales
Ara	Altar	Lupus	Wolf
Argo Navis	Ship Argo	Lynx	Lynx
Aries	Ram	Lyra	Lyre
Auriga	Charioteer	Mensa	Table
Boötes	Herdsman	Microscopium	Microscope
Caeium	Chisel	Monoceros	Unicorn
Camelopardus	Giraffe	Musca	Fly
Cancer	Crab	Norma	Rule (straightedge)
Canes Venatici	Hunting Dogs	Octans	Octant
Canis Major	Great Dog	Ophichus	Serpent-beater
Canis Minor	Little Dog	Orion	Orion (hunter)
Capricornus	Sea-Goat	Pavo	Peacock
Carina	Keel (of Argo)	Pegasus	Pegasus (winged horse)
Cassiopeia	Cassiopeia	Perseus	Perseus
Centaurus	Centaur	Phoenix	Phoenix
Cepheus	Cepheus	Pictor	Painter (or Easel)
Cetus	Whale	Pisces	Fishes
Chamaeleon	Chameleon	Piscis Austrinus	Southern Fish
Circinus	Compasses (art)	Puppis	Stern (deck)
Columba	Dove	Pyxis	Mariner's Compass
Coma Berenices	Berenice's Hair	Reticulum	Net
Corona Australis	Southern Crown	Sagitta	Arrow
Corona Borealis	Northern Crown	Sagittarius	Archer
Corvus	Crow	Scorpius	Scorpion
Crater	Cup	Sculptor	Sculptor
Crux	Southern Cross	Scutum	Shield
Cygnus	Swan	Serpens	Serpent
Delphinus	Dolphin	Sextans	Sextant
Dorado	Swordfish	Taurus	Bull
Draco	Dragon	Telescopium	Telescope
Equuleus	Little Horse	Triangulum	Triangle
Eridanus	River Eridanus	Triangulum Australe	Southern Triangle
Fornax	Furnace	Tucana	Toucan
Gemini	Twins	Ursa Major	Great Bear
Grus	Crane	Ursa Minor	Little Bear
Hercules	Hercules	Vela	Sails (of Argo)
Horologium	Clock	Virgo	Virgin
Hydra	Sea-Serpent	Volans	Flying Fish
Hydrus	Waternake	Vulpecula	Fox
Indus	Indian		

1 Equuleus
2 Delphinus
3 Pegasus
4 Pisces
5 Cetus
6 Aries
7 Triangulum
8 Andromeda
9 Lacerta
10 Cygnus
11 Sagitta
12 Aquila
13 Lyra
14 Cepheus
15 Cassiopeia
16 Perseus
17 Camelopardus
18 Auriga
19 Taurus
20 Orion
21 Lynx
22 Polaris
23 Ursa Minor
24 Draco
25 Hercules
26 Ophiuchus
27 Serpens
28 Corona Borealis
29 Boötes
30 Ursa Major
31 Gemini
32 Cancer
33 Canis Minor
34 Hydra
35 Leo
36 Leo Minor
37 Canes Venatici
38 Coma Berenices
39 Virgo

**SOUTHERN
HEMISPHERE**

1 Cetus
2 Sculptor
3 Aquarius
4 Piscis Austrinus
5 Capricornus
6 Grus
7 Phoenix
8 Fornax
9 Eridanus
10 Hydrus
11 Tucana
12 Indus
13 Sagittarius
14 Aquila
15 Corona Australis
16 Pavo
17 Octans
18 Dorado
19 Pictor
20 Columba
21 Lepus
22 Orion
23 Monoceros
24 Canis Major
25 Puppis
26 Carina
27 Volans
28 Chamaeleon
29 Apus
40 Triangulum Australe
1 Ara
2 Scorpius
43 Serpens
4 Ophiuchus
5 Lupus
6 Centaurus
7 Crux
8 Musca
9 Vela
0 Pyxis
1 Hydra
2 Sextans
3 Crater
4 Corvus
5 Libra
6 Virgo

The positions of the constellations
of the northern and southern
hemispheres.

Stars and Galaxies

You can tell stars from planets because their light seems to twinkle. Planets, which merely reflect the Sun's light, shine with a steady glow. The stars appear to move across the sky, but really this apparent motion is produced by the rotation of the Earth, just like the seeming movement of the Sun. Every star is a great glowing atomic furnace. It consists mainly of the two lightest gases, hydrogen and helium, which are burning all the time.

Galaxies are systems of stars. These are real systems, not apparent ones like the constellations. Galaxies have two main shapes, an ellipse or a spiral. Our own galaxy, the Milky Way, is a spiral galaxy. The galaxies are moving away from each other at ever-increasing speed. We know this because the lines of the spectrum of the light from each galaxy have moved toward the color red, a phenomenon that astronomers term red shift.

THE NEAREST STARS	
Name	Distance (light-years)
Proxima Centauri	4.38
Alpha-Centauri A	4.37
Alpha-Centauri B	4.37
Barnard's Star	5.90
Wolf 359	7.60
Lalande 21185	8.13
Sirius A	8.80
Sirius B §	8.80
Luyten 726–8 A	8.88
UV Ceti	8.88
Ross 154	9.44
Ross 248	10.28
Epsilon-Eridani	10.76
Luyten 789–6	10.76
Ross 128	10.83
61 Cygni A	11.09
61 Cygni B	11.09
Epsilon-Indi	11.20
Procyon A	11.40
Procyon B §	11.40
Struve 2398 A	11.52
Struve 2398 B	11.52
§ White dwarf.	

▽ Galaxies exist in groups. Our Milky Way Galaxy belongs to what scientists call the Local Group, of about 30 galaxies. This diagram shows the galaxies so far discovered at their correct distances apart, although their sizes are not to scale. The Milky Way Galaxy and the Andromeda Galaxy are by far the largest members of the group. There is another smaller spiral galaxy, but the other galaxies are all elliptical dwarfs.

THE BRIGHTEST STARS

Name	Constellation	† Apparent magnitude	Distance (light-years)
Sun	—	−26.74	—
Sirius	Canis Major	−1.45	8.8
Canopus	Carina	−0.73	196
Rigil Kent	Centaurus	−0.10	4.37
Arcturus	Boötes	−0.06	37
Vega	Lyra	0.04	26
Capella	Auriga	0.08	46
Rigel	Orion	0.11	815
Procyon	Canis Minor	0.35	11.4
Achernar	Eridanus	0.48	127
Hadar	Centaurus	0.60	391
Altair	Aquila	0.77	16
Betelgeuse	Orion	0.80	652
Aldebaran	Taurus	0.85	68
Acrux	Crux	0.90	260
Spica	Virgo	0.96	261
Antares	Scorpius	1.00	424
Pollux	Gemini	1.15	36
Fomalhaut	Piscis Austrinus	1.16	23
Deneb	Cygnus	1.25	1630
Mimosa	Crux	1.26	490
Regulus	Leo	1.35	85

† A measure of brightness; the lower the number, the brighter the star.

△ There are millions of spiral galaxies, like our own Milky Way Galaxy. Each one turns very slowly, like a vast wheel of stars in space. This photograph of a nearby spiral galaxy gives us a good idea of what our own Galaxy must look like. The arms of this galaxy are more "open" than the arms of our own star system, however, and the central nucleus is smaller.

The Sun

The Sun provides us with light and heat, so it is extremely important to us. But it is really a very ordinary star, of the kind that astronomers call a "yellow dwarf." It has been shining for at least five billion years and it is certain to go on shining for at least five billion more.

Deep inside the Sun the temperature reaches millions of degrees. At such a temperature atoms of its main gas, hydrogen, join together to make the gas helium. This process is called fusion. Scientists are trying to make nuclear power plants here on Earth that will work in the same way.

The Sun's surface is seething as hot gases well up from underneath. On the surface we can see dark markings, known as sunspots. These spots come and go, and they appear to reach their maximum number every 11 years. The sunspots are about 3,600°F (2,000°C) cooler than the temperature of the rest of the Sun's surface. During sunspot activity the magnetic radiation from the Sun's surface changes. These changes cause interference with radio communications and compass needles on Earth.

Sunspot
Prominence

△ The Sun looks bright because it is intensely hot. Yet the surface is dim and cool compared to the interior, which has a temperature of about 27 million degrees F.

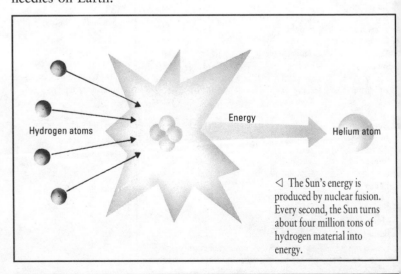

Hydrogen atoms

Energy

Helium atom

◁ The Sun's energy is produced by nuclear fusion. Every second, the Sun turns about four million tons of hydrogen material into energy.

Photosphere

Core

SUN STATISTICS

Diameter at equator: 865,000 miles (1,392,000 km)
Volume: 1,303,600 times Earth's volume
Mean density: 1.41 (water = 1)
Mass: 333,000 times Earth's mass
Gravity: 28 times Earth's gravity
Mean distance from Earth: 92,960,000 miles (149,000,000 km)
Escape velocity: 384 miles/sec (618 km/sec)
Surface temperature: 10,800°F (6,000°C)
Core temperature: circa 27,000,000°F (15,000,000°C)
Spins on axis in: 25.38 days
Orbits galaxy in: 225 million years
Speed of travel through space: 155 miles/sec (250 km/sec)
Distance from center of galaxy: 30,000 light-years
†Apparent magnitude: −26.74

† *A measure of brightness: the lower the number, the brighter the star.*

▽ The Sun's daily path
across the sky changes with
the seasons of the year. The
Sun is at its highest point in
the sky at midsummer, and
at its lowest point at
midwinter.

△ During an eclipse of the
Sun by the Moon, the glow
of the Sun's corona can be
seen.

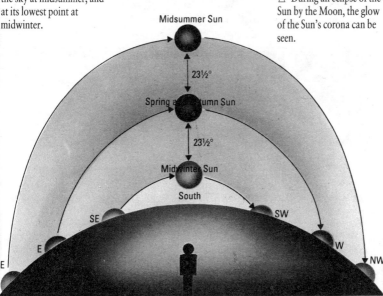

Midsummer Sun

23½°

Spring and Autumn Sun

23½°

Midwinter Sun

South

SE

SW

E

W

NE

NW

△ The Moon was first explored by humans between 1969 and 1972, when six teams of Apollo astronauts landed. This photograph shows the second man on the Moon, Edwin Aldrin, posing for the first man, Neil Armstrong, after the Apollo 11 landing of July 20, 1969.

The Moon

The Moon is a satellite of the Earth – that is, it circles around the Earth. It takes 27⅓ days to do so, slightly less than a calendar month. Its bright surface reflects the light of the Sun. When the Moon is directly between the Earth and the Sun we cannot see it. This is the new Moon. As the Moon moves on, a thin crescent of light appears. The first quarter is when half the surface is lit.

Later, we see all the surface – the full Moon. Up to this point we say the Moon has been "waxing." After this it starts to "wane." When half is lit again the Moon is in its last quarter. The sunlit portion gets smaller until the Moon vanishes.

The diameter of the Moon is 400 times smaller than that of the Sun, but the Moon is 400 times closer to the Earth. As a result, we see the Moon and Sun as about the same size. At certain times of the year, the Moon comes directly between us and the Sun and blots out the Sun from our sight for a few minutes. We say that an eclipse of the Sun has occurred. If the Earth's shadow comes between the Sun and the Moon, there is an eclipse of the Moon.

△ We call the varying appearance of the Moon its "phases." First comes the new Moon. As the Moon waxes, a thin crescent appears and gets bigger until half the surface is lit. We call this the Moon's first quarter. Next comes the gibbous Moon; then the full Moon. As the Moon wanes, the sunlit portion gets smaller, until it disappears at the next new Moon.

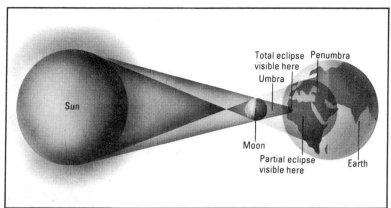

△ An eclipse of the Sun, or solar eclipse, happens when the Moon blocks the Sun's light from reaching the Earth. A total eclipse can be seen only from within the umbra – a region of shadow a few hundred miles across. Around it is a less shadowy area, the penumbra.

MOON STATISTICS

Diameter at equator: 2,160 miles (3,476 km)
Volume: 1/49 Earth's volume
Density: 3.34 (water = 1)
Mass: 1/81 Earth's mass
Gravity: 1/6 Earth's gravity
Closest distance from Earth: 221,460 miles (356,400 km)
Farthest distance from Earth: 252,710 miles (406,700 km)
Mean distance from Earth: 238,860 miles (384,400 km)
Spins on axis in: 27⅓ days
Orbits Earth in (sidereal month): 27⅓ days
Synodic month (new Moon–new Moon): 29½ days

▷ We only see one face of the Moon. When the Moon was newly formed it was made of molten rock, spinning around once in a few hours. As it cooled, a hard skin or crust formed on the outside. The Earth's gravity, pulling at this crust, slowed the spin down and raised a "bulge" a few miles high on one side. Now this bulge is always turned inward, and the Moon keeps the same face toward the Earth.

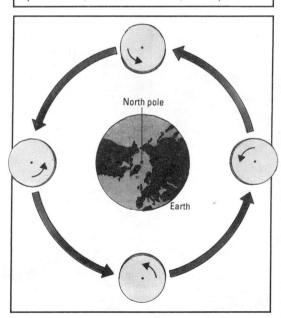

HOW THE PLANETS FORMED

1. In the beginning, there was a spinning ring of gas and dust particles, circling the Sun.

2. The solid particles began to stick together, forming larger bodies, made mostly of carbon and ice.

3. The bodies became as big as planets, and began to "pull" against each other. Some of the very small ice bodies became comets.

4. Eventually there were just nine large bodies going around the Sun in orbits: the major planets.

5. In time, the planets' orbits stabilized.

The Solar System

Nine planets orbit the Sun. We call the Sun's satellites the *solar system,* "solar" meaning "of the Sun." The Earth is the third planet in distance from the Sun and – so far as scientists are aware to date – it is also the only planet on which there is life. The farther a planet is from the Sun, the longer its year – the time it takes to go once around the Sun. The Earth takes 365¼ days. Mercury, the nearest to the Sun, takes only 88 days. Pluto, the most distant planet, has a year more than 247 Earth-years long.

In between the orbits of two of the planets, Mars and Jupiter, are thousands of smaller bodies called the asteroids or minor planets. The largest of these minor planets, Ceres, is only 427 miles (687 km) across. Most of the asteroids are less than 60 miles (95 km) in diameter. We do not know if these little planets are debris that resulted from the break-up of a larger planet, or whether they just failed to form one body when the solar system began.

FAMOUS COMETS

Comets are small heavenly bodies made up of dust and ice. They have been described as "dirty snowballs". They orbit the Sun in very long ellipses, and some take thousands of years to complete one circuit of their orbit.

Name	First observed	Orbital period (years)
Halley's Comet	240 BC	76
Encke's Comet	1786	3.3
Great Comet of 1811	1811	3,000
Pons-Winnecke Comet	1819	6.0
Biela's Comet	1826	6.7
Great Comet of 1843	1843	512.4
Donati's Comet	1858	2,040
Schwassmann-Wachmann Comet	1925	16.2
Arend-Roland Comet	1957	10,000
Ikeya-Seki Comet	1965	880
Kouhoutek's Comet*	1975	–
Comet West	1976	–

*observed from Skylab and Soyuz spacecraft

THE PLANETS AND THEIR STATISTICS

Name	Average distance from Sun, millions of miles	(km)	Diameter at equator miles	(km)	Circles Sun in:	Turns on axis in:
Sun	–	–	865,000	(1,392,000)	–	25⅓ days
Mercury	36	(58)	3,015	(4,850)	88 days	59 days
Venus	67	(108)	7,545	(12,140)	224 days	244 days
Earth	93	(150)	7,926	(12,756)	365¼ days	23:56 hours
Mars	142	(228)	4,220	(6,790)	687 days	24:37 hours
Jupiter	483	(778)	88,600	(142,600)	11.9 years	9:50 hours
Saturn	887	(1,427)	74,700	(120,200)	29.5 years	10:14 hours
Uranus	1,783	(2,870)	30,500	(49,000)	84 years	11 hours
Neptune	2,794	(4,497)	31,200	(50,000)	164.8 years	15:48 hours
Pluto	3,660	(5,900)	1,800	(3,000)	247.7 years	153 hours

▷ This view of the Sun and planets shows how small the Earth is compared with the four "giant" planets. But even the giants are tiny compared with the Sun.

▽ The nine planets of our system (in order from the Sun)
1. Mercury
2. Venus
3. Earth
4. Mars
5. Jupiter
6. Saturn
7. Uranus
8. Neptune
9. Pluto

ASTRONOMY TERMS

asteroids Thousands of small bodies that orbit the Sun between the orbits of Mars and Jupiter.

astrobiology Study of life on other worlds.

astronomical unit (AU) Mean distance between Earth and Sun. 93,000,000 miles (150,000,000 km).

astrophysics Branch of astronomy concerned with physical nature of heavenly bodies.

aurora Phenomenon of the atmosphere seen around the polar regions, in form of colorful displays of light, attributed to sunspot activity. Northern Lights – Aurora Borealis; Southern Lights – Aurora Australis.

big bang theory See *Universe*.

black holes Supposed regions of space of intense gravitational force caused by collapse of star.

celestial sphere Imaginary sphere in which heavenly bodies seem to be projected from point of observation.

chromosphere Layer of crimson gas around the Sun.

comet Heavenly body consisting of the head, a relatively small, star-like nucleus surrounded by *coma*, a glowing cloud, with, usually, a *tail* millions of miles long made up of dust and gas. Comets, visible near the Sun, orbit it with periods of a few to thousands of years.

constellation Apparent grouping of stars together within definite region of the sky; 88 officially recognized and designated.

corona Sun's pearly-white outer layer of gas, extending more than a million miles, visible only during eclipse.

eclipse Obscuration of one heavenly body by another.

equinox Instant when the Sun is directly over our Equator, making equal day and night; occurs about March 21 and September 23.

evening star Planet seen in western sky after sunset, especially Venus.

galaxy Vast system of stars (billions). Millions of galaxies exist, regular ones having spiral or elliptical forms.

halo (1) Luminous ring seen around Moon or Sun, caused by light refraction through high clouds. (2) Stars surrounding Milky Way in halo style.

interstellar space Beyond the Solar System, among the stars.

light-year Distance traveled by light in 1 year, 5.88 trillion miles, or 9.46 trillion km.

meridian Imaginary line in sky passing through poles of celestial sphere and directly over observer.

meteor Phenomenon caused by small body entering Earth's atmosphere and emitting light; estimated 100 million per day.

meteorite Meteor reaching Earth before burning up; lumps of stone (*aerolites*) or iron (*siderites*) up to a 50-ton specimen found near Grootfontein, Namibia.

Milky Way Our galaxy; contains estimated 200 billion stars; spiral type.

moon Any natural satellite of planet. Earth's Moon is our only natural satellite.

▽ On June 21, the north pole is inclined toward the Sun, bringing midsummer to the northern hemisphere while the south has midwinter. On December 21 the situation is reversed.

The Seasons

Summer solstice
June 21

Vernal equinox March 21

Autumnal equinox September 23

Winter solstice
December 21

morning star Planet seen in eastern sky before sunrise, especially Venus.
nebula (Lat. *mist*) Hazy mass of gases and particles in space.
Northern Lights See *Aurora*.
orbit Path of one celestial body around another.
parsec Unit of distance equal to 3.258 light-years.
photosphere Visible surface of the Sun.
planetarium Projection instrument that demonstrates motions of heavenly bodies.
planets The nine major bodies moving in orbit around the Sun.
quasar Quasi-stellar radio sources – mysterious distant objects in the universe, powerful sources of radio waves and light.
radio astronomy Branch concerned with study of radio energy emitted by stars or regions in space.
radio source A single source of radio emission in space.
radio telescope Instrument that collects radio waves from space.
red shift Spectra of galaxies shift toward the red, indicating receding of galaxies.
satellite A body, natural or artificial, that orbits a celestial body.
shooting star Common type of meteor, caused by objects as small as 1 mm (less than 1/16 inch) in diameter.
siderite See *Meteorite*.
solar flare Eruption of radiation on the Sun.
Solar System The Sun and its satellites.
solar wind Permanent particle radiation from the sun.

△ The Aurorae, or Northern and Southern Lights, are brilliant displays in the atmosphere.

solstice Instant when the Sun is farthest from Earth's Equator, making longest or shortest day; occurs about June 21 and December 21.
Southern Lights See *Aurora*.
star Heavenly body generating its own heat and light; nearest after Sun is Proxima Centauri (4.28 light-years); 5,000 stars are visible to the naked eye. Brightness is measured in terms of *star magnitude*.
steady-state theory See *Universe*.
Sun Our star, basis of the Solar System, a glowing ball of gases, mainly hydrogen and helium. (See *Chromosphere, Corona, Photosphere*.)
sunspots Dark patches on the Sun, 2,000°C cooler than normal; maximum activity in 11-year cycles; origin unknown (see *Aurora*).
transit Passage of Mercury or Venus across the Sun's disk.
universe Everything that exists – matter, space, energy. Most astronomers set its age at 15 billion years; the universe seems to be expanding, like an inflating balloon.
Big bang theory suggests explosion of "primeval atom" 100 million light-years in diameter – hence the expanding universe;
steady-state theory suggests infinite universe, no beginning or end, matter continuously being created, changing, and "aging."
zenith Point in heavens directly overhead.

▽ A photograph of meteor tracks. Such brilliant displays as this are rare.

APOLLO

Escape
tower

THIRD
STAGE

Liquid-
hydrogen
tank

Liquid-
oxygen
tank

One J2
engine

Liquid-
hydrogen
tank

Liquid-
oxygen
tank

SECOND
STAGE

Five J2
engines

Liquid-
oxygen
tank

FIRST
STAGE

Kerosene
(RP-1)
tank

Stabilizer
fins

Fairing

Five F1
engines

△ Cutaway view of the three-stage Saturn 5 rocket launcher used for the American-manned Apollo flights.

Exploring Space

Only 60 years ago, the idea that people might one day fly in space and walk on the Moon seemed as far-fetched as any modern science fiction story. But it suddenly came close on October 4, 1957, when radio signals were picked up from space. They came from *Sputnik 1*, a tiny Soviet satellite and the first man-made object to orbit the Earth.

Four years later came the first manned space flight, by the Russian cosmonaut Yuri Gagarin. American manned space flights followed. The first Moon landing was made on July 20, 1969, by the American astronauts Neil A. Armstrong and Edwin E. Aldrin, while their colleague Michael Collins orbited the Moon in a vehicle called the command module, ready to pick them up for the return to Earth.

The first series of manned Moon landings was completed by the United States in the early 1970s. The next target is Mars, where the Soviets plan to land a mission in the 1990s.

However, the most important aspects of space exploration have been the practical uses of Earth satellites and the scientific knowledge of our solar system that we have gained. Satellites keep a regular watch on the world's weather. Weathermen can actually see bad weather and potential disaster-makers such as hurricanes as they approach land, and can warn people to take the necessary precautions. Satellites have photo-graphed every part of the Earth's surface, and confirmed the accuracy of our maps. They have also confirmed the growing hole in the ozone layer above Antarctica, first detected in 1985.

One of the biggest benefits has been in the field of communications. If a satellite orbits the Earth at a speed matching the Earth's rotation, it becomes "fixed" in space above

Spacecraft continues in orbit

Third stage separates

Third stage fires and thrusts spacecraft into orbit

Second stage is jettisoned when its fuel is gone

Escape tower is jettisoned

Second stage fires

First stage is jettisoned when its fuel is gone

Lift-off: first stage fires

△ How a three-stage rocket launches a spacecraft. The first stage fires at lift-off. When its fuel is used up, it separates and falls away. The second and third stages fire in turn to give the spacecraft sufficient speed to enter orbit.

one point on the ground. A group of three communications satellites placed around the world can receive radio and television signals from almost every part of the globe and "bounce" them back to receiving stations on Earth.

In this way we can now use satellites to relay telephone calls. Radio and TV can bring you events as they happen on the opposite side of the world.

Unmanned space probes have been sent to land on or fly past every one of the planets in our solar system. They have photographed the planets in close-up and relayed the pictures back to Earth. In this way we have discovered that water must once have existed on Mars and that Jupiter has 16 moons, three more than we can detect by telescope.

Only one kind of engine works in space – the rocket. When fuel is burned inside a rocket engine, it produces large volumes of gas. The gas exerts great pressure on the surface inside the engine. The pressure around the sides is the same. The upward pressure on the top is much greater than the pressure on the bottom. This is because the gas can escape through a nozzle at the bottom of the engine. Because the pressure at the top is much stronger than the pressure at the bottom, the result is an upward thrust which drives the rocket along.

Perhaps the most exciting developments are still going on: the creation of space laboratories where scientific work impossible within Earth's gravity can be carried out.

STEPS INTO SPACE

1957 First artificial Earth satellite: Russians launch *Sputnik 1* on October 4, heralding Space Age; November 3, Russians launch *Sputnik 2*, containing dog Laika, first mammal in space.

1958 On January 31, Americans launch their first satellite, *Explorer 1*.

1959 Russians launch *Lunik 1* (first probe to go near Moon), *Lunik 2* (first to crash-land on Moon), and *Lunik 3* (first photographs of hidden side of Moon).

1960 U.S. launches *Tiros 1*, first Earth weather satellite (pictures of cloud cover).

1961 First man in space: Russian cosmonaut Yuri Gagarin makes one orbit in *Vostok 1* on April 12. First American astronaut Alan Shepard makes sub-orbital flight on May 5.

1962 First American in orbit, John Glenn makes 3 orbits in *Friendship 7* (Mercury craft). *Ranger 4* becomes first U.S. craft to reach Moon. First commercial communications satellite, *Telstar 1*, begins relaying TV programs across Atlantic.

1963 First woman in space is Russian cosmonaut Valentina Tereshkova.

1964 Russians launch *Voskhod 1* with Vladimir Komarov, Boris Yegorov, and Konstantin Feoktistov aboard; first craft with more than one spaceman (made 16 orbits).

1965 Alexei Leonov makes first space walk.

1966 Russia's *Luna 9* makes soft landing on Moon and returns TV pictures. Neil Armstrong and Dave Scott make first space docking with unmanned craft. First American soft landing on Moon by *Surveyor 1*.

1967 First space disasters: three U.S. astronauts and one Soviet cosmonaut die.

1968 First recovery of unmanned lunar probe, Russian *Zond 5*, from Indian Ocean on September 21. First manned lunar flight: *Apollo 8* (Frank Borman, James Lovell, William Anders) completes 10 orbits.

1969 First docking of two manned spacecraft, with exchange of cosmonauts by space walk (*Soyuz 4* and *5*). In July *Apollo 11* lands lunar module on Moon: American astronaut Neil Armstrong becomes first man to walk on Moon. Second Moon landing (*Apollo 12*) in November.

◁ *Top*: Sputnik 1 was the first space satellite. *Center*: The first Soviet cosmonauts flew in Vostok spacecraft. *Bottom*: Telstar was the first communications satellite.

1970 *Apollo 13* has narrow escape from disaster. Russians soft-land unmanned *Luna 17* on Moon and use 8-wheeled *Lunokhod 1*, first propelled vehicle on Moon. Russian probe *Venera 7* lands on Venus (December 15) and transmits data back.

1971 *Apollo 14* makes 3rd manned Moon landing. Three cosmonauts make longest space flight to date (23 days 17 hr 40 min), but die on return. *Apollo 15* makes 4th Moon landing. U.S. probe *Mariner 9* becomes first artificial satellite of Mars.

1972 Americans launch *Pioneer 10* on 21-month mission to Jupiter. *Apollo 16* and *Apollo 17* make final Moon landings, bringing back lunar samples.

1973 Americans launch *Skylab 1*, unmanned portion of their first manned orbiting space station, including workshop and telescope mount. *Skylab 2, 3,* and *4* launched, each with three astronauts.

1974 *Mariner 10* (launched by U.S. 11-3-73) passes Venus and flies close to Mercury (March 29) for the first close-up look.

1975 First joint Russian-American mission in space: *Soyuz 19* and *Apollo 18* dock while orbiting Earth. Astronauts and cosmonauts carry out exchange visits and experiments. Russian probes *Venera 9* and *Venera 10* soft-land on Venus.

1976 *Helios B,* a research spacecraft carrying American and German instrumentation, comes within 27 million miles (43.4 million km) of the Sun. Soviet spacecraft *Luna 24* makes a soft landing on the Moon to take soil samples with automatic scoop.

1977 The Soviet craft *Soyuz 24* docks successfully with orbiting *Salyut 5* space laboratory one day after launch. The U.S. launches two *Voyager* spacecraft to fly to Jupiter and Saturn.

1978 Two Soviet spacecraft dock with the orbiting *Salyut* space laboratory (January 11) thus achieving the first triple link-up in space.

1980 Western Europe's *Ariane* rocket makes first test flight. *Voyager 1* flies past Saturn. Its instruments reveal that Saturn's rings are more numerous and complex than had been thought.

1981 America's shuttle *Columbia* makes first test flight of 54½ hr, orbiting the Earth and gliding back to a perfect landing on a desert airstrip. *Voyager 2* flies near Saturn, before going on to visit Uranus and Neptune.

△ The American Mercury capsule was just big enough for one astronaut. The Mercury program of manned spaceflights ended in 1963, after six flights, four of them orbital.

△ In 1983 the Pioneer spacecraft became the first object launched from Earth to leave the solar system.

◁ The American space shuttle was the first reusable spacecraft. Its Soviet counterpart is a roughly similar design. Shuttle craft are meant to ferry payloads scientists and satellites into Earth orbit.

1983 U.S. launches space shuttle *Challenger* on a six-day mission. The crew includes a woman, Dr. Sally Ride.
1984 Three Soviet cosmonauts return to Earth after spending a record time in space of almost nine months. A Russian woman cosmonaut becomes the first woman to walk in space. The first repairs are carried out in space, using space shuttle *Challenger* to mend the Solar Max satellite.
1986 The *Challenger* tragedy causes a delay in the Shuttle program. *Voyager 2* sends back detailed photographs of the moons of Uranus. Russians launch space station *Mir*.
1987 Russians send three more spacecraft to link up with space station *Mir*. U.S. and Soviet Union sign an agreement to cooperate on the exploration and use of space.
1988 U.S. shuttle *Discovery* makes successful flight in September, first since *Challenger* disaster. In November the Russians launch their first space shuttle, the unmanned *Buran*. In December the U.S. shuttle *Atlantis* sets off on a secret mission.

△ The Soviet MIR space station is a permanently manned orbital laboratory. Soviet cosmonauts can remain on board for as long as a year.

SPACE ACCIDENTS

1967, January First space accident: three U.S. astronauts (Ed White, Gus Grissom, Roger Chaffee) die in *Apollo 1* launch pad fire.

1967, April Cosmonaut Vladimir Komarov is killed when *Soyuz 1* crashes into ground.

1970, April Moon-bound *Apollo 13* is damaged by an explosion on the third day of its journey, but loops around the Moon and back to Earth.

1971, June After a record flight the three-man crew of Soviet spacecraft *Soyuz 11* are killed by a last-minute pressure failure.

1986, January U.S. space shuttle *Challenger* explodes on takeoff, killing all seven on board.

1988, September Three Soviet cosmonauts almost fail to return following a computer failure.

▽ The Voyager spacecraft showed the planet Saturn's rings in clearer detail than ever before. They are numerous and more complicated than had been previously suspected. This picture was taken from the dark side of the giant planet, at a distance of 434,970 miles (700,000 kilometers).

▽ Skylab was an American space station launched in 1973. Three astronauts could live in the crew quarters within the orbital workshop, a converted third stage Saturn rocket. Three crews visited Skylab, successfully repairing damage caused during its launch. Skylab was burned up in the Earth's atmosphere in 1979.

Solar array wing ripped off at launch

Refrigeration system radiator

Crew quarters

Instrument unit

APOLLO TELESCOPE MOUNT

Experiment compartment

array (4 wings)

ORBITAL WORKSHOP

Solar array wing

MULTIPLE DOCKING ADAPTER

Apollo Command and Service Module

Planet Earth

An atmosphere containing the element oxygen and an abundant supply of its compound, water, is found on planet Earth, and nowhere else in the solar system. These two ingredients are vital for life, which began here probably about 3½ billion years ago. During that unimaginable span of time, continents have formed and re-formed, Ice Ages have come and gone, living things have evolved, and some have become extinct.

Our Earth is one of nine planets that orbit the Sun. It ranks fifth in size. It is the only one with abundant water and an atmosphere containing oxygen – the two things necessary for life. Space probes have not detected any definite signs of life on the other planets.

Some form of life on Earth may have begun as long ago as 3½ billion years. But the abundant life we see today has been in existence for only about 600 million years. That is less than one-eighth of the Earth's age. During that time many species (kinds) of plants and animals have come into existence and died out again. Geologists divide the past 600 million years of Earth's history into periods. There is a chart showing these periods and the kinds of living things that flourished during them on pages 30–31.

Although the continents appear to have always been where they are now, this is not so. Millions of years ago, all the continents were part of one supercontinent known as Pangaea. About 200 million years ago this huge supercontinent began to break up, and the separate continents gradually moved to where they are now. This process is called continental drift. The continents are still moving. The Atlantic Ocean, for example, is growing wider by at least 2 inches (5 cm) a year, as America drifts to the west.

△ The two main gases in the atmosphere are nitrogen, 78 percent, and oxygen, 21 percent. There is also an increasing amount of carbon dioxide and small quantities of other gases, water vapor, dust, and salt particles.

The continents rest on plates. There are about 20 covering the surface of the Earth's crust. As the plates move, some of them bump into one another. Such collisions happen very slowly. Some of them thrust up mountains, such as the ranges of western North and South America and the Himalayas of Asia. At such places, one plate may be sliding under another. New material is welling up under the oceans to replace the lost part of the plate, and to push the plates along. The plates also slide sideways against one another. One place where this is happening is the San Andreas Fault, in California. The plates do not move smoothly, but in jerks. When a jerk happens, we get an earthquake.

Many factors influence the world's climate and weather. From time to time, large parts of the Earth's surface are covered with thick sheets of ice. Scientists think these Ice Ages – also called glacials – occur every few million years. We are now in one of the warmer periods, called interglacials. During Ice Ages so much of the ocean water is locked up as ice that the sea level falls. That is how there was once a strip of land connecting Alaska to Siberia, and another linking Britain to the rest of Europe.

The most recent Ice Age lasted until about 10,000 years ago. During the Ice Age a large part of northern North America and Europe were covered with a sheet of ice up to 9,800 ft (3,000 m) thick.

During the Ice Age there were a great many glaciers or ice rivers. As glaciers creep slowly over the land they wear it away, smoothing out mountains and gouging out deep valleys. If you see very jagged mountains, such as the Rockies, you can be sure that they are not very old – in Earth history terms, that is. But low, smooth mountains have been shaped by the ice. You can still see glaciers in cold mountain regions.

EARTH'S VITAL STATISTICS

Age: About 4.6 billion years.

Diameter: From Pole to Pole through the Earth's center, 7,930 miles (12,700 km); across the Equator through the Earth's center 7,930 miles (12,760 km).

Circumference: Around the Poles 24,860 miles (40,070 km); around the Equator 24,900 miles (40,070 km).

Area: Land 57,400,00 sq miles (148,800,000 sq km) = 29 percent; water 139,500,000 sq miles (361,300,000 sq km) = 71 percent.

Volume of the oceans: 317 million cubic miles (1.3 billion cu km).

Average height of land: 2,757 ft (840 m) above sea level.

Average depth of oceans: 12,450 ft (3,795 m) below sea level.

EARTH'S LONG HISTORY

Era	Period	Epoch	Millions of years ago
Cenozoic	Quaternary	Recent (Holocene)	
			0.01
		Pleistocene	
			2
	Tertiary	Pliocene	
			5
		Miocene	
			25
		Oligocene	
			35
		Eocene	
			60
		Paleocene	
			65
			65
Mesozoic	Cretaceous		
			145
	Jurassic		
			210
	Triassic		
			245
			245
Paleozoic	Permian		
			285
	Carboniferous		
			360
	Devonian		
			410
	Silurian		
			440
	Ordovician		
			505
	Cambrian		
			570
			570

Pre-Cambrian time stretches back to the formation of the Earth, about 4.6 billion years ago

Highlights of plant and animal life

Modern human beings emerged and civilization began.

Ice Age in northern hemisphere, wooly mammals survived the cold.

"Ape-men" appeared. Many large mammals died out as the weather got colder.

Many apes in Africa. Herds of mammals grazed on the spreading grasslands.

Early apes appeared. Many modern mammals began to evolve. Flowering plants increased.

Primitive mammals, including early horses and elephants. Plants mostly modern types.

Mammals evolved rapidly after most reptiles had died out.

Dinosaurs and many other reptiles died out at the end of the period. Ammonites disappeared. First flowering plants.

Dinosaurs ruled the land. Flying reptiles. First birds. Ammonites common. Some small mammals.

First dinosaurs and large sea reptiles. First mammals. Ammonites common. Cycads and Bennettitaleans evolved. Conifers spread. Luxuriant forests.

Reptiles increased. Amphibians less important. Trilobites died out. Primitive conifers and ginkgoes.

Amphibians increased. First reptiles. Clubmosses, ferns and horsetails in coal-forming swamps.

The age of fishes (bony and cartilaginous). Amphibians evolved. Land plants more common.

Giant armored fishes. First land/marsh plants. Large sea scorpions – terrors of the seas.

First vertebrates (jawless fishes). Graptolites and trilobites abundant. Echinoderms and brachiopods spread.

Fossils abundant. Graptolites, trilobites, primitive shellfish, corals, crustaceans, etc.

Life began about 3.5 billion years ago. Oldest known fossils are organisms in Fig-Tree cherts (3.5 b yrs) and stromatolites (2.8 b yrs). But fossils rare – probably because creatures were soft-bodied (e.g. jellyfish, worms).

Earthquakes and Volcanoes

Earthquakes and volcanoes often seem to go together. They are most likely to occur in areas where two plates meet (see page 38). Most of the world's active volcanoes occur in a band around the edge of the Pacific Ocean, called the "Ring of Fire," that continues north of Australia through New Guinea and Indonesia.

Volcanoes are also likely to occur over "hot spots," places in the Earth's crust where there are weaknesses. Many Pacific islands are the tops of old volcanoes which were once over such hot spots, before the plates moved on. Inside a volcano, lava (hot liquid rock) spouts up from a central vent. As the lava cools it forms solid rock again.

▽ What happens during a volcanic eruption. Pressure forces molten rock or magma (1) from the mantle to the surface through a weakness in the crust called a vent (2). Other vents may cut through the volcano (3). A dyke is formed (4) as magma forces its way through a cleft in the rocks above.

△ Low volcanoes (1) are made of liquid lava. This spreads out before it hardens. Cone volcanoes (2) are made from thick lava, which may form a plug. Pressure inside the volcano can blow out the plug (3).

NOTABLE EARTHQUAKES

Shensi Province, China, 1556: Over 800,000 people perished – more than in any other earthquake.

Lisbon, Portugal, 1755: About 60,000 people died, and shocks were felt as far away as Norway.

San Francisco, 1906: An earthquake and the fires it caused destroyed the center of the city.

Kwanto Plain, Japan, 1923: Some 570,000 buildings collapsed. This was the costliest earthquake ever, as measured by damage to property.

Tangshan, China, 1976: About 242,000 people were reported killed in this city.

Lebu, Chile, 1977: The strongest earthquake shock ever recorded.

Armenia, U.S.S.R., 1988: 45,000 people died; 20,000 people were injured; 400,000 people were made homeless and 3 cities were destroyed.

THE RICHTER SCALE

The intensity of an earthquake is measured by the Richter scale, which was devised by Charles F. Richter in 1935. Taking some extremely weak tremors as a base, he gave these a value of near 0, then gave values of 1, 2, 3, and so on to more intense quakes. Each number on the Richter Scale represents a tenfold increase over the lower number. Quakes are measured on a machine called a seismograph. The most severe earthquakes have measured as much as 9 on the Richter Scale. These include an earthquake in the Pacific Ocean in 1906 and another in Japan in 1933. The earthquake in Mexico City in 1985 measured 8·1 on the Richter scale.

Earthquakes which measure over 5 on the Richter scale are considered major. They may cause major damage such as the collapse of buildings and may kill people if the center is located in a populated area. The Mexico City earthquake of 1985 injured thousands of people and killed 7,200.

▽ Shock waves spread out from the epicenter of an earthquake.

△ San Francisco after the 1906 earthquake.

THE EARTHQUAKE ZONES OF THE WORLD

The World's Water

Nearly three-quarters of the Earth's surface is covered by water. The oceans are mostly very deep. Near land the seas are shallower, because part of each continent slopes down under the sea at what is called the continental shelf. Several parts of the oceans are very deep indeed. They are called ocean trenches, and they occur where one plate of the Earth's crust is sliding under another. The deepest of these trenches is the Marianas Trench, in the Eastern Pacific. It is 36,198 ft (11,033 m) deep. The deepest trench in the Atlantic Ocean is the Puerto Rico Trench in the West Indies, which is 28,374 ft (8,648 m) deep.

The water of the oceans is salty. It is always being evaporated by the heat of the Sun, forming clouds which eventually fall as rain. Rain collects on land to form ponds and lakes, and flows back down rivers to the sea. Some water collects in huge natural reservoirs deep underground. There are stores of such water under the dry Sahara desert. Much of it fell as rain thousands of years ago.

△ Most of the Earth's surface is watery, as this pie chart shows.

△ Spring tides are high because the Sun's gravitational pull is combined with the Moon's. Neap tides are low because the Moon and Sun are pulling at right angles to each other.

SIZE OF THE OCEANS

	Sq miles	Sq km
Pacific Ocean	70,000,000	181,000,000
Atlantic Ocean	41,000,000	106,000,000
Indian Ocean	28,400,000	73,500,000
Arctic Ocean	5,540,000	14,350,000

▽ This diagram shows the relative sizes of the four major oceans.

LONGEST RIVERS

	Miles	Km
Nile (Africa)	4,160	6,695
Amazon (South America)	4,000	6,440
Chang Jiang (China)	3,964	6,380
Mississippi-Missouri-Red River (North America)	3,710	5,970
Ob-Irtysh (U.S.S.R.)	3,362	5,410
Huang He (China)	2,903	4,672
Zaïre (Africa)	2,900	4,667
Amur (Asia)	2,744	4,416
Lena (U.S.S.R.)	2,734	4,400
Mackenzie (Canada)	2,635	4,240
Mekong (Asia)	2,600	4,180
Niger (Africa)	2,590	4,170

LARGEST LAKES

	Sq miles	Sq km
Caspian Sea (Asia/Europe)	143,244	371,000
Superior (North America)	31,700	82,103
Victoria (Africa)	26,828	69,484
Aral Sea (Asia)	24,904	64,496
Huron (North America)	23,000	59,569
Michigan (North America)	22,300	57,757
Tanganyika (Africa)	12,700	32,893
Baykal (Asia)	12,162	31,499
Great Bear (North America)	12,096	31,328
Malawi (Africa)	11,150	28,878

▽ Five lakes make up North America's Great Lakes. They are Superior, Michigan, Huron, Erie, and Ontario. Shown here is Erie.

△ This bar graph shows the world's longest rivers.

World Record Breakers

The world contains many natural features, such as deserts and mountains, which are outstanding in size. Here is a selection. It has proved very difficult to measure some of them. For example, several measurements have been made of Mount Everest, which do not quite agree. Several different ways of measuring the depth of the Marianas Trench have been tried, again giving slightly different readings. The figures given here are the best available.

△ One of nature's most violent phenomena: an erupting volcano spews out lava in Iceland.

DEEP, LONG, AND HIGH

Greatest ocean depth: 36,198 ft (11,033 m), Marianas Trench, Pacific Ocean.
Deepest underwater gorge: 5,900 ft (1,800 m), near Esperance, Western Australia.
Longest gorge: 217 miles (349 km), Grand Canyon, Arizona.
Highest navigated lake: Titicaca, on the borders of Peru and Bolivia, 12,500 ft (3,810 m) above sea level.
Deepest lake: Baykal, Central Asia, 6,365 ft (1,940 m).

HIGHEST MOUNTAINS

	feet	meters
Asia		
Everest (Himalaya-Nepal/Tibet)	29,028	8,848
Godwin Austen (Pakistan/India)	28,250	8,611
Kanchenjunga (Himalaya-Nepal/India)	28,208	8,597
Makalu (Himalaya-Nepal/Tibet)	27,824	8,480
Dhaulagiri (Himalaya-Nepal)	26,801	8,169
Nanga Parbat (Himalaya-India)	26,660	8,126
Annapurna (Himalaya-Nepal)	26,504	8,078
South America		
Aconcagua (Andes-Argentina)	22,834	6,960
North America		
McKinley (Alaska Range)	20,320	6,194
Africa		
Kilimanjaro (Tanzania)	19,340	5,895
Europe		
Elbruz (Caucasus-U.S.S.R.)	18,481	5,633
Mont Blanc (Alps-France)	15,771	4,807
Antarctica		
Vinson Massif	16,864	5,140
Australasia		
Jaja (New Guinea)	16,500	5,029

▷ The great waterfalls of the world are awesome spectacles.

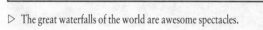

FAMOUS WATERFALLS

	Drop (ft)	(m)
Africa		
Tugela (Africa)	2,014	614
Asia		
Jog or Gersoppa (India)	890	272
Australasia		
Sutherland (New Zealand)	1,904	580
Wallaman (Australia)	1,137	347
Europe		
Mardalsfossen, Southern		
(Norway)	2,149	655
Gavarnie (France)	1,385	422
North America Yosemite		
(U.S.A., Cal.)	2,425	739
Della (Canada, B.C.)	1,443	440
South America		
Angel (Venezuela)†	3,212	979
Glass (Brazil)	1,325	404

† World's highest waterfall

EROSION FACTS

Weight of soil and rock removed by rivers is about 363 tons a year from each square mile (140 from each square kilometer) of the Earth's crust.

Thickness of land worn away by rivers is about 1 ft (30 cm) a year as estimated for the United States.

Deepest gorges cut by rivers are those made by the rivers Indus, Brahmaputra, and Ganges in India–Pakistan; they are more than 3 miles (5 km) deep.

DESERTS

	Sq miles	Sq km
Sahara (Africa)	3,500,000	9,096,000
Australian Desert	600,000	1,550,000
Arabian Desert	500,000	1,300,000
Gobi (Asia)	500,000	1,300,000
Kalahari (Africa)	200,000	518,000
Chihuahuan		
(U.S.A. and Mexico)	140,000	363,900
Mojave (U.S.A.)	15,000	39,000

▷ Sand dunes in Colorado. The Earth's desert regions are the driest and most inhospitable environments for plants, animals, and people.

FACTS ABOUT VOLCANOES

Active volcanoes: There are about 535 of these, 80 below the sea.

Largest known eruption: Tamboro, Indonesia, in 1815. The volcano threw out about 36 cubic miles (about 150 cubic km) of matter and lost 4,100 ft (1,250 m) in height.

Greatest disaster: 35,000 people were drowned by a giant wave unleashed when Krakatoa, Indonesia, exploded in 1883.

Greatest volcanic explosion: About 1470 B.C., Santorini, in the Aegean Sea, exploded with possibly 130 times the force of the greatest H-bomb.

FACTS ABOUT ICE

More than one-tenth of all the land on Earth is covered by ice at any given time.

Largest ice sheet is the Antarctic Ice Sheet, covering 5 million square miles (13 million sq km).

Longest glacier is the Lambert-Fisher Ice Passage in Antarctica. It stretches over 300 miles (500 km).

Largest iceberg ever recorded was an Antarctic iceberg seen in 1956. It covered 12,000 square miles (31,000 sq km), an area bigger than Belgium.

LARGEST ISLANDS

	Sq miles	Sq km
Greenland	840,000	2,183,000
New Guinea	317,000	821,000
Borneo	280,100	727,900
Madagascar	226,658	589,081
Baffin Island	195,928	509,214
Sumatra	182,860	431,982
Honshu	87,805	228,204
Great Britain	84,200	218,800
Victoria Island	83,896	218,045
Ellesmere Island	75,767	196,917

▽ About 200 million years ago there was a single huge land mass. It later split into two supercontinents, which eventually, after millions of years of drift, formed the continents we see today. Millions of years from now, the continents will have drifted still farther. For example, North and South America will probably have separated.

500 million years ago

325 million years ago

175 million years ago

50 million years ago

Drifting Continents

Although its inhabitants are unaware of its daily changes, the Earth is in a constant state of flux. Movements beneath the crust cause variations in the surface features which are revealed over a period of millions of years.

The Earth's crust is very thin compared with the diameter of the globe. It varies from 20 miles (32 km) thick under the continents to 5 miles (8 km) under the oceans. It lies over a layer of very hot rock called the mantle.

Scientists think that the mantle, which is so hot that its rock can melt, is constantly moving. It has convection currents, like those you see when a pan of thick soup is cooking on the stove. The theory is that it is these convection currents which move the plates along, causing continental drift. The movement is circular, welling up in the mid-ocean ridges, and going down at the ocean edges, as under the west coast of South America.

On a world map Africa and South America look as though they should fit together, and that is exactly what they did. The surprising thing is that India was separate from the rest of Asia. When it collided with Asia the force of the collision slowly pushed up a huge range of mountains, the Himalayas.

▽ Where two plates meet, rocks either are pushed up to form mountains or ridges or sink down into the Earth's mantle to create trenches.

The Weather

The atmosphere – the layer of air around the Earth – is constantly moving because it is unevenly heated by the Sun. Huge masses of warm air from the Equator and cold air from the Poles flow around the world, meeting each other. The warm air rises and the cold air sinks, and this movement causes the winds.

The air picks up water vapor evaporated from the oceans in the tropics, and rises, getting cooler. The vapor condenses into tiny droplets of water in the cool air and forms clouds. If it cools further, the droplets unite to form larger drops, which fall as rain. On very cold days the droplets form snowflakes. From storm clouds small pieces of ice may fall as hailstones.

△ The atmosphere of the Earth acts like an insulating wrapping, stopping the planet from getting too hot or too cold.

WEATHER EXTREMES

Hottest shade temperature recorded: 136°F (57.7°C) at Al'Aziziyah, Libya, on September 13, 1922.

Coldest temperature recorded: −128.6°F (−89.2°C) at Vostock, Antarctica, on July 21, 1983.

Highest average annual rainfall: 463 inches (11,770 mm) at Tutunendo, Colombia.

Driest place on earth: Arica, Chile, averages 0.030 inches (0.76 mm) of rain per year.

Greatest tides: 53.4 ft (16.3 m) Bay of Fundy, Nova Scotia, Canada.

Strongest surface wind recorded: 231 mph (372 km/h) at Mt. Washington, New Hampshire, in 1934.

BEAUFORT SCALE

In 1805 Admiral Sir Francis Beaufort worked out a scale for measuring wind speed. The scale is numbered from 1 to 12 and represents wind force out in the open, 33 feet (10 meters) above the ground.

No.	Wind force	mph	km/h	Observable effects
0	calm	<1	<1.6	smoke rises vertically
1	light air	1–3	1.6– 4.8	direction shown by smoke
2	slight breeze	4–7	6.4– 11.3	felt on face; wind vanes move
3	gentle breeze	8–12	12.9– 19.3	leaves, twigs move; flags extended
4	moderate breeze	13–18	20.9– 29.0	dust, paper, small branches move
5	fresh breeze	19–24	30.6– 38.6	small trees sway; flags ripple
6	strong breeze	25–31	40.2– 50.0	large branches move; flags beat
7	moderate gale	32–38	51.5– 61.2	whole trees sway; walking difficult
8	fresh gale	39–46	62.8– 74.0	twigs break off; walking hindered
9	strong gale	47–54	75.6– 86.9	slight damage – chimney pots, slates
10	whole gale	55–63	88.5–101.4	severe damage; trees uprooted
11	storm	64–72	103.0–115.9	widespread damage
12	hurricane	>73	>117.5	devastation

TYPES OF CLOUDS

Clouds consist of masses of water drops or ice crystals in the atmosphere. They form when moisture in the air condenses.

Altostratus: A grayish sheet of cloud, with a hazy Sun above.
Altocumulus: Fleecy bands of cloud with blue sky between.
Cirrus: High, wispy clouds made of particles of ice.
Cirrocumulus: Thin, high lines of cloud with rippled edges.
Cirrostratus: Milky, thin, high cloud producing a halo around the Sun.

Stratus: Low, gray, sheet-like cloud covering the sky.
Nimbostratus: Low, gray, sheet-like cloud producing steady rain.
Stratocumulus: Like a low, dark, heavy kind of altocumulus.
Cumulus: A white heaped-up cloud usually seen in fair weather.
Cumulonimbus: A towering cloud that may give heavy showers.

▷ Lightning is a huge electric spark.

FACTS ABOUT STORMS

Most thundery region on Earth: The tropics and nearby regions. More than 3,000 thunderstorms occur there every night of the year.
Fiercest storm winds: Those whirling around in a tornado. They are thought to reach speeds of 500 mph (800 km/h).
Speed of lightning: The fastest flashes move at 87,000 miles a second (140,000 km/sec).
Tornadoes: A tornado is a storm that moves across the land at about 40 mph (65 km/h). It measures only about 650 ft (200 m) across, but its whirling winds can cause severe damage.

SOME WEATHER TERMS

climate The average weather conditions of a place. Climate figures are averages of figures collected over a number of years, so extremes of heat and cold, drought and flood are hidden.

hurricane A severe tropical storm with spiraling winds and very low air pressure. The wind does a great deal of damage, and the accompanying rain and high tides cause floods.

Mediterranean climate Summers are hot and dry; winters are warm and wet. Such a climate is found around the Mediterranean Sea and also in central California and Perth, Western Australia.

monsoon The word means season and usually refers to winds that bring an exceptionally wet season for part of the year. The most spectacular monsoon climates are in Asia.

temperate lands Those parts of the world between the tropics and the Polar areas that have a cold season and a hot season. Places such as the Mediterranean which have warm winters may be called warm temperate.

precipitation When used of the weather, refers to rain and snow.

▽ A depression or cyclone is an area of low air pressure. This satellite photograph shows a hurricane, a severe tropical cyclone. Hurricane winds spiral at up to 210 mph (340 km/h).

△ Weather forecasting has been aided by weather satellites like this one. Such satellites can spot and track weather systems as they develop.

▽ All maps are projections: from a globe (**A**), a cone (**B**) or a cylinder (**C**). The Mollweide projection (**D**) shows the entire surface of the Earth.

A

B

Making Maps

It is impossible to make a completely accurate flat map of a curved surface such as the Earth, which is a sphere. So mapmakers make "projections" from a globe. Imagine a transparent globe touching a flat surface at one point. If a light could be placed in the center of the globe, it would throw a shadow of the lines of latitude and longitude onto the paper. This projection (**A**) becomes more and more distorted away from the point of contact.

If you put a cone of paper on the globe, the light in the globe would give what is called a conical projection (**B**).

If you put a cylinder of paper around the globe, the resulting map would look like (**C**), the familiar projection invented by the Flemish cartographer Gerhardus Mercator in the 1500s. But the north and south of the map are badly distorted, and the lines of latitude appear to be parallel to each other, which they are not.

Flat maps of a small area of the world – for example, New England – can be much more accurate, because the Earth's surface does not curve so much over such a comparatively short distance.

C

D

MAP TERMS

atlas A book of maps.

globe A ball painted or printed to show the Earth in its true shape.

legend A small table that explains what the various symbols on a map mean.

political map A map in which the political boundaries of the various countries are shown, usually in different colors.

road map A map especially designed to help drivers find their way.

thematic map A map that shows a certain aspect of geography, such as rainfall or population.

topographic map A map that shows the rivers, mountains, and other physical features of the landscape.

Time Zones

The Earth rotates on its axis once every 24 hours. As a result the local time – by the Sun – changes by about 4 minutes for every 1° of longitude. Therefore we cannot use the same time all over the world. So the world has been divided into 24 time zones, each representing a difference of roughly 1 hour.

Within a zone, the time is the same. But if you cross into the next zone, you have to put your watch back (going west) or forward (going east) by 1 hour. The zone lines are not always straight, but follow country boundaries. In large countries such as the United States there are several time zones. For example, when it is noon in San Francisco, it is 1 pm in Denver, Col., 2 pm in Houston, Tex., and 3 pm in Washington D.C.

The line of longitude, or meridian, at 0° passes through Greenwich, in London; this line is also called the Greenwich meridian. Exactly halfway around the world from 0° is the 180th meridian. Along most of it runs the International Date Line, where every new calendar day begins. People living just east of this line are almost a day behind those who live just west of it.

△ The Earth rotates on its axis once in 24 hours. This gives us day and night. At any one moment, part of the Earth is facing the Sun, and people there have their clocks set at noon. On the opposite side of the Earth it is midnight.

▽ This map shows the world divided into time zones. The lines zigzag in some places to follow country borders where possible.

International Time Zones

PLANET EARTH GLOSSARY

atmosphere The layer of moving air that surrounds the Earth. It consists of nitrogen, oxygen, water vapor, and other gases. The atmosphere becomes thinner away from the Earth.

axis An imaginary straight line around which a spinning object rotates. The Earth's axis goes from the North Pole, through the center of the Earth, to the South Pole.

block mountains Blocks of land raised up by vertical movements between faults in the Earth's crust.

canyon A deep, steep-sided valley, usually cut by a river in a *desert* area. The most famous is the Grand Canyon.

coral Coral is made by tiny creatures called polyps that live in warm sunny seas. They build skeletons outside their bodies. When they die new polyps build on the old skeletons to form coral reefs.

core The inner part of the Earth.

crust The outer layer of the Earth.

delta The Greek letter Δ (delta) is used to describe an area of sediments deposited at the mouth of some rivers, such as the Mississippi and the Nile.

desert A dry area where few plants grow. The Sahara is the largest desert; the Atacama is the driest.

dunes Mounds or ridges of sand. They are found on some sandy coasts and in sandy *deserts*.

earthquake A sudden movement within the Earth's *crust* which causes shock waves which make the Earth's surface shake. Earthquake tremors are recorded on a seismograph.

estuary The mouth of a river where it enters the sea. Usually it is much wider than the rest of the river and it has tides.

fault A more or less vertical break in the Earth's crust, along which the rocks have moved. The rocks may move upward, downward, or sideways.

fiord (fjord) A long, steep-sided inlet of the sea in a mountainous coastal area, as in Norway. Originally it was a valley eroded by a glacier. After the glacier melted, the valley was drowned as the sea level rose.

fold mountains Mountains formed by folding layers of rocks. When parts of the Earth's crust move together from each side, the rocks in between are folded.

geyser A hot spring which throws out a jet of hot water regularly or occasionally. The best-known geysers are in the United States, Iceland and New Zealand.

glacier A mass of ice that moves slowly downhill. It follows the easiest route – usually along a river valley which it deepens and straightens.

iceberg A lump of ice that has broken off from one of the two polar ice caps and floats in the sea. Only about one-tenth of an iceberg shows above water level.

latitude and **longitude** These are lines drawn on a globe. Lines that run through the poles north to south are called lines of longitude. The Equator and lines parallel to it are lines of latitude.

meander A bend in a river, usually in soft, relatively flat ground.

▽ The curved lines on a globe are lines of latitude (east-west) and lines of longitude (north-south).

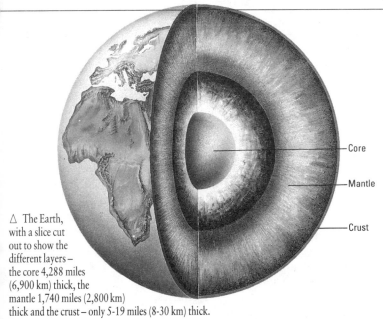

△ The Earth, with a slice cut out to show the different layers – the core 4,288 miles (6,900 km) thick, the mantle 1,740 miles (2,800 km) thick and the crust – only 5-19 miles (8-30 km) thick.

- Core
- Mantle
- Crust

oasis An area in a desert with water at or near the surface. Crops can be grown, and people can live there.

peninsula An area of land almost surrounded by water, but not completely cut off from the mainland.

plain A lowland area with a fairly level surface, though there may be hills. The North European Plain and the Great Plains of North America are examples of very large plains.

plateau An upland area with a fairly level surface, though a plateau may have some hills and may be divided by deep valleys.

sedimentary rocks Rocks formed from sediments (small rock particles) which once accumulated on land or sea. Clay, sandstone, and limestone are examples of sedimentary rocks.

tropics Lines of latitude marking where the Sun is directly overhead on midsummer's day. On June 21 the Sun is overhead at the Tropic of Cancer. On December 21 it is overhead at the Tropic of Capricorn.

▽ Fold mountains are formed when the Earth's crust squeezes rock layers upward.

Fold mountains

Faults

Countries of the world

There are over 5 billion people in the world today living in more than 160 countries and speaking over 3,000 languages. Before World War II, Britain, France, and other European countries ruled large empires; since that time most colonies have gained independence and, together with their former rulers, joined the United Nations in an attempt to keep world peace and form fruitful political and economic alliances.

There are more than 160 independent countries in the world. In addition, there are a number of countries that are not independent. They are either part of larger countries or are colonies, dependent territories, or associated states. Many of them have internal self-government.

Examples of countries that are part of larger bodies include England, Scotland, and Wales, which are part of the United Kingdom; and French Guiana, which is the overseas French *département* of Guyane Française, giving it the same status as the political divisions of mainland France.

There are few colonies left. They include Anguilla in the West Indies, Bermuda, and Gibraltar, which are all British colonies. American Samoa, in the Pacific Ocean, is an example of a dependent territory. Others include the Australian territories of Christmas Island and the Cocos Islands, the Chilean territory of Easter Island, and the Ecuadorean territory of the Galápagos Islands.

Associated states tend to have a greater measure of self-government than dependencies. Some are difficult to classify: for example, the West Indian island of Puerto Rico is completely self-governing, but its people are United States citizens, and it sends a (non-voting) representative to Congress.

△ An assembly of Indian princes. Until its independence in 1947, India was the jewel in Britain's imperial crown. The British Empire was the largest and most diverse in history.

Former empires

Before World War II (1939–1945) many European countries had large empires, consisting of a mixture of dominions, colonies, protectorates, and so-called "spheres of influence," places that were virtually independent but relied for defense and other aid on a European country. Many lands of the Middle East were in this group. The Empire of India was administered by Britain, but many of its states were effectively self-governing.

The largest empires were the British and French empires. Smaller empires were controlled by Belgium, Italy, The Netherlands, Portugal, and Spain. The Spanish empire originally included most of South America, but those colonies fought for, and won, independence in the early 1800s. Portugal's empire included Brazil.

After World War II most of the colonies began to press for independence. The European nations were glad to let them have it, partly because administering such large overseas lands was becoming too expensive, and partly because public opinion everywhere was in favor of self-government for all peoples. The process began with the break-up of the Indian Empire in 1947, but the largest number of new independent countries came into being in the 1960s, when most of the African states won their freedom.

Peoples of the world

The total population of the world is over 5 billion. The population is growing at the rate of 1.6 percent a year. The number of people being born is greater than the number who are dying – there are about 29 births per thousand population, with deaths at 11 per thousand.

People live longer in the industrialized countries than in those that are developing. The place to be if you want to reach old age is Japan, where a newborn baby can expect to

▽ At the present time, as the graph shows, the population of the world is increasing rapidly. This is sometimes called a population explosion. Rates of increase vary in different parts of the world. For example, in the United States the increase is small (only 0.9 percent per year), while in Africa and South America the population is increasing at 2.7 percent.

6000 million (forecast)

over 4000 million

1608 million

728 million

1750
1900
1980
2000

∇ The human race can be divided into three main groups. Caucasoids include northwestern Europeans, most Indians, and the Aborigines of Australia. Mongoloids comprise mainly the peoples of China and Japan and the Indians of North and South America. They are characterized by high cheek bones and small noses, straight black hair and yellowish skin. Negroids are African people and usually have black curly hair, broad noses, and large lips.

Caucasoid

Mongoloid

Negroid

live to the age of 77. In the United States and Britain life expectancy is about 75 years. At the other end of the scale, in Afghanistan the life expectancy is about 37 years (recent war contributes to the low figure). In many African countries it is about 45 years. In most countries, women live longer than men.

All humans belong to the same species, but over thousands of years groups living in different parts of the world have evolved great varieties of size, skin color, hair, and eyes. For example, people living in countries where there is almost continuous hot sunshine have evolved darker skins, which partially protect against harmful rays of the Sun.

The result is that there are many different kinds of people. These different kinds are called races, but scientists do not agree on what constitutes a race. The most common difference is in skin color, and that has led to the unpleasant trait of racism: the misguided belief that people of one color are inferior to those of another. Racism has led to much bloodshed and barbarity.

Improved communications has meant that the world has increasingly become a great melting pot of racial types. The United States and Britain are examples of multiracial societies – that is, they have people of different races living side by side.

Languages
One thing that divides people is the language they speak. There about 160 main languages – that is, those spoken by 1,000,000 or more people. But altogether there are at least 3,000 separate languages, and countless dialects.

The languages with the most speakers are Mandarin Chinese (788,000,000), English (420,000,000), Hindi (300,000,000), Spanish (296,000,000), and Russian (285,000,000). Most languages are spoken in a limited area: for example, few people outside China speak Mandarin Chinese.

Many languages are spoken only in a single community of a few thousand people. For example, Papua New Guinea has a population of only 3,400,000, yet more than 700 languages are spoken there.

By contrast, several languages are spoken by people of many lands, and are used as international languages. English, Spanish, and French are among them. In many former French colonies of Africa people speak so many different local languages that French has been retained as the official language.

Other countries have two official languages: Kenya, a former British territory, uses the local Swahili and also English. India, which has 14 major languages and more than 160 others, with 700 dialects, has Hindi as its first official language, but many people use English as a common language.

Another barrier to communications has been the number of different alphabets in use. The Western alphabet – in which this book is written – is used in more countries than any other, even in those where it is not the main alphabet employed. It is one of the easiest to learn and to write, and it can be readily adapted to many languages.

Other important alphabets include Arabic, the Cyrillic script used in the Soviet Union, Greek, and the scripts used for Hindi and its related language Urdu. Chinese has a different system of writing, using about 50,000

△ The world's peoples speak and read many languages. Newspapers reflect this rich variety of cultures.

△ Soldiers of a U.N. peace-keeping force. The U.N. has no army of its own but relies on contingents of troops from member states, who also pay the cost of such operations. U.N. forces act as observers and "police" in trouble spots, endeavoring to hold "peace-lines," between warring factions.

▽ The emblem of the United Nations. The olive branches symbolize peace.

characters, each representing a word. Most Chinese use only about 10,000 characters, and a simplified version of the system was introduced in the 1950s. However, one advantage of the Chinese system is that the Chinese people, who speak many dialects and pronounce their words in many ways, can read written Chinese even when they cannot understand what other people are saying.

International organizations

Over the centuries, countries have formed alliances of all kinds, for trade or political reasons. Some alliances were the result of conquest. Others, especially the British Empire, were created for purposes of trade. Many of the empire-builders of the 1800s sincerely believed that they were also bringing benefits to underdeveloped countries.

Many alliances have existed for mutual defense, such as the *Entente Cordiale* between Britain and France of 1904. Russia joined it in 1907 to make a *Triple Entente*, which pledged the three countries to support each other in the event of war. The alliance came into action in 1914 when World War I broke out.

A different kind of alliance came into being in 1920 as a result of World War I. It was the League of Nations, formed with the express purpose of maintaining world peace. The League had some success in stopping small wars, but it was unable to prevent the outbreak of World War II in 1939, or many of the conflicts leading up to it. However, out of World War II came a new body, the United Nations, which took over the role of the League of Nations.

The United Nations

The United Nations was formed in 1945 by 50 countries, headed by the United States, Britain, and the Soviet Union, who had been allies in World War II. Today nearly all the independent countries of the world are members. The member countries send representatives to the United Nations Assembly, which meets for one three-month session every year. Emergency special sessions may be called in between the regular meetings if a crisis develops.

More frequent meetings are held by the Security Council, which has representatives from 15 countries. The United States, Britain, France, China, and the Soviet Union are permanent members, while 10 other countries are elected by the General Assembly to serve for two years at a time. The Security Council makes its decisions by a majority vote, with nine being the minimum number of votes for a majority. However, the five permanent members have the right of veto on any Security Council resolution.

The Commonwealth

A smaller world body is the Commonwealth. It consists of 49 countries, mostly former British colonies, that were part of the old British Empire. It developed from the empire, and its member countries originally acknowledged the British sovereign as their head of state. Now that 25 Commonwealth countries are republics, with their own heads of state, Queen Elizabeth II is regarded as "Head of the Commonwealth".

Unlike the United Nations, the Commonwealth has no charter or treaty. It is described as "a free association" of countries that are equal in status, and have their common background in the old empire. The Commonwealth exists for those countries' mutual assistance, cooperation, and benefit. The Commonwealth Secretariat, based in London, acts as a coordinating body. Heads of government meet every two years at a Commonwealth Conference to discuss business. Each conference is held in a different member country, and is opened by the Queen.

▽ Members of the Commonwealth incorporate the likeness of Queen Elizabeth II in the design of their stamps.

UNITED NATIONS: MEMBER COUNTRIES

Country	Joined*	Country	Joined	Country	Joined
Afghanistan	1946	Central African		Greece	1945
Albania	1955	Republic	1960	Grenada	1974
Algeria	1962	Chad	1960	Guatemala	1945
Angola	1976	Chile	1945	Guinea	1958
Antigua and		China †	1945	Guinea-Bissau	1974
Barbuda	1981	Colombia	1945	Guyana	1966
Argentina	1945	Comoros	1975	Haiti	1945
Australia	1945	Congo	1960	Honduras	1945
Austria	1955	Costa Rica	1945	Hungary	1955
Bahamas	1973	Côte d'Ivoire	1960	Iceland	1946
Bahrain	1971	Cuba	1945	India	1945
Bangladesh	1974	Cyprus	1960	Indonesia	1950
Barbados	1966	Czechoslovakia	1945	Iran	1945
Belgium	1945	Denmark	1945	Iraq	1945
Belize	1981	Djibouti	1977	Ireland, Rep. of	1955
Benin	1960	Dominica	1978	Israel	1949
Bhutan	1971	Dominican Republic	1945	Italy	1955
Bolivia	1945	Ecuador	1945	Jamaica	1962
Botswana	1966	Egypt	1945	Japan	1956
Brazil	1945	El Salvador	1945	Jordan	1955
Brunei	1984	Equatorial Guinea	1968	Kenya	1963
Bulgaria	1955	Ethiopia	1945	Kuwait	1963
Burkina Faso	1960	Fiji	1970	Laos	1955
Burundi	1962	Finland	1955	Lebanon	1945
Byelorussian S.S.R.	1945	France	1945	Lesotho	1966
Cambodia	1955	Gabon	1960	Liberia	1945
Cameroon	1960	Gambia	1965	Libya	1955
Canada	1945	Germany, East	1973	Luxembourg	1945
Cape Verde	1975	Germany, West	1973	Madagascar	1960
		Ghana	1957	Malawi	1964

U.N.: PRINCIPAL ORGANS

General Assembly consists of all members, each having one vote. Most of work done in committees: (1) Political Security, (2) Economic & Financial, (3) Social, Humanitarian & Cultural, (4) Decolonization (including Non-Self- Governing Territories), (5) Administrative & Budgetary, (6) Legal.

Security Council consists of 15 members, each with one vote. There are five permanent members – China, France, U.K., U.S.A. and U.S.S.R. – the others being elected for two-year terms. Main object: maintenance of peace and security.

Economic and Social Council is responsible under General Assembly for carrying out functions of the U.N. with regard to international economic, social, cultural, educational, health, and related matters.

Trusteeship Council administers Trust Territories.

International Court of Justice is composed of 15 judges (all different nationalities) elected by U.N. Meets at The Hague.

The Secretariat is composed of the Secretary-General, who is chief administrative officer of the U.N. and is appointed by the General Assembly, and an international staff appointed by him. Secretary-Generals:

Trygve Lie (Norway)	2-1-46 to 4-10-53
Dag Hammarskjöld (Sweden)	4-10-53 to 9-17-61
U Thant (Burma)	11-3-61 to 12-31-71
Kurt Waldheim (Austria)	1-1-72 to 12-31-81
Javier Pérez de Cuéllar (Peru)	1-1-82 to

Country	Joined*	Country	Joined	Country	Joined
Malaysia	1957	St. Kitts-Nevis	1983	United Kingdom	1945
Maldives, Rep. of	1965	St. Lucia	1979	United States	1945
Mali	1960	St. Vincent and		Uruguay	1945
Malta	1964	the Grenadines	1980	Vanuatu	1981
Mauritania	1961	São Tomé e Príncipe	1975	Venezuela	1945
Mauritius	1968	Saudi Arabia	1945	Vietnam	1976
Mexico	1945	Senegal	1960	Western Samoa	1976
Mongolian P.R.	1961	Seychelles	1976	Yemen Arab Republic	1976
Morocco	1956	Sierra Leone	1961	Yemen P.D.R.	1967
Mozambique	1975	Singapore	1965	Yugoslavia	1945
Myanmar	1948	Solomon Islands	1978	Zaïre	1960
Nepal	1955	Somali Republic	1960	Zambia	1964
Netherlands	1945	South Africa	1945	Zimbabwe	1980
New Zealand	1945	Spain	1955		
Nicaragua	1945	Sri Lanka	1955		
Niger	1960	Sudan	1956		
Nigeria	1960	Surinam	1975		
Norway	1945	Swaziland	1968		
Oman	1971	Sweden	1946		
Pakistan	1947	Syria	1945		
Panama	1945	Tanzania	1961		
Papua New Guinea	1975	Thailand	1946		
Paraguay	1945	Togo	1960		
Peru	1945	Trinidad and Tobago	1962		
Philippines	1945	Tunisia	1956	*The U.N. came into existence	
Poland	1945	Turkey	1945	in 1945.	
Portugal	1955	Uganda	1962	†In 1971 the U.N. voted for the	
Qatar	1971	Ukrainian S.S.R.	1945	expulsion of Nationalist China	
Romania	1955	U.S.S.R.	1945	and the admittance of	
Rwanda	1962	United Arab Emirates	1971	Communist China in its place.	

UNITED NATIONS AGENCIES

FAO	Food and Agriculture Organization	ITU	International Telecommunications Union
GATT	General Agreement on Tariffs and Trade	UNCLOS	United Nations Conference on the Law of the Sea
IAEA	International Atomic Energy Agency	UNCTAD	United Nations Conference on Trade and Development
IBRD	International Bank for Reconstruction and Development (World Bank)	UNEF	United Nations Emergency Fund
		UNESCO	United Nations Educational, Scientific, and Cultural Organization
ICAO	International Civil Aviation Organization		
IDA	International Development Association	UNICEF	United Nations Children's Emergency Fund
IFAD	International Fund for Agricultural Development	UNIDO	United Nations Industrial Development Organization
IFC	International Finance Corporation	UPU	Universal Postal Union
ILO	International Labor Organization	WHO	World Health Organization
IMCO	Inter-Governmental Maritime Consultative Organization	WIPO	World Intellectual Property Organization
IMF	International Monetary Fund	WMO	World Meteorological Organization

Other International Groups

There are a great many small international groups. Some exist to look after mutual defense interests; these include the North Atlantic Treaty Organization, the Warsaw Pact, and the Arab League.

Others are concerned with trade. Examples of these groups include the European Community (the "Common Market"), COMECON (Council for Mutual Economic Assistance), and the Latin American Integration Association.

MEMBERS OF INTERNATIONAL ORGANIZATIONS

COMECON: Bulgaria, Cuba, Czechoslovakia, East Germany, Hungary, Mongolia, Poland, Romania, U.S.S.R., Vietnam.

Commonwealth: Antigua and Barbuda, Australia, Bahamas, Bangladesh, Barbados, Belize, Botswana, Brunei, Canada, Cyprus, Dominica, Fiji, Gambia, Ghana, Grenada, Guyana, India, Jamaica, Kenya, Kiribati, Lesotho, Malawi, Malaysia, Maldives, Malta, Mauritius, Nauru, New Zealand, Nigeria, Papua New Guinea, Pakistan, St. Kitts-Nevis, St. Lucia, St. Vincent and the Grenadines, Seychelles, Sierra Leone, Singapore, Solomon Islands, Sri Lanka, Swaziland, Tanzania, Tonga, Trinidad and Tobago, Tuvalu, Uganda, United Kingdom, Vanuatu, Western Samoa, Zambia, Zimbabwe.

European Community (Common Market): Belgium, Denmark, France, Greece, Ireland, Italy, Luxembourg, Netherlands, Portugal, Spain, United Kingdom, West Germany.

NATO (North Atlantic Treaty Organization): Belgium, Canada, Denmark, France, West Germany, Greece, Iceland, Italy, Luxembourg, Netherlands, Norway, Portugal, Spain, Turkey, United Kingdom, United States.

Organization of American States: Antigua and Barbuda, Argentina, Bahamas, Barbados, Bolivia, Brazil, Chile, Colombia, Costa Rica, Cuba, Dominica, Dominican Republic, Ecuador, El Salvador, Grenada, Guatemala, Haiti, Honduras, Jamaica, Mexico, Nicaragua, Panama, Paraguay, Peru, St. Kitts-Nevis, St. Lucia, St. Vincent and the Grenadines, Surinam, Trinidad and Tobago, United States, Uruguay, Venezuela.

Warsaw Pact: Bulgaria, Czechoslovakia, East Germany, Hungary, Poland, Romania, U.S.S.R.

OTHER INTERNATIONAL ORGANIZATIONS

ASEAN	Association of South-East Asian Nations
EFTA	European Free Trade Association
OAU	Organization of African Unity
OECD	Organization for Economic Development and Co-operation
OPEC	Organization of Petroleum-Exporting Countries

Gazetteer of Independent Countries
In the gazetteer that follows, all independent countries of the world are described in alphabetical order. One non-independent country, Namibia (South-West Africa), is included. The League of Nations assigned it to South Africa to administer in 1920.

Since 1971 the United Nations has regarded South Africa's continued rule of Namibia as illegal, and it pressed for the country to become independent. Moves toward independence began in 1989.

For many countries a small map appears next to the relevant article to show the area that the country covers and which are its neighboring countries.

At the end is a ready-reference chart of all the independent countries. It includes each nation's area, population, and capital.

Independent Countries A–Z

AFGHANISTAN, a landlocked republic in southeastern Asia. The land is mostly mountainous: major ranges include the Hindu Kush and the Pamirs. The north is arid. Rainfall generally averages 12 in (300 mm). Temperatures vary from 120°F (49°C) in the south in summer to −15°F (−26°C) in winter in the mountains. Nearly 80 percent of the workers are farmers. Only 10 percent of the land is cultivable, mostly in irrigated valleys. Many people are nomads: sheep are the most numerous animals. Natural gas is exported, but mining and manufacturing are small-scale. Islam was introduced in the 8th century. Modern Afghanistan was founded in 1747 by an Afghan chief, Ahmad Shah. A republic was declared in 1973.

ALBANIA, the smallest European communist nation, borders the Adriatic Sea. The climate on the dry coast is Mediterranean in type. The land is mostly mountainous. Farmland covers 17 percent of Albania, with fertile basins in the wetter uplands where the rainfall averages 71 in (1,800 mm). Scrub and oak and pine forest cover 44 percent of the land and pasture another 25 percent.

Farming is collectivized and 62 percent of the workforce is employed on farms. But mining and manufacturing are the leading industries. Ottoman Turks introduced Islam in the 15th century. Albania became independent in 1912 and a kingdom in 1928. After World War II a communist republic was set up. Albania officially became an "atheist state" in 1967.

ALGERIA, a large republic bordering the Mediterranean Sea in North Africa. The Sahara, which covers 85 percent of the nation, yields oil and natural gas, and oil accounts for 90 percent of the exports. People are moving from the countryside to the towns. Of the workers, agriculture now employs 30 percent, industry 25 percent, and services 45 percent. Most people live in the northern Atlas mountain region and the fertile coastal plains. Barley, fruit, grapes, olives, vegetables, and wheat are grown. Livestock are raised in the uplands. Islam and the Arabic language were introduced in the 7th century, but Berber languages survived in some areas. France ruled Algeria from 1848 until it become independent in 1962.

ANDORRA, a tiny, mountainous co-principality in the Pyrenees between France and Spain. Sovereignty is technically exercised by the "co-princes," the Spanish Bishop of Urgel and the French President, but an elected, 28-member General Council effectively rules the state. Tourism is the main industry. Tobacco is the chief cash crop.

ANGOLA, a republic in west-central Africa, including the small enclave of Cabinda. Behind the narrow coastal plain are plateaus. The climate is generally warmest and wettest in the north. Savanna covers much of the country, with forests in the south and northeast. Most people speak Bantu languages. The main groups are the Ovimbundu, the Mbundu, and the Kongo. Tribalism has divided the nationalist movement in Angola. About 60 percent of the people are farmers, mostly at subsistence level. The main food crops are cassava and corn. Mining is becoming increasingly important. Angola was a Portuguese colony until it became independent in 1975.

ANTIGUA, including the smaller and also low-lying islands of Barbuda and the uninhabited Redonda in the Leeward Islands, was a British colony but became an independent nation in the Commonwealth in 1981. The British monarch is its Head of State. Antigua exports cotton and rum, but tourism is the most important industry in this dry, sunny country. Discovered by Christopher Columbus in 1493, Antigua was named after a church in Seville, Spain. Most Antiguans are descendants of African slaves, but some are of European or Middle Eastern origin.

ARGENTINA, South America's second largest nation after Brazil, extends north-south through more than 32° of latitude. As a result the climate varies considerably. There are four main regions. The tropical, largely forested north is comparatively little developed. The west is arid, except around "oases" where such towns as Mendoza and Tucumán have grown up, rising in the far west to the Andes Mountains. Here, on the border with Chile is Mt. Aconcagua, the highest mountain in the western hemisphere. Southern Argentina, called Patagonia, consists of sparsely populated, windswept and semi-arid plateaus. In the far south is

half of the barren and cold archipelago Tierra del Fuego. The fourth and most densely populated region is the central *pampas* (or plains) which cover nearly 25 percent of the country. The soils of the pampas are fertile and the climate is mild. The *pampas* lie to the northwest and south of Buenos Aires, the elegant capital city. About 90 percent of the people are of European descent, another 8 percent being *mestizos* of mixed White and Indian origin, and 2 percent pure Indians. Argentina is one of the world's leading food producers. Dairy products, hides, corn, meat, oats, vegetable oils, wheat, and wool are major products. About 11 percent of the country is cultivated, and pastureland covers another 41 percent. In recent years, mining (for coal and oil) and manufacturing have become important. The cities are growing quickly, and eight out of ten people live in them. The Spanish explorer Juan de Solás was the first European to see the Rio de la Plata estuary, into which the Paraguay and Uruguay rivers flow, in 1516. The first permanent Spanish settlers arrived in 1535. Spanish rule continued until independence in 1816. Argentina has been disturbed by political and economic turmoil. Between 1946 and 1987, the Republic of Argentina had 15 presidents, seven of whom were deposed.

AUSTRALIA, the world's sixth largest country, has very few people for its size, because large tracts are desert or semi-desert. About 90 percent of the people live in towns, with more than 50 percent concentrated in the four largest cities. The western part of Australia is a vast plateau, broken by occasional mountain ranges. The central plains extend from the Gulf of Carpentaria in the north to the Great Australian Bight in the south. These plains include the Great Artesian Basin, comprising western Queensland, the southeast of the Northern Territory, the northeast of South Australia and the northern part of New South Wales. Here artesian wells tap ground water that originally fell as rain on the Great Dividing Range in the east, and which has seeped through aquifers beneath the plains. The Lake Eyre basin in the southwest of the Great Artesian Basin is usually dry and covered by salt. The highest peak in the Great Dividing Range, an uplifted block of land, is Mt. Kosciusko, in that part of the Range called the Australian Alps. The Range continues in the island state of Tasmania in the southeast, which is separated from the mainland by the shallow Bass Strait. In the northeast is the Great Barrier Reef, the world's longest reef, 1,260 miles (2,027 km) long. Australia's chief rivers are the Murray and its tributaries, including the Darling, in the southeast. The climate varies according to the latitude. The north is tropical with summer monsoon rains. In the south, winters are cooler and rains are brought by the prevailing westerlies. However, about two-thirds of Australia is too dry for farming. The tropical region in the north contains tropical forest and savanna, and crops, such as sugar-cane, flourish in Queensland. Deserts cover most of Western Australia, the southern part of Northern Territory, much of South Australia and the eastern parts of New South Wales. The mid-latitude grasslands are west of the Great Dividing Range in south-central Queensland and central New South Wales. The coastlands of New South Wales and southeastern Victoria form a warm temperate zone, where eucalyptus forests grow. The southwestern part of Western Australia and parts of South Australia and western Victoria have a Mediterranean climate, with much scrub woodland vegetation. The cool, temperate climate of Tasmania supports forests of beech and eucalyptus. Australia has a wide range of animals, including kangaroos, koalas, platypuses and wallabies. Birds include the flightless emu and cassowary and the lyre bird. The first people in Australia were probably the Tasmanian Aborigines, who were driven into Tasmania by the Australian Aborigines, who arrived from Asia about 16,000 years ago. The Tasmanian Aborigines became extinct in 1876, and contact with Europeans caused the Australian Aborigines to decline in numbers. Today there are about 100,000 Australian Aborigines, but many are of mixed ancestry. About 80 out of 100 Australians are of British origin. Many recent settlers have come from other parts of Europe. Australia has vast mineral reserves and is a major world producer of bauxite, iron ore, and lead. Other metal ores, coal, and oil are also mined, together with thorium and uranium. The main product of the country is wool. Beef and dairy products are of great importance particularly in the north and east. Only about 2 percent of the land is cultivated, but yields are high and crops are varied because of the wide climatic range. Manufacturing industries are mostly in the towns and cities. The main steel centers are Newcastle, Wollongong, and Whyalla. Dutch navigators landed in northern and eastern Australia in the early 17th century, and in 1788 a British convict settlement was established on the present site of Sydney. In 1793 the first free settlers arrived. Gold rushes in the 1850s and 1890s accelerated immigration. Australia is a member of the Commonwealth, and the British monarch, represented by a governor-general, is Head of State.

AUSTRIA, a federal republic in central Europe. The Alps cover about 75 percent of the land, and tourism is a major industry, especially winter sports. The Danube river valley in the north is the chief farming region. Livestock are also important: the uplands contain much summer pasture. Forests occupy about 40 percent of the land. Iron ore and lignite are mined, forming the basis of the iron and steel industry. Vienna is the main manufacturing and cultural center and more than half the people live in towns. Austria, part of the Holy Roman Empire, became a possession of the Hapsburg family in 1282. From 1438 this family supplied all but one of the Holy Roman Emperors. After the Empire ended (1806), the Hapsburg ruler became Emperor of Austria. In 1938 Germany annexed Austria. It became a federal republic in 1955.

BAHAMAS, a group of 14 large and about 700 small islands with a mild climate, to the southeast of Florida. Tourism is the main industry. Christopher Columbus discovered the islands in 1492; the island of San Salvador was possibly his first landing place. The Bahamas became a British colony in 1717. Full independence within the Commonwealth was achieved in 1973. About 85 percent of the people are descendants of African Blacks (former slaves).

STATISTICS

To see the statistics of each country's area and population, plus its capital, turn to pages 102–106.

BAHRAIN, a densely populated island nation in the Persian Gulf. The capital, Manama, is on the largest island, also called Bahrain. This hot, arid country is an important oil producer, and revenue from oil sales has been used to provide free education, health care, and other services. The Arabs occupied Bahrain in the 7th century. In 1861, it became a British protectorate. It became a fully independent sheikhdom in 1971.

BANGLADESH, a densely populated country in Asia, is one of the world's poorest. It has a tropical monsoon climate, with hot, dry winters and hot, wet summers. It is mostly flat, largely occupying the fertile deltas of the Ganges, Brahmaputra, and other rivers. The rivers are the main transport arteries, but they often flood, causing disease and starvation. Coastal floods are also caused when cyclones in the Bay of Bengal drive the sea inland. About 71 percent of the mainly Muslim Bengali population is engaged in agriculture. In 1980 only 11 percent of the population was urban. Formerly part of British India, Bangladesh became the province of East Pakistan in 1947. A bitter civil war between East and West Pakistan in 1971 ended with the secession of East Pakistan, which became the People's Republic of Bangladesh.

BARBADOS, the most easterly island in the West Indies, is mostly flat with a mild climate. More than 90 percent of the people are descendants of African slaves, the rest being white or of mixed origin. Sugar and sugar products (molasses and rum) are the main products, but tourism is now the chief industry. Barbados was a British colony from 1628 to 1966, when it became an independent member of the Commonwealth.

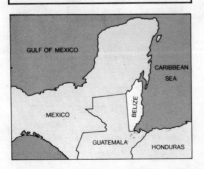

BELGIUM, a densely populated, prosperous industrial nation in western Europe. Two-thirds of the land is flat, but the largely forested Ardennes rise in the southeast. The navigable Meuse and Scheldt rivers drain the fertile central plains. Antwerp, near the mouth of the Scheldt, is the main port. The climate is mild. Three languages are spoken: Flemish (a Dutch dialect) in the north; French by the Walloons in the south; and German by a small group in the southeast. Conflict between Flemish- and French-speakers has led to rioting and complaints about discrimination. More than 70 percent of the people are town-dwellers. The lowlands are intensely cultivated. Most farms are small and many farmers also have jobs in industry. The main crops are cereals, notably wheat, flax, potatoes, and sugar beet. Coal is mined in the northeastern Campine (Kempen) region, which has become a major industrial area. The older industrial areas are in the south, in the Sambre-Meuse valley. This zone is based on coalfields which extend from Mons to Liège, but extraction of the coal has become expensive and the region has declined in consequence. Antwerp is a major industrial center, some industries being based on imported oil, as is Brussels, whose varied industries produce luxury goods such as lace. Textiles are important, particularly in Flanders; the main center is Ghent. Belgium came under the Austrian Hapsburgs in 1477 and the Spanish Hapsburgs in 1506. After a spell of independence (1598–1621), it came successively under Spain, Austria, France, and the Netherlands. It declared its independence in 1830. The Kingdom of Belgium is a constitutional, representative, and hereditary monarchy, with an elected Senate and Chamber of Deputies. Belgium is a founder member of the European Community.

BELIZE, which faces the Caribbean Sea in Central America, is flat in the north, with uplands in the south. Forests flourish, and sugar cane is the chief cash crop in this hot, wet nation. More than half the people are Creoles; most of the others are of Mayan Indian, Black, Carib, or European descent. Belize was declared a British colony in 1862, although neighboring Guatemala has claimed it since 1821. Belize became an independent country within the Commonwealth in 1981.

BENIN, a People's Republic on the Gulf of Guinea in West Africa. Behind the sandy coast are low plateaus, with the highest land in the northwest. The formerly forested south has an equatorial climate, but winters are dry in the tropical northern savanna. The Black African population is divided into 50 groups, the largest being the Fon, Adja, Bariba, and Yoruba. Nearly half the people work in agriculture. The most important food crops are corn, beans, rice, and millet, and the chief cash crop is palm kernels and oil. Oil was discovered offshore in the late 1970s. Benin (known as Dahomey until 1975) was ruled by France from the 1890s to 1960, when it became independent.

BHUTAN, a mountainous landlocked kingdom between China and India. Most people, who are of Tibetan or Hindu Nepalese origin, live in fertile valleys where the climate is warm and wet. Nine out of every 10 workers are in agriculture. Some rice, fruit, and timber are exported. Most manufactures and fuels must be imported. Contact with the West began in 1774. An elected National Assembly can dismiss the king. India has responsibility for Bhutan's foreign affairs.

BOLIVIA, a landlocked republic in South America. The Andes mountains in the southwest contain a central plateau, the Altiplano, where most Bolivians live. It has a cool climate, contrasting with the hot Amazon rain forests in the northeast. Lake Titicaca, the world's highest navigable lake, is on the border with Peru. More than half of the people are American Indians, a third are *mestizos* and the rest of European origin. Agriculture employs 51 percent of the people, but mining is the most valuable

industry. Bolivia is the world's 2nd largest tin producer, and antimony, copper, lead, oil, natural gas, silver, and wolfram are also mined. Spain ruled Bolivia from 1532 to 1825, when it won independence.

BOTSWANA, a thinly populated, landlocked republic in southern Africa. Most of the country is a plateau, and the climate is warm. The rainfall is three times as heavy in the north as in the southwest. The Kalahari, a semi-desert, covers 84 percent of the country, and only a few nomadic Bushmen live there. Most people belong to the Bantu-speaking Tswana group, including the Bamangwato and Bangwaketse. Minerals now dominate the rapidly developing economy: diamonds, copper, and nickel are the main exports. Most people work in agriculture. Arable land covers only 2 percent of the country, but cattle farming is important. Beef, skins, and textiles are also exported. Other farmers raise corn and millet. Botswana became the British protectorate of Bechuanaland in 1885. In 1966 it became fully independent within the Commonwealth.

STATISTICS
To see the statistics of each country's area and population, plus its capital, turn to pages 102–106.

BRAZIL, the world's 5th largest nation, occupies nearly half of South America. In the north, the equatorial Amazon basin contains the world's largest rain forest, which is now being reduced as economic development proceeds. The Amazon river is the world's 2nd longest, with a greater volume than any other. It is navigable into Peru. South of the forest is a huge tropical grassland. This region is still little developed despite the inauguration, in its heart, of the new capital of Brasília in 1960. The northeast around Recife and Salvador has a forested coastal plain, but the inland plateaus are dry: long droughts cause much hardship to an already impoverished population. The central coastal region is the most densely populated and includes the great industrial cities of São Paulo and Rio de Janeiro. Inland are fertile plateaus and pleasant, mineral-rich highlands. The plateaus near São Paulo are Brazil's main coffee-producing region. The southern region around Porto Alegre has a temperate climate; pastoral farming is important. About 75 percent of Brazil's population is of Portuguese or other European origin. There are many people of mixed European/Indian/Black African descent; color prejudice is almost absent. Agriculture provides work for two-fifths of the people. Brazil leads the world in producing bananas and coffee, and it is among the top world producers of beef, veal, cocoa, cotton, corn, sugar cane, soya beans, and tobacco. It is Latin America's leading producer of vehicles, steel, and cement. Brazil was a Portuguese colony from 1500 to 1822, when it became an empire. It became a republic in 1889.

BRUNEI, a small Sultanate in northwestern Borneo. Behind the narrow coastal plain, the interior is rugged and forested. The climate is tropical. Some 68 percent of the people are of Malay origin and 25 percent are Chinese. Oil is the main product. Natural gas, rubber, and timber are also exported. Brunei was a British protectorate between 1888 and 1971. It became independent in 1984.

BULGARIA, a Communist People's Republic facing the Black Sea in southeastern Europe. The climate is transitional between Mediterranean and continental, the latter prevailing in the north and in the mountains. The mountains include the Balkans in the north and the higher Rhodope Mountains in the south. The capital, Sofia, is in a fertile mountain basin. The River Danube plain is in the north, but the central plains are the main farming region, producing fruit, mulberry leaves, attar of roses, sugar beet, tobacco, and wine. Lignite, copper, iron ore, and oil are mined, and manufactures include cement, iron and steel goods, and textiles. COMECON countries account for 80 percent of Bulgaria's trade. Tourism is increasing. The Turks ruled Bulgaria from 1396. Bulgaria became independent in 1878.

BURKINA FASO, formerly Upper Volta, a West African republic. Low plateaus cover most of the country. The east is in the River Niger basin; the center and west are drained by the Black, Red, and White Volta rivers. Burkina Faso has a hot, tropical climate. The main rainy season is July–October, but droughts are common. Most people are Blacks; the Mossi (48 percent) are the largest single group. Four-fifths of the people farm the land, raising cattle, sheep, and goats. Cotton and other cash crops are grown in the south and southwest. The country was ruled by France from 1896 to 1960, when it became independent.

BURUNDI, a small, densely populated, landlocked republic in east-central Africa. Part of Lake Tanganyika is in the Rift Valley in the west, with highlands and high plateaus in the east. There are a few pygmies, but the main ethnic groups are the Bantu-speaking Hutu (85 percent) and the Hamitic Tutsi (13 percent). Agriculture employs 85 percent of the people. Most are subsistence farmers. The Tutsi entered the area from the north in the 17th century. They founded a feudal society under their *mwami* (king), making the Hutu serfs. Burundi was ruled by Germany from 1890 to 1916, and was under Belgian administration until independence in 1962. Hutu attempts to overthrow the Tutsi government have all failed, leading to the deaths of thousands of Hutu.

CAMBODIA is a South-East Asian nation. It was originally called Cambodia, then, briefly, the Khmer Republic, and then Kampuchea. Much of the land is low-lying, in the drainage basin of the lower Mekong River; hills surround the plain. Cambodia has a tropical monsoon climate, and dense forests cover nearly half the land. Khmers make up 90 percent of the population. There are Chinese and Vietnamese minorities. The economy is based on agriculture, mainly on growing rice. The country was a French colony from 1863 to independence in 1953.

CAMEROON, a republic in west-central Africa, bordering the Gulf of Guinea. Behind narrow coastal plains are plateaus that slope down in the north to the Lake Chad basin. The main uplands are on the western border; the highest peak is the volcanic Mt. Cameroon on the coast. The equatorial south is forested; the tropical center contains wooded savanna; the drier north has open grassland. Most people are Blacks, speaking one of about 200 Bantu or Sudanic languages. Agriculture employs eight out of 10 people. Mining (for bauxite and oil) is becoming important. After being ruled by Germany, Britain, and France, Cameroon became completely independent in 1961.

CANADA, the world's 2nd largest nation after the U.S.S.R. There are seven main regions. The *Appalachian region* in the northeast is an extension of the Appalachian region in the U.S.A. The *St. Lawrence and Lower Great Lakes* region is Canada's most densely populated. The *Canadian Shield* is a vast region of ancient rocks, mineral deposits, and innumerable lakes and rivers. The *Hudson Bay* lowland is a plain between the Canadian Shield and Hudson Bay. The *Western Interior Plains* are between the Canadian Shield and the *Western Mountains*, which include the Canadian Rockies and the Coast Range. In the far north are the bleak *Arctic Islands*. Canada has extremely cold winters, especially north of the Arctic Circle. Southern Canada has warm, moist summers. Forests cover 35 percent of Canada. There are also vast grasslands and tundra regions. The origins of the people are as follows: British (45 percent), French (29 percent), German (6 percent), Italian (3 percent), and Ukrainian (3 percent). Most of the rest come from other parts of Europe. American Indians and Inuit number 289,000 and 17,500 respectively. Canada has two official languages, English and French. Quebec is the main French-speaking province. Only 7.2 percent of the land is cultivated, but Canada is one of the world's leading producers of barley, fruit, oats, wheat, rye, and timber. Livestock ranching and dairy farming are also important. Canada is among the top six world producers of asbestos, copper, gold, iron ore, lead, molybdenum, natural gas, nickel, potash, silver, uranium, and zinc. But more important than mining is manufacturing. The chief industrial area is the St. Lawrence and Lower Great Lakes region. Much traffic is carried along the St. Lawrence Seaway, the world's longest artificial seaway. The

CANADA

STATISTICS

To see the statistics of each country's area and population, plus its capital, turn to pages 102–106.

Dominion of Canada, comprising Quebec, Ontario, Nova Scotia, and New Brunswick, was established in 1867. Canada is now a federation of 10 self-governing provinces and two territories, and a Commonwealth member.

CAPE VERDE, an island republic west of Senegal in West Africa. The 10 large islands and five islets are of volcanic origin. The climate is tropical, but the rainfall is very unreliable. Most people are of mixed Portuguese and African origin; 28 percent are classed as "pure" Africans. Most people are subsistence farmers, but severe droughts in the 1970s forced many people to emigrate, and the government has had to provide work for destitute farmers. Portugal claimed the islands in 1460. Independence was achieved in 1975.

CENTRAL AFRICAN REPUBLIC, a landlocked nation, consists largely of plateaus high above sea-level. The climate is warm, and there is heavy rainfall in the south of the country. The south is forested, but wooded savanna covers most of the land. Wildlife is abundant. Most people speak Sudanese languages. Nearly nine out of every 10 people work on the land. Diamonds are mined and large uranium deposits have been found, but manufacturing is on a small scale. The country became part of French Equatorial Africa in the 1880s. It became independent in 1960.

CHAD, a landlocked nation in north-central Africa. Lake Chad, the remains of an inland sea, is in the west. Southern Chad is savanna-covered, but sandy deserts and bare rocky uplands, notably the high Tibesti massif, are in the north. About 100 languages are spoken in Chad. In the south, where most of the population lives, most people are

Blacks. Muslim Arabs and Berbers live in the north. Cultural divisions have caused much civil conflict and periodic war since the mid-1960s. Agriculture employs 86 percent of the workers in this poor nation. Cotton is the chief crop. Chad became a French colony in 1897 and an independent republic in 1960.

CHILE, a long, narrow country stretching through 38° of latitude in South America. From west to east there are generally three regions: coastal uplands, central lowland basins and valleys, and the high Andes. In the glaciated south, the coastal uplands are islands, the central lowlands becoming arms of the sea. Chile's climate changes north-south. The north is hot and arid, including the rainless Atacama Desert with its large mineral reserves. Central Chile, where most Chileans live, has hot summers and mild, moist winters. The forested south, with its beautiful fiords, is cool; heavy rain falls in all seasons. Cape Horn, South America's stormy tip, is in the far south. People of mixed European and Indian origin make up 68 percent of the population, Europeans 30 percent, and Araucanian Indians 2 percent. Agriculture provides work for about 15 percent of the people. The main farm products are barley, fruit, corn, wheat, oats, rice, and wine. Minerals include copper, which makes up 48 percent of the exports, molybdenum, iron ore, nitrates, and oil. Chile has one of the largest fishing industries in the world. Manufacturing industries are powered mainly by hydroelectricity. Chile was a Spanish colony for about 300 years before becoming independent in 1818.

CHINA, the world's 3rd largest country, contains about 20 percent of the world's population. The land is extremely varied. In the northeast is the basin of the Huang He, one of the world's longest rivers. It cuts through a clay-rich plateau which has colored its waters yellow. To the north lie the central plain and eastern highlands of Manchuria. To the south, beyond the Qin Ling Mountains, lies the Chang Jiang basin of Central China. The Chang Jiang is Asia's longest river. China's third important river basin is that of the Xi Jiang in the southeast, south of the South China Highlands. Outer or Western China contains the high and vast Tibetan plateau which rises in the south to

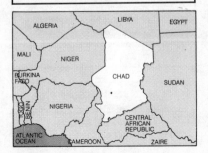

the Himalayan range, crowned by Mt. Everest. In the far west are other ranges, including the lofty Pamirs and Tien Shan. Northeastern China contains some large deserts, including the vast Tarim and Dzungaria basins. The Gobi desert straddles the frontier between Nei Monggol (in China) and Mongolia. The climate varies from north to south. Northeastern China has bitterly cold winters and warm summers, with moderate rainfall. Central China has milder winters and more rainfall, while south-eastern China has a sub-tropical monsoon climate. About 94 percent of the population are Han, or true, Chinese. But there are also large national minorities, including Manchus, Mongols, Tibetans, and Uighurs, who maintain their own cultures. The population is densest in the fertile river basins and along the coasts of eastern China. Some 25 percent of the population lives in urban areas. The rural population has been encouraged to live in communes, which are groups of villages where up to 20,000 people work together, share the produce, and receive wages that are geared to production. More than half the people work on the land. China leads the world in millet, rice, and tobacco production. It is among the top three producers of barley, cotton, peanuts, corn, potatoes, silk, sorghum, tea and wheat. It has more pigs than any other country, plus cattle, sheep and goats. There is also an important fishing industry. China has huge mineral resources—many untapped. It is among the world's top producers of antimony, asbestos, coal, iron ore, mercury, tin, and tungsten. The oil industry is expanding. The main industrial centers are in Manchuria, Sichuan, and the large cities. Coal is the main source of energy for manufacturing. China's written history goes back 3,500 years, and it is one of the world's oldest living civilizations. Its inventions have included gunpowder, paper, printing, porcelain, and silk. It was ruled by emperors until it became a republic in 1912. War with Japan (1937–45) was followed by civil war between the Nationalists and Communists. The Communists, under Mao Zedong, were victorious in 1949, and the People's Republic of China was established.

COLOMBIA, a republic in northwestern South America, includes three ranges of the Andes, whose high, fertile valleys contain most of the people. In eastern Colombia, grasslands merge into the forests of the upper Amazon and Orinoco basins. The coastal lowlands are hot and wet. The highlands are cooler and less rainy. The grasslands have dry winters but wet summers. More than two-thirds of the people are of mixed American Indian and European origin; most others are of pure American Indian, European, or African descent. The chief export, coffee, is grown in the highlands. Seventy percent of the people live in urban areas. Spaniards opened up the region in the early 16th century. Spanish rule was overthrown in 1819.

COMOROS, an island Federal and Islamic Republic, lies at the northern end of the Mozambique Channel. Geographically, there are four islands: Njazidja, Nzwani, Mahoré (or Mayotte), and Mwali. The republic contains three of them, but Mayotte is a French territory. The islands are mountainous; Mt. Kartala is an active volcano. The population is mixed, including elements from Africa, Asia, and Europe. These tropical islands have few resources and most people are subsistence farmers. They came under French protection in 1886–1909 and became a colony in 1912. In 1946 they became a French overseas department. Comoros, apart from Mayotte, became independent in 1976.

STATISTICS

To see the statistics of each country's area and population, plus its capital, turn to pages 102–106.

CONGO, a People's Republic in equatorial Africa. Behind a narrow coastal plain is an upland region; the north is a swampy plain drained by the Congo (Zaïre) and Oubangui rivers. High temperatures and heavy rainfall, except on the coast, have encourged the growth of rain forests and wooded savanna. Most people speak Bantu languages (including Kongo, Téké and Mbochi); 12,000 pygmies live in central Congo. About one-third of the people work on the land, and a third in industry: oil extraction and processing industries are especially important. Discovered by Europeans in 1482, Congo later became a slave trade center. French rule was established in the 1880s. Full independence was achieved in 1960.

COSTA RICA, a Central American republic, has coastlines on the Caribbean Sea and the Pacific Ocean. Inland it is mountainous with volcanic peaks. Fertile plateaus lie between the mountains. About 70 percent of the people live in the largest of these, the Central Plateau. More than 80 percent of the population is of European origin. Most non-whites are of mixed European and American Indian origin. The main cash crop is coffee. Costa Rica is one of the more prosperous nations of Central America. Spain ruled the country from around 1530 to 1821. Dictatorships and revolutions marred its early years of independence, but it has enjoyed democracy since 1919.

CÔTE D'IVOIRE (Ivory Coast), a republic in West Africa with a coastline on the Gulf of Guinea. Behind the broad coastal lowlands are high plains. The main highlands are in the northwest: the highest peak, Mt. Nimba, is on the Côte d'Ivoire-Liberia-Guinea border. The south has an equatorial climate. The north is often scorched by the northeasterly Harmattan, a wind from the Sahara. There is some forest in the south, but savanna is the main type of vegetation. About 60 languages and dialects are spoken by the Black peoples, but French is the official language. The Côte d'Ivoire is prosperous by African standards, but prosperity is confined mostly to the southeast. Four-fifths of the people farm the land. The Côte d'Ivoire leads the world in cocoa production and is the 4th largest coffee producer. There is some mining, but the processing and consumer goods industries make a larger contribution to the economy. The Côte d'Ivoire became a French colony in 1893, and achieved independence in 1960.

CUBA, the largest nation in the West Indies. Small islands, reefs, and mangrove swamps skirt much of the coast. More than half of the land is flat and fertile. Forested mountain ranges occupy about 25 percent of the land, the rest being gently undulating country. The climate is tropical, with heavy rainfall. About 75 percent of the people are descendants of Spaniards, the rest being Blacks or mulattos. About two-thirds of the people are town-dwellers, and a quarter work on the land. About 34 percent of Cuba is cultivated, most farms being government-owned. Sugar and its byproducts, molasses and rum, are the main products. Minerals, tobacco, bananas, and fish are also exported. Columbus discovered Cuba in 1492, and Spain ruled it between 1511 and 1898. U.S. influence was strong in the 20th century until Communist guerrillas seized power in 1959.

CYPRUS, an island republic in the north-eastern Mediterranean Sea. There are fertile coastal plains and a broad central plain (the Mesaoria). The Kyrenia and Karpass mountains are in the north and the Troödos mountains in the south. The climate is typically Mediterranean. Greek Cypriots form 80 percent of the population, Turkish Cypriots 18 percent, and Armenian, Maronite, and other minorities also live there. Most people feel themselves to be Greeks or Turks rather than Cypriots. About 60 percent of the land is cultivated; one-third of the workforce is employed in farming. Agriculture supplies about half of the exports, and minerals (notably copper) about 30 percent. Cyprus was a British colony from 1927 to 1960, when it gained independence. In 1974 Turkish forces occupied the north. The island was partitioned, the northern 40 percent being proclaimed the "Turkish Cypriot Federated State."

CZECHOSLOVAKIA, a landlocked communist republic in Eastern Europe. The saucer-shaped Bohemian plateau, bounded by mountains, is in the east. It is drained by the upper Elbe (the Vltava), on which Prague stands. Moravia, in the center, is largely

WORLD ATLAS

O C E A N

80   2   60   3   40

L

O   C   E   A   N

Severnaja
Zemlja

Wrangel I.

Bering Sea

Aleutian Islands

180

Nordvik   New Siberian Is.   Nižnie
Kolymsk
Chatanga   Verkhoyansk   Zyr'anka   Anadyr
Okamenskoje   4

nka   Tura   Lena   Yakutsk   Petropavlovsk
Kamčatskij
Kamčatka Penin.

Arctic Circle

b   e   r   i   a

Krasnojarsk   Lake   Čita   Ochotsk   Sea of Okhotsk
Baykal   Irkutsk   Ulan-Ude   160

al   Socialist Republics   Jakutsk   Sakhalin
OCIALIST REPUBLICS   Kamsomolsk   Sea of Okhotsk
Nikolajevsk-na-Amure   Soveckaja Gavan'
Kyzyl   Blagoveščensk   Hokkaidó   K
Manchuria   Ussurijsk   Otaru   Kushiro   Sapporo
MONGOLIA   Harbin   Vladivostok   Hakodate

Ulan Bator   Changchun   Fushun   160
Shenyang   NORTH   P'yongyang   Sendai   20
Nei Monggol Zizhiqu   KOREA   Seoul   Kyoto   Yokohama
Beijing   Lushun   SOUTH   Pusan   Tokyo
Hohhot   Dalian   KOREA   Hiroshima   Nagoya
Yinchuan   Tianjin   Yellow   Shikoku   Osaka
Taiyuan   Jinan   Sea   Kitakyushu   Kyushu
Xining   Qingdao   Nagasaki   Kagoshima
Zhengzhou   Xuzhou   Shanghai
Lanzhou   Xi'an   Nanjing   East
CHINA   Hangzhou   China Sea   Tropic of Cancer
Chengdu   Wuhan   Nanchang   Ryukyu Is.
Chongqing   Changsha   Fuzhou   Taipei
Guiyang   Guangxi Zhuangzu   TAIWAN   5
Kunming   Guangzhou
Macau   Hong-Kong
(Port.)   (U.K.)
Hainan

Bonin Is.
(Japan)
Kazan

Mariana Is.
(U.S. Trust Terr.)

P   A   C   I   F   I   C   O   C   E   A   N

AUSTRALIA

140

ARCTIC OCEAN

Shetland (U.K.)
Faeroe (Den.)
Reykjavik
ICELAND
Denmark Strait
Greenland Sea
Jan Mayen (Nor.)
C. Patersen
GREENLAND
Godhavn
Godthaab
Davis Strait
Baffin Bay
Thule
Etah
Baffin Island
Hudson Str.
Southampton Island
Ellesmere I.
C. Morris Jesup
Devon I.
Pr. of Wales I.
G. of Boothia
Queen Elizabeth Islands
Parry Islands
Melville I.
North Pole
Sverdrup Is.
Hudson Bay
Churchill
Fort Severn
Arctic Circle
Banks Island
M'Clure Str.
Victoria Island
Great Bear Lake
Coppermine
Yellowknife
Great Slave Lake
Hay River
Fort Nelson
Beaufort Sea
Mackenzie
Norman Wells
Fort Wilson
Fort Chimo
Hebron
Schefferville
Fort George
Inoucdjouac
Labrador
L A B R A D O R
Moosonee
Cochrane
Chicoutimi
Quebec
Sept Iles
Gulf of St. Lawrence
Anticosti I.
C. Breton I.
Halifax
C. Chidley
Battle Harbour
Island of Newfoundland
C. Race
L. Winnipeg
Nelson
Lynn Lake
Mc Murray
Athabaska
L. Saskatoon
Regina
Edmonton
Calgary
Jasper
Prince George
Prince Rupert
Queen Charlotte Is.
Vancouver I.
Victoria
Seattle
Vancouver
ROCKY MOUNTAINS
C A N A D A
Whitehorse
Dawson
Juneau
Skagway
Alexander Archipelago
Mt. St. Elias 5489
Cordova
Anchorage
Seward
Mt. McKinley 6194
Fairbanks
Fort Yukon
Kotzebue
Pt. Barrow
Barrow
UNITED STATES
Alaska
Kodiak I.
Alaska Pen.
Nunivak I.
Bering Sea
St. Lawrence I.
C. Pr. of Wales
Bering Str.
Wrangel I.
Anadyr
Siberia
PACIFIC OCEAN

180 170 160 150
A B C D E F G H I J K L M N O P Q R S T U

Copyright. Vallardi Industrie Grafiche

NORTH AMERICA

UNITED STATES
MEXICO
BAHAMAS
CUBA
HAITI
DOMINICAN REP.
Santo Domingo
Puerto Rico (U.S.)
JAMAICA
HONDURAS
GUATEMALA
BELIZE
EL SALVADOR
NICARAGUA
COSTA RICA
PANAMA
Canal Zone (U.S.)
VENEZUELA
COLOMBIA

Caribbean Sea
Gulf of Mexico
PACIFIC OCEAN
Greater Antilles
Yucatán Str.
Florida
L. Michigan

Bermuda Is. (U.K.)

Havana
Nassau
Santiago de Cuba
Port-au-Prince
Kingston
San José
Managua
Tegucigalpa
Belmopan
San Salvador
Guatemala
Caracas
Maracaibo
Barranquilla
Cartagena
Panamá
Medellín
Bogotá

New York
New Haven
Philadelphia
Baltimore
Washington D.C.
Buffalo
Cleveland
Pittsburgh
Toronto
Toledo
Detroit
Chicago
Milwaukee
Minneapolis
St. Paul
Des Moines
Omaha
Kansas City
Topeka
Wichita
Oklahoma City
Tulsa
St. Louis
Indianapolis
Cincinnati
Columbus
Nashville
Knoxville
Memphis
Atlanta
Birmingham
Montgomery
Jackson
New Orleans
Houston
Galveston
Corpus Christi
San Antonio
Austin
Dallas
Fort Worth
Columbia
Charleston
Savannah
Jacksonville
Tampa
Miami
Raleigh
Richmond
Norfolk
Columbus
Pierre
Casper
Cheyenne
Denver
Mt. Elbert 4399
Santa Fé
Albuquerque
El Paso
Ciudad Juárez
Chihuahua
Phoenix
Tucson
Mexicali
Tijuana
San Diego
Los Angeles
San Bernardino
Las Vegas
Fresno
Mt. Whitney 4418
Carson City
Reno
Sacramento
Oakland
San Francisco
Salt Lake City
Great Salt Lake
Pocatello
Boise City
Snake
Nuevo Laredo
Matamoros
Monterrey
Saltillo
Torreón
Durango
Culiacán
Mazatlán
Guaymas
Ciudad Obregón
Hermosillo
La Paz
Guadalajara
León
S. Luis Potosí
Querétaro
Mexico City
Puebla
Oaxaca
Veracruz
Tampico
Tuxpan
Mérida
C. Catoche
Acapulco
Manzanillo
Tehuantepec

Mississippi
Missouri
Ohio
Arkansas
R. Grande

Rocky
Sierra Nevada
Lower California
G. of California
Revilla Gigedo Is.
Pta. Eugenia
C. Falso
Clipperton (Fr.)
C. Mendocino
Tropic of Cancer

West from 100 Greenwich

Km
0   500   1000

ATLANTIC

Tropic of Cancer

S. Paulo (Braz.)
Fernando de Noronha (Braz.)
Equator

C. São Roque
Natal
Rio Gr. do Norte
Paraíba
Pernambuco
Recife
Maceió
S. Alagoas
Sergipe
Juàzeiro
João Pessoa

Fortaleza (Ceará)
Teresina
Parnaíba
Piauí
Maranhão
São Luís
Belém
Pará
Santarém
Óbidos
Macapá
Amapá
Cayenne
French Guiana
SURINAM
Paramaribo
New Amsterdam
Georgetown
GUYANA

D West from 60 Greenwich E

Barbuda (U.K.)
ANTIGUA
Guadeloupe (Fr.)
DOMINICA
Martinique (Fr.)
ST. LUCIA
BARBADOS
Bridgetown
ST. VINCENT
GRENADA
Port-of-Spain
TRINIDAD AND TOBAGO
Lesser Antilles
Puerto Rico (U.S.)
San Juan
St. Kitts (U.K.)
Virgin Is. (U.K., U.S.)
Curaçao (Neth.)

Roraima 2810
Roraima
Ciudad Bolívar
Cumaná
Caracas
Valencia
Maracay
S. Cristóbal
Maracaibo
VENEZUELA
S. Fernando de Atabapo
Amazonas
Barcelona
Manaus
Boa Vista
Moura
Manicoré
Borba
Humaitá
Pôrto Velho
Rondônia
Riberalta
Acre
Cruzeiro do Sul
Rio Branco

BAHAMAS
Nassau
Havana
Santa Clara
CUBA
Santiago de Cuba
Guantánamo
HAITI
Port au Prince
DOMINICAN REP.
Santo Domingo
JAMAICA (U.K.)
Kingston
Greater Antilles
Caribbean Sea
Cayman (U.K.)

Florida
Tampa
Miami
UNITED STATES
Florida Str.
Yucatán Channel
Gulf of Mexico
Mérida
Yucatán
MEXICO

Barranquilla
Cartagena
Medellín
Manizales
Cali
Buenaventura
Magdalena
Bogotá
COLOMBIA
Pasto
ECUADOR
Quito
Guayaquil
Cuenca
Chimborazo 6272
Cocos I. (Costa.)
Malpelo I. (Col.)
Galápagos Islands (Ecuad.)

PANAMA
Panamá
Canal Zone
San José
COSTA RICA
NICARAGUA
Managua
Nicaragua
San Salvador
EL SALVADOR
Tegucigalpa
HONDURAS
Belmopan
BELIZE
GUATEMALA

Chiclayo
Trujillo
Chimbote
Cerro de Pasco
Piura
Cajamarca
Iquitos
PERU
Cuzco
Ucayali
Pta. Parinas

BRAZIL
Amazonas
Pará
Tocantins
Carolina
Caratinga

PACIFIC

Copyright. Vallardi Industrie Grafiche

Map labels

O   C   E   A   N

Trindade (Braz.)
Martin Vaz (Braz.)

Caravelas
Espirito Santo
Dignantina
Vitória
Campos
Piragora
Rio de Janeiro
Belo Horizonte
Rio de Janeiro
São Paulo
Ribeirão Preto
São Paulo
Campinas
Santos

Minas Gerais
Gerais
São Paulo

Goiânia
Uberaba
Corumbá
Pto. Alegre
Paranaguá
Paranaguá
Curitiba
Blumenau
Sta Catalina
Florianópolis

Paraná
Concepção
Paraná

PARAGUAY
Asunción
Sta Cruz
Sucre
Cochabamba
Oruro
Potosí
Uyuni
Jujuy
S.Salvador de Jujuy
Salta
S.Miguel de Tucumán
Catamarca

Antofagasta
Copiapó
La Serena
Valparaíso
Santiago
Talca
Concepción
Temuco
Valdivia
Pto. Montt
Chiloé I.

Arequipa
Mollendo
Arica
Iquique
Tocopilla
Cajama
Lacama Desert
Tarapacá
Tattal

Villarica
Resistencia
Corrientes
Santa Fé
Córdoba
Aconcagua
San Juan
Mendoza
Rosario
San Luis
Buenos Aires
La Plata
Paraná
Santiago del Estero
La Rioja

Río Grande do Sul
Pto. Alegre
Río Grande
Pelotas
Salto
URUGUAY
Montevideo
Paysandú
Río de la Plata
Mar del Plata
Bahía Blanca
Viedma
Rawson
Neuquén
S.Carlos de Bariloche

Comodoro Rivadavia
Deseado
Sta Cruz
Río Gallegos
Magellan's Str.
Tierra del Fuego
Punta Arenas
Co. Yogan 2469
C. Horn
Ushuaia

Falkland Is. (U.K.)
South Georgia (U.K.)

Wellington I.
Pto. Aisén

San Ambrosio (Chile)
San Felix (Chile)
Juan Fernández Is. (Chile)
Tropic of Capricorn

O   C   E   A   N

Km
0   500   1000

CHINA

Hang chou
Nan chang
Chang sha
Fu chou
Canton
Macau (Port.)
Hong Kong (U.K.)

East China Sea

JAPAN
Kagoshima

Ryukyu Is.
Amami
Daito
Okinawa

Bonin Is.
(Ogasawara)

Volcano Is.
(Kazan)

Marcus
(Minami Tori)

Tropic

1

Taipei
TAIWAN
Tai nan

20

Parece Vela
(Okino)

PACI

Agrihan

Mariana Is.

Saipan

Guam
(U.S.)

Wake

Marshall Island

(U.S. Trust Terr.)

Laoag

Luzon

Quezon City
Manila
Batangas
Legaspi

PHILIPPINES

Mindoro
Samar

Palawan
Iloilo

Mindanao

Zamboanga
Davao

Sulu Arch.

Sandakan

Brunei

Sarawak

Borneo

Celebes
Sea

Manado

South China Sea

2

MICR

Caroline Islands

Yap
Uithi Is.
Palau Is.

Hall Is.
Truk Is.

Nomoi Is.

Eniwetok

Kwajalein

Jaluit

Kusaie

Ratak Chain

Ralik Chain

MELL

NAURU

Ocean I.

Balikpapan
Palu
Sulawesi
(Celebes)
Bandjarmasin
Buru
Seram
Ambon

Halmahera

Sorong

Irian Jaya

New
Guinea

Djajapura

PAPUA
NEW GUINEA

Madang

Admiralty Is.

New Ireland

Bismarck
Archipelago

New
Britain

Rabaul

Bougainville

SOLOMON

St. Isabel

Malaita

IS.

S. Cristôbal

Santa Cruz Is.

A

INDONESIA

Ujung
Pandang

Banda Sea

Flores Sea

Surabaya

Lesser Sunda Islands

Bali
Lombok
Sumbawa
Flores
Sumba

Dili

Timor

Tanimbar

Aru Is.

Merauke

Daru

Torres Strait
C. York

Samarai

Port Moresby

Bairiki

Guadalcanal

NESI

M

Tar

3

Arafura Sea

Timor
Sea

Melville I.

Arnhem
Land

Darwin

Cape
York
Pen.

Coral
Sea

NEW
Caledonia

VANUATU REPU

Port Vila

(France)

Loyal
Isla

Nournea

Gulf of
Carpentaria

Newcastle
Waters

Wyndham

Broome

Derby

NORTHERN

TERRITORY

Normanton

Townsville

Great Barrier Reef

QUEENSLAND

Mackay

Rockhampton

Barcaldine

Brisbane

C. Byron

Norfolk Is.

Tasman

20

N.W.
Cape

Onslow

Great Sandy
Desert

Cloncurry

Sea

WESTERN

Gibson Desert

AUSTRALIA

AUSTRALIA

Carnarvon

Gt. Victoria
Desert

Oodnadatta

L. Eyre

SOUTH

AUSTRALIA

Bourke

Broken
Hill

NEW SOUTH

Darling

Murray

WALES

Newcastle

Sydney

Canberra

Kosciusko
2228

NE

Geraldton

Kalgoorlie

Port Augusta

Perth
Fremantle
Albany

Great Australian
Bight

Adelaide

VICTORIA

Melbourne

Bass Strait

ZEALA

Mt.

4

S.

AUSTRALIAN

BASIN

TASMANIA

Launceston

Hobart

Invercargil
Stewart

40

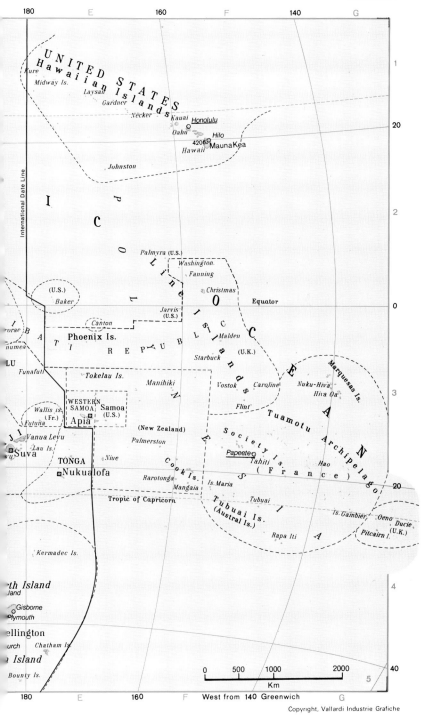

180   E   160   F   140   G

Kure

UNITED STATES

Hawaiian Islands

Midway Is.

Laysan

Gardner

Necker

Kauai

Oahu   Honolulu

Hilo

4206   MaunaKea

Hawaii

20

Johnston

International Date Line

I

C

P

O

L

Palmyra (U.S.)

Washington

Fanning

Christmas

Equator

0

(U.S.)

Baker

Jarvis
(U.S.)

O

C

Canton

Malden

Phoenix Is.

(U.K.)

I   B

orae

humea

LU

A

T

I

R

E

P

U

B

L

Starbuck

C

Funafuti

Tokelau Is.

Manihiki

N

I

Line Islands

S

O

Vostok   *Caroline*

Nuku-Hiva
Hiva Oa

Marquesas Is.

E

C

A

N

Wallis Is.
(Fr.)

WESTERN
SAMOA

Samoa
(U.S.)

Flint

Tuamotu

Futuna

Apia

(New Zealand)

Archipelago

Vanua Levu

Palmerston

Society Is.

Lau Is.

Suva

Niue

(F r a n c e)

TONGA

Cook Is.

Papeete

Tahiti

Hao

Nukualofa

Rarotonga

Is. Maria

20

Mangaia

Tropic of Capricorn

Tubuai

Is. Gambier

Oeno

Tubuai Is.
(Austral Is.)

Ducie

Rapa Iti

A

Pitcairn I.

(U.K.)

Kermadec Is.

th Island
land

4

Gisborne

lymouth

ellington
urch

Chatham Is.

a Island

Bounty Is.

0   500   1000   2000

40

Km

180   E   160   F   West from 140 Greenwich   G

5

FLAGS OF THE WORLD

Flags of the World

Afghanistan

Albania

Algeria

Andorra

Angola

Antigua
and Barbuda

Argentina

Australia

Austria

Bahamas

Bahrain

Bangladesh

Barbados

Belgium

Belize

Benin

Bhutan

Bolivia

Botswana

Brazil

Brunei

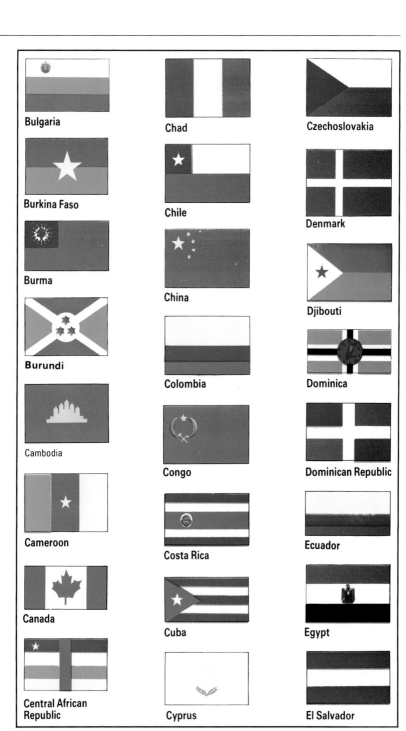

Bulgaria

Chad

Czechoslovakia

Burkina Faso

Chile

Denmark

Burma

China

Djibouti

Burundi

Colombia

Dominica

Cambodia

Congo

Dominican Republic

Cameroon

Costa Rica

Ecuador

Canada

Cuba

Egypt

Central African Republic

Cyprus

El Salvador

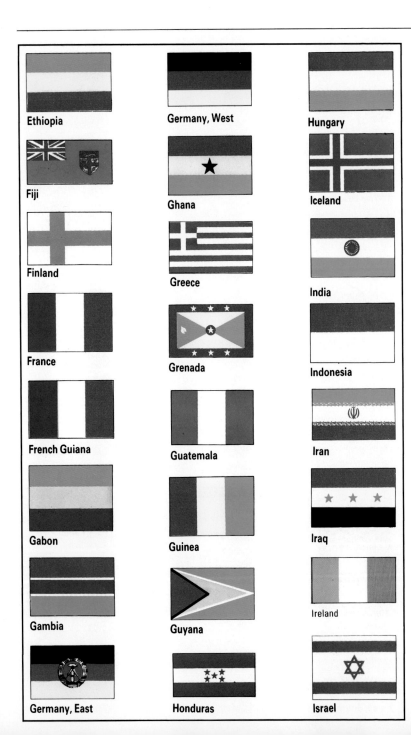

Ethiopia

Germany, West

Hungary

Fiji

Ghana

Iceland

Finland

Greece

India

France

Grenada

Indonesia

French Guiana

Guatemala

Iran

Gabon

Guinea

Iraq

Gambia

Guyana

Ireland

Germany, East

Honduras

Israel

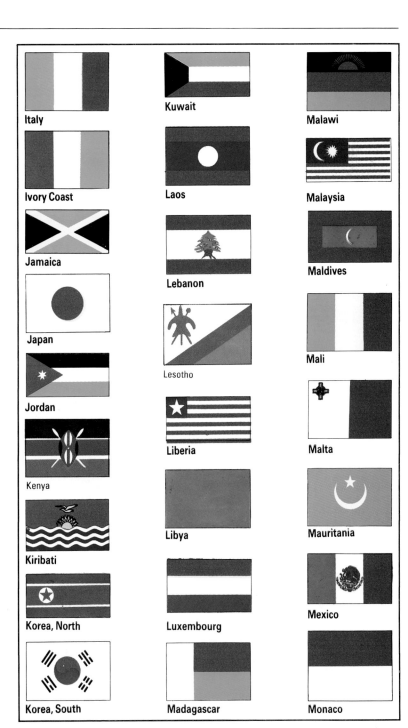

Italy

Ivory Coast

Jamaica

Japan

Jordan

Kenya

Kiribati

Korea, North

Korea, South

Kuwait

Laos

Lebanon

Lesotho

Liberia

Libya

Luxembourg

Madagascar

Malawi

Malaysia

Maldives

Mali

Malta

Mauritania

Mexico

Monaco

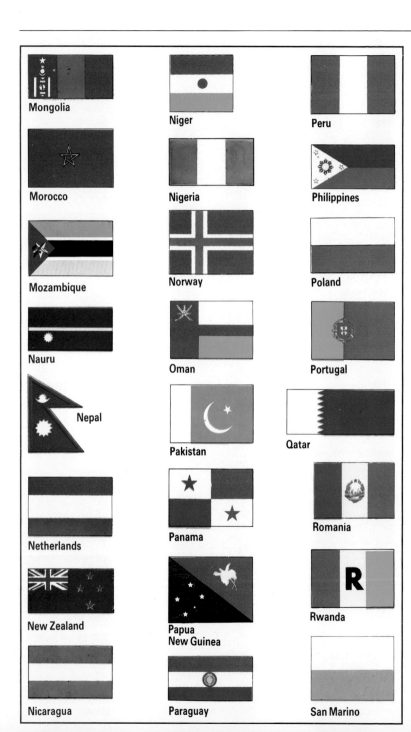

Mongolia

Morocco

Mozambique

Nauru

Nepal

Netherlands

New Zealand

Nicaragua

Niger

Nigeria

Norway

Oman

Pakistan

Panama

Papua New Guinea

Paraguay

Peru

Philippines

Poland

Portugal

Qatar

Romania

Rwanda

San Marino

Saudi Arabia

Senegal

Sierra Leone

Singapore

Solomon Islands

South Africa

Spain

Sri Lanka

St Christopher Nevis

St Lucia

St Vincent and Grenadines

Sudan

Surinam

Swaziland

Sweden

Switzerland

Syria

Tanzania

Thailand

Togo

Tonga

Trinidad and Tobago

Tunisia

Turkey

Tuvalu

**UAE
(United Arab Emirates)**

Uganda

United Kingdom

Uruguay

USA

USSR

Vanuatu

Vatican City

Venezuela

Vietnam

Western Samoa

Yemen AR

Yemen PDR

Yugoslavia

Zaire

Zambia

Zimbabwe

truck

heading

Inglefield clip

staff or pole

grommet

sleeve

halyard

Red Cross

Red Crescent

Magen David

lowland, with rivers draining into the Danube. Slovakia, in the east, is mainly upland, with some plains in the south. The climate is continental. The people include the Czechs (65 percent of the population), in Bohemia and Moravia, the Slovaks (30 percent), and various minorities. Industry, which is nationalized, is the main occupation. The country is rich in coal and lignite and has many metal ores, although metals are imported. Farmland covers 55 percent of the country. Crops include barley, hops, rye, sugar beet, and wheat. The republic was created in 1918, and became a communist state in 1948.

DENMARK, the smallest but most densely populated nation in northern Europe. It consists of the low-lying Jutland peninsula and about 500 islands, the largest of which, Sjaelland, contains the capital, Copenhagen. Two thirds of the land is fertile farmland or pasture. Animal products (bacon, butter, cheese, and eggs) are particularly important, as is sea fishing. The leading sector of the economy is manufacturing. Products include silverware, furniture, processed food, chemicals, engineering goods, machinery, and ships. The Faeröe Islands and Greenland are semi-independent parts of Denmark. They are governed by home rule.

DJIBOUTI, a small republic on the Red Sea in northeastern Africa. The land is mostly hot desert. The people include the Somali-speaking Issas, the nomadic Afars, both of whom are Muslims, and some Europeans, Arabs, and other foreigners. Stock raising is the main occupation. The country became a French colony in 1881, called French Somaliland. In 1967 it was renamed the Territory of the Afars and Issas. It became independent in 1977, calling itself Djibouti.

DOMINICA, volcanic island republic in the Windward Islands in the eastern Caribbean Sea. Its wet tropical climate supports dense forests. Most people are Blacks or of mixed origin. There is a small Carib American Indian community, mostly of mixed origin. Agriculture and tourism are the main industries. Dominica was under British rule from 1805 until independence in 1978.

DOMINICAN REPUBLIC, a nation occupying the eastern half of Hispaniola, an island in the West Indies. The land is mountainous and the climate tropical. Rain forests are widespread, and the valleys are fertile. More than 70 percent of the population is of mixed Black and European descent, 15 percent is White, and 10 percent is Black. More than half the workers are in agriculture. Sugar is the chief export. Bauxite, nickel, gold, and silver are mined and there is some light industry. Tourism is increasingly important. Columbus discovered Hispaniola in 1492. Spain lost the area to France in 1795 but ruled it again in 1809–21. From 1822 to 1844 Haitians occupied the area. The Dominican Republic was founded in 1844; its history has been marred by violence and civil war.

ECUADOR, a republic on the Equator in northwestern South America, includes the 15 Galápagos Islands to the west. The Pacific coastlands have a high average annual temperature. The Andes ranges are much cooler. The hot Amazon basin occupies eastern Ecuador. More than half the people

---

STATISTICS

To see the statistics of each country's area and population, plus its capital, turn to pages 102–106.

are American Indians. There are also people of European, African, and mixed descent. Fewer than half the people work on the land. Oil is the leading industrial product. The Incas ruled the area from about 1470 until Spaniards conquered it in 1533. Independence was achieved in 1822, and Ecuador became a separate republic in 1830.

EGYPT, an Arab Republic in northeastern Africa. The fertile, irrigated Nile valley contains 99 percent of the population, although it covers less than 4 percent of the country. The Nile flows through Egypt. Near the Mediterranean Sea it divides into two branches, the Dumyat (Damietta) and Rashid (Rosetta), which enclose the triangular delta. The rest of Egypt is desert. The western (Libyan) desert contains several large oases and depressions, notably the Qattara depression, which is below sea level. The eastern, or Arabian, desert rises to highlands that border the Red Sea. But the highest peak, Jabal Katrinah, is in the Sinai peninsula, east of the Suez Canal. This international waterway, opened in 1869, links the Mediterranean and Red seas. Average temperatures in Egypt are high, and rainfall is low. Most Egyptians are Arabs, but there are Berber, Nubian, and Sudanese minorities. Egypt is a poor country, although it is the 2nd most industrialized in Africa. Nearly half the people live in urban areas. Energy comes mainly from hydroelectric stations, especially at the Aswan High Dam. Manufactures include cement, chemicals, plastics, steel, sugar, and textiles. Some phosphates, iron ore, and oil are mined. Just over half the people work on the land. The chief export is cotton, but most farmers are peasants (*fellahin*) who practice subsistence farming. Tourism is important. Ancient Egypt's pyramids and other monuments are special attractions. Ancient Egypt's history is divided into 30 dynasties. The first began in 3100 B.C., when Upper and Lower Egypt were united. It reached its peak under King Thutmose III (1490–36 B.C.). From 525 B.C. Egypt was mostly under foreign rule. In 30 B.C. it became part of the Roman Empire, and in A.D. 395 it was the center of the Coptic Christian Church. Arabs occupied Egypt in 639–642, introducing Islam and Arabic. In 1517 Egypt became part of the Ottoman Empire. It was under British control 1881–

1922, when it became an independent kingdom. Egypt was declared a republic in 1953 and, in 1956, nationalized the Suez Canal.

EL SALVADOR, a densely populated republic in Central America, has a coastline on the Pacific Ocean. The country is mountainous. The climate is warm and wet. About 90 percent of the population is of mixed European and American Indian descent. Agriculture employs 52 percent of the workforce, the main crops being coffee and cotton. Spain conquered the area in 1526. Independence from Spain was achieved in 1821 and El Salvador became an independent republic in 1841.

EQUATORIAL GUINEA, a republic in west-central Africa, comprises Río Muni on the mainland and the islands of Bioko (formerly Fernando Póo) and Pagalu. The islands are volcanic; Río Muni contains hills and plateaus. The climate is equatorial. The Bantu Fang form the majority in Río Muni. Fang, Bubi (the original inhabitants), and Fernandinos (descendants of liberated slaves) live on the islands. Most people are farmers: coffee is the main crop. Spain took the territory in the 1840s. Independence was achieved in 1968.

ETHIOPIA, a republic in northeastern Africa. The highlands are divided into two blocks by the deep Rift Valley. Lowlands occur in the east near the Red Sea coast. The main river, the Blue Nile, flows from Lake Tana in the north. The lowlands are hot and arid, contrasting with the cooler, moister uplands. About 100 languages are spoken: most belong to the Cushitic, Semitic, and Nilotic families. Cushites include the nomadic Galla, the largest single ethnic group. The Amhara, who form the ruling class, speak a Semitic language, while Nilotic languages are spoken by Negroid people in the east. Four out of five people work on the land. Coffee makes up about 75 percent of the exports. Ethiopia is the home of an ancient monarchy which embraced Christianity in the 4th century. The monarchy was abolished in 1974.

FIJI, a nation in the south-central Pacific. Two mountainous, volcanic islands, Viti Levu and Vanua Levu, make up 87 percent of the total area, although there are 320 other small islands. About 48 percent of the people are Indians (mainly Hindus); 44 percent are Melanesians; there are also Europeans, Chinese, and other Pacific islanders. Agriculture is the main activity and tourism is important. Discovered in 1643, the islands became a British colony in 1874 and an independent nation within the Commonwealth in 1970.

FINLAND, a republic in northeastern Europe. It contains 55,000 lakes, and water covers 9 percent of the country. Much of Lapland, in the north, is within the Arctic Circle. Winters are long and severe, but the short summers are warm. Forests cover more than four-fifths of the country and timber has been the mainstay of the economy. Farming is confined mainly to the far south. Russia occupied Finland in 1809, but Finland declared itself independent in 1917 and, became a republic in 1919.

FRANCE, the 2nd largest nation in Europe after the U.S.S.R. Mountain ranges (the French Alps, which contain France's highest peak, Mont Blanc, and the lower Jura Mts.) form the southeastern border. The Vosges Mts. are in the northeast, overlooking the Rhine rift valley, and the scenic Massif Central is in south-central France. The northwest peninsula, including Brittany, is lower but also scenic, with a superb indented coastline. The Paris basin is a saucer-shaped depression enclosed by rings of hills with outward facing scarps. The Aquitaine basin in the southwest is a low plain, partly fringed by coastal sand dunes. It extends to the high Pyrenees along the border with Spain. The Rhône-Saône valley, in the south-east between the Massif Central and the southeastern mountains, ends in the marshy Camargue. The climate varies from the moist,

temperate north to the Mediterranean coastlands, with their hot, dry summers and mild, moist winters. The climate also changes from west to east. Rain falls all the year round except in the Mediterranean region. Several minority languages are spoken: Breton, a Celtic tongue, in Brittany; Basque in the Western Pyrenees; Catalan in the eastern Pyrenees; Provençal in the southeast; and German in the northeast. Foreign-born people, including Portuguese, Algerians, Spaniards, and Italians, make up 6.5 percent of the population. Some 78 percent of the people live in towns. The chief mineral resource is iron ore, notably in Lorraine. Some coal, oil, and natural gas are mined. Energy also comes from hydroelectric stations and the River Rance tidal power station in Brittany. There is a wide range of manufacturing industries. Paris is known especially for its luxury and fashion products; Lyon is known for textiles; Marseille and Bordeaux are major industrial ports; and Lille, on the northwestern coalfield, is the center of a large industrial region. Farming is also important, and nine out of every 100 people work on the land. A high proportion of the farms are small and unmechanized, but France is a leading producer of wheat, barley, oats, flax, and sugar beet and has a lot of livestock, including dairy cattle. France is famous for its quality wines and cheeses. The tourist industry is a major source of foreign earnings. France is a founder member of the European Community. The Romans conquered the country (then called Gaul) in

STATISTICS
To see the statistics of each country's area and population, plus its capital, turn to pages 102–106.

the 50s B.C.. In A.D. 486 the country became an independent kingdom. The monarchy was overthrown by the French Revolution of 1789. After years of turmoil, during which France was successively a republic, an empire, a monarchy, a republic again and then once more a monarchy, it finally settled down as a republic in 1875.

GABON, a republic on the Equator in west-central Africa. Behind the coastal plain are plateaus and mountains. Most of Gabon is in the River Ogooué drainage basin. Average annual temperatures and rainfall are high. Rain forests cover 75 percent of the land. About 40 languages are spoken: the Bantu-speaking Fang form the largest ethnic group; a few pygmies form the smallest. About 70 percent of the population is engaged in agriculture, the chief cash crops being cocoa, coffee, palm oil, and bananas. But the main wealth of Gabon comes from oil and natural gas, manganese, and uranium. France established a settlement on the coast in 1842 and founded Libreville for free slaves in 1849. Gabon became a French colony in the 1880s and an independent republic in 1980.

GAMBIA, in West Africa, is the smallest nation in mainland Africa. It is a narrow strip of land bordering the Gambia River, being entirely enclosed by Senegal except along its short Atlantic coast. The climate is tropical. Wooded savanna covers much of the land. The largest of the five main ethnic groups are the Mandingo and the Fulbe (or Fulani). Eighty-five out of every hundred people work on the land. The only major cash crop is peanuts. Tourism is expanding rapidly. Gambia became a British colony in 1888. Full independence was achieved in 1965, and Gambia became a republic in 1970.

GERMANY, EAST, officially the German Democratic Republic, a communist country in Eastern Europe. The Baltic seacoast is fringed by sand bars and lagoons. The north is part of the North European Plain, with many lakes and marshes and vast areas of heathlands. Soil fertility is generally low. The south, which is more fertile, contains low plateaus and mountains, including the Harz Mountains and the Thüringer Wald in the southwest and the Erzgebirge in the southeast. The main rivers are the Elbe,

which flows into West Germany, and the Oder-Neisse rivers, which form the frontier with Poland. The climate is continental, and rainfall is moderate. About 77 percent of the population lives in urban areas, working in industry and services. East Germany is now one of the world's top 10 industrial powers. Most factories are government-owned. About one-third of the output comes from engineering industries. Consumer goods, precision and optical goods, chemicals, textiles, and plastics are all important. The main industrial centers are the Dresden, Erfurt, Gera, Halle, Karl-Marx-Stadt and Leipzig districts in the south and the area around Berlin. Mines produce lignite, potash, copper, iron ore, nickel, tin, and uranium. Agriculture employs 10 percent of the workforce. Barley, oats, potatoes, rye, sugar beet, and wheat are leading crops. Germany was partitioned after World War II, and East Germany, including East Berlin, corresponds to the former Soviet Occupation Zone. It has been independent since 1949.

GERMANY, WEST, officially the Federal Republic of Germany. The coasts on the Baltic and North seas are fringed by sandy islands and dunes. The northern plains are drained by the Elbe, Weser, and Ems rivers. The natural vegetation is moorland and heath, but large areas have been cleared for farming. Central Germany contains hills, plateaus, and low horsts (block mountains). The leading region is the industrial Ruhr valley, with its rich coalfield. Southwestern Germany, the chief farm region, includes horsts that border the Rhine rift valley. The horsts include the Black Forest and the Odenwald. The southeast is an upland zone which includes the scenic Bavarian Alps in the far south. The Danube, which rises in the

Black Forest, is Europe's 2nd longest river after the Volga in the U.S.S.R. It drains much of the southeast. The center and south have slightly warmer summers and colder winters than the north. Rainfall is moderate. After World War II millions of refugees from East Germany and eastern Europe flooded in; nearly 25 percent of West Germans today are former refugees. Also in recent years, many immigrants or "guest workers," from Turkey, Yugoslavia, Italy, and other places have found jobs in the country: there were 1.6 million such workers in West Germany in 1987. West Germany is a highly industrialized nation, having achieved an "economic miracle" since 1945. The largest city, West Berlin, is an enclave in East Germany. Hamburg and Bremen are the chief seaports, but the river port of Duisburg, at the confluence of the Ruhr and Rhine, has a greater annual tonnage of shipping than Hamburg. The ships ply to Rotterdam in the Netherlands, which handles a substantial part of German trade. West Germany is the world's 8th largest coal-producer (the main coalfields being the Ruhr, Aachen, and Saar), the 3rd largest producer of lignite and it also produces some potash, salt, metal ores, and oil. Chemical and iron and steel industries underpin the economy. Other major industries include electrical engineering, machinery, textiles, and vehicles. Agriculture employs only 4 percent of the workforce, but farming remains important. The main crops in the north are potatoes and rye. In the central uplands and southwest, crops include fruit, grapes (for wine), hops, tobacco, sugar beet, and wheat. The southeast is mainly pastoral. West Germany is a member of the European Community. For hundreds of years, Germany was a loose federation of small states. It was united in 1871 under the leadership of Prussia, whose king became emperor, After World War II it was split into two, West Germany becoming a federal republic in 1949.

GHANA, a republic in West Africa. It is mostly low-lying and contains the man-made Lake Volta. The most fertile region is in the hilly southwest. The only highlands are in the southeast. The climate is hot and wet, with more rain in the southwest than elsewhere. The people are Blacks, and they speak about 100 languages and dialects. Agriculture

employs 54 percent of the workforce. The main crop and export is cocoa. Bauxite, diamonds, gold, and manganese are mined, but manufacturing is small-scale. Portuguese mariners reached Ghana in 1471. The area was the British colony of Gold Coast from 1875 until independence in 1957. Ghana became a republic in 1960.

GREECE, a republic in southeastern Europe. It contains the southern part of the mountainous and deeply indented Balkan peninsula and many islands. The southern Peloponnesus is linked to the north by the narrow Isthmus of Corinth. The northern part of the peninsula contains the Pindus Mts. and Greece's highest peak, Mt. Olympus. It also includes the Plain of Thessaly, the largest lowland apart from the coastal plains of Macedonia and Thrace in the northeast. Islands make up 20 percent of the area of Greece. The Cyclades are 220 islands east of the Peloponnesus in the Aegean Sea. The South Sporades (or Dodecanese), including Rhodes, are Aegean islands nearer to Turkey than Greece. The North Sporades are north-east of Euboea. The Ionian Islands, including Corfu, lie off the west coast. In the south, the largest island, Crete, covers 3,217 sq miles (8,331 sq km). The climate is Mediterranean, with hot, arid summers and mild, moist winters, but winters are severe in the mountains. Greece has many processing industries, and manufactures are now the leading exports. Only one-third of the land is cultivable. Citrus fruits, grapes, olives, tobacco, and wheat are major crops. Sheep, goats, and cattle are raised. Tourism brings

STATISTICS
To see the statistics of each country's area and population, plus its capital, turn to pages 102–106.

in foreign exchange. The merchant navy, one of the world's largest, is another money-earner. Thousands of Greeks emigrate every year, finding work especially in Australia, West Germany, and the U.S. Greece came under Roman rule in 146 B.C., and formed part of the Ottoman (Turkish) empire from A.D. 365 to 1830, when it became independent. Greece is a member of the European Community.

GRENADA, a West Indian nation, the southernmost in the Windward Islands. The land is mountainous and largely forested. Temperatures remain very warm throughout the year. Descendants of African slaves form the largest ethnic group. Most of the rest are of mixed Black and European descent. The main exports are cocoa, nutmegs, and bananas. Tourism is becoming important. Columbus discovered the island in 1498. In 1674–1763 it was a French colony. Thereafter, except for a period of French rule in 1779–83, it was ruled by Britain until it became a fully independent monarchy in the Commonwealth in 1974.

GUATEMALA, a Central American republic. Coastal lowlands face the Pacific Ocean in the southwest; a central highland region with 27 volcanoes, some active, is in the earthquake-prone center; a low forested plain covers the north; and there is a short Caribbean coastline. The altitude modifies the climate. The capital, Guatemala City, is in the hills and is pleasantly warm with heavy rainfall. The lowlands are hotter and generally wetter. More than 50 percent of the people are American Indians; most of the rest are of mixed European and American Indian origin. About half the people are farmers, mainly in the highlands. Coffee is the main crop. Mining is becoming important, especially for nickel. Spain conquered the area in the 1520s. Guatemala became independent in 1821.

GUINEA, a West African republic. Behind the Atlantic coastal plain is the Fouta Djallon plateau, where the Gambia, Niger, and Senegal rivers rise. The northeast contains the Upper Niger plains, while the southeast is mountainous, rising to Mt. Nimba on the border with the Côte d'Ivoire and Liberia. Guinea has a tropical monsoon climate and

savanna covers most areas. Most people are Blacks and a large number of tribal languages are spoken. Eight out of 10 people work on the land. The leading industry is bauxite mining: Guinea is the world's 2nd largest producer. It is a very important export for the country, together with a processed form called alumina. France annexed part of Guinea in 1849 and gradually extended its rule. In 1958 the people of Guinea voted to become independent.

GUINEA-BISSAU, a West African republic. The land is mostly low-lying, with a broad coastal plain and flat offshore islands. It has a tropical monsoon climate. Most people are Black, belonging to various tribal groups. There is a small mulatto community of Guinean and Cape Verdean descent. It has played an important part in the government. Most people are subsistence farmers. The main food crop is rice; the main cash crop is peanuts. There is no mining and little manufacturing. Portuguese explorers first sighted the coast in 1446. In 1836–79 Portugal ruled the country, as well as the Cape Verde Islands, establishing close ties that were to continue. A long guerrilla war began in 1963, led by Guineans and Cape Verdeans. Guinea-Bissau became independent in 1974, followed by Cape Verde in 1975.

GUYANA, a republic in northeastern South America. Behind the flat, cultivated coastal zone, the land rises to a hilly upland and then to the Guiana Highlands in the east and south. Forest covers 83 percent of the land with grassland in the highest mountain areas. The main river is the Essequibo. The climate is tropical. Most people live in the coastal zone: 51 percent are of Asian origin; 33 percent are descendants of Black African slaves; about 10 percent are of mixed origin; and 5 percent are American Indians who live mostly in the forested interior. Bauxite is the main resource, and diamonds and gold are also mined. The chief cash crop is sugar and the main food crop is rice. Guyana was the British colony of British Guiana until independence in 1966.

HAITI, a republic in the western part of the West Indian island of Hispaniola. The interior consists of wooded mountains: the Massif du Nord, the Massif de la Selle (in the southeast), and the Massif de la Hotte (in the southwest). Most people live on the fertile plains, which make up about one-fifth of the country. About 95 percent of the people are of Black African descent. The mulattoes, who form 5 percent, make up a social elite. Voodoo is the chief religion. Most people are subsistence farmers. The chief cash crops are coffee and sugar. Haiti was a French colony from 1697 to 1804, when a revolution brought independence.

HONDURAS, a wedge-shaped Central American republic. It has a coastline on the Caribbean Sea and an outlet to the Pacific Ocean through the Gulf of Fonseca. Behind the hot and humid Caribbean coastal plain, there are mountains and high plateaus with a healthy climate. Most Hondurans are of mixed European and American Indian origin. Honduras is Central America's poorest nation. Nearly two-thirds of the people are farmers. Bananas and coffee are the main cash crops. Forests cover 45 percent of the country and timber is exported. Some lead, zinc, and silver are also exported, and there are many, mostly small, manufacturing and processing industries. Spain ruled Honduras between 1525 and 1821. It was part of a Central American Federation but became fully independent in 1838.

HUNGARY, a landlocked People's Republic in Eastern Europe. It is mostly low-lying and drained by the Danube and the Tisza, its tributary. The fertile, hilly Little Alföld is in the northwest. It is separated from the Great Alföld, or Hungarian Plain (56 percent of the country), by a limestone ridge, the Bakony Forest. Low mountains northeast of Budapest are renowned for their wine. Winters are cold and summers hot. Hungarians, or Magyars, are of Finno-Ugric and Turkic descent, mixed with local peoples. Industry is developing rapidly. Bauxite, coal, and some other minerals are produced, but many raw materials must be imported. More than 50 percent of the factories, all of which are nationalized, are in or around Budapest. Farming employs 18 percent of the workforce. Arable land, orchards and vineyards cover 53 percent of the land, pasture 14 percent, and forests 17 percent. Corn and wheat are the main crops. Hungary

and Austria jointly controlled the Austro-Hungarian Empire from 1867 until it broke up in 1918. Hungary became a communist state in 1948.

ICELAND, an island republic in the North Atlantic Ocean. Large snowfields, glaciers, volcanoes, hot springs (which are used to heat homes in Reykjavík, the capital), and a deeply indented coastline are features of this rugged island. The warm North Atlantic Drift keeps the southern coasts ice-free in winter. Summers are cool. Less than 1 percent of the land is cultivated; the main crops are hay, potatoes, and turnips. Fishing is the main industry. Norwegian Vikings colonized Iceland in A.D. 874. In 1262 it was united with Norway and, in 1380, it came under Denmark. Independence was achieved in 1918. In 1963 it acquired a new volcanic island, Surtsey, which appeared from the sea.

INDIA, the world's 7th largest country in area, but the 2nd largest in terms of population. The Himalayan mountains in the north include India's highest peak, Nanda Devi. In the northwest Kashmir contains parts of the Karakoram and Hindu Kush ranges. The Indus, Ganges, and Brahmaputra rivers rise in the Himalayas. The fertile northern plains of India are densely populated. To the south, the Vindhya range borders the Deccan, a huge, triangular-shaped plateau. It is bounded by two other ranges: the Western Ghats and the lower Eastern Ghats. The main rivers, the Cauvery, Krishna, and Godavari, flow from west to east into the Bay of Bengal. The climate and vegetation vary greatly. The highest mountains have an Arctic climate; the Thar desert borders Pakistan; Cherrapunji in the northeast holds the world rainfall record for one year – 1,041.8 inches (26,461 mm) were recorded in 1860–61; and the Deccan lies in the tropics. Most of India has three seasons: winter in October–February, when it is cool and dry; the hot season in March–June; and the rainy season, June–September, when monsoon

STATISTICS

To see the statistics of each country's area and population, plus its capital, turn to pages 102–106.

winds are drawn into eastern India from the southwest. Hundreds of languages are spoken in India, but the government recognizes only the two official languages, Hindi and English, and 14 other national languages: Assamese, Bengali, Gujerati, Kannada, Kashmiri, Malayalam, Marathi, Oriya, Punjabi, Sanskrit, Sindhi, Tamil, Telegu, and Urdu. India is a mainly poor agricultural nation; 74 percent of the workers farm the land. India is the world's top producer of peanuts, hemp, sugar cane and tea; the 2nd leading producer of millet, rice, and sorghum; the 3rd largest producer of coconuts, copra, and tobacco; and the 4th producer of cotton and wheat. It has more cattle than any other nation, but Hinduism forbids their slaughter. India has various minerals, including bauxite, coal, iron ore, and manganese. Manufacturing has expanded greatly since 1947; the chief products are textiles, but there is also much heavy industry. Various kings ruled India until 1858, when Britain took over. Independence was achieved in 1947 when British India was partitioned into the mainly Hindu India and the Muslim Pakistan.

INDONESIA, a republic in South-East Asia made up of more than 13,000 islands. The largest regions are Kalimantan (part of Borneo), Sumatra, West Irian (part of New Guinea), Sulawesi (Celebes), and Java, the most densely populated island. There are many mountain ranges and more active volcanoes than in any other country: 77 have erupted in recent times. The climate is equatorial, hot and wet all the year round. Rain forests cover large areas. Most people are of Malay origin, mixed with Melanesians and Australasians, and at least 70 languages are spoken. Agriculture employs 60 percent

of the workforce. Rice is the main food. Coffee, copra, palm oil and kernels, rubber, tea, and tobacco are major cash crops. Forestry is important. Indonesia is the leading oil producer in the Far East. Manufacturing is important, including shipbuilding, textiles, cement, and chemicals. Indonesian princes adopted Islam in the 16th century as a political weapon against Portuguese traders. It gradually replaced Hinduism. Dutch influence began in the late 16th century, and the territory became Dutch in 1799. The Republic of Indonesia was formed in 1949.

IRAN, a republic in southwestern Asia. Around a barren plateau, which contains the Dasht e Kavir (Great Salt Desert) and the Dasht e Lut (Great Sand Desert), are mountains: the highest are the northern Elburz Mts.; the Zagros Mts. in the west and south; and several ranges in the east. The only fertile areas are near the Caspian Sea and in mountain foothills. The central plateau is arid and hot, but the Zagros Mts. can be bitterly cold. About 90 percent of the people are Shia Muslims. Two-thirds of the people are Persian in type and one-fourth are Turki. There are some Arabs, and Sunni Muslim Kurds live in the north. Forty percent of the people are farmers. Cereals, fruit, cotton, and tobacco are grown. Income from oil has been used to develop heavy industries and improve social services. Ancient Persia was a powerful empire between 550 and 330 B.C. The country was Islamized in A.D. 641. Iran was ruled by a shah (king) until 1979, when it became an Islamic Republic.

IRAQ, a republic in southwestern Asia. It contains Mesopotamia, the valleys of the Tigris and Euphrates rivers, where the ancient civilizations of Babylonia and Assyria arose. There are swamps in the south where the two rivers join, deserts in the west, and mountains in the northeast. Summers are hot and winters cool. More than half of the people are Shia Muslims. Sunni Muslim Kurds live in the north, forming about 15 percent of the population. Oil production dominates the economy. The main crops that are grown include dates, cereals, rice, tobacco, pulses, and cotton. Manufacturing is expanding. Iraq was Islamized in A.D. 637, and in 1638 it became part of the Ottoman Empire. British forces occupied Iraq in World War I and stayed until it became an independent monarchy in 1932. In 1958, however, the monarchy was overthrown and a republic was proclaimed.

IRELAND, REPUBLIC OF, occupies 80 percent of the island of Ireland. It contains 26 counties, divided into four provinces: Connacht, Leinster, Munster, and Ulster. The six northeastern counties of Ulster constitute Northern Ireland, which is part of the United Kingdom. Central Ireland is a lowland, containing areas of peat bog and some rich farmland. A broken rim of uplands surrounds the plain. The highest peak, Carrantuohill, is in County Kerry in the southwest. The River Shannon is the longest river in the British Isles. Along its course are several lakes, including Lough Ree and Lough Derg. Ireland has mild, wet winters and cool, wet summers. Most people are of Celtic or mixed Celtic and English descent. About 30 percent speak Irish, but English is used in daily life. Farming forms the basis of the economy. Arable land and pasture cover two-thirds of the land. Major crops are barley, hay, oats, potatoes, sugar beet, and wheat, and cattle, sheep, and pigs are raised. There are many processing industries. The only large-scale manufacturing industries are in Dublin and Cork; most of the minerals and raw materials needed are imported. Fishing employs about 9,000 men. Tourism is important. The main exports are chemicals, computers, meat, dairy products, and textiles. The Normans invaded Ireland in the 12th century and the island came under English rule. Much of Ireland's subsequent history was concerned with a struggle against English rule. In 1801 the Act of Union created the United Kingdom of Great Britain and Ireland. In 1919–21 the Irish fought for independence, finally achieving dominion status as the Irish Free State. Northern Ireland remained part of the U.K. Ireland became a republic in 1949. It is a member of the European Community.

ISRAEL, a Middle Eastern republic created in 1948. The Galilee highlands, containing Mt. Meron, are in the north. To the east is an extension of the East Africa Rift Valley, enclosing the Sea of Galilee (Lake Tiberias), the River Jordan, and, in the south, the Dead Sea. South of the Galilee Highlands are fertile plains and hilly regions. The Negev, in the far south, is desert. The coast has a Mediterranean climate; the rainfall decreases inland and to the south. More than 80 percent of the people are Jews: the rest are Arabs. Israel makes most industrial products, and diamond finishing is the most valuable industry. Farming is efficient because of extensive irrigation and co-operative and collective farming methods. Cereals, citrus fruits, cotton, olives, tobacco, and vegetables are important. About 1 million tourists visit Israel yearly. Israel is part of the ancient land of Palestine. It was the cradle of Judaism and Christianity. Britain ruled Palestine from 1917 to 1948.

ITALY, a republic in southern Europe. It consists largely of a long peninsula projecting like a boot between the Adriatic Sea to the east and the Ligurian and Tyrrhenian seas to the west. The scenic Alps, Italy's highest region, form a broad arc in the north. They overlook the North Italian plain, which consists mainly of the Po River drainage basin. This is Italy's most densely

ATLANTIC OCEAN — SCOTLAND — NORTH SEA — NORTHERN IRELAND — REPUBLIC OF IRELAND — IRISH SEA — WALES — ENGLAND — ST GEORGE'S CHANNEL

STATISTICS

To see the statistics of each country's area and population, plus its capital, turn to pages 102–106.

populated region. The Po is Italy's longest river. The Apennine Mts. occupy much of peninsular Italy. Within the Apennines are many fertile valleys and basins, and there are some rich coastal plains. Most rivers are short. The most important are the Arno, on which Florence stands, and the Tiber, which flows through Rome. In the southwest are a series of volcanoes: Vesuvius is near the port of Naples; Stromboli and Vulcano in the Lipari Islands; and Etna, Europe's highest volcano, in Sicily. Sicily is the largest of Italy's 70 or so islands. Italy's second largest island is Sardinia to the west. Southern Italy is subject to earthquakes; it lies near a subduction zone in the Earth's crust. Southern Italy has hot, dry summers and mild winters. Winter rainfall is highest in the mountains and it increases northward. Winters are colder in the more Continental North Italian plain. The Alps are cold and snowy. Oil and natural gas are extracted in the North Italian plain and in Sicily, but oil and coal have to be imported. Hydroelectric projects are numerous and supply 30 percent of Italy's electricity. Generally, Italy lacks minerals, and metal ores are major imports. Leading industrial products include textiles, especially silk; engineering goods, including transportation; equipment and motor vehicles; office and household equipment; chemicals; and iron and steel. The chief industrial region is the triangular area formed by Turin, Milan, and Genoa. Farmland covers about two-thirds of the land, but agriculture employs only 13 percent of the workforce. Major crops include barley, citrus and other fruits, grapes (for wine-making), corn, olives, sugar beet, tobacco, vegetables, and wheat. Italy is a major milk producer, and its cheeses, such as Gorgonzola, are famous. There is a huge tourist industry. The Romans ruled Italy for about a thousand years until A.D. 476. It then became a series of small city-states, but was unified as a kingdom in 1861. It became a republic in 1946, and is a founder member of the European Community (E.C.).

JAMAICA, a West Indian island nation. The land is mainly mountainous, with spectacular scenery. The coast has a tropical climate, although the Blue Mountains have a very high average annual rainfall. The coasts are drier. More than 75 percent of the people are Blacks, 14 percent are of mixed Black and White origin, and there are minorities of Asians, Afro-Asians, and Whites. Jamaica is the world's 3rd largest producer of bauxite, the main export. Bananas and sugar are the main farm products. About three people out of ten work on the land. Tourism is a major industry. Discovered by Columbus in 1494, Jamaica was ruled by Spain until 1655, when the English captured it. Full independence within the Commonwealth was achieved in 1962.

JAPAN, an island nation in the Far East that is separated from the Asian mainland by the Sea of Japan. There are 4 large islands (Honshu, Hokkaido, Kyushu, and Shikoku) and about 3,000 small ones, including the Ryukyu island chain that stretches toward Taiwan. The islands are largely mountainous, the most rugged region being the Japanese Alps on Honshu, including the highest peak Fujiyama, a dormat volcano southwest of Tokyo which last erupted in 1707. Japan contains more than 160 volcanoes; 54 are active. Earthquakes are common; about 1,500 occur every year, but most cause little damage. Japan has a monsoon climate, with plentiful rain. The heaviest rains fall in June–July and September–October and typhoons are common. Most people are descendants of people who came from mainland Asia and Pacific islands. Japan is Asia's most prosperous and industralized nation. About eight people out of ten live in towns. Some minerals, including coal and copper, are mined, but the amounts are generally too small for the needs of manufacturers. Hence, many materials, including iron ore and oil, must be imported. Japan has a wide range of light and heavy industry. It is the world's 2nd largest manufacturer of cars and is a leading producer of many different types of electronic equipment. It is the world's 3rd largest producer of electrical energy, after the U.S. and the U.S.S.R. Japan leads the world in producing motorcycles, merchant ships, and television sets. Most of Japan is too mountainous for farming; forests cover nearly 70 percent of the land. Farming produces rice, barley, fruit, soya beans, and wheat. Japan has a large fishing fleet, but has to import some types of food. According to tradition, Japan's monarchy dates from 660 B.C. Emperors have ruled Japan, at least in name, ever since. After World War II, Japan adopted a constitutional monarchy, and became one of the world's leading industrial powers.

JORDAN, a kingdom in southwestern Asia. Its official name is the Hashemite Kingdom of Jordan. The fertile western uplands (the West Bank, occupied by Israel) overlook the Rift Valley which contains the River Jordan and the Dead Sea. The valley continues south to the Gulf of Aqabah, Jordan's only outlet to the sea. The east consists mainly of barren uplands. About 87 percent of Jordan is desert. Some highland regions are cooler and have adequate rainfall. Most people are Arabs. Farmers grow fruit and vegetables and

raise sheep and goats. The main export is phosphates. British forces occupied what is now Israel and Jordan in World War I. Transjordan became a separate country in 1923 and full independence was achieved in 1946.

KENYA, an East African republic. Behind the narrow coastal plain is a large grassy or savanna-covered plateau broken by volcanic mountains, including the highest peak, Mt. Kenya. The East African Rift Valley in Kenya contains lakes Nakuru, Naivasha, and Turkana. Part of Lake Victoria is in the south-east. The climate on the coast is equatorial, but it is much cooler on the plateau. Only 15 percent of Kenya has a reliable rainfall. There are about 40 language groups: the largest are the Kikuyu and Luo. Farming is the main occupation, employing about eight people out of every ten. The chief cash crops are coffee and tea, and cattle, sheep, and goats are raised. Manufacturing is growing rapidly. The wildlife, scenery, and beaches attract many thousands of tourists each year. Kenya became a British protectorate in 1895, a colony in 1920, and independent in 1963. It remains a member of the Commonwealth.

KIRIBATI, an island republic in the Central Pacific. It includes Ocean (Banaba) Island, the 16 Gilbert Islands, eight of 11 Line Islands (the rest are uninhabited U.S. dependencies), and the eight Phoenix Islands. The climate is hot and generally wet. Most people are Micronesians. Copra is the only export. The

STATISTICS

To see the statistics of each country's area and population, plus its capital, turn to pages 102–106.

Gilbert and Ellice Islands became a British protectorate in 1892. The Ellice Islands became a separate country, Tuvalu, in 1975. Kiribati (pronounced *Kiribas*) became fully independent in 1979.

KOREA, NORTH, officially the Democratic People's Republic of Korea. The northern part of a peninsula, North Korea is mostly mountainous, the population being concentrated in coastal plains in the east. Only 16 percent of the land is cultivable, but nearly half the people are farmers. Rice is the main crop in irrigated areas: corn, millet, and wheat grow in drier places. There are many minerals—coal, copper, iron ore, lead, manganese, nickel, tungsten, and zinc. The country has developed many light and heavy industries. Korea was partitioned in 1945, and North Korea became a communist state. War raged between the two Koreas from 1950 to 1953. Despite a treaty, North Korea is still committed to reunification

KOREA, SOUTH, a republic in the Far East. The land is mostly mountainous with many islands in the west. Winters are dry, but rainfall is plentiful over the year. Forests cover 70 percent of the land. Since partition, industry has overtaken agriculture. Tungsten is the chief mineral; small deposits of many other minerals occur. The chief manufactures are light consumer goods, but chemical and heavy industries are growing. The chief crops are rice and other grains and tobacco. Livestock raising and fishing are also important. Korea became a united kingdom in the 7th century A.D. It was occupied by Mongols between the 13th and 14th centuries and it was conquered by China in 1627. Korea became a Japanese colony in 1910. It became the two countries of North and South Korea in 1945.

KUWAIT, a small emirate at the head of the Persian Gulf. This low-lying, desert nation has low and erratic rainfall. The average summer temperature is hot. Winters are cooler. Most people are Arabs. Kuwait is one of the world's 10 top oil producers, and revenue from oil sales finances one of the world's most elaborate welfare states. In 1899 Kuwait accepted British protection for certain rights. Kuwait became independent in 1914, but Britain remained responsible for Kuwait's foreign policy until 1961, when Kuwait became fully independent.

LAOS, a poor, landlocked People's Democratic Republic in South-East Asia. Forested mountains and plateaus cover much of the country; most people live in the Mekong River plains. Laos has a tropical monsoon climate, with most rain in May–September. The Lao-Lum (or Valley Lao, a Thai people) make up 56 percent of the population; the Lao-Theung, consisting of many groups of animist tribes in the uplands, make up 34 percent; and the Lao-Soung, including the Meo and Yao who are nomadic farmers, make up 9 percent. Among the minorities, the Chinese and Vietnamese are important in business. Four out of five people work on the land. Rice is the main food crop; timber and coffee are the main exports. Tin is the only important mineral. A united kingdom was established in what is now Laos and northern Thailand in the 14th century. Laos became a French protectorate in 1893, and became independent in 1954.

LEBANON, a Middle Eastern republic. Behind the narrow coastal plain are the western Lebanon Mts., an interior plateau containing the fertile Bekaa valley, and the Anti-Lebanon Mts. in the east. The climate is Mediterranean in type. Most people are Arabs, but only 60 percent of them are Muslims; the rest are Christians. Lebanon has long been a financial and commercial base, and in normal times it has a major tourist industry. Hence, services are the leading sector of the economy, followed by industry and agriculture. Consumer goods are manufactured and cereals and fruit are the main farm products; 38 percent of the land is cultivated. Lebanon was the heart of the ancient Phoenician Empire. It came under the Romans in 64 B.C. and under Ottoman rule from 1517. France ruled Lebanon from 1918 to 1946, when it became a fully independent republic. Since 1975 it has suffered civil war.

LESOTHO, a landlocked kingdom enclosed by South Africa. It was formerly called Basutoland. Mostly mountainous, it includes the high Drakensberg range, but most people live in the western lowlands and the southern Orange River valley. The climate is continental, with warm, moist summers and cold, dry winters. The people, called Basotho, speak Sesotho and English. Agriculture employs one-third of the workforce. The chief food crops are cereals and vegetables. The main exports are wool, mohair, and alluvial diamonds. The nation became a British protectorate in 1884 and an independent kingdom in 1966.

LIBERIA, a republic in West Africa. Behind the coastal plain, with its mangrove swamps and savanna country, are forested plateaus and grassy highlands. The climate is very warm, with heavy rainfall. There are 16 main language groups. The 50,000 or so Americo-Liberians, descendants of freed slaves, have been important in ruling Liberia. About 70 percent of the people work the land, growing rubber, cassava, and rice. Iron ore is the country's main product. Liberia has a large merchant navy: many foreign ships register in Liberia because of the low fees. In 1822 the American Colonization Society founded Monrovia, now the capital, for freed slaves. In 1847 Liberia became an independent republic.

LIBYA, a nation in north Africa, officially the Socialist People's Libyan Arab Jamahiriyah. (*Jamahiriyah* means "state of the masses".) About 95 percent of Libya is desert or semi-desert. The land rises toward the south. Most people live in the northeastern and northwestern coastal plains, where temperatures are high and rainfall is moderate. Most are of Arab or Berber origin. Libya is a wealthy country because of its oil. The main food crops are cereals, dates, olives, and vegetables. The Turks controlled Libya from 1551 to 1911, when Italy occupied Tripoli. Italy lost Libya in World War II, after which Libya became independent, first as a monarchy (1951) and later as a republic (1969).

LIECHTENSTEIN, a small principality, lies between Austria and Switzerland, with which it has close links. It uses Swiss currency and is united with Switzerland in a customs union. The Rhine and Ill river plains are in the north, with mountains in the south. Farming includes the cultivation of cereals, fruit and vines, and cattle rearing. Light industry, the sale of postage stamps, and tourism are leading sources of revenue. Liechtenstein was founded in 1719. It was part of the German Confederation from 1815, but it has been independent since 1866. It is a constitutional monarchy.

LUXEMBOURG, a Grand Duchy between Belgium, France, and West Germany. The north is part of the Ardennes plateau, with fertile lowlands in the south. The climate is mild and moist. Iron ore is the chief resource and there are large iron and steel works. About 52 percent of the land is farmed: barley, oats, potatoes, sugar beet, and wheat are major crops. Luxembourg became a Grand Duchy in 1354. It has been under the control of Spain, Austria, France, and the Netherlands, but has been independent since 1890, when it broke away from the Netherlands. It is a constitutional monarchy, and became a founder member of the European Community in 1957.

MADAGASCAR, an island republic separated from the African mainland by the Mozambique Channel. A high plateau covers about 66 percent of the country; volcanic peaks, such as the Massif du Tsaratanana,

---

STATISTICS

To see the statistics of each country's area and population, plus its capital, turn to pages 102–106.

rise above it. The coastal plain in the east is narrow; broader lowlands are in the west. The forested east coast is hot and humid. The grassy and savanna-covered plateau is cool, with abundant rainfall. The northwest is wet but the southwestern lowlands are semi-desert. The people are of Indonesian and African origin; the largest of the main 18 groups is the Merina. The people speak Malagasy, which is based on the Merina language. Farmers form 86 percent of the workforce. Rice is the main food, and coffee, cloves, and vanilla are exported. There is little mining, but there are many small processing industries, and oil refining is important. The Portuguese discovered the island in 1500. France made it a protectorate in 1885. Independence was achieved in 1960.

MALAWI, a landlocked republic in southern Africa. It includes part of Lake Malawi (Nyasa) in the East Africa Rift Valley. The River Shire flows from the lake into the Zambezi in Mozambique. There are scenic highlands west of Lake Malawi, but the highest peak, Mt. Mlanje, is east of the River Shire. The highlands are wetter and cool. The people speak a number of Bantu languages. Two out of every five workers are engaged in agriculture. Corn is the chief food crop. Tobacco accounts for 49 percent of the exports and tea for 24 percent. In 1891 the territory became the British Central African Protectorate; it was renamed Nyasaland in 1907. It became independent within the Commonwealth as Malawi in 1964 and declared itself a republic in 1966.

MALAYSIA, a southeast Asian monarchy. It contains the southern Malay peninsula, and Sabah and Sarawak in northern Borneo. Forested mountains cover large areas. The most important lowlands are in the Malay peninsula. The climate is tropical. The Malay peninsula contains 84 percent of the population. In the country as a whole, 47 percent are Malays, 34 percent are Chinese, 9 percent are Indians and Pakistanis, 5 percent are Dayaks, and 5 percent belong to other groups. Tin is the main mineral, and Malaysia is the world's leading tin producer. Some oil is also produced, and manufacturing is increasing. Half the people are farmers, growing rubber, palm (for oil), and rice. Timber is also important. Portuguese traders reached Malacca in 1509, but the Dutch took over in 1641. Malaya, Sabah, and Sarawak were all under British protection from the 1800s until 1963, when the independent country of Malaysia was formed. At first Singapore was part of it, but broke away in 1965. Malaysia's Constitution provides that the 9 Rulers of the Malay states elect one of their number every 5 years to be *Yang di-Pertuan Agong* (Supreme Head of the Federation).

MALDIVES, an island republic 400 miles (650 km) southwest of Sri Lanka. It includes about 2,000 coral islands. Fishing is the main industry. Coconuts, millet, and fruit are grown. The Maldives came under British protection in 1887. Full independence was achieved in 1965.

MALI, a landlocked republic in northwestern Africa. Plains cover most of Mali, with uplands in the northeast and south. The River Niger flows in a broad arc through southern Mali. The climate is warm. The south has adequate rainfall; the north is desert. There are people of Arab and Berber origin, such as Tuaregs, and some of mixed origin, such as the Fulbe (Fulani). But more than 80 percent of the population is Black. Almost 90 percent of the people work on the land. The chief cash crop is cotton. In 1880 France made the area a protectorate. Full independence was achieved in 1960.

MALTA, a Mediterranean island republic, south of Sicily, includes Malta, Gozo, Comino, and two islets. It has warm summers and mild winters. Most people are of Arab, Italian, and English descent. More people work in manufacturing than in agriculture or fishing. Tourism is important. Malta was a

British colony from 1814 until it gained independence in 1964.

MAURITANIA, an Islamic republic in north-western Africa. Low plateaus cover most of the country, which lies largely in the Sahara. But the fertile Senegal River plains are in the southwest. Average annual temperatures are between 77°F and 90°F (25–32°C), and there are large daily variations in the Sahara. The average rainfall is 26 inches (660 mm) per year in the savanna-covered south. The north has little rainfall. About 80 percent of the population is of Arab and Berber origin. The others are Blacks. Agriculture, particularly livestock rearing, employs eight out of ten workers. Sea fishing is important, but the chief resource is iron ore: Mauritania is Africa's 3rd largest producer. Copper is also mined. France ruled Mauritania from 1903 to 1960, when it won independence.

MAURITIUS, an island nation east of Madagascar in the Indian Ocean. It includes the mountainous, volcanic island of Mauritius and Rodrigues, which is about 350 miles (560 km) to the east. The climate is warm and humid. The people are of Asian Hindu descent (53 percent), Asian Muslim descent (17 percent), and European, mixed, and African descent (28 percent). Sugar and its byproducts form the basis of the economy. Tourism is increasing. Britain captured Mauritius from France in 1810. It achieved independence in the Commonwealth in 1968.

MEXICO, a republic in North America. It is largely mountainous, with high plateaus and volcanic peaks. The lowlands are in the Yucatan peninsula and along the Pacific and Gulf of Mexico coasts. The chief mountain ranges are the Sierra Madre Occidental and the Sierra Madre Oriental, which enclose the central plateaus. These are dotted with lakes and volcanoes: one, Citlaltépetl, is Mexico's highest peak. Most of the long peninsula, Lower or Baja California, is separated from the rest of Mexico by the Gulf of California. It is a rugged, arid region. Mexico straddles the Tropic of Cancer, but there are three main climatic regions determined by the altitude: the tropical *tierra caliente*, the mild *tierra templada*, in which Mexico City is situated; and the high *tierra fría* with its cold winters. Rainfall in central Mexico is adequate, but the northwest is arid. People of mixed European and American Indian origin form 55 percent of the population; American Indians 29 percent and Europeans 15 percent. Crops include coffee, cotton, corn, sisal, and sugar. Cattle, sheep, goats, and pigs are reared. Mexico is a major oil producer. Coal, copper, gold, iron ore, lead, manganese, mercury, silver, zinc, and other minerals are mined. Textiles and steel are leading manufactures. Spain ruled Mexico from 1521 to 1821. The country became a republic in 1824.

MONACO, a tiny principality on the Mediterranean Sea in southeastern France. There are four districts: Monaco-Ville, the capital; la Condamine, a resort area; Monte-Carlo, a luxury resort with a famous casino; and Fontvieille. French currency is used. Monaco became fully independent in 1861. It is a constitutional monarchy.

MONGOLIA, a landlocked People's Republic in northern Asia. A featureless plateau covers much of Mongolia, with mountains in the west and the Gobi desert, which covers

STATISTICS
To see the statistics of each country's area and population, plus its capital, turn to pages 102–106.

one-third of the country, in the south. The main rivers are the Selenga, which flows into Lake Baykal, and the Kerulen, a tributary of the Amur River. The climate is severe. Most people were formerly nomadic herdsmen, but all farmland is now organized in large state or collective farms: these farms own 80 percent of the animals—sheep, goats, cattle, and horses—that are reared. Some oil, coal, and other minerals are produced, but manufacturing is small-scale. The Mongol Empire became powerful in the 13th century under Genghis Khan. Mongolia became a Chinese province in 1691 and an independent Buddhist kingdom in 1912. In 1924 the communist Mongolian People's Republic was set up.

MOROCCO, a monarchy in northeastern Africa. The folded Atlas ranges cover much of the country: the highest point is Djebel Toubkal in the High Atlas range. The Anti-Atlas in the south is an uplifted rim of the African plateau. The fertile Rharb-Sebou lowlands and the Moulouya valley are in the north. Low plateaus border the narrow coastal plain in central Morocco. The north has a Mediterranean climate, but the south is cooler. The south and east merge into the Sahara. Most people are Arabs. About 30 percent are Berbers, and there is a small European minority. Over half the people work on the land. Barley, citrus fruit, grapes, and wheat are important crops, and sheep, cattle, and goats are reared. Forestry and fishing are also important, but the main resource is phosphates. Iron ore, lead, manganese, oil, zinc, and other minerals are mined. France ruled most of Morocco from 1912, although Spain held the north. Morocco became an independent kingdom in 1956.

MOZAMBIQUE, a People's Republic in southeastern Africa. Coastal plains cover 44 percent of the land, plateaus and hills 43 percent, and uplands 13 percent. Lake Nyasa (Malawi) is shared with Malawi and Tanzania. There is a manmade lake behind the Cabora Bassa Dam on the Zambezi river. The center and north have a tropical climate. The far south is subtropical. The rainfall is generally low. There are 12 major Bantu-speaking tribes and more than 30 minor ones. Agriculture employs 67 percent of the people in this poor nation. Leading crops are cashew nuts, copra, cotton, peanuts, corn, rice, sisal, sugar cane, and tobacco. Some coal is mined, and the towns contain some industries. Portugal became established in Mozambique in the early 16th century. A guerrilla war (1964–74) preceded independence in 1975. The Constitution of 1978 vests power in the sole political party, FRELIMO, and declares socialism to be the national objective.

MYANMAR, formerly Burma, a Socialist republic in southeastern Asia. The north, east, and west are mountainous, but the southern valleys of the Irrawaddy and Sittang rivers are fertile. The Irrawaddy delta is one of the world's great rice-growing areas. The climate is tropical, with heavy rainfall in the delta. Two-thirds of the people are Tibeto-Burmese, and there are many small groups of isolated hill peoples. Half the people are farmers. Forests cover half the country and teak is a major product. Many minerals, including oil and natural gas, are mined. Britain took Burma between 1823 and 1855. It became independent in 1948. Burma changed its name to Myanmar in 1989.

NAMIBIA, a South African-ruled land moving toward independence. Behind the coastal plain (the Namib desert) is the central plateau. The Kalahari, a semi-desert, is in the east. The north is tropical and the south subtropical. The Namib is almost rainless; the northern interior is the wettest place. The people include Europeans (12 percent), people of mixed origin (6 percent), Khoisan and related peoples, including Nama (Hottentots) and Bushmen (16 percent), and Bantu-speaking people, who make up the rest of the population. Diamonds, lead, tin, zinc, and uranium are mined. In 1920 the League of Nations mandated South Africa to rule the country. United Nations attempts to achieve independence for Namibia intensified in 1989.

NAURU, an island republic close to the Equator in the western Pacific Ocean. A raised atoll, it contains rich phosphate deposits on which the economy is based. Half the people are Polynesians, while the rest are other Pacific islanders, Chinese, or Europeans. The League of Nations mandated Britain to rule Nauru in 1920. Full independence was achieved in 1968 with "special member" Commonwealth status.

NEPAL, a landlocked monarchy between China and India. It includes some of the world's highest peaks in the Himalayas, including Mt. Everest on the Chinese border.

Two-thirds of Nepal is mountainous. There are temperate valleys and warm plains near the Indian border. The people are of Tibetan or Indian descent, including the warlike Gurkhas. Most people are farmers, but manufacturing is developing. The country is a constitutional monarchy.

NETHERLANDS, a prosperous monarchy, is one of the Low Countries. It is at the western edge of the North European Plain. About 40 percent of the country is below sea-level at high tide: the sea is held back by dikes which enclose polders (reclaimed areas), which make up more than 25 percent of the land. The center of the country consists of the flood plains of the Rhine and Maas (Meuse) rivers, and their branches (the Ijssel, Lek, and Waal). The Schelde river enters the sea in the southwest. The coastal region contains many islands, deep estuaries, marshes, sand dunes, and polders. The highest land is in the southeast (Limburg). The Netherlands is one of the world's most densely populated nations. Nearly 70 percent of the land is farmed, but only six out of every 100 people work on it. Most farms are small, but the yields are among the world's highest. Butter, cheese, and eggs are major products. Leading crops include flowers and bulbs, potatoes, sugar beet, and wheat. There is little mining apart from the extraction of natural gas and oil. The chief manufacturing region is the Randstadt, a ring of cities around the polders of the west-center: Rotterdam with its port Europoort, The

STATISTICS

To see the statistics of each country's area and population, plus its capital, turn to pages 102–106.

Hague, Haarlem, Amsterdam, and Utrecht. Eindhoven is another industrial center. Petroleum products, ships, radio and television sets, textiles, and china and earthenware goods are major products. The country has been independent almost continuously since the late 16th century.

NEW ZEALAND, a member nation of the Commonwealth, in the southwestern Pacific Ocean. It contains two large islands, North Island and South Island, with Stewart Island, the Chatham Islands, and some smaller islands. North Island, where most people live, contains fertile plains, a volcanic central plateau, and fold mountain ranges in the east. Active volcanoes include Ngauruhoe and Tongariro. Lake Taupo in the center is in a crater of an extinct volcano. North of the lake, hot springs are utilized to produce electricity. The eastern fold mountains continue in South Island as the Southern Alps, which reach their highest point in Mt. Cook. Glaciers flow down high valleys, and the southwestern coast is glaciated with scenic fiords. The major lowlands include the Canterbury Plains in the east and the Otago plateau in the southeast. New Zealand has a cool, temperate climate. Nine out of 10 New Zealanders are of European, mostly British, origin; 8 percent are Maoris; and 1 percent other Pacific peoples. Farming is efficient and yields are high. Wool, beef, lamb, mutton, and dairy products are the leading exports. Arable farming is less important than livestock, but cereals, fruit, tobacco, and vegetables are all important. New Zealand has a few minerals, including some coal and ironsands. Nearly 70 percent of the electricity, however, is generated by hydroelectric stations. Maoris probably settled in New Zealand in the 14th century. The Dutch navigator Abel Tasman reached New Zealand in 1642. British settlers went to New Zealand in the early 1800s, and it

became a British colony in 1841. It became an independent dominion in 1907. The British monarch, represented by a Governor-General, is Head of State.

NICARAGUA, a Central American republic. Forested plains border the Caribbean Sea. In the center is a highland region with some active volcanoes. It is broadest and highest in the north. The Pacific coastlands contain two huge lakes, Managua and Nicaragua. The country has a hot and humid climate. About 80 percent of the people are of mixed White and American Indian origin, 10 percent are Blacks, and 4 percent are pure American Indians. Coffee, cotton, and meat are major products. Gold, silver, and copper are mined, and manufacturing is expanding. Spain conquered Nicaragua in the early 16th century. The country became independent in 1821, but in 1823–38 it was part of the Central American Federation. It was torn by rebellion in the 1980s.

NIGER, a poor landlocked republic in north-central Africa. The highest peaks are in the Aïr massif in the north; plateaus and plains cover most of Niger. The only river is the Niger in the southwest. The north is mostly in the hot Sahara, although there is some pasture in the Aïr massif. Nomadic Tuaregs live in the Sahara, but most of the people are Black Africans, who live in the south. Most of them are engaged in agriculture. Live animals, animal products, peanuts and vegetables are important products. Niger has large uranium deposits. The country was a French colony from 1900 to 1960, when it became independent.

NIGERIA, a Federal Republic in West Africa, and Africa's most populous nation. Most of the country is drained by the Niger and Benue rivers. North of these rivers are the high plains of Hausaland and higher plateaus. The land descends to the Sokoto plains in the northwest and the Lake Chad internal drainage basin in the northeast. South and west of the Niger River are hilly uplands bordered by a broad coastal plain which extends to the huge, swampy Niger delta. In the southeast the land rises to mountains on the Cameroon border. The climate is equatorial. Forest is the typical vegetation in the south, with savanna in the north and semi-desert in the Chad basin. About 250 languages and dialects are spoken in Nigeria, but English is the official language. The largest groups are the Muslim Hausa and Fulani in the north, the Ibo in the southeast and the Yoruba in the southwest. More than half the people work on the land. Oil is Nigeria's main source of wealth. Revenue from oil sales is being used to diversify the economy and to improve Nigeria's towns, including the building of a new federal capital at Abuja in central Nigeria. Southern Nigeria was a center of the slave trade from the 15th century. Britain abolished the slave trade in 1807 and extended its control over the country. Nigeria became independent in 1960 and a republic in 1963.

NORWAY, a monarchy in the western part of the mountainous Scandinavian peninsula. The Kjölen mountains form much of the border with Sweden. In the south there is an extensive region of high plateaus and mountains, including the highest peak, Galdhöppigen. The only large lowlands are in the southeast. Although a third of Norway lies within the Arctic Circle, the climate is mild, especially in winter, when the western coasts are warmed by the North Atlantic Drift. Even at North Cape, Norway's and Europe's most northerly point, the sea never freezes. Norway is thinly populated. Only 2 percent of the land is cultivated, and food must be imported. Coniferous forests cover 26 percent of the land, and the pulp and paper industry is important. Fishing is the main activity for people who live in the fiords or on the 50,000 or so islands. Capelin, cod, haddock, and mackerel are the most important fish. A large part of the catch is processed for export. Norway has rich oil reserves in the North Sea; since the 1970s it has become Western Europe's 2nd largest oil producer. Iron ore, copper, lead, and zinc are also mined, and a high proportion of Norway's exports come from the electro-metallurgical, electro-chemical, and paper industries. Hydro-electric power stations provide electricity for most purposes. Norway's large merchant shipping fleet is another major source of income. Between 1380 and 1814 Norway was united with Denmark under Danish rule. After a brief period of independence, Norway entered into a union with Sweden. In 1905 Norway broke away and became independent again as a constitutional monarchy.

OMAN, a Sultanate in the southeastern corner of the Arabian peninsula. Behind the fertile northern coast (the Batinah northwest of Muscat) is a barren upland that merges into an arid interior plateau. The only other fertile region is in the far south (Dhufar). The climate is hot, with hardly any rain. Arabs make up 90 percent of the population. There are also some Indians, Iranians, Blacks, and Pakistanis. Most people are farmers or fishermen, but the oil industry dominates the economy. Oil is the main source of wealth. Dates, dried fish, limes and other fruit, tobacco, and vegetables are also produced. Fish, particularly sardines are caught in the Gulf of Oman and the Arabian Sea. Britain established a special relationship with the area in 1891. Oman is now an independent, absolute monarchy, but retains ties with Britain.

STATISTICS
To see the statistics of each country's area and population, plus its capital, turn to pages 102–106.

PAKISTAN, an Islamic Republic in southern Asia. The land is mountainous in the north, where the Hindu Kush and Himalayas rise. Central and southern Pakistan contain fertile plains drained and irrigated by the Indus River and its tributaries. The southwest includes the arid Baluchistan plateau, and the Thar Desert is in the southeast. Winters are cold in the mountainous north, and cold northeasterly winds chill the northern plains in November–February. In the hot season, March–May, temperatures are high. Rainfall is higher in the north than in the south. Pakistanis are descendants of the many peoples who have invaded the area. Several languages are spoken, including Urdu, Punjabi, Sindhi, Pashto, and Baluchi. More than two thirds of the people of this extremely poor country live in rural areas. Agriculture is the main activity. Leading crops are rice, winter wheat, cotton, corn, and sugar cane. Hydroelectricity is important, and Pakistan has large reserves of natural gas. Textiles, cement, sugar, and fertilizers are leading manufactures. The Indus valley was the home of early civilizations dating from 2500 B.C. Islam was introduced in the 8th century A.D. Pakistan was part of the Indian Empire, and under British rule from the late 1700s until 1947, when Pakistan became a separate Muslim state. In 1971 East Pakistan broke away to become Bangladesh. Pakistan rejoined the Commonwealth in 1989.

PANAMA, a narrow Central American republic linking North and South America. Behind the Pacific and Caribbean coastal plains the interior is mountainous, the highest peak being Mt. Chiriqui in the west. Panama is at its narrowest at the point where the Panama Canal cuts through to link the Atlantic and Pacific oceans. The United States governed the Panama Canal Zone, a strip of land along the canal, until 1979, when it reverted to Panama, although the U.S. retains control over the canal itself until 1999. Panama has a tropical climate. More than 75 percent of the people are of mixed White and American Indian descent. Bananas, rice, and sugar cane are major crops and there are copper reserves. Panama became independent from Spain in 1819 as part of Colombia, and a separate nation in 1914.

PAPUA NEW GUINEA, a nation in the southwestern Pacific Ocean. It consists of the eastern part of New Guinea, the Bismarck Archipelago, including Manus Is., New Britain, and New Ireland; Bougainville and Buka in the northern Solomon Is.; the D'Entrecasteaux Is.; the Louisiade Archipelago and the Trobriand Is.; and about 600 smaller islands. New Guinea contains forested mountain ranges and broad, swampy river valleys. There are 40 active volcanoes in the north; this volcanic zone extends eastward through the islands. The climate is hot and humid, but the uplands are cooler. About 700 languages are spoken by the various tribal groups, a few of which have never come into contact with Western civilization. Most of them farm the land. The main resource, copper, is mined on Bougainville. Coffee, cocoa, copra, timber, and fish are other major products. The territory was under Australian rule from 1906 until 1975, when it achieved independence as a monarchy in the Commonwealth.

PARAGUAY, a landlocked republic in South America. Its main river, the Paraguay, divides it into the Chaco, a thinly populated, flat region of marsh and scrubland in the west, and a fertile plain and hills, rising to the Paraná plateau, in the east. The climate is subtropical. About 75 percent of the people are of mixed American Indian and White descent, 21 percent are of European origin, and 3 percent are pure American Indians. Half the people work in agriculture. Cotton and soya beans are major crops. Forestry is also important: the bark of the quebracho tree is used to make tannin. Yerba maté, the plant from which a green tea is made, grows wild. Mining is unimportant, and most manufacturing is involved in processing farm products. Paraguay broke away from the former Spanish Empire in 1811.

PERU, a republic in western South America. Behind the narrow, arid coastal plain are high Andean ranges. These mountains, which reach their highest peak at Mt. Huascarán, contain the headwaters of the Amazon River, notably the Maranon and Ucayali. Lake Titicaca, the world's highest navigable lake, straddles the border with Bolivia. Eastern Peru is in the low Amazon basin. The climate is tropical, but the highlands are cooler. People of mixed American Indian and White origin and a roughly equal number of pure American Indians make up the bulk of the population. Sugar, cotton, coffee, and wool are leading crops. Fishing is a major industry. Peru produces oil and a variety of minerals, which provide its main wealth. These include copper, lead, zinc, silver, and iron ore. Spain ruled Peru from the 1500s until independence in 1821.

PHILIPPINES, a southeast Asian republic consisting of more than 7,000 islands. The largest, Luzon and Mindanao, together make up two-thirds of the land area. The large islands are volcanic and mountainous, but many islands are small coral outcrops. The country has a tropical monsoon climate. The plains are hot and humid; the uplands are cooler. Most Filipinos are of Malay-Polynesian origin. There are also some people of Pygmy, European, and mixed descent. The Philippines is Asia's only predominantly Christian country. Rice and corn are the main food crops. Coconut products and sugar cane are major cash crops. Copper is the leading mineral. Textiles, footwear, chemicals, beverages, and food are leading manufactures. Spain ruled the Philippines from 1565 to 1898, when the archipelago was ceded to the United States. It became independent in 1946.

POLAND, a People's Republic in Eastern Europe. Behind the lagoon-fringed Baltic coast is a broad plain, the northern part of which is covered mainly by infertile glacial deposits and forest. The central lowlands, in which Warsaw, Poznań, and Lódź are situated, are more fertile. A low plateau in the south rises to the Sudeten Mts. in the southwest and the Carpathians in the southeast. The plateau contains much fertile land, and the major industrial region built around the Upper Silesian coalfield. The south is drained by the Oder and Vistula river systems. Summers become warmer from north to south. Farmland covers 60 percent of Poland; unusually for a communist country, 75 percent is privately owned. Cereals, potatoes, and sugar beet are major crops, and farmers raise cattle, pigs, poultry, and sheep. Poland is the world's 4th largest coal producer, and it has large reserves of copper, lignite, lead, nickel, salt, sulphur, and zinc. But much iron ore for the large steel industry is imported. It is now one of the world's 15 top industrial nations. Poland's frontiers have changed several times in the last 200 years. In 1795 it disappeared from the map when it was partitioned among Austria, Prussia, and Russia. Poland was proclaimed an independent republic in 1918, but in 1939 it was divided between Germany and the U.S.S.R. It again became independent in 1945, and a communist government was set up. All attempts by the government to nationalize farmland and discourage religious worship have failed.

STATISTICS
To see the statistics of each country's area and population, plus its capital, turn to pages 102–106.

PORTUGAL, a republic in the Iberian peninsula of southwest Europe. Much of the land is an extension of the Spanish meseta; there are plateaus and continuations of the central Sierras of Spain. Lowlands border the coast. Portugal has hot, dry summers and mild, moist winters, but the rainfall decreases and temperatures increase from north to south. Cereals are the main crops. About 12 percent of the land is devoted to vineyards and olive groves. Forests cover one-third of Portugal, which leads the world in cork production. In fishing, sardines, and cod form the bulk of the catch. Portugal produces coal, copper, and some iron ore. Manufacturing, including iron and steel, chemicals, and textiles, is increasing, as is tourism. Portugal's modern frontiers were established in the 13th century, and Spain recognized Portugal as an independent kingdom in 1385. In the 15th century Portugal initiated the Age of Exploration and built up a large overseas empire, now gone, in the 1400s and 1500s. In 1910 the monarchy was abolished and a republic proclaimed. Between the 1930s and early 1970s Portugal had a very limited form of democracy, but in 1974 full democracy was restored.

QATAR, an Arab Emirate occupying a peninsula in the Persian Gulf. This hot, arid, and mostly desert nation has little agriculture, although fruit and vegetables are grown. Oil dominates the economy, and its revenues have been used to finance an elaborate welfare state. After being under Turkish rule, Qatar became a British protectorate in 1916, and fully independent in 1971 when Britain withdrew from the Gulf.

ROMANIA, a socialist Republic on the Black Sea. Transylvania forms the heart of Romania. It includes a central plateau surrounded by the Bihor Mts. to the west, the Carpathians to the east, and the Transylvanian Alps to the south, where the country's highest peak is situated. In the far west are fertile plains. Other plains lie in the east and south. They are drained by the River Danube and its tributaries. A limestone plateau (Dobrogea) borders the Black Sea coast. The climate is continental. The people are descendants of several peoples, including the Romanized Dacian tribes of the Danube valley, and Slavs. The Romanian language is

based on Latin but contains many Slav words. Farmland covers 63 percent of the country; most is government-owned. Cereals, potatoes, oilseeds, and sugar beet are major crops and cattle, pigs, and sheep are raised. There are rich mineral resources, including oil and natural gas, coal, lignite, copper, chromite, gold, iron ore, manganese, and zinc. Manufacturing is increasing. Romania was formed in 1861 by the union of Moldavia and Walachia, two provinces. It became a communist state in 1947 after the king abdicated.

RWANDA, a small, poor, landlocked republic in east-central Africa. The East Africa Rift Valley in the west contains part of Lake Kivu. It is bordered by highlands that descend in a series of plateaus to the River Kagera in the east. It has an equatorial climate. Bantu-speaking Hutu form 90 percent of the population. There are also Nilo-Hamitic Tutsi and Pygmy, European, and Asian minorities. Most people farm the land. The main cash crop is coffee. Cassiterite, the chief ore of tin, is mined, and there are various small-scale manufacturing industries. Rwanda was ruled successively by Germany and Belgium before independence in 1962.

SAINT CHRISTOPHER AND NEVIS,

popularly St. Kitts-Nevis, an island country in the Leeward Islands of the West Indies. It consists of the two small islands of St. Christopher, where most of the people live, and Nevis. The country has a warm climate with good rainfall. Most of the people are descendants of Black Africans. The country earns its living from tourism and growing cane sugar. Britain ruled the two islands from 1713 until independence in 1983.

SAINT LUCIA,

a picturesque island nation in the Windward Is. in the West Indies. Volcanic in origin, it has a tropical climate; bananas, cocoa, coconut oil and copra, and textiles are exported. Tourism is developing. The island was ruled by Britain from 1814 until it achieved full independence within the Commonwealth in 1979.

SAINT VINCENT AND THE GRENADINES,

a West Indian nation in the Windward Is., consists of the volcanic island of St. Vincent and the small islands that make up the Northern Grenadines. The climate is tropical. Most people are Blacks or of mixed origin. Farming is the main activity, but tourism is expanding. It was a British colony from 1805, and became a full independent member of the Commonwealth in 1979.

SAMOA, WESTERN,

a Pacific island nation northeast of Fiji. The largest islands are Savai'i and Upolu. There are also two small islands, Manono and Apolima, and several uninhabited islets. The islands are volcanic in origin and have a tropical climate. The people are Polynesians, and Christianity is the main religion. The chief products are bananas, cocoa, and coconuts. The country was ruled successively by Germany and New Zealand until it became a fully independent monarchy in 1962. It became a member of the Commonwealth in 1970.

SAN MARINO,

Europe's smallest independent republic. It is landlocked and situated in central Italy, south of Rimini. Its capital is on the slopes of Mt. Titano, a spur of the Apennines. Most people are farmers, but tourism is the main industry. Building stone, textiles, and wine are exported. San Marino was founded in the A.D. 300s.

SÃO TOMÉ AND PRÍNCIPE,

an African island republic in the Gulf of Guinea. It includes the volcanic island of São Tomé, Príncipe to the north, and some smaller islands. The people are descendants of slaves from the mainland and Europeans. Agriculture is the main activity. From 1522 the islands were governed as a province of Portugal until independence in 1975.

SAUDI ARABIA,

a kingdom occupying much of the Arabian peninsula. Behind the narrow, Red Sea coastal plain is a highland zone, including the Hejaz in the north and the Asir highlands in the south. To the east of these there are plateaus that slope gently toward the Persian Gulf coastal plain. The plateaus, which cover 90 percent of the country, include the Nafud Desert in the north and the Rub'al-Khali (the "Empty Quarter") in the south. The lowlands are hot, but the higher land is cooler. Rainfall is low, and hardly any

---

STATISTICS

To see the statistics of each country's area and population, plus its capital, turn to pages 102–106.

falls in the Rub'al-Khali. Most Saudis are Muslim Arabs. Mecca, the birthplace of the Prophet Muhammad, and Medina are the two holiest places of Islam. The economy is dominated by oil; only the U.S.S.R. and U.S. produce more. There is a small amount of manufacturing and agriculture, but the country cannot yet produce all the food it requires and has to import most of its food. The country was under the nominal rule of the Ottoman Turks from 1517 to 1916, when they were driven out. In 1927 the Sultan of Nejd, Abd Al-Aziz Ibn Saud, founded modern Saudi Arabia and became its king.

SENEGAL, a West African republic. It is mostly low-lying and covered by savanna. There is a low plateau in the southeast. Senegal is drained by the Senegal, Saloum, Gambia, and Casamance rivers. The climate on the coast is pleasant, but the interior is hot. The rainfall increases from the arid north to the south. Most of the people are Black Africans. Three-quarters of them work in agriculture, growing peanuts and raising cattle, sheep, and goats. The capital, Dakar, is West Africa's most industrialized city. Tourism is growing. France ruled Senegal as a colony from 1887. It became an independent republic in 1960.

SEYCHELLES, an Indian Ocean island republic northeast of Madagascar. There are about 90 islands. The rugged Mahé, or Granitic, islands make up 80 percent of the area; the rest are flat coral islands. The largest island, Mahé, contains the capital, Victoria. The climate is tropical. Most people are Creoles, of mixed French and African origin. There are also some Chinese, Europeans, and Indians. Tourism and agriculture are the main activities. Britain ruled the islands from 1810 until independence in the Commonwealth in 1976.

SIERRA LEONE, a West African republic. Behind the broad coastal plain are interior plateaus and mountains. The climate is tropical, and rainfall is heavy. Most people are Black Africans: there are 18 main groups. A minority is composed of descendants of freed slaves. Rice is the main food crop, and coffee, cacao, and palm kernels are the chief cash crops. Diamonds and bauxite are the chief exports. Forestry and fishing are expanding, as is manufacturing, and tourism is being developed. In 1787 Britain founded Freetown, the capital, as a settlement for freed slaves. Sierra Leone was a colony from 1808 until full independence in 1961. The country became a republic in 1971.

SINGAPORE, a prosperous island republic off the southern tip of the Malay peninsula. A causeway links Singapore Island to the mainland. There are many islets, that make up 8 percent of the country. The climate is hot and humid. The main groups of people are Chinese (76 percent), Malays (15 percent), and Indians (7 percent). The country has four official languages—Chinese, English, Malay, and Tamil. There is little agriculture. Manufacturing is extremely important. The many products include ships, chemicals, electronic equipment, machinery, steel, and textiles. Other important industries are oil refining, and food and timber processing. The port of Singapore is one of the world's largest, and Singapore is a major financial center. Britain took over the island in 1824. It was part of Malaysia from 1963 but it became a separate republic in 1965.

SOLOMON ISLANDS, an island nation in the Commonwealth in the southwestern Pacific. It lies to the east of New Guinea. The largest of the Solomon Islands is Guadalcanal, which, like the other large islands in the group, is volcanic and mountainous. The climate is equatorial. Most people are Melanesians. Agriculture, forestry, and fishing are the main activities: copra, timber, and palm-oil are major exports. The Solomons became a British protectorate in 1893–99. Full independence was achieved in 1978.

SOMALI REPUBLIC, in the Horn of Africa, faces the Gulf of Aden in the north and the Indian Ocean to the east. Behind the narrow northern coastal plain are highlands containing Somalia's highest peaks. The south consists of plateaus and plains. It contains the only permanent rivers: the Wabi Shebele and the Juba. Rainfall increases from the north to the south. Temperatures are high throughout the year. The main types of vegetation are semi-desert and savanna. Nearly all the people are Muslims. About 75 percent are nomads, herding goats, sheep, camels, and cattle. The main arable areas are in the southern river valleys. The north became a British protectorate in 1884, while Italy took the south in 1905. The two territories merged and became an independent republic in 1960.

SOUTH AFRICA, a republic since 1961. The interior is a vast, saucer-shaped plateau, with an uptilted rim. The Orange and Limpopo rivers drain much of the plateau. Around the plateau, the land descends in steps to the sea. Most of South Africa has a subtropical climate, and a low rainfall; about 50 percent is arid. The population includes Black Africans (70.2 percent), people of European origin (17.5 percent), people of mixed descent (9.4 percent), and Asians (2.9 percent). The Whites control the country. Since 1948 a policy of apartheid has been pursued, whereby each ethnic group is supposed to develop separately. Hence, 10 African tribal Homelands have been set up for the main Black groups, including the Zulu, Xhosa, Tswana, Sepedi, and Seshoeshoe. South Africa produces most of the non-communist world's gold and many other minerals, including asbestos, coal, diamonds, copper, iron ore, manganese, tin, uranium, and zinc. Industry produces nearly all the goods the country needs, and farms grow most of its food. The chief food crop is corn, but a wide variety of cash crops is produced. Forestry, fishing, and tourism are also important. During the 1800s Boers (Dutch settlers) and British settlers clashed over South Africa and fought two wars. In 1910 the country was united as the Union of South Africa, an independent member of the Commonwealth. Since 1948 the White minority government of South Africa has been increasingly criticized for its racial separatism. In 1961 South Africa declared itself a republic and left the Commonwealth.

STATISTICS

To see the statistics of each country's area and population, plus its capital, turn to pages 102–106.

SPAIN, a kingdom in the Iberian peninsula. Most of Spain is a *meseta*, or plateau, which is broken by several mountain ranges, including the Sierra de Gredos and the Sierra de Guadarrama near the capital, Madrid. The fold ranges of the Pyrenees and the Cantabrian Mts. are in the north, while the Sierra Nevada in the south contains Mulhacén, Spain's highest peak. The coastal plains vary in width. Some, like those around Alicante and Valencia, are fertile. Four major rivers, the Duero, Tagus, Guadiana, and Guadalquivir, rise in the Meseta and discharge into the Atlantic. The Ebro River rises in the Cantabrian Mts. and flows into the Mediterranean. The Balearic Islands (notably Majorca, Minorca, and Ibiza) form a province in the Mediterranean. The volcanic Canary Islands, off southern Morocco, consist of two provinces: Las Palmas de Gran Canaria and Santa Cruz de Tenerife. The northern Atlantic coast region has mild, wet winters and cool summers; the south has warmer summers. The national language of Spain is Castilian Spanish. Basque, which is not clearly related to any other language in the world, is spoken in the north in the provinces bordering the Bay of Biscay. Catalan is spoken in the northeast and Galician in the northwest. In 1980, regional governments were established for the Basques and Catalans, and in 1981 a similar government was set up in Galicia. In 1980 74 percent of Spain's people lived in urban areas, as compared with 57 percent in 1960. This change reflected a fall in the relative importance of agriculture in the economy. Industry employs 43 percent of the population, services 39 percent, and agriculture 18 percent. Important minerals include coal, iron ore, copper, lead, and zinc. Hydroelectric and nuclear power stations supply half Spain's electrical energy. The leading manufacturing centers are Madrid and the Mediterranean port of Barcelona. Textiles are the leading manufactures, but Spain has a wide range of light and heavy industry. Tourism is a major source of foreign exchange. Crops vary according to the climate; irrigation is practiced in many arid areas. Barley, citrus fruit, grapes (for wine), olives, potatoes, wheat, and vegetables are leading crops. Spain is Europe's 3rd largest wine producer. There is a large fishing fleet. Moors from Morocco invaded Spain in 711, and occupied a large part of it. They were driven out by 1492. The modern kingdom of Spain came into being in 1479, when the two small kingdoms of Castile and Aragon were united. Spain built up a huge overseas empire, but lost most of it in the early 1800s. The country is a member of the European Community.

SRI LANKA, called Ceylon until 1972, is a South Asian island republic and member of the Commonwealth. It is mostly low-lying; the central highlands, which cover less than 20 percent of the land, reach their highest peak in Pidurutalagala. The climate is tropical, with moderate to heavy rainfall and high temperatures. Most people are Sinhalese, but 18 percent are Tamils and 7 percent are Moors. About 36 percent of Sri Lanka is cultivated. Rice is the main food. Tea, rubber, and coconuts are the main cash crops. Gemstones and graphite are mined, and there is a variety of manufacturing industries. The Sinhalese, from northern India, conquered the island in the 6th century B.C., Tamils arrived in the 11th century A.D. and Arabs (Moors) in the 12th and 13th centuries. The country was the British colony of Ceylon from 1796 until independence in 1948. It became the republic of Sri Lanka in 1972.

SUDAN, Africa's largest nation. The land is mostly flat. It includes much of the Upper Nile basin. Highlands border the Red Sea plains in the northeast, the Darfur highlands are in the west, but the highest peak, Kinyeti, is in the far south. The average annual temperature is high. Rainfall varies from extremely low in the north to plentiful. Much of Sudan is desert, but large areas of *sudd* (masses of floating plants) occur in the Nile region. In the north most people are Muslim Arabs, Hamites and Blacks; Blacks predominate in the south. Agriculture is the main occupation, producing cotton for export. Farmers raise cattle, sheep, and goats. Many people grow barely enough food to eat; droughts, floods, and famine have been a severe problem. Britain and Egypt ruled Sudan jointly as a condominium from 1899. The country became fully independent as a republic in 1956.

SURINAM, a republic in northeastern South America, formerly called Dutch Guiana. Behind the wide, marshy coastal plain are savanna-covered hills that rise to forested highlands. The climate is tropical and the rainfall plentiful. About 35 percent of the people are Creoles of mixed African and European origin, 35 percent are East Indians, 15 percent are Javanese, 9 percent are descendants of runaway slaves, 2 percent are Chinese, and 2 percent are pure American Indians. Farming is confined to the coastal plain. Fruit, rice, and sugar cane are major crops. Forestry is also important, but the most valuable resource is bauxite. Surinam was a Dutch colony from 1667 until independence in 1975.

SWAZILAND, a landlocked kingdom in southern Africa between South Africa and Mozambique. There are 4 regions aligned north-south, forming rolling grasslands and open plains dotted with bushes. Rainfall is higher in the west than in the east. The Swazis are Black Africans speaking the Bantu language, siSwati. Most of them live in rural areas. The main crops are citrus fruits, cotton, corn, pineapples, rice, sorghum, sugar cane, and tobacco, and people raise cattle, goats, and sheep. Asbestos and coal are mined, and there are various factories in the towns. Tourism and remittances from Swazis working abroad are sources of foreign exchange. Britain ruled Swaziland from 1902 until independence in the Commonwealth was achieved in 1968.

SWEDEN, a Scandinavian European monarchy. Norrland, north of latitude 61° North, contains vast coniferous forests and many streams and lakes in the valleys. Mountains run along the border with Norway; the highest peak, Kebnekaise, is in the northwest. In the far north of this thinly-populated region is part of Lapland, where some Lapps still follow their traditional nomadic way of life. South of Norrland, between Göteborg and Stockholm, is the Central Lake region, where lakes Vänern and Vättern are situated. This region has a milder climate than Norrland. South of the Lake region are the infertile southern uplands. Scania, in the far south, is the most fertile region. Most of Sweden has long, cold winters and short, warm summers. Sweden is one of the world's most prosperous nations. It has little coal, but hydroelectric and nuclear power stations produce most of

STATISTICS
To see the statistics of each country's area and population, plus its capital, turn to pages 102–106.

its electric energy. There are major reserves of metal ores, notably iron ore. Steel and steel products are the chief manufactures. Forests cover 57 percent of Sweden, and timber and wood pulp are major exports. Only 8 percent of the land is cultivated: cereals, potatoes, sugar beet, and cattle fodder are grown. Sweden was united with Denmark and Norway in 1397. It broke away in 1523. From 1814 to 1905 it was again united with Norway.

SWITZERLAND, a landlocked federal republic in Europe. The Jura Mts. run from northeast to southwest along the border with France. These mountains are separated by a central plateau, the *Mittelland*, from the spectacularly scenic Alps, which make up 60 percent of Switzerland. The plateau contains 75 percent of the population. It has many lakes, between Lake Geneva in the southwest and Lake Constance in the northeast. Switzerland contains the headwaters of the Inn, Rhine, Rhône, and Ticino rivers. The average annual temperature range on the plateau is low to moderate, with moderate rainfall. The mountains are colder and wetter, although much of the precipitation falls as snow. Switzerland is a multilingual nation: 69 percent of the population speak German, 18 percent French, 12 percent Italian, and 1 percent Romansch (which is related to Latin). Dairy farming is the main agricultural activity. Cereals, potatoes, sugar beet, and fruits are grown, and wine is produced. Switzerland is highly industrialized. Its precision instruments made it famous, but chemicals, processed foods, glassware, machinery, metal products, and textiles are all important today. Tourism is a major source of foreign exchange. Switzerland was formed by a league of cantons (provinces) and won independence

from the Holy Roman Empire in 1648. The country has remained neutral in all wars since 1815. There are 23 self-governing cantons, and a federal parliament in Bern.

SYRIA, an Arab republic in southwestern Asia. Behind the coastal plain, with its Mediterranean climate, is a low mountain range that overlooks the fertile River Orontes valley. The River Euphrates drains the inland plains in the north. The highest peaks are in the Anti-Lebanon range in the southwest. To the east, the land slopes down to the hot Syrian desert. The rainfall decreases from west to east: about 60 percent of Syria has very low rainfall. About 90 percent of the people are Arabs, 6 percent are Kurds, and there is a Palestinian minority. Cotton is the leading crop. Oil is produced and manufacturing is increasing. Tourism is important in peaceful times. Syria was under foreign rule for most of its history, finally winning independence in 1946.

TAIWAN, an island republic (formerly called Formosa) off the coast of China. It is largely mountainous, with fertile plains in the west. The climate is tropical. Nearly all the people are Chinese. Rice, sugar cane, sweet potatoes, and tea are major crops. Taiwan produces coal, some oil and natural gas, and various metals. But manufactures, including textiles and electrical goods, dominate the exports. Taiwan became Chinese in the 1680s. Japan ruled it between 1895 and 1945. When the Communists took over China in 1949, their Nationalist opponents set up a government on Taiwan. The economy expanded rapidly with U.S. aid. Taiwan represented China in the U.N. until 1971, when the People's Republic of China was admitted instead.

TANZANIA, a united republic in East Africa, consisting of mainland Tanganyika and the coral islands of Zanzibar and Pemba. Most of Tanganyika is a high plateau broken by arms of the East African Rift Valley; the western arm encloses lakes Nyasa (Malawi) and Tanganyika; the eastern arm contains smaller salt lakes. Lake Victoria lies in the northwest. There are mountains in the north and south. Mt. Kilimanjaro is Africa's highest peak. The climate is equatorial, but is cooler on the plateau. Savanna vegetation is the most common. The wildlife is rich, and national parks cover 3 percent of the land; tourism is expanding. The people are divided into 120 tribal groups. About 94 percent of the people speak Bantu languages. Others speak Cushitic and Khoisan tongues. The majority of Tanzanians work on the land. Major crops are coffee, cotton, cashew nuts, and sisal. Zanzibar is a leading producer of cloves. Diamonds are mined, but manufacturing is small-scale. Britain ruled Tanganyika under mandate from 1919 until independence in 1961. Zanzibar, a British protectorate from 1890, became independent in 1963 but joined with Tanganyika in 1964, adopting the official title of the United Republic of Tanzania. The country concentrates on rural development.

THAILAND, a southeast Asian kingdom, called Siam until 1939. The fertile Chao Phraya river basin, the main farming region, is bordered by mountains in the east, west, and north, where the highest peak, Inthanon, is situated. Northeastern Thailand, a plateau drained by the Mekong River, is infertile. The climate is tropical, and most areas have plentiful rainfall. About 85 percent of the people are Thais. There is a sizable Chinese community, tribesmen in remote areas (Karen, Khmu, Mao, and Yao), Malays, and Indians. Three-quarters of the people work on the land. The main products are rice, rubber, and tin. Manufacturing is increasing. The Thai state was founded in the 14th century. Its area was reduced in the 19th century but it remained independent. It was an absolute monarchy until 1932, when it became a constitutional monarchy.

TOGO, a West African republic. The Togo-Atacora Mts. in the center separate a low plateau in the north from the fertile southern plains. The climate is tropical. The rainfall increases from the coast inland. There are about 30 tribal groups among the Black African population. Farming is the main activity: cocoa and coffee are the leading crops. Phosphates make up 39 percent of the exports, but manufacturing is small-scale. Togo was a German protectorate from 1884. France and Britain divided it between them during World War I. In 1957 the western (British) section joined Ghana. French Togo was made a fully independent republic in 1960.

STATISTICS
To see the statistics of each country's area and population, plus its capital, turn to pages 102–106.

TONGA, or the Friendly Islands, an island kingdom in the South Pacific. The 169 islands and islets are divided into 3 groups: Vava'u in the north; Ha'apai in the center; and Tongatapu in the south, where the capital is situated. There are both coral and volcanic islands. The climate is pleasant. Most people are Polynesians. The country is basically agricultural. Coconuts and bananas are leading products and some are exported. The islands were a British protectorate from 1900 until independence within the Commonwealth was achieved in 1970.

TRINIDAD AND TOBAGO, a West Indian republic of two islands close to South America. Trinidad covers 94 percent of the country. Both islands are hilly and have a tropical climate. The people include Blacks, (45 percent), East Indians (35 percent), people of mixed origin (17 percent), Europeans (2 percent), and Chinese (1 percent). Oil is the main product. Other exports include asphalt and natural gas. Citrus fruits, cocoa, coffee, and sugar cane are grown. Sugar is used in the production of rum and molasses. Columbus discovered the islands in 1498. They were ruled by Britain from 1802 until independence within the Commonwealth in 1962. Trinidad and Tobago became a republic in 1976.

TUNISIA, a North African republic. An extension of the Atlas Mts. is in the north, surrounded by plains. A depression containing salt lakes, the Chott el-Djerid, is in the center. Saharan plateaus are in the south. The country becomes drier from north to south. Most people are Arabs or Berbers. Nearly half the people work in agriculture. Major crops are cereals, olives, grapes (for wine), fruit, and vegetables. Fishing is important. Mining for oil, phosphates, and metal ores is increasing; manufacturing is also growing. Tourism is important. The Arabs conquered Tunisia in A.D. 647. France made Tunisia a protectorate in 1883. Full independence as a monarchy was achieved in 1956 and a republic was proclaimed in 1957.

TURKEY, a republic partly in Europe but mostly in Asia. European Turkey lies west of the Dardanelles, the Sea of Marmara, and the Bosporus. These waterways link the Mediterranean and Black seas. European Turkey is a fertile, low-lying region. Asian Turkey (Anatolia) has fertile coastal plains with a Mediterranean climate. Central Anatolia, a mainly flat plateau, has a very low rainfall. About 90 percent of the people speak Turkish; Kurds make up 7 percent of the population. Nearly 31 percent of Turkey is cultivated. Major crops include barley, cotton, grapes (for wine), fruit, nuts, raisins, sugar beets, and wheat, and large numbers of cattle, sheep, and goats are raised. Turkey produces coal and lignite, chromium, and some iron ore, copper, and oil. Manufactures include iron and steel, petroleum products, paper, cement, chemicals, textiles, and machinery. Tourism is growing. Ottoman Turks captured the former Byzantine capital, Istanbul (then called Constantinople), in

1493, and built up a huge empire stretching north into Europe and south and west into southwestern Asia and northern Africa. It was ruled by sultans. The Ottoman Empire declined in size during the 1700s and 1800s, and finally disappeared in 1918, during World War I. In 1923 Turkey became a republic.

TUVALU (formerly the Ellice Islands), an independent member of the Commonwealth north of Fiji in the South Pacific. The islands are coral atolls. The people are Polynesians. Coconuts and copra are major products. The Gilbert and Ellice Islands became a British protectorate in 1892. The Ellice Islands broke away from the Micronesian Gilbert Islands (now Kiribati) in 1975 to become Tuvalu. Full independence was achieved in 1978.

UGANDA, a landlocked republic in equatorial Africa. Part of Africa's largest lake, Victoria, is in the southeast; the marshy Lake Kyoga is in the center; and lakes Edward and Mobutu Sese Seko are in the Rift Valley in the west. The Ruwenzori Range borders the Rift Valley. Most of Uganda is a high plateau, warm with plentiful rainfall. Uganda has about 40 tribal groups. Two-thirds of the people, including the largest single group, the Baganda, speak Bantu

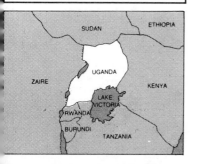

languages. Some Nilotic languages are also spoken. Most people are farmers. Coffee, cotton, tea, bananas, and skins are produced, and copper is mined. Manufacturing is developing. Uganda was under British rule for about 70 years until independence in 1962.

UNION OF SOVIET SOCIALIST REPUBLICS, the U.S.S.R., is the world's largest nation. It spreads from eastern Europe right across Asia to the Pacific Ocean. The European part, west of the Ural Mts., covers 25 percent of the country, but it contains 75 percent of the population. Much of the land, including the fertile Ukraine, is flat, but there are many hilly areas. Major rivers are the Dniepr and Don, which flow into the Black Sea, and the Volga, which empties into the Caspian Sea. The Caspian Sea is the world's largest lake, while the Volga, is Europe's longest river. The Caucasus in the south contain Mt. Elbruz, which is Europe's highest point. East of the Urals is the West Siberian Plain, drained by the River Ob. Between the Yenisey and Lena rivers is the central Siberian plateau. In the far east is a series of mountain ranges. The southeast, which is drained by the Amur River, contains Lake Baykal, the world's deepest lake. South of the West Siberian plain are the Kazakh plateaus; several mountain ranges, including the Pamir, Altai, and Tien Shan; and in the west the plains around the Aral Sea. The climate varies from the Arctic north to the warm Mediterranean climate along the Black and Caspian sea coasts. Inland areas have a continental climate, with freezing winters. The north-west and the Caucasus region are the wettest places. There are deserts east of the Caspian Sea (the Kara Kum and the Kyzyl Kum). About 60 languages are spoken in the U.S.S.R. The largest groups are Russians (52.2 percent), Ukrainians (16 percent), Uzbeks (4.8 percent), Byelorussians (3.6 percent), Kazakhs (2.5 percent), Tatars (2.4 percent), Azerbaijanis (2.1 percent), Armenians (1.6 percent), Georgians (1.4

STATISTICS

To see the statistics of each country's area and population, plus its capital, turn to pages 102–106.

percent), Moldavians (1.1 percent), Tadzhiks (1.1 percent), Lithuanians (1.1 percent), and Turkmenians (0.8 percent). The U.S.S.R. is divided into 15 republics. The largest, the Russian Soviet Federal Socialist Republic (R.S.F.S.R.) covers 76 percent of the country. Arable land covers 10 percent and pasture 17 percent of the land. Crops vary with the climate. The U.S.S.R. is a world leader in producing apples, barley, coniferous wood, milk, mutton, lamb and goat's meat, oats, potatoes, rye, sugar beet, and wheat. Forests cover about one-third of the U.S.S.R. Most of the land and all industry are government-owned, but most farm workers have a private plot. The U.S.S.R. has vast mineral resources. It leads the world in asbestos, coal, oil, iron ore, lead, manganese, mercury, nickel, potash, and silver production. But manufacturing is the chief economic sector. The main industrial areas are the Moscow region, the Ukraine; the Urals; Transcaucasia; and the area around Leningrad. Only the U.S. produces more electrical energy than the U.S.S.R., which is the world's top steel producer. Russia was invaded by Mongol hordes in the 1200s. By 1480 the principality of Moscow had driven out the Mongols and begun to unify Russia. The grand princes of Moscow took the title of *tsar* (emperor). Tsars ruled Russia until 1917, when a revolution brought the Bolsheviks (communists) to power under Lenin. In 1922 the country took the name Union of Soviet Socialist Republics; it is also often called the Soviet Union. After World War II the U.S.S.R. became a super-power.

UNITED ARAB EMIRATES, an oil-rich federation of seven emirates (formerly the Trucial States), with coastlines on the Persian Gulf and the Gulf of Oman. The emirates are Abu Dhabi, Ajman, Dubai, Fujairah, Ras al Khaimah, Sharjah, and Umm al Qaiwain. The main resource of this flat, hot, desert nation is oil. About 70 percent of the people are Arabs. The rest are Iranians or other Asians. Britain was responsible for the states' armed forces and foreign relations from 1820 to 1971.

UNITED KINGDOM OF GREAT BRITAIN AND NORTHERN IRELAND, an island monarchy off the west coast of Europe. It is known as Britain or the U.K. Great Britain consists of England, Scotland, and Wales. The Channel Islands (Jersey, Guernsey, and Guernsey's dependencies: Alderney, Brechou, Great Sark, Herm, Jethou, Lihou, and Little Sark) and the Isle of Man in the Irish Sea are dependencies of the British Crown, but they are largely self-governing. Scotland has three main land regions. The highlands are divided by Glen More into the rugged northwestern Highlands and the Grampians, which include the U.K.'s highest mountain, Ben Nevis. The main island groups are Orkney and Shetland to the north and the Hebrides to the west. The central lowlands are the most densely populated region, with coalfields, the leading cities, and much farmland. Scotland's southern uplands are mainly a farming region. Northern England contains the Cumbrian Mts. (or the Lake

District), with England's highest peak, Scafell Pike, and the Pennines which run north–south. Coalfields near the edge of the Pennines have stimulated the growth of major industrial regions. England's other highland region includes Exmoor and Dartmoor in the southwest. Lowland England contains many fertile plains, crossed by ranges of low hills. Wales is a mainly highland country, rising to Snowdon. South Wales contains a large coalfield on which a major industrial region has been built. Northern Ireland contains uplands and plains. In the east Lough Neagh is the U.K.'s largest lake. The U.K.'s longest rivers are the Severn and the Thames, on which the capital, London, stands. The U.K. has a moist, temperate climate, moderated by the warm North Atlantic Drift (Gulf Stream). Nine out of ten people live in towns. Farming is highly efficient but much food is imported. Major crops are cereals, potatoes, sugar beets, and green vegetables. Cattle, sheep, and pigs are raised. Fishing is an important source of food. The U.K.'s industrial economy was originally based on its abundant coal and iron ore resources. Coal-mining has declined, but the economy has been boosted by the exploitation of oil and natural gas in the North Sea. Manufactures are extremely varied. Invisible earnings from banking, insurance, tourism, and other services make a vital contribution to the economy. The U.K.'s early history is one of successive invasions by Iberians, Celts, Romans, Angles, Saxons, Jutes, Norsemen, and finally, in 1066, Normans, who conquered England. In 1282 England overran Wales and annexed it. In 1603 the Scottish king, James VI, also became king of England, though the two countries were not finally united until 1707. England began the conquest of Ireland in the 1100s, but it was not until 1801, after much bloodshed, that Ireland became part of the United Kingdom of Great Britain and Ireland. The southern part of Ireland broke away in 1922 and is now independent. In the 1700s and 1800s the U.K. became the first country to change the basis of its economy from agriculture to industry. From the 1960s onward many Blacks and Asians from the Commonwealth settled in the U.K., transforming it into a multiracial society. In 1973 the U.K. joined the European (Economic) Community (E.C.).

UNITED STATES OF AMERICA, a federal republic and the world's 4th largest nation. The bulk of the U.S. lies between Canada and Mexico. The 49th state, Alaska, is in north-western North America, while the 50th state, Hawaii, is in the north Pacific Ocean, about 2,400 miles (3,870 km) southwest of San Francisco. Alaska and Hawaii became states in 1959. The main part of the U.S. contains five land regions. The southern coastal plains are broadest around the Gulf of Mexico. The Atlantic coastal plains are broadest in the south and narrowest in New England. The Atlantic coast is deeply indented and contains several natural harbors. West of the Atlantic seaboard are the Appalachian Mts., running roughly from Newfoundland (Canada) in the northeast to Alabama in the south. The central (interior) lowlands stretch westward from the Appalachians. In the north are the five Great Lakes. To the south, the central plains are drained by the Mississippi River and its tributaries, notably the Missouri and Ohio. To the west are the higher Great Plains. Beyond these plains the land rises to the western highlands, made up of the folded Rocky mountains, the Sierra Nevada range, and the Cascade range, where the volcano Mt. St. Helens erupted in 1980. The Colorado River in the southwest has carved the Grand Canyon. The Pacific slope contains fertile valleys and coastal ranges. One feature is the 597 miles (960 km) long San Andreas Fault in California. Movements along the fault cause earthquakes. Alaska also has much earthquake and volcanic activity, and the Alaska range contains North America's

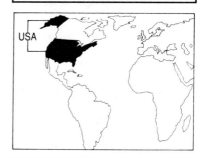

STATISTICS
To see the statistics of each country's area and population, plus its capital, turn to pages 102–106.

highest peak, Mt. McKinley. Hawaii consists of a string of volcanic and coral islands. The climate varies greatly from Arctic conditions in Alaska to deserts in the southwest, including Death Valley, the U.S.'s lowest point at 282 ft (86 m) below sea level, and a humid, sub-tropical climate in the southeast. California has a pleasant Mediterranean climate, but much of the interior has a continental climate, with hot summers, cold winters, and a relatively low annual rainfall. About 83 percent of the people are of European descent, and 12 percent are Black, the descendants of slaves. A few are American Indians, the earliest inhabitants. There are also Asians. Farming is highly efficient, and the U.S. is among the world's top producers of cotton, fruit, corn, oats, soya beans, sugar beets, tobacco, timber, wheat, and livestock. The U.S. is one of the world's top producers of copper, iron ore, oil and natural gas, lead, phosphates, sulfur, and uranium. The U.S. is the world's most industrialized nation, accounting for about half of the world's industrial goods. The first inhabitants, American Indians, entered North America at least 30,000 years ago, crossing the Bering Strait from Asia. They traveled over a huge sheet of ice covering the Strait at that time. Europeans discovered the continent in the 1490s, and quickly began settling. The United States was founded in 1776 by 13 British colonies which rebelled and declared themselves independent. The new country grew quickly to include all the territory between the Mexican and Canadian borders. After World War II the U.S. was established as one of the world's super-powers.

URUGUAY, a South American republic facing the Atlantic Ocean. It is mostly low-lying, with hills in the north. The River Negro,

a tributary of the Uruguay on the western border, drains the central region. Temperature and rainfall are both moderate. More than 90 percent of the people are of European descent. Most others are of mixed European and American Indian descent. About 89 percent of the land is farmed; 90 percent of this is pasture, grazing cattle and sheep; livestock products are the chief exports. Crops include fruit, corn, rice, sugar, and wheat. There are processing, oil refining, light engineering, transport, chemical, and textile industries. From 1726 Uruguay was part of the Spanish Empire. It became an independent nation in 1828.

VANUATU, an island republic in the south-western Pacific Ocean, formerly called the New Hebrides. There are about 80 islands which are mountainous and volcanic. The climate is tropical and the rainfall is generally abundant. Most people are Melanesians. Copra and fish are exported. Tourism is growing. Britain and France jointly ruled the islands from 1906 until independence in 1980.

VATICAN CITY STATE, the world's smallest independent state, is in north-western Rome, on a hill on the right bank of the Tiber River. It contains the government of the Roman Catholic Church, headed by the Pope, and the magnificent St. Peter's Basilica. It has been the residence of the Pope since the 5th century and was formerly the hub of the Papal States in central Italy. Its independence was officially recognized in 1929 when the Lateran Treaty was signed.

VENEZUELA, an oil-rich republic in northern South America. The hot Maracaibo lowlands surround Lake Maracaibo, a freshwater lake open to the sea, beneath which are the largest known oil deposits in the continent. Overlooking the lowlands are the Venezuelan highlands, extensions of the Andes. The central plain is drained by the Orinoco, one of the world's longest rivers. This plain is covered by llanos (savanna). The south-eastern Guiana Highlands are thinly populated. They contain the world's highest waterfall, Angel Falls, with a drop of 3,212 ft (979 m). A lot of the southern part of this region is covered with tropical forests. The climate is equatorial. About 70 percent of the people are mestizos (of mixed White and American Indian origin), 18 percent are Blacks or mulattos, 10 percent are Whites, and 2 percent are American Indians. About four people out of five live in the towns. The chief resource is oil; Venezuela is a leading producer and most is exported to the United States. Other minerals, including diamonds, gold, and iron ore, are being exploited, and manufacturing has been expanding quickly. Particularly important are textiles, lumber, and products and chemicals derived from oil and natural gas. Coffee, cotton, corn, rice and sugar cane are major crops; beef and dairy cattle are raised in the central plains. Spain ruled the area from the 16th century. It was liberated from Spain in 1821, but became part of a republic called Gran Colombia until 1830.

VIETNAM, a Socialist Republic in South-East Asia. The northern Red River delta is ringed by hills and mountains, including Fan Si Pan, the nation's highest peak. In central Vietnam, a narrow coastal plain is backed by the Annamite range. In the far south is the huge delta of the Mekong River. Temperatures are high throughout the year in the south, but are cooler in the north. The rainfall is generally abundant. About 84 percent of the people are Vietnamese (Kinh). There are also Khmers, Thais, and various tribal groups. Rice, corn, sugar cane, sweet potatoes, and cotton are major crops. Farmers raise cattle and pigs. Fishing is also important. The north is rich in minerals, including coal, lignite, bauxite, chromite, iron ore, manganese, and titanium. Manufacturing has been steadily increasing. From the 1880s Vietnam was part of the colony of French Indo-China. In 1954 it was given independence as two countries, North Vietnam and South Vietnam. War between the two started in 1959. It ended with the defeat of South Vietnam and the reunification of the country as a Socialist Republic with close relations with the U.S.S.R. in 1976.

YEMEN ARAB REPUBLIC (North Yemen) is in the southwestern Arabian peninsula. The Red Sea coastal plain, called the Tihama, is backed by mountains. The coastal plain is hot with very low rainfall and has little population. The highlands have more rain and contain Arabia's best farmland. Most people are Arabs; 90 percent live in rural areas. Agriculture is the main occupation. Cereals,

STATISTICS

To see the statistics of each country's area and population, plus its capital, turn to pages 102–106.

sesame, coffee, cotton, fruit, and vegetables are grown and hides and skins are important products. Oil deposits were discovered in the early 1980s and oil production is an important industry. Some salt is mined and manufacturing is expanding. From A.D. 897 Yemen was ruled by an *imam*, a religious and political leader. Yemen was part of the Ottoman Empire in 1849–1918. In 1962 the *imam* was overthrown and a republic proclaimed.

YEMEN PEOPLE'S DEMOCRATIC
REPUBLIC, in the southern Arabian peninsula, was formerly the Federation of South Arabia, including Aden. Behind the narrow coastal plain are mountains, a fertile valley (the Hadhramawt), and large deserts in the east. Temperatures are high and the rainfall low in Aden, but parts of the Hadhramawt have moderate rain. Most people are Arabs. The chief crops are cereals; cotton is the main cash crop. Farmers keep goats and sheep. Fishing is also important. Aden has an oil refinery, and oil products, made from imported oil, are exported. Transit trade is generally important. In 1839 Britain annexed Aden, which became a major strategic and trading center after the opening of the Suez Canal in 1869. The country became independent in 1967.

YUGOSLAVIA, a Socialist Federal Republic on the Adriatic Sea. Large areas are mountainous; the mountains are extensions of the Alpine system. The mountains on the coast have been submerged, so former ridges now form long, narrow islands parallel to the coast, and former valleys are inlets. There are more than 600 islands along the coast. To the north and east is hill country descending

to the interior plains drained by the Danube river system. The coastal climate is typically Mediterranean, but the interior plains, the main farming region, have a continental climate. Most people are South Slavs: the Serbs and Croats are the two largest groups; the Slovenes live in the north; and the Montenegrins and Macedonians live in the south. Various non-Slav minorities live mainly in the east and south. The division of Yugoslavia into six republics reflects its cultural diversity. About half the people live in towns, but more and more people are leaving country areas to seek better-paid jobs in the cities. Farmers grow cereals, cotton, fruit, olives, sugar beets, sunflower seeds, and tobacco, and raise sheep, pigs, and cattle. Forestry is important. Yugoslavia has many mineral resources and manufacturing has steadily expanded since 1945. Yugoslavia was founded in 1918 as a union of the independent countries of Serbia and Montenegro with lands formerly ruled by Austria and Turkey. It became a communist country after World War II.

ZAÏRE, a republic in west-central Africa, is the continent's 2nd largest nation. Most of the country lies in the drainage basin of the River Zaïre (formerly Congo), which is one of the world's longest at 3,000 miles (4,828 km). There are highlands and plateaus in the south and east along the Rift Valley, where Zaïre's border passes through lakes Tanganyika, Kivu, Edward, and Mobutu Sese Seko (formerly Albert). The climate is equatorial. There is rainforest in the center and savanna in the north and south. About 200 language and ethnic groups live in Zaïre. About two-thirds of the people speak Bantu languages; Hamitic, Nilotic, Sudanic, and pygmy languages are also spoken. Agriculture is the chief occupation. The chief cash crops are coffee, cotton, palm products, and rubber. Fishing is important, but livestock can be reared only in areas free from the disease-carrying tsetse fly. The main mining region is Shaba, where copper (the most valuable export), cobalt, manganese, silver, uranium, and zinc are mined. Some oil is produced, and diamonds are mined in the Kasai provinces. Hydroelectricity is being developed and manufacturing is growing. The country became the personal property of King Leopold of Belgium in 1884, and later became the colony of the Belgian Congo. Independence came in 1960.

ZAMBIA, a landlocked republic in south-central Africa, called Northern Rhodesia until 1964. It consists mostly of a high plateau. In the south and east are the Zambezi and Luangwa rivers. The Zambezi has been dammed to form Lake Kariba, which Zambia shares with Zimbabwe. Kariba's hydroelectric plants have given Zambia an abundance of electrical energy. Parts of lakes Mweru and Tanganyika are in Zambia, as is the entire Lake Bangweulu. The main mountains are in the northeast. The climate is tropical. Wildlife is abundant in the savanna, which covers most of Zambia. Six major Bantu languages and 66 dialects are spoken. The chief resource is copper, which accounts for 90 percent of the exports. Cobalt, lead, and zinc are also exported, as are corn and tobacco, the main cash crop. There are processing and metal industries. After more than 50 years under British protection the country became independent in 1964.

ZIMBABWE, a landlocked republic in southern Africa, formerly called Rhodesia. The north is in a deep trough through which the River Zambezi flows. Lake Kariba, a man-made lake on the Zambezi, is shared with Zambia, as is the electricity produced at Kariba dam. Central Zimbabwe (the high veld) has a pleasant climate. The lowlands in the south, drained by the Limpopo River, are much hotter and arid. About 96 percent of the people are Black Africans who speak Bantu languages. The largest groups are the Ndebele in the south and the Shona in the north. Most other people are of European descent. European farming is efficient but African farming is mostly at subsistence level. Tobacco, sugar cane, tea, and fruit are the leading cash crops. Asbestos, chrome, coal, and gold are mined. Manufacturing is important in the towns. Between 1898 and 1923, Southern Rhodesia (as Zimbabwe was then called) was ruled by a British High Commissioner based in South Africa. In 1923 it became a self-governing British colony. In 1965 the White government declared independence, but Britain refused to agree because the Black majority had little power. Finally independence with a majority Black government was achieved in 1980.

STATISTICS

To see the statistics of each country's area and population, plus its capital, turn to pages 102–106.

Country Data by Continents

EUROPE

Country	Area sq miles	Area sq km	Population	Capital
Albania	11,100	28,750	3,200,000	Tirana
Andorra	188	486	56,000	Andorra la Vella
Austria	32,374	83,850	7,500,000	Vienna
Belgium	11,780	30,507	9,900,000	Brussels
Bulgaria	42,823	110,910	9,000,000	Sofia
Czechoslovakia	49,365	127,855	15,700,000	Prague
Denmark	16,633	43,080	5,100,000	Copenhagen
Finland	130,120	337,006	5,000,000	Helsinki
France	221,207	572,923	55,800,000	Paris
Germany, East (German Democratic Republic – D.D.R.)	41,768	108,178	16,700,000	East Berlin
Germany, West (Federal Republic of Germany)	95,975	248,574	61,200,000	Bonn
Greece	51,146	132,467	10,100,000	Athens
Hungary	35,919	93,030	10,600,000	Budapest
Iceland	39,790	103,053	251,000	Reykjavík
Ireland, Republic of	27,137	70,284	3,700,000	Dublin
Italy	116,303	301,223	57,400,000	Rome
Liechtenstein	62	160	30,000	Vaduz
Luxembourg	998	2,585	369,000	Luxembourg City
Malta	122	316	358,000	Valletta
Monaco	0.6	1.6	29,000	Monaco
Netherlands	15,770	40,844	14,700,000	Amsterdam; The Hague is the seat of government
Norway	125,180	324,217	4,200,000	Oslo
Poland	120,727	312,680	38,400,000	Warsaw
Portugal (including Azores and Madeira)	35,553	92,082	10,200,000	Lisbon
Romania	91,700	237,500	23,200,000	Bucharest
San Marino	24	62	23,000	San Marino
Spain	194,896	504,728	39,800,000	Madrid
Sweden	173,730	449,960	8,400,000	Stockholm
Switzerland	15,940	41,287	6,500,000	Bern
United Kingdom	94,226	244,044	56,700,000	London
U.S.S.R.	8,649,496	22,402,090	287,000,000	Moscow
Vatican City State	108.7 acres	0.44	1,000	Vatican City
Yugoslavia	98,766	255,803	23,800,000	Belgrade

NORTH AND CENTRAL AMERICA

Country	Area sq miles	Area sq km	Population	Capital
Antigua and Barbuda	170	443	86,000	St. John's
Bahamas	5,380	13,934	247,000	Nassau
Barbados	166	430	256,000	Bridgetown
Belize	8,867	22,965	179,000	Belmopan
Canada	3,851,790	9,976,090	25,400,000	Ottawa
Costa Rica	19,575	50,700	2,900,000	San José
Cuba	44,218	114,524	10,600,000	Havana
Dominica	290	750	76,000	Roseau
Dominican Republic	18,816	48,733	7,300,000	Santo Domingo
El Salvador	8,260	21,393	5,500,000	San Salvador
Grenada	133	344	87,000	St. George's
Guatemala	42,042	108,888	9,400,000	Guatemala City
Haiti	10,714	27,750	6,200,000	Port-au-Prince
Honduras	43,277	112,087	5,100,000	Tegucigalpa
Jamaica	4,232	10,960	2,400,000	Kingston
Mexico	761,604	1,972,545	88,100,000	Mexico City
Nicaragua	50,193	130,000	3,700,000	Managua
Panama	29,208	75,648	2,400,000	Panama
Saint Christopher (St. Kitts) and Nevis	100	262	40,000	Basseterre
Saint Lucia	238	616	128,000	Castries
Saint Vincent and the Grenadines	150	388	112,000	Kingstown
Trinidad and Tobago	1,980	5,128	1,300,000	Port-of-Spain
United States	3,618,770	9,372,570	247,500,000	Washington, D.C.

SOUTH AMERICA

Country	Area sq miles	Area sq km	Population	Capital
Argentina	1,065,189	2,758,826	32,600,000	Buenos Aires
Bolivia	424,165	1,098,582	6,900,000	La Paz (seat of government); Sucre (legal capital)
Brazil	3,286,470	8,511,917	154,000,000	Brasília
Chile	292,257	756,942	12,900,000	Santiago
Colombia	439,735	1,138,908	31,800,000	Bogotá
Ecuador	109,483	283,560	10,500,000	Quito
Guyana	83,000	214,970	800,000	Georgetown
Paraguay	157,047	406,750	4,500,000	Asunción
Peru	496,222	1,277,440	21,800,000	Lima
Surinam	63,037	163,265	380,000	Paramaribo
Uruguay	68,037	176,215	3,000,000	Montevideo
Venezuela	352,143	912,046	19,200,000	Caracas

ASIA

Country	Area sq miles	Area sq km	Population	Capital
Afghanistan	251,773	652,090	16,600,000	Kabul
Bahrain	258	668	483,000	Manama
Bangladesh	55,598	143,998	112,800,000	Dhaka
Bhutan	18,147	47,000	1,500,000	Thimphu
Brunei	2,226	5,765	267,000	Bandar Seri Begawan
Cambodia	69,898	181,035	6,860,000	Phnom Penh
China	3,705,390	9,596,915	1,069,600,000	Beijing
Cyprus	3,572	9,250	700,000	Nicosia
India	1,266,595	3,280,466	833,400,000	Delhi
Indonesia	735,268	1,904,335	187,700,000	Jakarta
Iran	636,293	1,647,990	51,000,000	Teheran
Iraq	167,924	434,920	17,600,000	Baghdad
Israel	7,847	29,324	4,500,000	Jerusalem
Japan	145,856	377,765	123,200,000	Tokyo
Jordan	37,737	97,738	3,000,000	Amman
Korea, North	46,540	120,538	22,000,000	Pyongyang
Korea, South	38,025	98,484	45,200,000	Seoul
Kuwait	6,880	17,820	2,000,000	Al Kuwait
Laos	91,428	236,797	4,000,000	Vientiane
Lebanon	4,015	10,400	2,900,000	Beirut
Malaysia	127,316	330,868	17,000,000	Kuala Lumpur
Maldives	115	298	202,000	Malé
Mongolia	604,247	1,564,992	2,100,000	Ulan Bator
Myanmar (formerly Burma)	261,789	678,030	39,900,000	Yangon (formerly Rangoon)
Nepal	56,136	145,392	18,800,000	Katmandu
Oman	82,030	212,457	1,400,000	Muscat
Pakistan	310,403	803,940	110,400,000	Islamabad
Philippines	115,830	300,000	62,000,000	Manila
Qatar	4,247	11,000	342,000	Doha
Saudi Arabia	839,996	2,175,580	12,700,000	Riyadh
Singapore	224	580	2,700,000	Singapore
Sri Lanka	25,332	65,610	17,500,000	Colombo
Syria	71,498	185,180	12,200,000	Damascus
Taiwan	13,885	35,962	20,300,000	Taipei
Thailand	198,456	514,000	55,000,000	Bangkok
Turkey	301,380	780,573	55,400,000	Ankara
United Arab Emirates	32,000	82,900	1,500,000	Abu Dhabi
Vietnam	128,400	332,557	66,700,000	Hanoi
Yemen Arab Republic	75,290	195,000	6,900,000	San'a
Yemen People's Democratic Republic	128,560	332,966	2,500,000	Aden

AFRICA

Country	Area sq miles	Area sq km	Population	Capital
Algeria	918,497	2,378,896	25,100,000	Algiers
Angola	481,353	1,246,700	9,000,000	Luanda
Benin	43,483	112,620	4,600,000	Porto Novo
Botswana	231,804	600,370	1,200,000	Gaborone
Burkina Faso	105,870	274,200	7,700,000	Ouagadougou
Burundi	10,760	27,836	5,200,000	Bujumbura
Cameroon	185,568	480,620	10,900,000	Yaoundé
Cape Verde	1,750	4,532	337,000	Praia
Central African Republic	240,534	622,980	3,000,000	Bangui
Chad	495,756	1,284,000	5,700,000	N'Djamena
Comoros	838	2,170	459,000	Moroni
Congo	132,046	342,000	2,000,000	Brazzaville
Côte d'Ivoire	124,503	322,460	11,800,000	Abidjan
Djibouti	8,494	22,000	327,000	Djibouti
Egypt	386,650	1,001,420	54,800,000	Cairo
Equatorial Guinea	10,832	28,055	389,000	Malabo
Ethiopia	471,776	1,221,894	47,800,000	Addis Ababa
Gabon	103,346	267,665	1,100,000	Libreville
Gambia	4,360	11,295	840,000	Banjul
Ghana	92,098	238,537	14,800,000	Accra
Guinea	94,964	245,976	6,100,000	Conakry
Guinea-Bissau	13,948	36,125	929,000	Bissau
Kenya	224,960	582,644	23,700,000	Nairobi
Lesotho	11,716	30,344	1,700,000	Maseru
Liberia	38,250	99,067	2,500,000	Monrovia
Libya	679,359	1,759,532	4,300,000	Tripoli
Madagascar	226,657	587,040	11,100,000	Antananarivo
Malawi	45,747	118,484	8,100,000	Lilongwe
Mali	478,764	1,240,000	8,500,000	Bamako
Mauritania	397,954	1,030,700	1,800,000	Nouakchott
Mauritius	790	2,046	1,000,000	Port Louis
Morocco	172,413	446,547	25,400,000	Rabat
Mozambique	309,484	801,560	15,300,000	Maputo
Namibia	318,260	824,292	1,200,000	Windhoek
Niger	489,189	1,267,000	7,400,000	Niamey
Nigeria	356,667	923,763	115,200,000	Lagos
Rwanda	10,169	26,338	7,300,000	Kigali
São Tomé and Príncipe	372	963	114,000	São Tomé
Senegal	75,750	196,192	7,700,000	Dakar
Seychelles	170	443	70,000	Victoria
Sierra Leone	27,700	71,740	4,300,000	Freetown
Somali Republic	246,300	637,914	8,600,000	Mogadishu

AFRICA continued Country	Area sq miles	Area sq km	Population	Capital
South Africa	472,360	1,223,404	35,700,000	Pretoria (seat of government); Cape Town (legal capital)
Sudan	966,757	2,503,900	25,000,000	Khartoum
Swaziland	6,704	17,363	757,000	Mbabane
Tanzania	364,886	945,050	24,800,000	Dodoma
Togo	21,622	56,000	3,400,000	Lomé
Tunisia	63,170	163,610	7,900,000	Tunis
Uganda	93,354	241,785	16,800,000	Kampala
Zaïre	905,563	2,345,400	34,000,000	Kinshasa
Zambia	290,586	752,614	7,800,000	Lusaka
Zimbabwe	150,803	390,580	10,000,000	Harare

OCEANIA

Country	Area sq miles	Area sq km	Population	Capital
Australia	2,966,200	7,682,422	16,100,000	Canberra
Fiji	7,056	18,275	758,000	Suva
Kiribati	266	689	65,000	Tarawa
Nauru	8	21	8,000	Nauru
New Zealand	103,736	268,675	3,400,000	Wellington
Papua New Guinea	178,260	461,687	3,600,000	Port Moresby
Solomon Islands	10,640	27,557	314,000	Honiara
Tonga	270	700	108,000	Nuku'alofa
Tuvalu	10	26	9,000	Fongafale
Vanuatu	5,700	14,763	150,000	Port Vila
Western Samoa	1,133	2,934	169,000	Apia

CONTINENTS OF THE WORLD

PROVINCES AND TERRITORIES OF CANADA

Province or territory	Area sq miles	Area sq km	Population 1986	Capital
Alberta	255,300	661,187	2,400,000	Edmonton
British Columbia	366,276	948,599	2,900,000	Victoria
Manitoba	251,014	650,089	1,100,000	Winnipeg
New Brunswick	28,356	73,437	710,000	Fredericton
Newfoundland	156,194	404,518	568,000	St. John's
Northwest Territory	1,304,978	3,379,693	52,000	Yellowknife
Nova Scotia	21,426	55,491	873,000	Halifax
Ontario	412,606	1,068,586	9,100,000	Toronto
Prince Edward Is.	2,184	5,657	127,000	Charlottetown
Quebec	594,894	1,540,685	6,600,000	Quebec
Saskatchewan	220,121	570,113	1,000,000	Regina
Yukon Territory	207,088	536,326	23,0000	Whitehorse

STATES AND TERRITORIES OF AUSTRALIA

State or territory	Area sq miles	Area sq km	Population 1987 (est.)	Capital
Australian Capital Territory	939	2,432	268,000	Canberra
New South Wales	309,450	801,428	5,600,000	Sydney
Northern Territory	520,308	1,347,519	150,000	Darwin
Queensland	667,036	1,727,522	2,600,000	Brisbane
South Australia	380,091	984,377	1,400,000	Adelaide
Tasmania	26,379	68,322	449,000	Hobart
Victoria	87,889	227,618	4,200,000	Melbourne
Western Australia	975,973	2,527,621	1,500,000	Perth

REPUBLICS OF THE U.S.S.R.

Republic	Population 1986 (est.)	Capital	Republic	Population 1986 (est.)	Capital
Armenia	3,400,000	Yerevan	Lithuania	3,600,000	Vilnius
Azerbaijan	6,700,000	Baku	Moldavia	4,100,000	Kishinev
Byelorussia	10,000,000	Minsk	Russian S.F.R.S.	144,000,000	Moscow
Estonia	1,500,000	Tallinn	Tadzikistan	4,600,000	Dushanbe
Georgia	5,200,000	Tbilisi	Turkmenistan	3,300,000	Ashkhabad
Kazakhstan	16,000,000	Alma-Ata	Ukraine	51,000,000	Kiev
Kirgizia	4,100,000	Frunze	Uzbekistan	18,500,000	Tashkent
Latvia	2,600,000	Riga			

PROVINCES OF SOUTH AFRICA

Province	Area sq miles	Area sq km	Population	Seat of government
Cape of Good Hope	278,395	721,000	6,700,000	Cape Town
Natal	33,580	87,000	4,200,000	Pietermaritzburg
Transvaal	109,627	284,000	8,700,000	Pretoria
Orange Free State	49,869	129,000	1,700,000	Bloemfontein

STATES OF THE UNION

State	Capital	Area sq miles	Area sq km	Population 1987 (est.)
Alabama	Montgomery	51,609	133,667	4,083,000
Alaska	Juneau	1,518,800	3,933,670	534,000
Arizona	Phoenix	113,909	295,023	3,386,000
Arkansas	Little Rock	53,104	137,539	2,388,000
California	Sacramento	158,693	411,013	27,663,000
Colorado	Denver	104,247	269,998	3,296,000
Connecticut	Hartford	5,009	12,973	3,211,000
Delaware	Dover	2,057	5,328	6,644,000
Florida	Tallahassee	58,560	151,670	12,023,000
Georgia	Atlanta	58,876	152,488	6,222,000
Hawaii	Honolulu	6,450	16,705	1,083,000
Idaho	Boise	83,557	216,412	998,000
Illinois	Springfield	56,400	146,075	11,582,000
Indiana	Indianapolis	36,291	93,993	5,531,000
Iowa	Des Moines	56,290	145,790	2,834,000
Kansas	Topeka	82,264	213,063	2,476,000
Kentucky	Frankfort	40,409	104,659	3,727,000
Louisiana	Baton Rouge	48,523	125,674	4,461,000
Maine	Augusta	33,215	86,026	1,187,000
Maryland	Annapolis	10,577	27,347	4,535,000
Massachusetts	Boston	8,257	21,386	5,855,000
Michigan	Lansing	58,216	150,779	9,200,000
Minnesota	St. Paul	84,068	217,735	4,246,000
Mississippi	Jackson	47,716	123,584	2,625,000
Missouri	Jefferson City	69,686	180,486	5,103,000
Montana	Helena	147,138	381,086	809,000
Nebraska	Lincoln	77,227	200,017	1,594,000
Nevada	Carson City	110,540	286,297	1,007,000
New Hampshire	Concord	9,304	24,097	1,057,000
New Jersey	Trenton	7,836	20,295	7,672,000
New Mexico	Santa Fe	121,666	315,113	1,500,000
New York	Albany	49,576	128,401	17,825,000
North Carolina	Raleigh	52,586	136,197	6,413,000
North Dakota	Bismarck	70,665	183,021	72,000
Ohio	Columbus	41,222	106,764	10,784,000
Oklahoma	Oklahoma City	69,919	181,089	3,272,000
Oregon	Salem	96,981	251,180	2,724,000
Pennsylvania	Harrisburg	45,333	117,412	11,936,000
Rhode Island	Providence	1,124	3,144	986,000
South Carolina	Columbia	31,055	80,432	3,425,000
South Dakota	Pierre	77,047	199,551	709,000
Tennessee	Nashville	42,244	109,411	4,855,000
Texas	Austin	267,338	692,402	16,789,000
Utah	Salt Lake City	84,916	219,931	1,680,000
Vermont	Montpelier	9,609	24,887	548,000
Virginia	Richmond	40,817	105,716	5,904,000
Washington	Olympia	68,192	176,616	4,538,000
West Virginia	Charlestown	24,181	62,628	1,897,000
Wisconsin	Madison	56,154	145,438	4,807,000
Wyoming	Cheyenne	97,914	253,596	490,000
District of Columbia	(Washington)	67	174	626,000
Commonwealth of Puerto Rico	San Juan	3,435	8,897	3,286,000

THE STATES OF AMERICA

KEY
Conn. = Connecticut
Mass. = Massachusetts
N.H. = New Hampshire

History

The colorful pageant of history tells of the conflicts and achievements of the human race, of bloody wars and milestones of civilization. It is studded with the names of statesmen and conquerors, explorers, inventors, and artists; it also records the way ordinary people lived in times past. Records of daily life and world events have been kept since writing was invented 5,500 years ago; archaeologists search among ruins for clues to what happened before that in the two million years people have lived on Earth.

There are several different kinds of history. Social history tells of the everyday lives and customs of people living in a certain time and place. Economic history concentrates on the commerce and industry of nations. Military history narrates the campaigns of armies and navies and their leaders. Cultural history examines the arts produced by different peoples. But what most people mean by "history" is political history—the major events that shape the political boundaries of a state or nation; its laws; its relations with other countries; and the deeds of its rulers.

△ Alexander the Great (356-323 B.C.) was the greatest conqueror of the ancient world. He became ruler of Macedon at the age of 20.

Some rulers have had much more influence on the course of history than others. The most notorious have been the conquerors. Alexander the Great set out to conquer the whole world, as it was known in his day. From Macedonia, in Greece, he extended his empire over the Middle East, including Egypt, Persia (modern Iran), and Afghanistan, as far as the Indus River valley, now in Pakistan.

▽ Lord Protector of England and brilliant military strategist, Oliver Cromwell. He died in 1658.

Another conqueror was the French general Napoleon Bonaparte, who, at the height of his power, ruled most of Europe. Neither his career nor that of Alexander lasted long: Alexander died of fever at the age of 33; Napoleon was sent into exile at 46. By contrast, another great leader, George Washington, lived to be 67. He fought not to conquer but to liberate his country from colonial rule, and went on to become the first president of the United States.

The history of the whole world shows that people developed at very different times, and that great events in one part of the world were completely unknown to people living in other places. For example, while Roman soldiers were defending Hadrian's Wall, in northern Britain, against attacks from the Picts and Scots, across the Atlantic the Maya were beginning to build huge temple pyramids in Central America.

At the time Leif Ericsson discovered the land he called Vinland, in North America, the ancient Empire of Ghana was flourishing in West Africa; Polynesians were colonizing New Zealand; and in England the Saxon king Ethelred the Unready was paying Danish invaders large sums in gold to go away.

Human beings have lived on Earth for about two million years. The first humans appear to have lived in eastern Africa. By 100,000 years ago they had spread over most of Africa and Europe, and large parts of Asia. People migrated from Asia into North America less than 40,000 years ago, when they traveled across a huge ice sheet where the Bering Strait now is.

△ The Bayeux tapestry tells the story of the Norman conquest of England. At the battle of Hastings in 1066 William of Normandy defeated Harold Godwinsson, his rival for the English crown, and established Norman rule over England.

▽ At the battle of Austerlitz in 1805, the French emperor Napoleon won his greatest victory, defeating a combined army of Austrian and Russian troops.

People were unable to record the events of their times until the invention of writing, some 5,500 years ago. So we have to piece together the events before that from objects that ancient peoples have left behind, such as their cave dwellings, or the ruins of buildings.

In the Chronology of World History on pages 128–148 we deal only with events within the time of written history.

Major Wars

Over the centuries there have been hundreds of wars and thousands of battles. Indeed, even in times of apparent peace people have been fighting somewhere in the world. These are a few of the most important conflicts.

△ Greek hoplites were the "shock troops" of their day.

MAJOR WARS

Name	Date	Won by	Against
Peloponnesian War	431–404 B.C.	Peloponnesian League, led by Sparta, Corinth	Delian League, led by Athens
Punic Wars	264–146 B.C.	Rome	Carthage
Hundred Years War	1337–1453	France	England
Wars of the Roses	1455–1485	House of Lancaster	House of York
Thirty Years War	1618–1648	France, Sweden, the German Protestant states	The Holy Roman Empire, Spain
Civil Wars, English	1642–1651	Parliament	Royalists
Spanish Succession, War of the	1701–1713	England, Austria, Prussia, the Netherlands	France, Bavaria, Cologne, Mantua, Savoy
Austrian Succession, War of the	1740–1748	Austria, Hungary, Britain	Bavaria, France, Poland, Prussia, Sardinia, Saxony, Spain
Seven Years War	1756–1763	Britain, Prussia, Hanover	Austria, France, Russia, Sweden
American Revolutionary War	1775–1783	Thirteen Colonies	Britain
Napoleonic Wars	1792–1815	Austria, Britain, Prussia, Russia, Spain, Sweden	France
War of 1812	1812–1814	United States	Britain
Mexican-American War	1846–1848	United States	Mexico
Crimean War	1853–1856	Britain, France, Sardinia, Turkey	Russia
Civil War, American	1861–1865	23 Northern States (The Union)	11 Southern States (The Confederacy)
Franco-Prussian War	1870–1871	Prussia and other German states	France
Chinese-Japanese War	1894–1895	Japan	China

Name	Date	Won by	Against
Spanish-American War	1898	United States	Spain
Boer (South African) War	1899–1902	Britain	Boer republics
Russo-Japanese War	1904–1905	Japan	Russia
World War I	1914–1918	Belgium, Britain and Empire, France, Italy, Japan, Russia, Serbia, United States	Austria-Hungary, Bulgaria, Germany, Ottoman Empire
Chinese-Japanese War	1931–1933	Japan	China
Abyssinian War	1935–1936	Italy	Abyssinia (Ethiopia)
Civil War, Spanish	1936–1939	Junta de Defensa Nacional (Fascists)	Republican government
Chinese-Japanese War	1937–1945	China	Japan
World War II	1939–1945	Australia, Belgium, Britain, Canada, China, Denmark, France, Greece, Netherlands, New Zealand, Norway, Poland, South Africa, Soviet Union, United States, Yugoslavia	Bulgaria, Finland, Germany, Hungary, Italy, Japan, Romania
Korean War	1950–1953	South Korea and United Nations forces	North Korea and Chinese forces
Vietnam War	1957–1975	North Vietnam	South Vietnam, United States
Six-Day War	1967	Israel	Egypt, Syria, Jordan, Iraq
Civil War, Nigerian	1967–1970	Federal government	Biafra
Civil War, Pakistani	1971	East Pakistan (Bangladesh) and India	West Pakistan
October War	1973	Ceasefire arranged by U.N.: fought by Israel against Egypt, Syria, Jordan, Iraq, Sudan, Saudi Arabia, Lebanon	
Gulf War	1980–1988	Ceasefire arranged with U.N. help; fought by Iraq against Iran	

◁ Enola Gay, the USAAF B29 bomber that dropped the atomic bomb on Hiroshima on August 6, 1945. The use of atomic bombs against the cities of Hiroshima and Nagasaki forced Japan's surrender and ended World War II.

MAJOR BATTLES

490 B.C. Marathon Force of 10,000 Athenians and allies defeated 50,000 Persian troops, crushing a Persian invasion attempt.

A.D. 732 Tours The Franks under Charles Martel defeated the Muslims, halting their advance in western Europe.

1066 Hastings About 8,000 troops under Duke William of Normandy defeated an equal force under Saxon king Harold II. England came under Norman rule.

1415 Agincourt Henry V of England with 10,000 troops defeated 30,000 Frenchmen, and recaptured Normandy.

1453 Siege of Constantinople Ottoman Turkish army captured the city and destroyed the Byzantine Empire. The Turks gained a foothold in Europe.

1571 Lepanto Allied Christian fleet of 208 galleys under Don John of Austria defeated Ali Pasha's Turkish fleet of 230 galleys; last great battle with galleys (pictured below).

1588 Armada Spanish invasion fleet of 130 ships was defeated by 197 English ships.

1757 Plassey Robert Clive with an Anglo-Indian army of 3,000 defeated the Nawab of Bengal's army of 60,000, setting Britain on the road to domination in India.

1777 Saratoga British troops under John Burgoyne surrendered to American colonial forces under Horatio Gates. Defeat led France to join war against Britain.

1781 Yorktown Charles Cornwallis with 8,000 British troops surrendered to a larger force under George Washington, ending the American Revolutionary War.

1798 Nile Horatio Nelson commanding a British fleet of 15 ships destroyed a 17-ship French fleet under Francis Paul Brueys in Aboukir Bay, cutting off Napoleon Bonaparte's French army in Egypt.

1805 Trafalgar British fleet of 27 ships under Horatio Nelson shattered Franco-Spanish fleet of 33 ships, ending Napoleon's hopes of invading England.

1805 Austerlitz Emperor Napoleon I with 65,000 French troops defeated an 83,000-strong Austro-Russian army under the Austrian and Russian emperors.

1813 Leipzig Napoleon I with 190,000 French troops was surrounded and crushed by an allied force of 300,000 Austrian, Prussian, Russian, and Swedish troops.

1815 Waterloo A British, Dutch, and Belgian force of 67,000 fought off 74,000 French troops under Napoleon I until the arrival of the Prussian army.

1863 Gettysburg Union forces under George Meade defeated Robert E. Lee's Confederate army, a turning point in the American Civil War.

1914 Marne French and British armies halted German forces invading France.

1916 Verdun In a six-month struggle French forces resisted a major attack by German armies. French losses were 348,000 men, the German losses 328,000.

1917 Passchendaele British forces launched eight attacks over 102 days in heavy rain and through thick mud, gaining five miles (8 km) and losing 400,000 men.

1940 Britain German air force launched an attack lasting 114 days. The smaller Royal Air Force defeated the attack.

1942 Midway A 100-ship Japanese fleet led by Isoruku Yamamoto, aiming to capture Midway Island, was defeated by American fleet half the size, under Raymond Spruance.

1942 El Alamein British Eighth Army under Bernard Montgomery drove German Afrika Korps under Erwin Rommel out of Egypt and deep into Libya.

1942–3 Stalingrad Twenty-one German divisions tried to capture Stalingrad (now Volgograd), but siege was broken and Friedrich von Paulus had to surrender with more than 100,000 German troops.

1944 Normandy Allied forces under Dwight D. Eisenhower invaded German-held northern France in biggest-ever sea-borne attack.

1944–5 Ardennes Bulge Last German counterattack in west through Ardennes Forest failed; Germans lost 100,000 casualties and 110,000 prisoners.

△ World War II: German and Soviet troops fighting on the Eastern Front in 1941. The Germans failed to capture Moscow, and the severe Russian winter froze both men and machines.

▽ Chateau Wood devastated by gunfire during World War I. The war dragged on for four years, centered in Europe around the Western and Eastern fronts. Soldiers lived and fought in appalling conditions.

World Explorers

We owe our knowledge of the world to a number of brave men – and a few women – who had the urge to explore distant, unknown lands. They knew so little about the shape and size of the Earth, the earliest explorers needed real courage. For example, many of the Portuguese navigators trying to find a sea route to India thought the Earth was flat, and were afraid of falling off the edge of the world.

△ Henry the Navigator (1394–1460) encouraged Portugal's seafarers.

EXPLORATION AND DISCOVERY

Place	Achievement	Explorer or discoverer	Date
Pacific Ocean	discovered	Vasco Núñez de Balboa (Sp.)	1513
World	circumnavigated	Ferdinand Magellan and Juan Sebastian del Cano (Port. for Sp.)	1519–1521
Africa			
Congo (river)	discovered	Diogo Cão (Port.)	c. 1483
Cape of Good Hope	sailed around	Bartolomeu Dias (Port.)	1488
Niger (river)	explored	Mungo Park (Scot.)	1795
Zambezi (river)	discovered	David Livingstone (Scot.)	1851
Sudan	explored	Heinrich Barth (Germ. for G.B.)	1852–1855
Victoria Falls	discovered	Livingstone	1855
Lake Tanganyika	discovered	Richard Burton and John Speke (G.B.)	1858
Congo (river)	traced	Sir Henry Stanley (G.B.)	1877
Asia			
China	visited	Marco Polo (Ital.)	c. 1272
India (Cape route)	visited	Vasco da Gama (Port.)	1498
Japan	visited	St. Francis Xavier (Sp.)	1549
China	explored	Ferdinand Richthofen (Germ.)	1868

△ Marco Polo (1254–1324) journeyed to the court of the Chinese emperor Kublai Khan at Peking (Beijing) shown here on a map of 1459.

◁ Robert Peary (1856–1920)

△ Hernando Cortés (1485–1547)

△ Captain James Cook (1728–1779)

North America

North America	discovered	Leif Ericsson (Norse)	c.1000
West Indies	discovered	Christopher Columbus (Ital. for Sp.)	1492
Newfoundland	discovered	John Cabot (Ital. for Eng.)	1497
Mexico	conquered	Hernando Cortés (Sp.)	1519–1521
St. Lawrence (river)	explored	Jacques Cartier (Fr.)	1534–1536
Mississippi (river)	discovered	Hernando de Soto (Sp.)	1541
Canadian interior	explored	Samuel de Champlain (Fr.)	1603–1609
Hudson Bay	discovered	Henry Hudson (Eng.)	1610
Alaska	discovered	Vitus Bering (Dan. for Russ.)	1728
Mackenzie (river)	discovered	Sir Alexander Mackenzie (Scot.)	1789

South America

South America	visited	Columbus	1498
Venezuela	explored	Alonso de Ojeda (Sp.)	1499
Brazil	discovered	Pedro Alvares Cabral (Port.)	1500
Río de la Plata	discovered	Juan de Solis (Sp.)	1516
Tierra del Fuego	discovered	Magellan	1520
Peru	conquered	Francisco Pizarro (Sp.)	1532–1538
Amazon (river)	explored	Francisco de Orellana (Sp.)	1541
Cape Horn	discovered	Willem Schouten (Dut.)	1616

Australasia, Polar regions, etc.

Greenland	visited	Eric the Red (Norse)	c.986
Australia	discovered	unknown	1500s
Spitsbergen	discovered	Willem Barents (Dut.)	1596
Australia	visited	Abel Tasman (Dut.)	1642
New Zealand	sighted	Tasman	1642
New Zealand	visited	James Cook (Eng.)	1769
Antarctic Circle	crossed	Cook	1773
Antarctica	sighted	Nathaniel Palmer (U.S.)	1820
Antarctica	circumnavigated	Fabian von Bellingshausen (Russ.)	1819–1821
Australian interior	explored	Charles Sturt (G.B.)	1828
Antarctica	explored	Charles Wilkes (U.S.)	1838–1842
Australia	crossed (S–N)	Robert Burke (Ir.) and William Wills (Eng.)	1860–1861
Greenland	explored	Fridtjof Nansen (Nor.)	1888
Arctic	explored	Abruzzi, Duke of the (Ital.)	1900
North Pole	reached	Robert Peary (U.S.)	1909
South Pole	reached	Roald Amundsen (Nor.)	1911
Antarctica	crossed	Sir Vivian Fuchs (Eng.)	1957–1958

American Presidents

The president of the United States is one of the most powerful people in the world. Not only is he the country's head of state, but he is also the chief executive, whose duty is to make sure the law is carried out, and commander-in-chief of the armed forces. Forty-one men have held this office.

△ George Washington (1732–99)

AMERICAN PRESIDENTS

President (party)	Term
1 George Washington (F)	1789–1797
2 John Adams (F)	1797–1801
3 Thomas Jefferson (DR)	1801–1809
4 James Madison (DR)	1809–1817
5 James Monroe (DR)	1817–1825
6 John Quincy Adams (DR)	1825–1829
7 Andrew Jackson (D)	1829–1837
8 Martin Van Buren (D)	1837–1841
9 William H. Harrison* (W)	1841
10 John Tyler (W)	1841–1845
11 James K. Polk (D)	1845–1849
12 Zachary Taylor* (W)	1849–1850
13 Millard Fillmore (W)	1850–1853
14 Franklin Pierce (D)	1853–1857
15 James Buchanan (D)	1857–1861
16 Abraham Lincoln† (R)	1861–1865
17 Andrew Johnson (U)	1865–1869
18 Ulysses S. Grant (R)	1869–1877
19 Rutherford B. Hayes (R)	1877–1881
20 James A. Garfield† (R)	1881
21 Chester A. Arthur (R)	1881–1885
22 Grover Cleveland (D)	1885–1889
23 Benjamin Harrison (R)	1889–1893
24 Grover Cleveland (D)	1893–1897
25 William McKinley† (R)	1897–1901
26 Theodore Roosevelt (R)	1901–1909
27 William H. Taft (R)	1909–1913
28 Woodrow Wilson (D)	1913–1921
29 Warren G. Harding* (R)	1921–1923
30 Calvin Coolidge (R)	1923–1929
31 Herbert C. Hoover (R)	1929–1933
32 Franklin D. Roosevelt* (D)	1933–1945
33 Harry S. Truman (D)	1945–1953
34 Dwight D. Eisenhower (R)	1953–1961
35 John F. Kennedy† (D)	1961–1963
36 Lyndon B. Johnson (D)	1963–1969
37 Richard M. Nixon (R)	1969–1974
38 Gerald R. Ford (R)	1974–1977
39 James E. Carter (D)	1977–1981
40 Ronald Reagan (R)	1981–1989
41 George H. W. Bush (R)	1989–

◁ Thomas Jefferson (1743–1826)

▽ U.S. President F.D. Roosevelt with Winston Churchill and Joseph Stalin.

△ Ronald Reagan was succeeded as U.S. President by his two-term Vice-President, George Bush.

*Died in office. †Assassinated in office.
F = Federalist. DR = Democratic-Republican.
D = Democratic. W = Whig. R = Republican. U = Uni

British Prime Ministers

The power of Britain's monarchs has declined sharply over the past 300 years, so that today the duties of the Queen are largely ceremonial. The government of the country is conducted in her name, however, and she is informed on all aspects of home and foreign policy.

△ Mrs Thatcher, Britains first woman prime minister and the longest-serving premier this century.

Power now resides with a prime minister, Cabinet, and Parliament. The British constitution is not a written document but has evolved. Thus, the office of prime minister was not deliberately created. Instead, during the 18th century, powerful ministers both assumed the leadership of Parliament and worked closely with the king in governing the country. The first "prime minister" was Sir Robert Walpole, who was chancellor of the Exchequer and first lord of the Treasury under George I and George II. The prime minister is also a member of Parliament, representing a constituency in the House of Commons. The present prime minister, Margaret Thatcher, is the member for Finchley, an area of London.

SOME NOTABLE BRITISH PRIME MINISTERS

Robert Walpole (Whig) 1721–1742. First prime minister of Britain. Put the nation's finances in order after disaster of South Sea Bubble; strengthened position of House of Commons.

William Pitt the Elder (Whig) 1756–1761, 1766–1768. Pursued vigorous and successful war policy; established British supremacy (against French) in North America; sympathetic to American Colonists but opposed independence.

William Pitt the Younger (Whig) 1783–1801, 1804–1806. Steered Britain through early years of Napoleonic wars; worked for electoral reform, abolition of the slave trade, and Irish Catholic emancipation, none of which he lived to see.

Benjamin Disraeli (Conservative) 1868, 1874–1880. Ardent supporter of the Empire; secured for Britain nearly half ownership of vitally important Suez Canal.

William Ewart Gladstone (Liberal) prime minister four times, 1868–1894. Introduced many social reforms; extended voting rights, established a system of national education, fought for Irish Home Rule.

David Lloyd George (Liberal) 1916–1922. Social reformer who (as chancellor of the Exchequer) introduced social security; able wartime leader (World War I).

Winston Churchill (Conservative) 1940–1945, 1951–1955. Greatly loved for his inspiring leadership during World War II.

Clement Attlee (Labour) 1945–1951. Carried through an extensive program of economic reforms, including nationalization of many industries and the creation of the National Health Service.

Margaret Thatcher (Conservative) 1979– . Britain's first woman prime minister; introduced right-wing measures, notably privatization of state-owned industries.

European Monarchs

Until the beginning of this century European monarchs had considerable power, and their ambitions, beliefs, and private lives often influenced events. Listed here are a few of the important rulers with the dates of their reigns.

SOME IMPORTANT EUROPEAN MONARCHS

Charlemagne King of the Franks 768–814; crowned emperor of the "Romans" by the pope in 800 after conquering most of what is now Germany and northern Italy – the foundation of the Holy Roman Empire. He encouraged the first great rebirth of civilization since the beginning of the Dark Ages.

Alfred the Great Saxon King of England 871–899. He resisted Danish invaders and helped to build a stronger monarchy. A wise and well-loved king.

William I, the Conqueror, King of England 1066–1087. Originally duke of Normandy, in France. He invaded and subdued England, established feudal government, and introduced the French language, which was to influence the development of English.

Ferdinand and Isabella Joint rulers of Spain 1479–1516; Isabella died in 1504. Their marriage united the crowns of Aragon and Castile, and in 1492 they drove the last Moors from the Iberian Peninsula. They sponsored the voyages of Columbus, thus planting the Spanish flag in the New World.

Henry VIII King of England 1509–1547. His failure to father a male heir led him to divorce his queen, Catherine of Aragon, in defiance of the pope, which in turn led to England's break with the Roman Catholic Church. Henry had five more wives, one of whom produced a son, Edward VI, who died young.

▽ Henry VIII by Holbein.

Charles V Holy Roman Emperor 1519–1556 and king (Charles I) of Spain 1516–1556. The entire reign of this powerful ruler was dominated by conflict, as he repelled invasions by Turks, struggled with the French king Francis I for disputed lands, suppressed rebellions in the Low Countries, and tried in vain to stamp out Lutheranism in the Empire.

Ivan IV "the Terrible" Grand Duke of Moscow and first Tsar of Russia 1547–1584. Known mainly for his cruelty, he also established trade links with England and annexed Siberia.

Philip II King of Spain 1556–1598. Son of Emperor Charles V, he added extensive possessions in America to his vast European lands, which included the Low Countries. His Armada failed to conquer England.

Elizabeth I Queen of England 1558–1603. The daughter of Henry VIII by Anne Boleyn, she was called the "virgin queen" because she never married and was one of England's most capable and revered monarchs. She managed to steer a prudent course in the religious conflicts of her realm and to keep her country at peace. During her reign, England reached new heights of prosperity, artistic achievement and national pride.

Henry IV King of France 1589–1610. This well-loved monarch and astute statesman established religious tolerance in his country, after years of strife, and brought it increased prosperity.

Gustavus Adolphus King of Sweden 1611–1632. This famous warrior king enlarged his nation's domains and was the champion of the Protestant German states during the Thirty Years War.

Charles I King of Great Britain 1625–1649. Charles's good qualities – courage, piety, and intellect – were eclipsed by his political folly and highhandedness, which led to civil war between king and Parliament. He was executed for treason.

Louis XIV King of France 1643–1715. Called the "Sun King," this absolute monarch created a magnificent court at Versailles and made France the most powerful and prosperous nation in Europe. He also established its cultural supremacy for many years to come. His only blunder was abolishing religious freedom for Protestants, which drove many good citizens into exile.

Peter I, the Great Tsar of Russia 1689–1725. One of the most formidably energetic and capable rulers in history, Peter virtually recreated Russia, modernizing it in line with Western European standards. With the help of foreign expertise – and forced labor from his subjects – he reformed the army, created a navy, and built a new capital city, St. Petersburg (now Leningrad). Scarcely any aspect of Russian life remained unchanged.

Maria Theresa Queen of Hungary and Bohemia and Archduchess of Austria 1740–1780. Her sex prevented her from claiming the crown of the Holy Roman Empire (to which she was otherwise entitled); her husband Francis was given it instead, and she was "Empress" only through him. It was she, however, who ruled Austria and its dominions, and she did so in a shrewd and generally enlightened manner.

Frederick II, the Great King of Prussia 1740–1786. A brilliant military leader, Frederick was also one of the 18th century's "enlightened despots"; he introduced various liberal reforms, while still wielding absolute power. He was also a cultivated man, and his court at Potsdam was a magnet for writers, philosophers and composers.

George III King of Great Britain 1760–1820. He is famous for having lost the American Colonies and for going mad. However, Parliament and his ministers were partly responsible for the American disaster. During his later years, when he was mentally ill, his son George IV served as Regent. Earlier, he had been a popular monarch – the first Hanoverian king to find favor with the British.

Catherine II, the Great Empress of Russia 1762–1796. Born a German princess, Catherine acquired the Russian throne through marriage and kept it after her husband's death. She later acquired for Russia a large area of Poland. Serfdom was increased by Catherine, but she did institute a few reforms, including the virtual abolition of torture.

Louis XVI King of France 1774–1792. A weak king, who much preferred hunting to statecraft, Louis was trapped by a financial crisis, caused partly by France's military aid to the American Colonies. His political blundering and his willingness to be led by his queen, Marie Antoinette, led to his downfall and execution in the French Revolution.

Napoleon I Emperor of France 1804–1814. A Corsican army officer, he fought brilliantly for the French revolutionary government against its European enemies, rose quickly to become first consul, then had himself crowned emperor. He conquered most of Europe, installing members of his family as rulers from Holland to Italy. A European coalition finally defeated him and sent him into exile. His most enduring achievement is the French legal system, the Code Napoléon.

△ A 'penny black' portraying Queen Victoria.

Victoria Queen of Great Britain 1837–1901 and Empress of India. Although the British monarch's power was now much reduced, Victoria strongly influenced the nation's foreign policy, and her long reign saw the British Empire reach its zenith. Her many children married into other royal houses, and today most of the remaining European royalty are descended from her.

Napoleon III Emperor of the French 1852–1870. The nephew of Napoleon I, he first came to power as president in 1848, then staged a *coup*, making himself emperor. His reign, though repressive, brought France considerable prosperity. His attempt to establish an empire in Mexico, with the Archduke Maximilian as his puppet, was a disaster. After France was defeated by Prussia in 1870, he went into exile in England for the remaining three years of his life.

Popes

The pope is the head of the Roman Catholic Church. However, in the past the pope was the leader of the only Christian Church. The Eastern Orthodox Church broke away in 1054, and the Reformation, beginning in the 1500s, limited the power of the pope still more. But the pope remained an important political figure in Europe until the late 1800s, and even ruled parts of Italy directly.

△ Pope John Paul II.

POPES

List of popes and their dates of accession. Rival and doubtful popes are not included.

St. Peter	42	St. Anastasius I	399	St. Vitalian	657
St. Linus	67	St. Innocent I	401	Adeodatus II	672
St. Anacletus (Cletus)	76	St. Zosimus	417	Donus	676
St. Clement I	88	St. Boniface I	418	St. Agatho	678
St. Evaristus	97	St. Celestine I	422	St. Leo II	682
St. Alexander I	105	St. Sixtus III	432	St. Benedict II	684
St. Sixtus I	115	St. Leo I (the Great)	440	John V	685
St. Telesphorus	125	St. Hilary	461	Conon	686
St. Hyginus	136	St. Simplicius	468	St. Sergius I	687
St. Pius I	140	St. Felix III	483	John VI	701
St. Anicetus	155	St. Gelasius I	492	John VII	705
St. Soterus	166	Anastasius II	496	Sisinnius	708
St. Eleutherius	175	St. Symmachus	498	Constantine	708
St. Victor I	189	St. Hormisdas	514	St. Gregory II	715
St. Zephyrinus	199	St. John I	523	St. Gregory III	731
St. Callistus I	217	St. Felix IV	526	St. Zachary	741
St. Urban I	222	Boniface II	530	Stephen II (III)*	752
St. Pontian	230	John II	533	St. Paul I	757
St. Anterus	235	St. Agapetus I	535	Stephen III (IV)	768
St. Fabian	236	St. Silverius	536	Adrian I	772
St. Cornelius	251	Vigilius	537	St. Leo III	795
St. Lucius I	253	Pelagius I	556	Stephen IV (V)	816
St. Stephen I	254	John III	561	St. Paschal I	817
St. Sixtus II	257	Benedict I	575	Eugene II	824
St. Dionysius	259	Pelagius II	579	Valentine	827
St. Felix I	269	St. Gregory I (the Great)	590	Gregory IV	827
St. Eutychian	275	Sabinianus	604	Sergius II	844
St. Caius	283	Boniface III	607	St. Leo IV	847
St. Marcellinus	296	St. Boniface IV	608	Benedict III	855
St. Marcellus I	308	St. Deusdedit		St. Nicholas I	858
St. Eusebius	309	(Adeodatus I)	615	Adrian II	867
St. Melchiades	311	Boniface V	619	John VIII	872
St. Sylvester I	314	Honorius I	625	Marinus I	882
St. Marcus	336	Severinus	640	St. Adrian III	884
St. Julius I	337	John IV	640	Stephen V (VI)	885
Liberius	352	Theodore I	642	Formosus	891
St. Damasus I	366	St. Martin I	649	Boniface VI	896
St. Siricius	384	St. Eugene I	654	Stephen VI (VII)	896

Romanus	897	Lucius III	1181	Gregory XIII	1572
Theodore II	897	Urban III	1185	Sixtus V	1585
John IX	898	Gregory VIII	1187	Urban VII	1590
Benedict IV	900	Clement III	1187	Gregory XIV	1590
Leo V	903	Celestine III	1191	Innocent IX	1591
Sergius III	904	Innocent III	1198	Clement VIII	1592
Anastasius III	911	Honorius III	1216	Leo XI	1605
Landus	913	Gregory IX	1227	Paul V	1605
John X	914	Celestine IV	1241	Gregory XV	1621
Leo VI	928	Innocent IV	1243	Urban VIII	1623
Stephen VII (VIII)	928	Alexander IV	1254	Innocent X	1644
John XI	931	Urban IV	1261	Alexander VII	1655
Leo VII	936	Clement IV	1265	Clement IX	1667
Stephen VIII (IX)	939	Gregory X	1271	Clement X	1670
Marinus II	942	Innocent V	1276	Innocent XI	1676
Agapetus II	946	Adrian V	1276	Alexander VIII	1689
John XII	955	John XXI	1276	Innocent XII	1691
Leo VIII	963	Nicholas III	1277	Clement XI	1700
Benedict V	964	Martin IV	1281	Innocent XIII	1721
John XIII	965	Honorius IV	1285	Benedict XIII	1724
Benedict VI	973	Nicholas IV	1288	Clement XII	1730
Benedict VII	974	St. Celestine V	1294	Benedict XIV	1740
John XIV	983	Boniface VIII	1294	Clement XIII	1758
John XV	985	Benedict XI	1303	Clement XIV	1769
Gregory V	996	Clement V	1305	Pius VI	1775
Sylvester II	999	John XXII	1316	Pius VII	1800
John XVII	1003	Benedict XII	1334	Leo XII	1823
John XVIII	1004	Clement VI	1342	Pius VIII	1829
Sergius IV	1009	Innocent VI	1352	Gregory XVI	1831
Benedict VIII	1012	Urban V	1362	Pius IX	1846
John XIX	1024	Gregory XI	1370	Leo XIII	1878
Benedict IX	1032	Urban VI	1378	St. Pius X	1903
Gregory VI	1045	Boniface IX	1389	Benedict XV	1914
Clement II	1046	Innocent VII	1404	Pius XI	1922
Benedict IX†	1047	Gregory XII	1406	Pius XII	1939
Damasus II	1048	Martin V	1417	John XXIII	1958
St. Leo IX	1049	Eugene IV	1431	Paul VI	1963
Victor II	1055	Nicholas V	1447	John Paul I**	1978
Stephen IX (X)	1057	Callistus III	1455	John Paul II	1978
Nicholas II	1059	Pius II	1458		
Alexander II	1061	Paul II	1464		
St. Gregory VII	1073	Sixtus IV	1471		
Victor III	1086	Innocent VIII	1484		
Urban II	1088	Alexander VI	1492	*The original Stephen II died	
Paschal II	1099	Pius III	1503	before consecration, and was	
Gelasius II	1118	Julius II	1503	dropped from the list of popes in	
Callistus II	1119	Leo X	1513	1961; Stephen III became Stephen	
Honorius II	1124	Adrian VI	1522	II and the numbers of the other	
Innocent II	1130	Clement VII	1523	popes named Stephen were also	
Celestine II	1143	Paul III	1534	moved up.	
Lucius II	1144	Julius III	1550	†Benedict IX was driven from office	
Eugene III	1145	Marcellus II	1555	for scandalous conduct; but	
Anastasius IV	1153	Paul IV	1555	returned briefly in 1047.	
Adrian IV	1154	Pius IV	1559	**John Paul I died after only 33	
Alexander III	1159	St. Pius V	1566	days as Pontiff.	

Modern Leaders

Most modern leaders are not crowned heads but have come to power by other means, from democratic elections to bloody revolutions. They include courageous workers for peace and freedom as well as some of the most ruthless despots the world has ever seen.

SOME LEADERS OF THE 20TH CENTURY

Sun Yat-Sen First president of Chinese republic 1912–1913, and 1923–1925.

V. I. Lenin First premier of U.S.S.R. 1918–1924.

Benito Mussolini Fascist dictator of Italy, 1922–1943.

Mustafa Ataturk First president of Turkish republic 1923–1938.

Mohandas Gandhi (called "Mahatma" or "great soul") Leader of Indian struggle for independence, 1914–1947.

Hirohito Emperor of Japan 1926–1989.

Chiang Kai-Shek President of Chinese republic 1928–1931, and 1948–1975 (Nationalist China, Taiwan).

Haile Selassie Emperor of Ethiopia 1930–1934 and 1941–1947.

Abdul Aziz Ibn Saud First king of Saudi Arabia 1932–1953.

Adolf Hitler Nazi dictator of Germany (Third Reich, or "empire") 1934–1945.

Eamon De Valera Prime minister of Ireland 1937–1948, 1951–1954, 1957–1959; president 1959–1973.

Francisco Franco Dictator of Spain 1939–1975.

Henri Philippe Pétain Head of the Vichy government in France 1940–1944.

14th Dalai Lama Spiritual and political ruler of Tibet 1940–1959.

Joseph Stalin Premier of U.S.S.R. 1941–1953 (effective dictator from 1924).

Ho Chi-Minh Communist president of Vietnam 1945–1954, of North Vietnam 1954–1969.

Marshall Tito Communist prime minister of Yugoslavia 1945–1980 (president from 1953).

Charles de Gaulle President of France 1945–1946 and 1959–1969.

Juan Péron Dictator of Argentina 1946–1955 (with first wife, Eva), and president (with second wife, Estela, as vice-president) 1973–1974.

Jawaharlal Nehru First prime minister of India 1947–1964.

△ Jawaharlal Nehru (1889–1964) led India to independence from Britain in 1947, and became the country's first prime minister. His daughter was Indira Gandhi.

David Ben-Gurion First prime minister of Israel 1948–1953, and 1955–1963.

Konrad Adenaur Chancellor of West Germany, 1949–1963.

Chou En-Lai Premier of People's Republic of China 1949–1973.

Mao Tse-Tung Chairman of People's Republic of China 1949–1959, of Politburo until 1976.

King ibn Talal Hussein of Jordan 1952– .

Dag Hammarskjöld Secretary-General of the United Nations 1953–1961.

Nikita Khrushchev Premier of U.S.S.R. 1958–1964; first secretary of Communist Party 1953–1964.

Gamal Abdel Nasser Prime minister of Egypt 1954–1958; president of United Arab Republic (Egypt and Syria) 1958–1961.

Hendrik Verwoerd Prime minister of South Africa 1958–1966.

Fidel Castro Communist premier of Cuba 1959–

Kwame Nkoumah First president of Ghana 1960–1966.

Archbishop Makarios President of Cyprus 1960–1974, 1975–1977.

Julius Nyerere First president of Tanzania 1962– .

Jomo Kenyatta First president of Kenya 1964– .

Kenneth Kaunda First prime minister of North Rhodesia then first president of Zambia 1964– .

Ferdinand Marcos President of the Philippines 1965–1987.

Indira Gandhi Prime minister of India 1966–1977, 1980–1984.

Willy Brandt Chancellor of West Germany 1969–1974.

Yassir Arafat President of Palestine Liberation Organization (PLO) 1969– .

Golda Meir Prime minister of Israel 1969–1974.

Salvador Allende Socialist president of Chile 1970–1973.

Anwar El-Sadat President of Egypt 1970–1981.

Qaboos Bin Said Sultan of Oman, absolute ruler 1970– .

Colonel Moamer al-Gaddafi Libyan head of state 1970– .

Erich Honecker Leader of Communist Party in East Germany 1973–1989.

Nicolae Ceausescu Leader of Romanian Communist Party 1974–1989.

Leonid Ilyich Brezhnev President of U.S.S.R. 1977–1982.

Menachem Begin Prime Minister of Israel 1977–1983.

Robert Mugabe First prime minister of independent Zimbabwe 1982– .

François Mitterand President of France 1981– .

Helmut Kohl Chancellor of West Germany 1982– .

Ayatollah Khomeini Islamic leader of Iran 1978–1989.

Mikhail Gorbachev Premier of U.S.S.R. 1985– .

Benazir Bhutto Prime minister of Pakistan 1988– .

(*Note* Leaders of English-speaking countries are listed on pages 118–119.)

Assassinations

Assassination is the murder of a political leader or any other public figure. These killings are carried out for revenge, to remove a tyrant or a political opponent, or sometimes for financial gain. The word "assassin" originally meant an eater of hashish (a drug). A group of such drug-takers carried out many murders in Persia in the 1100s.

Assassinations have been a tragic feature all through history. One, the murder of archduke Franz Ferdinand of Austria in 1914, sparked off World War I. Four U.S. presidents have been assassinated, and so has one British prime minister, Spencer Perceval.

Perhaps the three most famous people to have been assassinated since the end of World War II are President Kennedy, whose killer evidently bore a political grudge against him; the Rev. Martin Luther King Jr., Black civil rights leader, by a white escaped convict; and songwriter and former Beatle, John Lennon, by a man who was mentally ill.

△ President Anwar El Sadat of Egypt worked for a peace treaty with Israel. He was assassinated in 1981.

126

HISTORIC ASSASSINATIONS

Victim	Details of assassination	Date
Philip II, king of Macedonia	Pausanias, young noble with a grudge	336 B.C.
Julius Caesar, Roman dictator	Stabbed by Brutus, Cassius, and others	44 B.C.
St. Thomas à Becket, English archbishop	Slain by four knights in cathedral	1170
James I of Scotland	Plot: Sir Robert Graham	1437
David Beaton, Scottish chancellor/ cardinal	Band of Protestant nobles in St. Andrews Castle	1546
Lord Darnley, husband of Mary Queen of Scots	Blown up; plot	1567
William the Silent, Prince of Orange	Shot by Balthasar Gérard	1584
Henry III of France	Stabbed by fanatic monk (Jacques Clément)	1589
Henry IV of France (de Navarre)	Stabbed by fanatic (François Ravaillac)	1610
Gustavus III of Sweden	Plot: shot by Johan Ankarström	1792
Jean Marat, French revolutionary	Stabbed in bath by Charlotte Corday	1793
Spencer Perceval, British prime minister	Shot by bankrupt broker John Bellingham	1812
Abraham Lincoln, U.S. president	Shot by actor, J. Wilkes Booth, in theater	1865
Alexander II, emperor of Russia	Nihilist bomb	1881
James Garfield, U.S. president	Shot at station by Charles Guiteau (grudge)	1881
Sadi Carnot, French president	Stabbed by anarchist	1894
Elizabeth, empress of Austria	By Italian anarchist at Geneva	1898
Humbert I, king of Italy	By anarchist at Monza	1900
William McKinley, U.S. president	Shot by anarchist, Leon Czolgosz, at Buffalo	1901
Francis Ferdinand, archduke of Austria	Alleged Serbian plot: shot in car by Gavrilo Princip at Sarajevo (sparked World War I)	1914
Rasputin, powerful Russian monk	By Russian noblemen	1916
Michael Collins, Irish Sinn Fein leader	Ambushed and shot	1922
"Pancho" Villa, former Mexican bandit/ rebel	Ambushed in car	1923
Paul Doumer, French president	Shot by mad Russian émigré, Paul Gorgoulov	1932
Engelbert Dollfuss, Austrian chancellor	Shot by Nazis in chancellery	193
Alexander I of Yugoslavia Jean Louis Barthou, French foreign minister	By Macedonian terrorist at Marseille	193
Leon Trotsky, exiled Russian communist leader	Axed in Mexico by Ramón Mercader	194
Mahatma Gandhi, Indian nationalist leader	Shot by Hindu fanatic, Nathuran Godse	194
Abdullah ibn Hussein, king of Jordan	In Jerusalem mosque	195
Anastasio Somoza, Nicaraguan president	Shot by Rigoberto López Pérez, in León	195
Carlos Castillo Armas, Guatemalan president	By one of own guards	195
Faisal II of Iraq	Military coup in Baghdad	195
S.W.R.D. Bandaranaike, Ceylonese premier	By Buddhist monk in Colombo	195
Patrice Lumumba, Congolese ex-premier	By Katanga secessionist regime	196
Rafael Trujillo Molina, Dominican Republic dictator	Car machine-gunned	196
Ngo Dinh Diem, S. Vietnamese president	By generals in coup	196
John F. Kennedy, U.S. president	Shot in car, in Dallas, Texas*	196
Malcolm X (Little), U.S. Black Muslim leader	Shot at rally	196
Hendrik Verwoerd, South African premier	Stabbed by parliamentary messenger, Dimitri Tsafendas (later ruled mentally disordered)	196
Rev. Martin Luther King Jr., U.S. Black civil rights leader	Shot on hotel balcony by James Earl Ray, in Memphis, Tennessee	19

△ Thomas à Becket is murdered by Henry II's knights.

△ Robert Kennedy, brother of murdered President John F. Kennedy, was himself assassinated in a Los Angeles hotel in 1968.

◁ Mahatma Gandhi led a nonviolent campaign to free India from British rule. He was assassinated by a Hindu fanatic shortly after India's independence.

bert F. Kennedy, U.S. senator	Shot by Arab immigrant, Sirhan Sirhan	1968
is Carrero Blanco, Spanish premier	Explosion under car; Basque terrorists (E.T.A.)	1973
ng Faisal of Saudi Arabia	Shot by nephew Prince Faisal ibn Musad	1975
ristopher Ewart-Biggs, British mbassador to Republic of Ireland	Car blown up by landmine planted by I.R.A.	1976
do Moro, five times prime minister of aly	Kidnapped by "Red Brigade" terrorists and later found dead	1978
Richard Sykes, British ambassador in he Hague	Shot by I.R.A.	1979
ey Neave, British Conservative M.P.	Car bomb at House of Commons; I.R.A.	1979
rl Mountbatten of Burma, uncle of ueen Elizabeth II	Explosion in sailing boat off coast of Ireland; I.R.A.	1979
astasio Somoza Debayle, president of caragua	Shot by revolutionaries during Sandinista coup	1980
n Lennon, musician/songwriter and -Beatle	Shot in street in New York by Mark David Chapman	1980
liam R. Tolbert, president of Liberia	Executed by army during coup	1980
ur Rahman, president of Bangladesh	Shot by army officers during abortive military takeover	1981
war El Sadat, president of Egypt	Shot by rebel soldiers	1981
nigno Aquino, Philippine opposition ader	Shot at airport on return from voluntary exile	1983
s. Indira Gandhi, Indian prime minister	Shot by her Sikh bodyguards	1984
f Palme, Swedish prime minister	Shot in street while walking home	1986

used, Lee Harvey Oswald, himself shot by Jack Ruby while awaiting trial.

CHRONOLOGY OF WORLD HISTORY

B.C.

*c.***3500** Sumerians develop flourishing civilization along Euphrates River.

*c.***3400** Upper and Lower Egypt united to form one nation.

*c.***2100** Abraham migrates from Ur.

*c.***2000** Bronze Age begins in northern Europe.

*c.***1750** Hammurabi of Bablyon draws up first known legal code.

1500s Shang Dynasty of China founded.

1570 Hyksos invaders of Egypt defeated.

1450 Minoan civilization flourishes in Crete: begins to decline soon after.

1410 Reign of Amenhotep III of Egypt: golden age of nation at height.

1400 Beginning of Iron Age in India and Asia Minor (Turkey).

1358 Tutankhamen becomes pharaoh of Egypt: restores old religion destroyed by his predecessor Akhenaton.

1292–1225 Rameses II pharaoh of Egypt; Abu Simbel temple built.

1230–1200 Israelites leave Egypt and make their way to Canaan (Palestine).

*c.***1100** Assyrian Empire founded in Mesopotamia.

*c.***1020** Saul becomes first king of Israel.

*c.***1000** Chou dynasty founded in China.

1000–961 David king of Israel.

922 Death of David's son Solomon: kingdom divided into Judah and Israel.

800s Homer composes the *Iliad* and the *Odyssey* in ancient Greece.

814 Phoenicians found Carthage.

776 Earliest known Olympic Games

753 Traditional date of founding of Rome

722 Assyrians conquer Israel.

689 Assyrians capture and destroy Babylon.

670 Assyrians ravage Egypt; destruction of Thebes and Memphis.

626 Nabopolassar liberates Babylon from Assyrian rule and becomes king.

612 Babylonians, Medes, and Scythians overthrow Assyrian Empire, destroying capital, Nineveh.

586 Nebuchadnezzar of Babylon seizes Jerusalem and takes people of Judah into captivity.

563 Siddhartha Gautama, later the Buddha, born at Lumbini, Nepal.

550–530 Reign of Cyrus the Great, founder of Persian Empire.

551 Birth of K'ung Fu-tzu – Confucius, Chinese philosopher.

539 Jews allowed to return to Jerusalem; rebuilding of city begins.

535–404 Persians rule Egypt.

510 Last king of Rome, Tarquin, deposed; city becomes republic.

499–494 Ionian war: Greek revolt against Persian rule.

494 Thirty cities of Latium form Latin League against Etruscans.

492 First Persian expedition against Athens ends when storm destroys Persian fleet.

490 Athenians crush second Persian expedition at Battle of Marathon.

485 Xerxes king of Persia.

480 Persian fleet defeated by Greeks at Battle of Salamis.

479 Greek soldiers rout Persians at Battle of Plataea; end of Persian attempt to subdue Greece.

460 Pericles becomes leader of Athenians.

◁ According to legend, the founders of Rome were Romulus and Remus, who as babies were suckled by a she-wolf.

431–421 Great Peloponnesian War between Athens and Sparta.

415–404 Second Peloponnesian War, ending with Spartan capture of Athens.

403 Thirty Tyrants seize power in Athens.

399 Philosopher Socrates put to death for teaching heresies to the young.

395–387 Corinthian War: coalition of Argos, Athens, Corinth, Thebes against Sparta; Sparta victorious.

391 Romans conquer Etruscans.

390 Gauls under Brennus sack Rome.

352–336 Philip II king of Macedon; rise of Macedon to power in Greece.

350 Persians suppress revolt of Jews.

338 Philip of Macedon conquers Greece.

336–323 Reign of Alexander III, the Great.

335 Alexander destroys Thebes.

332 Alexander conquers Egypt and Jerusalem, destroys Tyre.

331 Alexander overthrows Persian Empire, defeating Darius III and capturing Babylon.

326 Greeks under Alexander extend empire to Indus River, in what is now Pakistan.

323 Death of Alexander; birth of Euclid.

320 Egyptians under Pharaoh Ptolemy Soter capture Jerusalem.

305 Seleucus I Nicator founds Seleucid dynasty in Syria, Persia and Asia Minor.

305 Romans extend their rule over southern Italy.

301 Egyptians conquer Palestine.

295–294 Demetrius captures Athens and makes himself master of Greece.

290 Romans finally defeat Samnite attempt to usurp Roman power in Italy.

280 Achaean League of 12 Greek city-states formed.

274 Pyrrhus of Epirus conquers Macedonia; killed two years later.

264–241 First Punic War between Rome and Carthage; Carthage defeated and surrenders Sicily.

221 Ch'in dynasty (to 207); founded by Shih Huang-te, who builds the Great Wall.

218–201 Second Punic War.

218 Carthaginians under Hannibal cross Alps to invade Italy; defeat Romans at Trebbia.

△ The Carthaginian general Hannibal crossing the Alps in 218 B.C.

216 Hannibal defeats Romans at Cannae.

206 Romans under Scipio drive Carthaginians out of Spain.

202 Carthaginians defeated at Zama.

202 Han dynasty founded in China.

200–197 Romans drawn into war against Macedonia; Philip V of Macedon defeated.

192 Rome defeats Sparta.

182 Suicide of Hannibal to avoid capture by Romans.

171–167 Perseus of Macedonia attacks Rome; crushingly defeated; Roman rule in Macedonia.

168 Antiochus IV Epiphanes of Syria persecutes Jews and desecrates Temple in Jerusalem.

167 Revolt of Jews under Judas Maccabeus against Antiochus.

153 Jews win independence from Syrian rule.

149–146 Third Punic War ends in destruction of Carthage.

88–82 Civil war in Rome; Lucius Cornelius Sulla emerges victor.

87 Sulla defeats attack by Mithradates, King of Pontus, and captures Athens.

86 Civil war in China.

82 Sulla dictator of Rome.

73–71 Revolt of gladiators and slaves under Spartacus; defeated by consuls Gnaeus Pompeius (Pompey) and Licinius Crassus.

65 Roman armies under Pompey invade Syria and Palestine.

64 Romans occupy Jerusalem.

61 Gaius Julius Caesar becomes Roman governor of Spain.

60 Pompey, Crassus, and Caesar form First Triumvirate to rule Rome.

58–51 Caesar conquers Gaul and invades Britain; British pay tribute to Rome.

53 Death of Crassus in battle.

52 Pompey appointed sole consul in Rome.

49 Caesar crosses Rubicon River in Italy to challenge Pompey for power.

48 Pompey, defeated at Pharsalus, flees to Egypt and is assassinated.

47 Caesar appoints Cleopatra and her brother Ptolemy XII joint rulers of Egypt; Cleopatra disposes of Ptolemy.

45 Caesar holds supreme power in Rome.

44 Brutus, Cassius, and others murder Caesar.

43 Mark Antony, Marcus Lepidus, and Caesar's nephew Octavian form Second Triumvirate.

43 Cleopatra queen of Egypt.

36 Mark Antony marries Cleopatra; prepares to attack Octavian.

31 Battle of Actium: Octavian's fleet defeats Antony and Cleopatra, who commit suicide. Rome conquers Egypt.

27 Octavian emperor of Rome, with title of Augustus.

6 Romans seize Judea.

4 Birth of Jesus Christ at Bethlehem (probable date).

A.D.

9 Battle of Teutoburg Forest: German leader Arminius wipes out three Roman legions.

14 Augustus dies; succeeded by stepson Tiberius.

26 Pontius Pilate appointed Procurator of Judea.

27 Baptism of Jesus by John the Baptist.

30 Jesus crucified on Pilate's orders on charge of sedition.

32 Saul of Tarsus converted; baptized as Paul.

37–41 Caligula emperor of Rome; orders Romans to worship him as god.

41–54 Claudius emperor of Rome.

43–51 Roman conquest of Britain under Aulus Plautius.

◁ The most famous Roman – Julius Caesar (100–44 B.C.).

54–68 Reign of Emperor Nero.

64 Fire destroys Rome; Christians persecuted; St. Paul and St. Peter put to death.

65 Gospel of St. Mark probably written.

66–70 Revolt of Jews; subdued by Vespasian and his son Titus.

68 Suicide of Nero; Galba becomes emperor of Rome.

69–79 Reign of Vespasian.

77–84 Roman conquest of northern Britain.

79 Vesuvius erupts, destroying Pompeii, Herculaneum, and Stabiae.

98–117 Reign of Trajan; Roman Empire at greatest extent.

122 Emperor Hadrian (ruled 117–138) visits Britain; orders building of wall to keep out Picts and Scots.

132–135 Jewish revolt led by Simon Bar-Cochba suppressed; Romans disperse Jews from Palestine (*Diaspora*).

161–180 Marcus Aurelius emperor: Roman Empire at its most united.

177 Increased persecution of Christians in Rome.

***c.*200–800** Mayan Empire flourishes in Central America.

205–211 Revolts and invasions in Britain suppressed by Emperor Septimus Severus.

212	Emperor Caracalla (211–217) gives Roman citizenship to all free men in the empire.
220	Han dynasty in China ends.
226	Artaxerxes founds new Persian Empire.
249	Emperor Decius (249–251) inaugurates first general persecution of Christians.
253–259	Franks, Goths, and Alamanni cross empire's frontiers and invade Italy.
268	Goths sack Sparta, Corinth, Athens.
284–305	Reign of Diocletian.
285	Empire divided into West (based at Rome) and East (based at Nicomedia in Bythnia).
*c.***300**	Buddhism spreading throughout China.
303–313	New persecution of Christians.
306–337	Constantine the Great emperor of Rome.
313	Edict of Milan proclaims toleration for Christians throughout the Roman Empire.
314	Council of Arles: meeting of Christian leaders at which Constantine presides.
320	Gupta Empire founded in India.
324	Eastern and Western empires reunited under Constantine's rule.
325	First world council of Christian Church at Nicea in Asia Minor.
330	Foundation of Constantinople on site of village of Byzantium, as capital of Roman Empire.
360	Huns invade Europe; Picts and Scots cross Hadrian's Wall to attack north Britain.
369	Picts and Scots driven out of Roman province of Britain.
378	Battle of Adrianople: Visigoths defeat and kill Emperor Valens, and ravage Balkans.
379–395	Reign of Theodosius the Great; on his death, Roman Empire is again split up.
407	Roman troops leave Britain to fight Barbarians in Gaul.
410	Goths under command of Alaric sack Rome.
425–450	Jutes, Angles, and Saxons invade Britain.
451	Battle of Châlons: Franks and allies defeat Attila the Hun.

476	Goths depose Emperor Romulus Augustus, ending western Roman Empire; date generally regarded as beginning of Middle Ages.
481	Clovis king of Franks.
493	Theodoric the Ostrogoth conquers Italy.
496	Clovis converted to Christianity; increases Frankish power.
527–565	Justinian the Great, Byzantine (eastern Roman) emperor.
529–565	Justinian has Roman laws codified.
534	Franks conquer Burgundy.
534	Eastern Empire reconquers northern Africa from Vandals.
535	Byzantine troops occupy southern Italy.
550	St. David introduces Christianity into Wales.
552	Buddhism introduced into Japan.
554	Byzantine armies complete conquest of Italy.
563	St. Columba preaches Christianity to the Picts in Scotland.
568	Lombards conquer north and central Italy.
570	Prophet Muhammad born at Mecca.
581	Sui dynasty founded in China.
590	Gregory the Great becomes pope.
597	St. Augustine converts southeastern England to Christianity for Rome.
611–622	Persians conquer Palestine and Egypt; Jerusalem sacked.
616	Visigoths drive Romans from Spain.
618	T'ang dynasty founded in China.
622	The Hegira: Muhammad flees from Mecca to Yathrib, afterward called Medina.
624	Japan adopts Buddhism.
625	Muhammad begins dictating material later gathered into the *Koran*.
622–630	Byzantine emperor Heraclius drives Persians from Egypt and Palestine.
628	Muhammad enunciates principles of Islamic faith.
632	Death of Muhammad.
634–641	Muslim Arabs conquer Syria, Jerusalem, Mesopotamia, Egypt, and overthrow Persian Empire.
634–642	Oswald, king of Northumbria, introduces Celtic Christian Church to northern England.

646	Taikwa, Japanese edict of reform; Japanese begin to copy Chinese culture.
664	Synod of Whitby: Oswy, king of Northumbria, joins England to Church of Rome.
711–715	Spain conquered by Moors.
712	Islamic state set up in Sind, now part of Pakistan.
717–718	Arab siege of Constantinople fails.
720	Moors invade France.
732	Charles Martel of Franks defeats Moorish invaders at Poitiers.
752	Pepin the Short elected king of Franks.
756	Donation of Pepin: Franks agree to popes' controlling central Italy.
771–814	Reign of Charlemagne, king of Franks.
773–774	Charlemagne conquers Lombardy.
778	Moors defeat Franks at Roncesvalles.
781	Christian missionaries reach China.
786–809	Rule of Harun Al-Raschid as caliph of Baghdad.
787	First attacks by the Northmen (Vikings) on England.
800	Pope Leo III crowns Charlemagne as Roman emperor of the West.
814	Division of Charlemagne's empire following his death.

▽ Charlemagne (c.742–814), Frankish ruler and first Holy Roman emperor.

827–839	Egbert, first Saxon king claiming to rule all England.
832	Muslims capture Sicily.
c.850	Jainism and Hinduism established as main religions of northern India.
871–899	Reign of Alfred the Great in southern England.
874	Northmen begin settling in Iceland.
878	Treaty of Wedmore divides England between Saxons and Danes.
885	Paris besieged by Vikings.
896	Magyar tribes conquer Hungary.
906	Magyars begin invasion of Germany.
907	End of T'ang dynasty in China; civil war breaks out.
919–936	Reign of Henry I (the Fowler) of Germany.
926	Athelstan, king of England, conquers Wales and southern Scotland.
935	Wenceslaus of Bohemia murdered by brother.
936–973	Reign of Otto I, the Great, of Germany.
955	Battle of the Lechfeld: Otto the Great repulses Magyars.
960	Sung dynasty founded in China.
962	Revival of Roman empire in West: Pope John XII crowns Otto of Germany as Holy Roman emperor.
978	Ethelred II, the Unready, becomes king of England.
986	Eric the Red founds colonies in Greenland.
987	Hugh Capet elected king of Franks; Capetian dynasty founded.
988	Foundation of Al-Azhar University in Cairo.
994	London besieged by Olaf Trygvason of Norway and Sweyn of Denmark.
c.1000	Polynesian settlers reach New Zealand.
c.1000	Ancient Empire of Ghana flourishes in west Africa.
c.1000	Leif Ericsson of Norway discovers Vinland in North America.
1004–1013	Danes attack England, bought off by Ethelred II.
1014	Canute (Cnut) becomes king of Denmark and Norway.
1016	Canute also becomes king of England, deposing Ethelred.
1040	Macbeth murders Duncan, king of Scots, and becomes king.
1042–1066	Edward the Confessor, son of Ethelred, king of England.

1058	Malcolm III Canmore becomes king of Scots, having killed Macbeth in 1057 in battle near Aberdeen.
1066	Harold II chosen king of England; invasion of England by William of Normandy, who seizes throne.
1075–1122	Struggle between popes and German emperors over right to appoint bishops.
1076	Pope Gregory VII excommunicates German Emperor Henry IV.
1077	Penance at Canossa: Henry submits to the Pope.
1084	Normans under Robert Guiscard sack Rome.
1096–1099	First Crusade to free Holy Land (Palestine) from Muslim rule; capture of Jerusalem.
1100	William II (Rufus) of England shot while hunting; brother Henry I becomes king.
1106	Henry I wrests Normandy from elder brother Robert.
1113	Order of the Knights of St. John founded.
1119	Order of Knights Templars founded.
1122	Concordat of Worms ends disputes between emperors and popes.
1147–1149	Second Crusade: Christian armies disagree and crusade fails.
1152–1190	Frederick I (Barbarossa) king of Germany and Holy Roman emperor.

1154–1189	Reign of Henry II of England; much of France under English rule.
1174–1193	Rule of Saladin as Sultan of Egypt and Syria.
1182	Expulsion of Jews from France.
1187	Saladin captures Jerusalem.
1189–1192	Third Crusade, led by Frederick Barbarossa, Philip II of France, and Richard I of England; Acre and Jaffa captured.
1192–1194	Richard of England prisoner of Leopold of Austria and Emperor Henry VI.
1197–1212	Civil war in Germany following death of Emperor Henry VI; ends with election of Frederick II.
c.1200	Settlement of Mexico by Aztecs; Incas found their first kingdom in Peru.
1200–1450	German cities form Hanseatic League to promote their trade.
1202–1204	Fourth Crusade: crusaders, in debt to Venice, capture Constantinople for Venetians.
1206	Mongol leader Temujin proclaimed *Genghis Khan* (emperor within the seas).
1210	Francis of Assisi founds Franciscan order of monks.
1211–1222	Mongol invasion of China.
1212	Children's Crusade: 30,000 children from France and Germany set off to free Holy Land; many die.

▽ Routes taken by Crusaders to the Holy Land.

△ The seal of King John, as set upon Magna Carta in 1215.

1215 King John of England agrees to Magna Carta, statement of the rights of his subjects.
1215 St. Dominic founds Dominican order of friars.
1217–1221 Fifth Crusade fails to liberate Holy Land.
1223 Mongol invasion of Russia.
1224 Carmelite order of friars founded.
1228–1229 Sixth Crusade led by Emperor Frederick II regains Jerusalem.
1238 Mongol warriors capture Moscow.
1240 Russian hero Alexander Nevsky defeats Swedish force at River Neva.
1241 "Golden Horde" Mongol kingdom established on banks of River Volga.
1244 Muslims recapture Jerusalem.
1248 St. Louis (Louis IX of France) leads Seventh Crusade; captured by Muslims and ransomed in 1254.
1256 Foundation of Augustinian order.
1260–1294 Kublai Khan becomes ruler of Mongol Empire and founds Yüan dynasty in China.
1268 Egyptians capture Antioch, held by Christians.
1270 Eighth and last Crusade, led by St. Louis, who dies during it.
1271–1295 Marco Polo visits court of Kublai Khan, travels in Asia, and returns to Venice.
1273 Rudolf I of Hapsburg becomes Holy Roman Emperor, founding Hapsburg dynasty.
1282 Edward I of England conquers Wales.
1290 Expulsion of Jews from England.

1295 First truly representative parliament summoned in England.
1301 Edward I of England creates his son Edward as the first Prince of Wales.
1302 Papal Bull *Unam sanctam* proclaims papal superiority over national rulers.
1305–1378 Avignonese Papacy: seven popes based at Avignon in France because of unrest in Italy.
1306 Robert Bruce leads Scottish revolt against English rule.
1314 Scotland becomes independent after Bruce defeats English at Battle of Bannockburn.
1325 Aztecs found Tenochtitlán, now Mexico City.
1334–1351 The Black Death (bubonic plague) ravages Europe, killing one in four.
1337 Hundred Years War between England and France starts when Edward III of England takes title of King of France.
1339 English invasion of France begins.
1346 Edward III defeats French army at Battle of Crécy: longbow proved to be the most formidable weapon.
1356 English under Edward the Black Prince capture John II of France at Battle of Poitiers.
1360 First part of Hundred Years War ended by Treaty of Bretigny.
1368 Ming Dynasty begins in China.
1369 War breaks out again between England and France.
1369–1405 Reign of Tamerlane, Mongol ruler of Samarkand, and conqueror of much of southern Asia.
1371 Robert I becomes first Stuart king of Scotland.
1374 Peace between England and France, England having lost nearly all its French possessions.
1378–1417 The Great Schism: rival lines of popes elected, splitting the Church.
1396 Bulgaria conquered by Ottoman Turks.
1397 Union of Kalmar: Denmark, Norway and Sweden united under one king.
1400 Welsh revolt led by Owen Glendower.
1414 Lollards (heretics) persecuted in England.
1414–1417 Council of Constance called to heal Great Schism; Martin V elected pope.

1415	Henry V of England renews claim to French throne, and defeats French at Battle of Agincourt.
1420	Treaty of Troyes: Henry V acknowledged as heir to French throne.
1422	Deaths of Henry V and of Charles VI of France; renewed struggle for French throne.
1429	Joan of Arc raises English siege of Orléans; Charles VII crowned king at Rheims.
1431	Joan of Arc burned as witch.
1437	Portuguese naval institute founded by Prince Henry the Navigator.
c.1450	Invention of printing from movable type by Johannes Gutenberg.
1453	Hundred Years War ends, leaving England with Calais as only French possession.
1453	Ottoman Turks capture Constantinople, ending Byzantine Empire; taken as the end of the Middle Ages.
1455–1485	Wars of the Roses: civil wars in England between rival families of York and Lancaster.

△ Ivan the Great (1440–1505), first tsar of Russia.

1461–1485	House of York triumphant in England.
1475	Edward IV of England invades France; bought off by Louis XI.
1479	Crowns of Castile and Aragon united, making Spain one country.
1480	Ivan III, first tsar (emperor) of Russia, makes himself independent of Mongols.

▽ In 1453 Constantinople was captured by the Turks and the Byzantine Empire came to an end.

1483 Boy king Edward V of England deposed; possibly killed by uncle, Richard III.

1485 Richard III killed at Battle of Bosworth; Henry Tudor brings Lancastrians back to power as Henry VII.

1488 Bartolomeu Dias, Portuguese navigator, becomes first European to sail around Cape of Good Hope.

1492 Spaniards finally drive Moors out of Granada, last Muslim province.

1492 Christopher Columbus discovers West Indies while searching for westward route to eastern Asia.

1493 Inca empire in Peru at its height.

1497 John Cabot discovers Newfoundland; claims it for England.

1498 Vasco da Gama of Portugal discovers sea route to India by way of Cape of Good Hope.

1506 Work begins on St. Peter's Basilica, Rome; Donato Bramante, chief architect.

1508–1512 Michelangelo paints ceiling of Sistine Chapel in Vatican.

1516 African slave traffic to Americas begins.

1517 Beginning of Reformation: monk Martin Luther publishes *95 Theses* at Wittenberg, Germany.

1519–1555 Reign of Holy Roman Emperor Charles V, who has become king of Spain two years earlier.

1519–1521 First voyage around world; expedition led by Ferdinand Magellan, who dies during journey.

△ Title page of Martin Luther's Bible.

1519–1521 Conquest of Mexico by Spaniard Hernando Cortés.

1520 Field of Cloth of Gold: meeting between Francis I of France and Henry VIII of England.

1521 Diet of Worms (church conference) condemns doctrines of Martin Luther.

1524–1525 Peasants' War: revolt of German peasants defeated and peasants punished.

1525 Battle of Pavia: imperial forces defeat and capture Francis I of France.

1527 Sack of Rome by imperial forces; Pope Clement VII taken prisoner.

1529 Turkish armies advancing through Hungary besiege Vienna.

1530 Baber, founder of Mogul Empire in India, dies.

1532 Spaniards under Francisco Pizarro conquer the Incas of Peru.

1533 Henry VIII of England excommunicated by pope for divorcing Catherine of Aragon.

◁ Christopher Columbus (1451–1506) pioneered sea routes to the New World.

1534 Act of Supremacy: Henry VIII assumes leadership of the Church in England, and breaks with Rome.
1534 Society of Jesus (Jesuits) founded by Ignatius Loyola.
1541 John Calvin takes Reformation movement to Geneva.
1545–1563 Council of Trent marks beginning of Counter-Reformation.
1549 Book of Common Prayer introduced in England.
1553–1558 Reign of Mary I brings England into reconciliation with Rome.
1558 French capture Calais, last English possession in France.
1558–1603 Reign of Elizabeth I in England; return to Protestantism.
1562–1598 Religious wars in France between Roman Catholics and Huguenots (Protestants).
1567 Foundation of Rio de Janeiro.
1568 Mary, Queen of Scots, driven into exile; imprisoned by Elizabeth I of England.
1571 Battle of Lepanto: allied Christian fleet defeats Turkish fleet.
1572 Massacre of St. Bartholomew's Day in France; thousands of Huguenots killed.

1572 Active rebellion of the Netherlands against Spain begins.
1575 Bengal conquered by Akbar the Great.
1577–1580 Sir Francis Drake of England sails around the world.
1582 Pope Gregory XIII introduces reformed Gregorian calendar, which most Roman Catholic countries adopt.
1585–1589 War of the Three Henrys in France – Henry III, Henry of Navarre, Henry of Guise.
1587 Elizabeth I of England orders execution of Mary, Queen of Scots, found guilty of treason.
1587 Sir Francis Drake destroys Spanish fleet at Cádiz.
1588 Spanish Armada sets sail to invade England; defeated by English fleet.
1589 Assassination of Henry III of France; succeeded by Huguenot Henry of Navarre, who adopts Roman Catholicism.
1592 Conquest of Sind by Akbar the Great.
1598 Edict of Nantes: French Protestants gain political rights.

▽ Religious quarrels led to bloodshed: most terribly in the St. Bartholomew's Day massacre of 1572.

138

△ Captain John Smith founded the first permanent English colony in America, at Jamestown in Virginia.

△ A contemporary woodcut illustration of the execution by beheading of Charles I in 1649.

1600 English East India Company founded.
1602 Dutch East India Company founded.
1603 French East India Company founded.
1603 Death of Elizabeth I: James VI of Scotland becomes James I of England, uniting two countries under one crown.
1607 John Smith founds Colony of Virginia.
1609 Netherlands win independence from Spain.
1610 Henry IV of France assassinated; succeeded by Louis XIII, aged nine.
1610–1611 Henry Hudson discovers Hudson Bay; set adrift by his crew, following a mutiny.
1611 English and Scottish colonists begin settlement in Ulster.
1611 Publication of Authorized (King James) Version of the Bible.
1616 Dutch navigator Willem Schouten makes first-ever voyage around Cape Horn.
1618–1648 Thirty Years War in Europe; begins with revolt by Protestants in Prague.
1620 Pilgrim Fathers sail to America in *Mayflower*.
1625–1649 Reign of Charles I in England.
1626 Dutch colony of New Amsterdam (now New York) founded.

1629 Massachusetts colony founded.
1631 First colonists settle in Maryland.
1631 Sack of Magdeburg by Tilly; defeat of Tilly by Gustavus Adolphus of Sweden at Battle of Leipzig.
1633 Colonists settle in Connecticut.
1638 Japanese massacre Christians, and stop all foreign visitors to country.
1639 Colonists settle in New Hampshire and Maine.
1640 Financial crisis in England: Charles I summons Long Parliament.
1641 French colonize Michigan.
1642–1646 Civil War in England; Parliament in revolt against Charles I.
1642 Abel Tasman discovers New Zealand.
1643–1715 Reign of Louis XIV of France.
1643 Manchu dynasty founded in China.
1648 Peace of Westphalia: end of Thirty Years War.
1648 Second Civil War in England; crushed by Parliamentary forces.
1649 Charles I tried and executed for treason; England a republic.
1650–1651 Charles II tries to regain throne, but is defeated by Oliver Cromwell.
1652 Dutch pioneer Jan van Riebeeck founds first European settlement in South Africa.

△ The Great Fire of 1666 destroyed 14,000 buildings in London and burned for seven days. After the fire houses and churches were mainly built of brick or stone rather than timber.

1652–1654 War between Dutch and English.
1653 Oliver Cromwell becomes Lord Protector of England, Scotland, Ireland.
1660 Charles II restored to thrones of England and Scotland.
1664 English take New Amsterdam (New York) from Dutch.
1665–1667 Second Anglo-Dutch War.
1665 New Jersey colony founded.
1665 Great Plague ravages London.
1666 London destroyed by fire.
1667–1668 War of Devolution between France and Spain.
1668 Spain recognizes Portuguese independence.
1672–1674 Third Anglo-Dutch War; France allied to England.
1685 Louis XIV of France revokes Edict of Nantes; Huguenots flee from France.
1688–1689 Glorious Revolution in England: Roman Catholic James II deposed; Parliament offers throne to William III of Orange and his wife, James's daughter Mary II.
1689 France declares war on Spain and England.
1690 Battle of the Boyne: William III defeats James II, ending Stuart hopes.
1696–1725 Reign of Peter I, the Great, of Russia.

1700–1721 Great Northern War: Sweden fights other Baltic states.
1702 William III dies; succeeded by Anne, the last of the Stuart monarchs.
1701–1713 War of the Spanish Succession.
1704 Britain captures Gibraltar.
1707 Formal union of England and Scotland.

▽ Peter the Great (1672–1725), under whose rule Russia rose to be a power in western Europe. He modernized the army, changed the legal and administrative systems and encouraged education.

1709	Battle of Poltava: Charles XII of Sweden beaten by Peter the Great.
1714	Elector George of Hanover becomes King George I of England, ensuring Protestant succession.
1715–1774	Reign of Louis XV of France, great-grandson of Louis XIV.
1715	Jacobite (Stuart) rebellion in Britain fails.
1718	Quadruple Alliance of Britain, the Empire, France, and the Netherlands against Spain.
1721	Robert Walpole, world's first prime minister, becomes First Lord of the Treasury in Britain.
1733–1735	War of the Polish Succession.
1739	War of Jenkins' Ear between Britain and Spain.
1740–1786	Reign of Frederick II, the Great, of Prussia.
1740–1748	War of the Austrian Succession: dispute over Maria Theresa's right to inherit throne of Austria.
1745–1746	Second Jacobite rebellion in Britain fails.
1751	Robert Clive for Britain captures Arcot from French in India.
1755	Lisbon earthquake: 30,000 people die.
1756	Start of Seven Years War; Britain, Hanover, and Prussia against Austria, France, Russia, and Sweden.
1756	Black Hole of Calcutta; 146 Britons imprisoned in small room – most die.

1759	British capture Quebec from French.
1760–1820	Reign of George III of Britain.
1762	War between Britain and Spain.
1763	Peace of Paris ends Seven Years War.
1764	James Hargreaves invents the spinning jenny, marking start of Industrial Revolution in England.
1767	British government imposes import taxes on North American colonies.
1770	British navigator James Cook discovers New South Wales.
1770	Boston Massacre: British troops fire on American mob, killing five people.
1773	Boston Tea Party, protest against tea tax.
1775–1783	American Revolution.
1775	Battles of Lexington, Concord, and Bunker Hill.
1776	Declaration of Independence.
1777	Battle of Saratoga: a British army surrenders to Americans.
1778–1779	War of the Bavarian Succession between Austria and Prussia.
1778	France declares war on Britain to support American colonies.
1779	Spain joins war against Britain.
1781	British forces surrender at Yorktown, Virginia.

▽ On December 25th, 1776 George Washington led his troops across the icy Delaware to make a surprise attack on British forces.

▽ The guillotine was recommended by Dr. Joseph Guillotin and was introduced in 1792 during the French Revolution. Louis XVI was beheaded by its blade, as was Robespierre, who had himself instituted the bloody Reign of Terror.

1783 Peace of Paris: Britain recognizes independence of United States of America.
1785 First balloon crossing of English Channel.
1788 United States adopts Constitution.
1789 George Washington first president of the United States.
1789–1799 French Revolution begins with the fall of the Bastille, a prison.
1790 Washington, D.C. founded.
1792 France proclaimed a republic.
1792–1799 War of the First Coalition: Austria, Britain, the Netherlands, Prussia, Spain against France.
1793 Louis XVI of France executed; Reign of Terror (to 1794).
1796 Corsican general Napoleon Bonaparte conquers most of Italy for France.
1798 Napoleon Bonaparte in Egypt: cut off by Horatio Nelson's naval victory in Battle of the Nile.
1799 Coup d'état of Brumaire: Napoleon becomes first consul of France.
1799–1801 War of the Second Coalition.
1800 British capture Malta.
1801 Britain and Ireland united.
1803 Louisiana Purchase: United States buys Louisiana territory from France.

1804 Napoleon crowned emperor of France.
1805–1808 War of the Third Coalition: Austria, Britain, Naples, Russia, Sweden against France and Spain.
1805 Battle of Trafalgar: Nelson defeats French and Spanish fleets.
1805 Battle of Austerlitz: Napoleon defeats Austrians and Russians.
1806 Napoleon ends Holy Roman Empire, makes his brothers kings of Naples and Holland.
1807 Britain abolishes slave trading.
1808–1814 Peninsular War in Spain and Portugal against French invaders.
1809–1825 Wars of independence in Latin America.
1812 Napoleon invades Russia; forced to retreat, losing most of his army.
1812–1815 War between United States and Britain over searching of neutral shipping.
1813 Napoleon defeated at Battle of Leipzig; French driven from Spain.
1814 Napoleon abdicates; exiled to Elba.
1815 Napoleon tries to regain power; finally defeated at Battle of Waterloo and exiled to St. Helena.

▽ A caricature of Arthur Wellesley, Duke of Wellington (1769–1852), who was known as the Iron Duke.

A WELLINGTON BOOT
in the Head of the Army

△ Simon Bolívar (1783–1830). South American liberator; he led the struggle against Spanish rule.

1818 Chile becomes independent.
1819 United States gains Florida from Spain.
1819 Argentina becomes independent.
1821 Mexico and Peru gain independence.
1822 Greece and Brazil declare their independence.
1823 Monroe Doctrine: United States guarantees Western Hemisphere against European interference.
1825 Bolivia and Paraguay become independent.
1826 First photograph taken by Nicéphore Nièpce of France.
1830 July Revolution: Charles X of France deposed; Louis Philippe elected king.
1830 Belgium and Ecuador become independent.
1833 Slavery abolished in British colonies.
1836 Great Trek: Boer colonists move north from Cape Colony in South Africa.
1837–1901 Reign of Queen Victoria of Britain.
1839 Guatemala becomes a republic.
1841 New Zealand becomes British colony.
1841 Upper and Lower Canada united.
1842 China yields Hong Kong to Britain.
1844 First telegraph message sent by inventor Samuel F.B. Morse.
1846 Great Famine in Ireland: a million people die, a million emigrate.
1848 Gold discovered in California.
1848 Year of revolutions: in France, Berlin, Budapest, Milan, Naples, Prague, Rome, Venice, and Vienna.
1848 France becomes republic, with Louis Napoleon as president.

△ Karl Marx (1818–1883), German philosopher and founder of modern communist theory.

1848 Karl Marx and Friedrich Engels publish *Communist Manifesto*.
1849 Britain annexes Punjab in India.
1851 Australian gold rush begins.
1852 Napoleon III proclaimed emperor of the French.
1854–1856 Crimean War: Turkey, Britain, France, Sardinia against Russia.
1857–1858 Indian Mutiny; British government takes over rule from East India Company.
1861 Unification of Italy.
1861–1865 American Civil War; southern states secede and form Confederacy; war begins with Union attack on Ft. Sumter, S.C.

▽ Abraham Lincoln, a Republican whose party wanted to limit slavery, was elected president of the United States in 1860.

1863	Slavery abolished in United States; Battle of Gettysburg.
1865	Confederate General Robert E. Lee surrenders at Appomattox Court House.
1867	Canada proclaimed a Dominion.
1867	United States buys Alaska from Russia.
1867	Luxembourg becomes independent.
1869	Suez Canal opened.
1870–1871	Franco-Prussian War: fall of Napoleon III; France a republic again; Germany united under William of Prussia.
1876	Alexander Graham Bell invents the telephone.
1876	France and Britain take joint control of Egypt.
1877	Romania becomes independent.
1880–1881	First Boer War; Britain defeats Boer settlers in South Africa.
1884	Leopold II of Belgium sets up private colony in the Congo.
1887	First automobiles built in Germany.
1890	Battle of Wounded Knee, S.D., last major conflict between Indians and U.S. troops.
1896	Klondike gold rush begins.
1898	Spanish-American War: United States wins Guam, Puerto Rico, and Philippines; Cuba wins independence.
1899–1902	Second Boer War; British victory.

△ The Suez Canal was opened in 1869, opening up a faster sea route between Europe and the Orient.

1900	Boxer Rebellion in China.
1901	Australia becomes independent commonwealth.
1901	First radio signals sent across Atlantic.

▽ In South Africa British regular troops fought a bitter war against the Boer (Dutch settlers) guerrilla forces.

△ On 17 December 1903 the Wrights' airplane flew for the first time.

▽ Lenin addressing a crowd from a truck during the 1917 Russian Revolution.

1903 Wright brothers make first heavier-than-air flight.

1904–1905 Russo-Japanese War: Japan wins.

1905 Revolution in Russia: Tsar Nicholas II grants limited reforms.

1907 New Zealand becomes a dominion.

1909 Robert Peary reaches North Pole.

1910 South Africa becomes a dominion.

1911 Roald Amundsen reaches the South Pole.

1911–1912 Italo-Turkish War: Italy gains Tripoli and Cyrenaica.

1912 China proclaimed a republic.

1912–1913 First Balkan War.

1913 Second Balkan War.

1914–1918 World War I: begun by assassination of Archduke Ferdinand of Austria at Sarajevo.

1914 Panama Canal completed.

1915 Allies fail in Dardanelles campaign against Turkey.

1916 Easter Rebellion in Ireland fails.

1916 Battle of Jutland; defense of Verdun; Battle of the Somme; first use of tanks, by the British.

1917 Revolutions in Russia: Bolsheviks under Lenin seize control; United States enters the war; Battles of Aisne, Cambrai, Passchendaele.

1918 War ends after final German offensive fails; Treaty of Versailles signed; Germany becomes republic.

1920 League of Nations meets for first time; U.S. refuses to join.

1920 Civil war in Ireland.

1921 Southern Ireland becomes a dominion.

1922 Russia becomes the Union of Soviet Socialist Republics.

1922 Fresh civil war in Ireland.

1923 Turkey becomes a republic.

1924 First Labour government in Britain.

1926 General Strike in Britain.

1927 Charles Lindbergh makes first solo flight across Atlantic Ocean.

1929 Wall Street crash: start of world depression.

◁ The trench warfare of 1914–1918 created appalling conditions for front-line soldiers.

△ Adolf Hitler at a Nazi rally in Germany. His dream of a thousand-year German domination of Europe led to world war.

△ A U.S. B17 bombs Budapest in 1944. World War II was largely dominated by air power.

1933   Adolf Hitler becomes chancellor of Germany: burning of Reichstag.
1934   Hitler becomes Führer of Germany.
1935   Germany regains Saarland.
1935–1936   Italians conquer Ethiopia.
1936–1939   Civil War in Spain; Francisco Franco becomes dictator after Nationalists defeat Republicans.
1936   Germany reoccupies Rhineland.
1938   The Anschluss: Germany annexes Austria.
1938   Munich crisis: France, Britain, and Italy agree that Germany should take Sudetenland from Czechoslovakia.
1939   Germans occupy remainder of Czechoslovakia.
1939   Russo-German treaty.
1939–1945   World War II: Germany invades Poland; Britain and France declare war.

1940   Germans invade Denmark, Norway, Belgium, the Netherlands, and France; Britain and its Empire carry on fight.
1940   Battle of Britain: German air attack fails.
1941   Germans invade Greece, Yugoslavia, and Russia.
1941   Japanese attack on Pearl Harbor brings United States into war.
1942   Japanese capture Malaya, Singapore, Burma, and Philippines; Battle of El Alamein in Egypt marks turning point in war.
1943   Allies invade North Africa, Sicily, and Italy; German army surrenders at Stalingrad (now Volgograd).
1944   Allies land in Normandy, liberating France and Belgium; major Russian attack begins.
1945   Germany overrun from east and west; Hitler commits suicide; atomic bombs on Japan end war in East.
1946   First session of United Nations General Assembly.
1947   India, Pakistan, and Burma independent.
1948   Israel becomes independent.
1948   Russians blockade West Berlin.
1949   North Atlantic Treaty Organization formed.
1949   Communist rule established in China.
1950–1953   Korean War: United Nations force helps defend South Korea.

◁ The Allied victory at El Alamein, 1942, turned the tide in North Africa.

1953 Edmund Hillary and Tenzing Norgay are first men to climb Mount Everest.
1954 French Indochina becomes independent countries of Laos, Cambodia, South Vietnam, and North Vietnam after fierce communist attacks.
1956 Egypt becomes a republic; Suez Canal nationalized.
1956 Russia crushes Hungarian uprising.

◁ Edmund Hillary and Tenzing Norgay, first to climb Mount Everest, in 1953.

1956 Morocco, Tunisia, Sudan all independent.
1957 European Common Market set up.
1957 Ghana and Malaysia independent.
1958 Guinea becomes independent.
1959 Fidel Castro establishes communist rule in Cuba.
1960 Year of independence for Cameroon, Central African Republic, Chad, Congo (Brazzaville), Congo (now Zaïre), Cyprus, Dahomey, Gabon, Ivory Coast (now Côte d'Ivoire), Madagascar, Mali, Niger, Nigeria, Senegal, Somalia, Togo, Upper Volta (now Burkina Faso).
1961 First man in space: Yuri Gagarin.
1961 Mauretania, Mongolia, Sierra Leone, Tanzania become independent.
1962 Independence of Algeria, Burundi, Jamaica, Rwanda, Trinidad and Tobago, Uganda.
1963 Assassination of John F. Kennedy.
1963 Kenya and Kuwait become independent.
1964 Malawi, Malta, and Zambia become independent.

▽ The Hungarian uprising of 1956. Russian tanks move into Budapest to quell the people's demand for freedom.

△ Yuri Gagarin, of the Soviet Union, the first man in space; he remained in orbit for 89 minutes. He died in 1968 in an aeroplane crash.

1965	Gambia, Maldive Islands, Singapore become independent; Rhodesia proclaims own independence with White minority rule.
1967	Six-Day War: Israel defeats Arab countries.
1967	South Yemen becomes independent.
1968	Soviet troops occupy Czechoslovakia.
1968	Independence of Nauru, Equatorial Guinea.
1969	First man on Moon (Neil Armstrong).
1969	Civil disturbances in Northern Ireland begin to escalate.
1970	Bloodless coup led by Lon Nol topples Cambodia's Prince Sihanouk.
1970	Guyana and Fiji become independent.
1971	East Pakistan rebels and becomes independent as Bangladesh; Qatar, Bahrain also independent.
1973	American forces end military intervention in Vietnam War.
1973	Independence of Bahamas.
1973	The October War: Arab states attack Israel; war halted after five weeks.
1973	Arab oil-producing states raise oil prices; world economic crisis begins.
1974	President Richard M. Nixon resigns because of Watergate scandal.
1974	Portugal's African colonies win independence agreement.
1975	Communists win decisive victories in Indochina: South Vietnam surrenders to North Vietnam.
1975	Independence of Papua New Guinea, São Tomé and Príncipe, and Angola.
1975	Reopening of Suez Canal to shipping.
1975	Death of Spanish dictator Francisco Franco; Prince Juan Carlos crowned King of Spain.
1976	North and South Vietnam reunified.
1976	Independence for the Seychelles within the Commonwealth.
1976	Two earthquakes destroy Tangshan in China; more than 700,000 die.
1976	Death of China's Chairman Mao.
1977	President Sadat of Egypt and Prime Minister Begin of Israel meet to gain peace for Middle East.
1979	Cambodia changes its name to Kampuchea; the capital captured by Vietnamese and rebels.
1979	Kampala captured by Tanzanian troops and Ugandan exiles; General Amin forced to flee.
1979	Shah of Iran deposed; exiled Muslim leader, the Ayatollah Khomeini, returns to Iran, which is declared an Islamic Republic.
1979	Margaret Thatcher becomes Britain's first woman prime minister.
1979	90 people, including 63 Americans, taken hostage in Iran.
1979	Russian forces move into Afghanistan.
1980	Rhodesia becomes independent as Zimbabwe with Black majority rule.
1980	Gulf War begins between Iran and Iraq.
1981	Ronald Reagan becomes 40th President of the United States.
1981	American hostages in Iran freed.
1981	President Sadat of Egypt assassinated.
1981	Assassination attempts on President Reagan and Pope John Paul fail.
1982	Argentine annexation of Falkland Islands and South Georgia. A British task force reoccupies the islands.
1983	Famine hits Ethiopia.
1983	Yuri Vladimirovich Andropov is elected president of the U.S.S.R.
1984	Yuri Andropov dies; is succeeded as Soviet leader by Konstantin Chernenko.

148

△ Fans at the Live Aid concert (1985) are cooled down.

1984 Canadian P.M. Pierre Trudeau resigns.

1984 I.R.A. bomb intended to kill members of the British Cabinet wrecks Brighton hotel; four die, 30 injured.

1984 Indian P.M. Indira Gandhi assassinated by her Sikh bodyguards.

1984 Chemical leak kills 2,000 and injures 200,000 at Indian town of Bhopal.

1985 Konstantin Chernenko dies: succeeded as Soviet leader by Mikhail Gorbachev.

1985 International rock concert "Live Aid" raises £40 million (then about $56 million) for Ethiopia's starving people.

1986 Space shuttle *Challenger* explodes on launch, killing its crew of seven.

1986 Philippines President Marcos is expelled; succeeded by Mrs. Corazón Aquino.

1986 Nuclear reactor at Chernobyl, Ukraine, blazes; fallout affects much of Europe.

1987 British car ferry *Herald of Free Enterprise* capsizes at Zeebrugge; 188 people die.

1987 World stock markets crash.

1987 Soviet leader Mikhail Gorbachev ushers in era of *glasnost* (openness) and reform.

1987 President Reagan and Soviet leader Gorbachev sign agreement to dismantle all nuclear missiles with 300–3,400 miles (480–5,500 km) range.

1988 Piper Alpha oil platform in North Sea explodes, killing 167 people.

1988 Gorbachev proposes major cuts in nuclear and other weapons.

1988 Ceasefire halts the Gulf War.

1988 U.S. resumes space shuttle flights; Soviets launch their first shuttle.

1988 Earthquake kills 45,000 people in Soviet Armenia and injures 20,000.

1988 Benazir Bhutto becomes prime minister of Pakistan.

1988 Soviet astronauts complete a year in space.

1988 Terrorist bomb wrecks U.S. airliner over Scotland: 269 people killed.

1989 Emperor Hirohito of Japan dies after a record reign of 62 years.

1989 George Bush is sworn in as 41st President of the United States.

1989 Second earthquake in the U.S.S.R. kills at least 300 people in Tadzhikstan.

1989 Kampuchea changes its name back to Cambodia.

1989 Chinese government suppresses student pro-democracy demonstration; many people killed.

1989 Iran's Muslim leader Ayatollah Khomeni dies aged 86.

1989 The trade union Solidarity wins most of the 261 seats it can contest in Poland's first free elections for 45 years; one-party rule ends, and Tadeusz Mazowiecki, editor of Solidarity's newspaper, is elected prime minister.

1989 U.S. space probe Voyager 2 sends back pictures from Neptune, 2.8 billion miles away.

1989 Hungary's Communist party votes to change its name to Socialist party.

1989 At least 20,000 East Germans flee to West Germany through Hungary and Austria.

1989 About 100 people die as earthquake rocks San Francisco and Oakland.

SEVEN WONDERS OF THE WORLD*

Pyramids of Egypt Oldest and only surviving "wonder." Built in the 2000s B.C. as royal tombs; about 80 are still standing. The largest, the Great Pyramid of Cheops, at el-Gizeh, was 481 ft (147 m) high.

Hanging Gardens of Babylon Terraced gardens adjoining Nebuchadnezzar's palace said to rise from 75 to 300 ft (23–91 m). Supposedly built by the king about 600 B.C. to please his wife, a princess from the mountains, but they are also associated with the Assyrian Queen Semiramis.

Statue of Zeus at Olympia Carved by Phidias, the 40 ft (12 m) statue marked the site of the original Olympic Games in the 400s B.C. It was constructed of ivory and gold, and showed Zeus (Jupiter) on his throne.

Temple of Artemis (Diana) at Ephesus Constructed of Parian marble and more than 400 ft (122 m) long with over 100 columns 60 ft (18 m) high, it was begun about 350 B.C. and took some 120 years to build. Destroyed by the Goths in A.D. 262.

Mausoleum at Halicarnassus Erected by queen Artemisia in memory of her husband, King Mausolus of Caria (in Asia Minor), who died 353 B.C.. It stood 140 ft (43 m) high. All that remains are a few pieces in the British Museum and the word "mausoleum" in the English language.

Colossus of Rhodes Gigantic bronze statue of sun god Helios (or Apollo); stood about 117 ft (36 m) high, dominating the harbor entrance at Rhodes. The sculptor Chares supposedly labored for 12 years before he completed it in 280 B.C.. It was destroyed by an earthquake in 224 B.C..

Pharos of Alexandria Marble lighthouse and watchtower built about 270 B.C. on the island of Pharos in Alexandria's harbor. Possibly standing 400 ft (122 m) high, it was destroyed by an earthquake in 1375.

*Originally compiled by Antipater of Sidon, a Greek poet, in the 100s B.C.

Pyramids of Egypt   Pharos of Alexandria   Mausoleum at Halicarnassus

Hanging gardens of Babylon

Colossus of Rhodes   Temple of Artemis   Statue of Zeus

Human body

The human body is a miracle of coordination. The heart beats 70 times a minute, pumping blood through the veins and arteries, taking life-giving oxygen to the brain. The body fights off infection and repairs itself: wounds can heal and broken bones knit together. Three billion of the body's cells die every minute and are replaced; only the brain cells cannot be renewed, but these last 100 years. The brain sends messages to our 639 muscles; these respond, moving our 206 bones to command. Our senses keep us in touch with the world, transmitting information, pleasure, and pain.

The body is complicated and finely balanced. It is made up of many different parts; each has its own special job and yet the healthy body is dependent on their all working together.

We need to look after our bodies. We need to supply them with food, sleep, and exercise. However, much of the regular maintenance is done by the body itself. Most of the cells of your body are replaced regularly. Around three billion cells die every minute, but they are replaced by three billion new ones. Only the nerve cells, including those of the brain, are not replaced. However, they can live for about 100 years.

▽ The development of the human species has taken millions of years. Our earliest human-like ancestors lived in Africa some 4 million years ago.

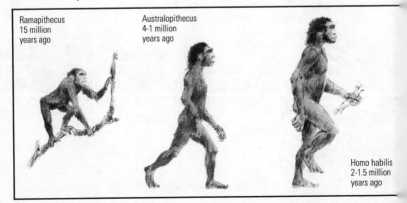

Ramapithecus
15 million
years ago

Australopithecus
4-1 million
years ago

Homo habilis
2-1.5 million
years ago

The body is also very good at repairing accidental damage. If cut, it does its best to stop the bleeding, and for all small cuts the normal body can do so without help. The skin heals up, leaving perhaps a small scar. Broken bones knit together to form strong new ones. The body fights off infection, with the help of its immune system.

Often, the work of doctors and surgeons is to give the body the best possible conditions to cure itself. Only when an injury is severe or a particularly virulent set of germs has invaded, are stronger methods needed, such as sewing up wounds, removing diseased tissue, or killing micro-organisms.

△ The body of an athlete is like a finely tuned engine. Training helps to develop body strengths and skills to a level far above the average.

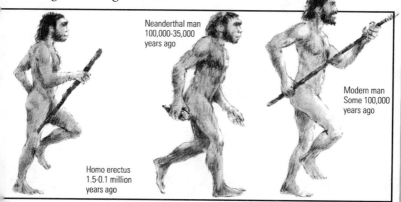

Neanderthal man 100,000-35,000 years ago

Modern man Some 100,000 years ago

Homo erectus 1.5-0.1 million years ago

152

Occasionally, part of the body breaks down completely. Today, we are able to replace some organs by the process of transplant surgery; for example we can give people new hearts and lungs, kidneys, or livers.

Groups of organs working together to perform a particular task are called systems. These are the body's seven systems and their functions.

The skeletal-muscular system provides a protective framework for the body and the means for moving it around.

The digestive system takes in food, processes it to keep the body running, and gets rid of waste material.

The urinary system balances the body's liquid intake. It plays a major part in clearing the body of waste products.

▽ The urinary system. The two kidneys (one of which has been cut away to show its structure) act as filters removing waste products and excess water from the blood. Urine produced in this way drips down the ureters into the bladder.

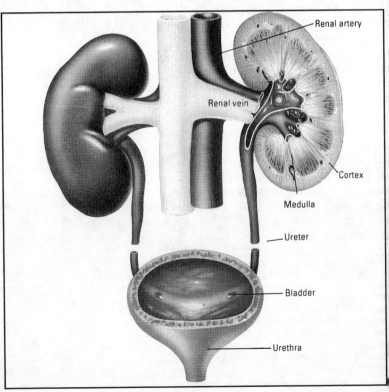

The *respiratory system* takes in oxygen every time you breathe in. Oxygen is needed by every part of the body. When you breathe out, the gas carbon dioxide (a waste product) is cleared out of your body. The respiratory system also gets rid of some moisture.

The *heart and circulatory system* takes the oxygen from the respiratory system and sends it all around the body in the blood. The blood picks up carbon dioxide and takes it back to the heart, which transfers it to the lungs for disposal.

The *nervous system* is the body's control system. The brain is the control center, and nerves carry messages to and from the brain, all over the body.

The *reproductive system* is the means by which babies are produced to carry on the human race. As in other animals, a sperm cell from a male is united with an egg cell in a female to start the reproductive process.

Various organs of the body take part in one or more of these systems. The glands make chemical substances that the body needs in order to keep running. The sense organs – eyes, ears, nose, taste buds, and the sense of feeling in the skin – supply the brain with information about the world around the body.

There are still many things about the body that we do not fully understand. One of the most wonderful is the mechanism that controls how we grow and develop as children – and what makes us stop growing when we have reached full size.

DNA double helix

HEREDITY

Heredity concerns the inheritance of characteristics from our parents' genes. The nucleus of all human cells (except eggs and sperm) contains 46 thread-like structures called **chromosomes**. These contain a chemical known as **DNA** (deoxyribonucleic acid), of which each molecule has a structure like a twisted ladder called a double helix (see right). The two parts of the "rungs" of this ladder are arranged in lots of different combinations which form coded instructions called **genes**.

154

The Skeleton

The skeleton is the main framework that supports your body. It is built up of bones. All bones are made of the same substances, mostly calcium. Bones are hard on the outside, but have a hollow center, filled with a soft substance called bone marrow. This is where red and white cells of the blood are made.

There are several different kinds of bone in the skeleton. The arms and legs have long bones; ankles, wrists, hands, and feet have short bones; and the shoulder blades and the skull are made up of flat bones. Broken bones knit together again if they are set (aligned) correctly and held in place by a splint or plaster while the body repairs the break.

The bones are linked together by joints, which allow the skeleton to be flexible. Some are hinge joints, such as those at the knee; some are pivot joints, which allow the bones to rotate against one another – the elbow has pivot and hinge joints. Some are ball and socket joints, such as those at the hips.

The main structure of the skeleton is built around the spine or backbone, which consists of 26 separate bones called vertebrae, with soft disks of cartilage between them as padding. The joints of the spine bend less than many other joints, such as those of the arms and legs.

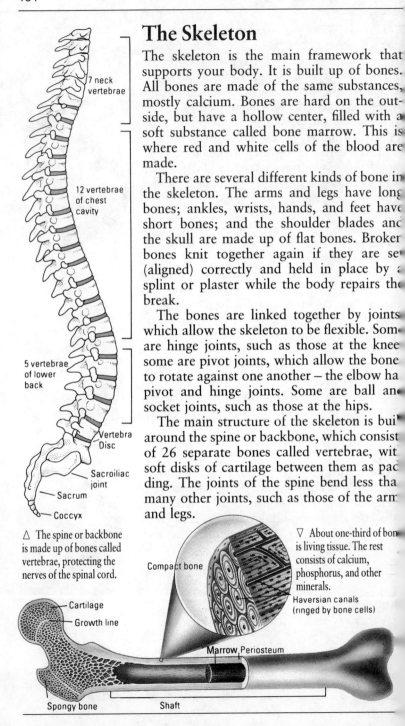

7 neck vertebrae

12 vertebrae of chest cavity

5 vertebrae of lower back

Vertebra
Disc
Sacroiliac joint
Sacrum
Coccyx

△ The spine or backbone is made up of bones called vertebrae, protecting the nerves of the spinal cord.

Compact bone

▽ About one-third of bone is living tissue. The rest consists of calcium, phosphorus, and other minerals.

Haversian canals (ringed by bone cells)

Cartilage
Growth line

Marrow Periosteum

Spongy bone   Shaft

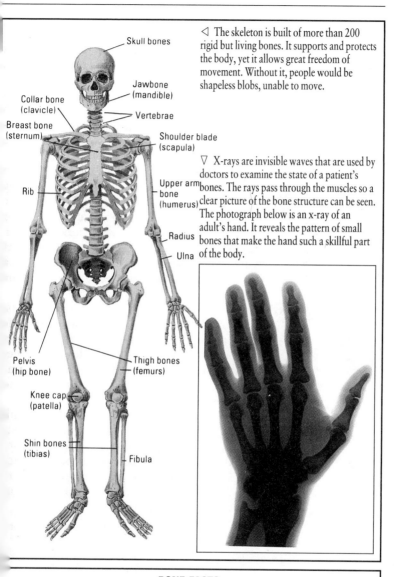

Skull bones

Jawbone (mandible)

Collar bone (clavicle)

Vertebrae

Breast bone (sternum)

Shoulder blade (scapula)

Rib

Upper arm bone (humerus)

Radius

Ulna

Pelvis (hip bone)

Thigh bones (femurs)

Knee cap (patella)

Shin bones (tibias)

Fibula

◁ The skeleton is built of more than 200 rigid but living bones. It supports and protects the body, yet it allows great freedom of movement. Without it, people would be shapeless blobs, unable to move.

▽ X-rays are invisible waves that are used by doctors to examine the state of a patient's bones. The rays pass through the muscles so a clear picture of the bone structure can be seen. The photograph below is an x-ray of an adult's hand. It reveals the pattern of small bones that make the hand such a skillful part of the body.

BONE FACTS

Number of bones in the adult human body is 206, but young children have more: the bones fuse together as the children grow.

Longest bone in the human body is the femur, or thigh bone. It is also the strongest.

Long bones are much stronger and lighter than reinforced concrete.

Smallest bone in the human body is the stapes or stirrup bone, one of three tiny bones in each ear.

Neck bones in the human body total seven – the same number as in a giraffe, whose neck may be 6 ft (1.8 m) long, or more.

The skull contains 22 bones, excluding the six tiny bones in the ears.

△ Striped or skeletal muscles have long striped cells with several nuclei in each cell.

△ Cardiac or heart muscles have shorter, less striped cells, which contain only one nucleus.

△ Smooth muscles are made of short, unstriped cells with one nucleus in each cell.

Muscles

Joints allow your bones to move, but the actual movements are produced by the muscles. Muscles are attached to your bones by strong bands of tissue called tendons. When muscles contract, they pull your bones. They can only pull, they cannot push, so most muscles come in pairs and work together to pull in turn. The brain sends them the instructions to contract or relax.

Muscle cells can shorten by up to one third of their length. When they contract the always shorten as much as they can. If all the cells in a muscle shorten at the same time the result is a jerky movement – for example when you snatch at something. But usually muscle cells contract in sequence, producing a smooth movement of the whole muscle.

There are three types of muscle in the human body. Most muscles are long and thin, and are made up of many cells arranged in fibers. The kind of muscles that move your arms and legs are called skeletal or striped muscles, because they look striped under a microscope. These are the voluntary muscles under the direct control of the brain, such as those you use when walking.

Other muscles, such as the diaphragm, are flat sheets of tissue. Smooth muscles appear unstriped. These are the involuntary muscles which work without direct control. They power all sorts of body functions, such as normal breathing and digestion, which must go on all the time whether you are awake or asleep. The third kind of muscle, found only in the heart, is a strong and specialized type called cardiac muscle.

MUSCLE FACTS

Number of muscles in the human body totals 639.

Largest muscle is the gluteus maximus, found in the buttock. It extends the thigh or the trunk.

Smallest muscle is the stapedius, a tiny muscle in the ear which controls movement of the stapes (stirrup bone).

40 per cent of your body weight consists of muscles.

Walking requires the use of 200 muscles.

HOW MUSCLES WORK

◁ Muscles are made up of bundles of fibers. As the fibers contract, the muscles become shorter and thicker. The muscle fibers are made up of muscle cells. The muscles of the arm work in pairs. As one contracts the other relaxes, straightening and bending the arm.

▽ Beneath the skin many muscles are partially contracted and ready for movement. In the face, short muscles control eye movements, facial expressions, speech, and chewing. In addition to the muscles we can control, there are 30 more that work automatically. These are the muscles of the heart, lungs, and digestive system.

△ 1. Breathing in: diaphragm contracts downward, chest inner space increases so pressure is greater outside than inside lungs. Air is breathed in.

△ 2. Breathing out: diaphragm arches upward, chest inner space decreases, so pressure inside lungs is greater than outside. Air is pushed out.

Lungs, Blood, and Heart

One substance that is essential for life is the gas oxygen, which forms about 21 percent of the air we breathe. Keeping the body supplied with oxygen is the work of the lungs and heart, with the help of the blood. Oxygen is drawn in by the lungs and transferred there to the blood. Blood is pumped around the body by the heart, carrying the oxygen to every living cell in the body.

When a person breathes in, the air is drawn through the nose and mouth. It passes down the trachea (windpipe), which branches into two tubes called bronchi. One bronchus leads to the left lung, the other to the right lung. In the lungs the bronchi branch into a mass of tiny twig-like bronchioles. The smallest bronchioles end in a bunch of tiny alveoli (air sacs). These absorb the oxygen from the air and pass it into the bloodstream.

The heart is a very efficient pump containing four chambers, the left and right atria a the top and the left and right ventricle below. Freshly oxygenated blood coming from the lungs flows into the left atrium. It i pumped through a one-way valve into the lef ventricle, and then around the body.

Blood returning from the body has lost it oxygen, but contains a waste product, carbo dioxide gas. This used blood comes into th right atrium, and is pumped through a valv into the right ventricle, and thence to th lungs to have the carbon dioxide remove and more oxygen added.

◁ Valves in the heart and veins control blood flow. Blood flowing forward forces valve flaps open.

▷ Blood attempting to flow backward forces flaps to close.

The blood is carried around the body in a series of tubes called blood vessels. Fresh blood from the heart flows through blood vessels called arteries. As with any pipe system, the arteries start large, and branch into smaller and smaller vessels, and finally into thin blood vessels called capillaries. The capillaries have thin walls which allow oxygen and food substances in the blood to pass into the body cells and waste products to be returned. Finally the blood flows back to the heart through a return system of veins.

The Heart

Vena cava

Aorta

ary artery

Pulmonary veins

Left atrium

Valve

alve

rium

Valve

Right ventricle

Valve

Left ventricle

BLOOD FACTS

Volume of blood in an average-sized adult is about 5¼ quarts (5 liters). Smaller people have less, larger people more.

Total number of red cells in the blood of an average man is 25 million million.

Blood groups There are four basic blood groups, A, AB, B, and O. Worldwide, Group O is the most common, but other groups are more common in various countries.

Total length of the blood vessels in an average-sized adult is about 100,000 miles (160,000 km).

HEART FACTS

The heart beats about 37 million times a year, or 70 times a minute.

The heart rests between beats; in a lifetime of 70 years, the total resting time is about 40 years.

Total weight of blood pumped every day by the heart is about 13 tons, or 3,600 gallons (13,640 liters)

Weight of the heart is about 11 oz (310 g) for a man, 9 oz (260 g) for a woman.

Largest artery is the aorta, which leaves the left ventricle of the heart. It is 1 inch (25 mm) across.

LUNG FACTS

The alveoli (air sacs) in the lungs total more than 600 million.

Walls of the air sacs cover between 600 and 1,000 sq ft (56–93 sq m).

Capacity of an adult's lungs is about 3 quarts (3 liters) of air.

Air is expelled and breathed in about 15 times a minute, a little over 1 pint (0.5 liter) at a time.

The diaphragm can move as much as 2 inches (50 mm) when breathing deeply.

The Brain and the Senses

The brain, nerves, and senses are the great control and communications system of the body. The brain is located in the skull. Messages to it come from the five senses – sight, hearing, smell, taste, and feeling. They tell the brain what is happening outside the body. The brain processes this information and issues instructions to the rest of the body in response.

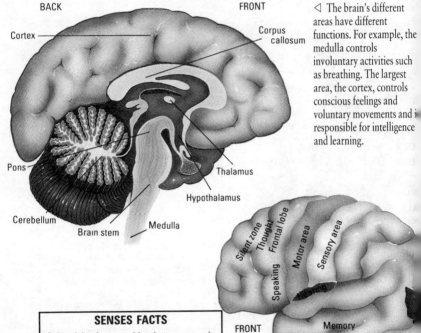

◁ The brain's different areas have different functions. For example, the medulla controls involuntary activities such as breathing. The largest area, the cortex, controls conscious feelings and voluntary movements and i responsible for intelligence and learning.

SENSES FACTS

Color vision is so sensitive that some people can distinguish as many as 300,000 different shades.

The human ear can distinguish more than 1,500 different musical tones.

The spiral canal of the inner ear is about the size of a pea, but if uncoiled it would be about 1½ inch (38 mm) long.

Taste buds on the tongue have specialized roles. Those on the tip detect sweet and salt flavors; those at the sides sour flavors; and those toward the back bitter flavors.

△ The cortex is the outer layer of a large, folded area called the cerebrum. The different functions of the cerebrum are shown above. T left side of the cortex controls the right side of the body. The right side controls the left. Sigh hearing, smell, and taste are controlled from sensory areas. Motor areas send messages to other parts of the body.

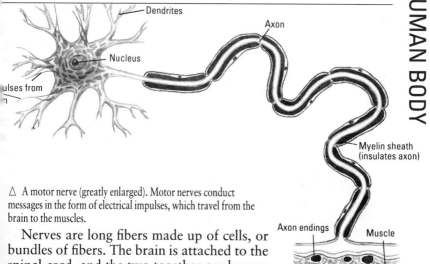

Dendrites

Axon

Nucleus

ulses from

Myelin sheath
(insulates axon)

△ A motor nerve (greatly enlarged). Motor nerves conduct messages in the form of electrical impulses, which travel from the brain to the muscles.

Axon endings

Muscle

Nerves are long fibers made up of cells, or bundles of fibers. The brain is attached to the spinal cord, and the two together are known as the central nervous system. The rest of the nerves, which extend all over the body, form the peripheral (outer) nervous system. Sensory nerves carry messages from the sense organs to the brain, while motor nerves carry messages from the brain to the muscles.

As you read this page, your brain is combining the letters into words and sentences. Some of this information will be stored as memories. Your brain is also sending messages to control your breathing rate, digestion of your food, and many other body functions. Because of your nervous system, you know where you are and what you are doing.

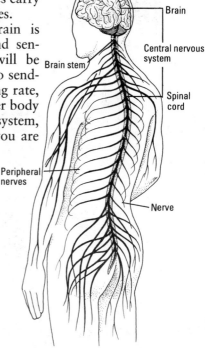

▽ The brain sends nerve impulses through the nerves within the spinal cord.

Brain

Central nervous system

Brain stem

Spinal cord

Peripheral nerves

Nerve

NERVOUS SYSTEM FACTS

Weight of an average adult brain is about 3 lb (1.4 kg)

Total number of nerve cells in the brain is about 12 billion. Once growing is complete, thousands of cells are lost every day and not replaced.

Nerve impulses travel at slightly over 200 mph (320 km/h).

The spinal cord is about 17 in (430 mm) long and about ¾ inches (20 mm) thick. It weighs about 1½ oz (43 g), and contains 31 pairs of spinal nerves which control the body's muscles.

△ The reproductive organs of a woman. From puberty, a mature egg is released from the ovary about every 28 days.

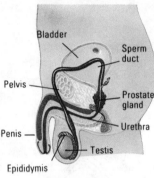

△ The reproductive organs of a man. Sperm are produced in the testes and mature in the epididymus. They travel to the penis in a fluid that is made in the seminal vesicles and prostate gland.

Reproduction

A baby begins its life when a sperm cell from its father meets an ovum – an egg cell – from its mother inside the mother's body. When the ovum is fertilized by the sperm, the two cells unite to form one cell, which then divides until a ball of 64 cells attaches itself to the lining of the uterus. The baby develops very quickly and has all its organs after about 12 weeks.

The baby takes about nine months to become fully formed and ready to be born. At birth powerful muscles in the uterus (womb) contract and force the baby out through the mother's vagina.

DID YOU KNOW?

The **uterus** is only about the size and shape of a pear, but during pregnancy it can stretch to about 12 in (30 cm) in length.

The **epididymis** is nearly 20 ft (6 m) long if uncoiled.

A **baby girl** is born with several thousand immature ova in her ovaries. Only a few hundred of these cells mature and are released during her lifetime.

The **testes** are outside the body in the scrotum because a cooler temperature helps the production of sperm.

An **ovum** from the mother and a **sperm** from the father each has 23 DNA-coded chromosomes in its nucleus.

A **mature sperm** is about 1/500 in (1/20 mm) long. Out of hundreds of millions of sperm released together, only one fertilizes the ovum.

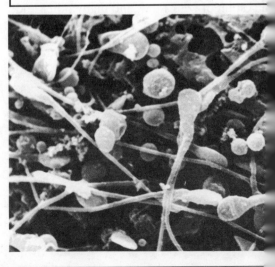

▷ A magnified photograph of spermatozoa. Each sperm consists of a head and a tail.

REPRODUCTION GLOSSARY

afterbirth The discarded placenta.
amnion Protective "bag" filled with fluid in which the fetus develops.
cervix Opening at the bottom of the uterus.
conception Fertilization.
contractions Regular movements by the muscles of the uterus to push the fully-grown baby out of the mother's body.
copulation Sexual intercourse, after which a man's sperm may fertilize a woman's ovum.
embryo A baby in its first eight weeks of development.
epididymis Coiled tube in which sperm are stored.
fallopian tubes Pair of tubes leading from the ovaries to the uterus.
fertilization Fusion of sperm and ovum.
fetus A developing baby after the first eight weeks.
labor The period during which the mother experiences contractions.
menstruation Monthly discharge of unfertilized egg and blood from the vagina.
ovaries Pair of organs in which a woman's egg cells are stored.
ovum (plural ova) The female egg cell.
penis Male external organ for passing water and copulation.
placenta Tissue that forms in the uterus to link the mother's blood supply to her baby.
pregnancy Condition in which a woman is carrying a baby.
scrotum The pouch of skin outside the body containing a man's testes.
semen The mixture of sperm and special fluids produced by a man.
sperm The male cells.
testes (singular testis) Male organs in which sperm is produced.
twins Two children conceived at the same time; identical twins result from the splitting of an embryo at a very early stage; non-identical twins result from the fertilization of two ova.
umbilical cord Tube linking fetus to mother through the placenta.
urethra Tube inside the penis through which semen leaves a man's body.
uterus Hollow female organ where fertilization and development take place.
vagina In a woman, the canal leading from the cervix to the exterior of the body.
womb The uterus.

△ An ovum is about 0.1–0.2 mm in diamater. In just nine months, one fertilized ovum will divide to form the two million cells that make up the tissues, organs and fluids of the new-born baby's body.

▽ An ultrasound picture of a baby in the womb. A scan may be given to check the size, health, and position of the baby, and to see if the mother is carrying twins. The scan uses waves to pick up the outline of the baby. It is a safer method than an x-ray.

The Digestive System

The digestive system is the body's fuel processing plant. The food and drink you consume is turned partly into materials to rebuild and replace the body's cells, and partly into energy.

The body produces chemical substances called enzymes, which digest (break down) the food so it can be absorbed. Digestion begins in the mouth, where saliva contains the first of the many enzymes. In the stomach more chemicals are poured on the food to break it down still further. From the stomach the partly digested food goes through the long tube called the small intestine, where most digestion is done. Liquids are processed by the kidneys, which filter out any substances the body still needs.

▽ The stomach squeezes and moves food along, as gastric juices break down the food into a kind of soup. In the small intestine, bile and other juices mix with the soup. Fats, sugars, proteins, and vitamins move into the bloodstream. Finally water and waste move into the large intestine. Solid waste is evacuated by way of the rectum.

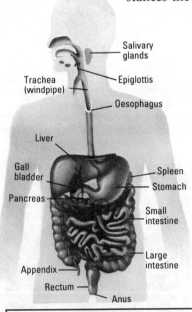

Salivary glands
Trachea (windpipe)
Epiglottis
Oesophagus
Liver
Gall bladder
Pancreas
Spleen
Stomach
Small intestine
Large intestine
Appendix
Rectum
Anus

DIGESTION FACTS

The gullet, or esophagus, is a tube about 10 in (250 mm) long and ½–1 in (12–25 mm) in diameter. It takes food from the mouth to the stomach.

The stomach contains the powerful hydrochloric acid, which breaks down food and kills germs; it is protected against the effects of this acid by a lining of mucus (a slimy substance which coats the walls).

The small intestine is about 20 ft (6 m) long. It is about 1½ in (40 mm) in diameter. Here food is digested and absorbed. Remaining material passes into the large intestine.

The large intestine is about 5 ft (1.5 m) long and 2 in (50 mm) in diameter. Much of the water from the undigested material is absorbed at this point.

The appendix is a thin pouch about 3½ in (90 mm) long. It seems to have no function in the human digestive system, though it has an important role in grass-eating animals.

FOOD FACTS

Cholesterol, a fat in eggs and dairy products; too much can increase the risk of a heart attack.
Insufficient iron can lead to anemia. Iron is found in meat, fruit, and vegetables.

Too much salt in the diet can lead to high blood pressure.
Scurvy, a disease producing swollen gums and inflamed skin spots, can result from not having enough Vitamin C (found in fruit and vegetables).

The Dangers of Drugs

Drugs are chemical substances used on the human body, mainly as medicines to cure illnesses. They are made from plants, animal products, and minerals. Many of the plant and animal product drugs have been replaced with synthetic versions made in laboratories.

Some drugs, if taken to excess, can become addictive – that is, the user cannot do without them. These include many medicinal drugs, such as painkillers and sleeping pills, as well as illegal drugs such as heroin and cocaine.

People vary in their reaction to different drugs. Some people become addicted to alcohol, for example, whereas others do not. Nearly all drugs, however, will harm the body in one or more ways, if they are used to excess. For example, sniffing, or "snorting," cocaine will eventually damage the mucus membrane of the nose. Marijuana has been found to harm certain brain cells. And the link between ordinary cigarettes and such diseases as emphysema and lung cancer is now well established. It is estimated that some 300,000 deaths in the United States each year are related to smoking.

Some of the effects that accompany the taking of drugs may not wear off for weeks, while continued use of drugs may lower the body's natural immunity system, making it less able to withstand infection.

Certain kinds of drug abuse are especially dangerous in girls and women. Some drugs can harm the female reproductive organs and even cause birth defects. Babies born of mothers addicted to heroin are already addicted at birth.

In recent years drug abuse has become an extremely serious problem in the United States, especially among young people, including schoolchildren. At even mild levels, drug-taking impairs performance in school, and severe addiction robs the person of the

Addictive Drugs

Alcohol

Cannabis

Cocaine

Heroin

Syringe

Barbiturates

Glue

Aerosol

△ Some of the substances used by drug addicts: alcohol, cannabis, cocaine, barbiturates, and amphetamines, glue (in cans, tubes and aerosols).

INFORMATION AND HELP

National Clearinghouse for Alcohol and Drug Information (NCADI) (address: PO Box 2345, Rockville MD 20852). This federal government organization provides free information on all aspects of drug use and can also put people in touch with local centers dealing with drug-related problems.

Alcoholics Anonymous is a self-help organization with groups meeting in all parts of the country. The local phone book will have the number of the nearest contact.

There are many other national and local organizations dedicated to helping people with drug problems, some of which have toll-free telephone numbers. These include:

1-800-662 HELP (National Institute on Drug Abuse Information and Referral line); Monday through Friday 8:30 a.m. – 4:30 p.m.

1-800-COCAINE (Cocaine Helpline) Monday through Friday 9:00 a.m. – 3:00 a.m.; Saturday and Sunday 12 noon – 3:00 a.m.

will to do anything except take another dose of the drug he or she is hooked on.

In addition to the threats posed by the drug itself, there are other threats linked to certain drugs. People who drive while intoxicated are much more likely to cause an accident than when sober. Another danger these days is the risk of getting AIDS through injecting drugs with a contaminated needle.

FACTS ABOUT DRUGS

alcohol A depressant, it releases inhibitions, dulls senses, and slows reflexes. Over a period of time it can damage organs, especially the liver.

amphetamines Addictive drugs, also called "uppers." After a short period of elation the user feels depressed and persecuted and may behave violently. A new illegal amphetamine, called "ecstasy," kills certain kinds of brain cell.

barbiturates Sometimes used as sleeping drugs; they can quickly become addictive; they may cause death if used with alcohol.

cocaine A dangerously addictive stimulant, especially in "freebase" forms such as "crack," which are smoked and reach the brain almost immediately. Cocaine increases the heart rate and narrows the blood vessels and can cause a cardiac arrest or stroke. An overdose can cause death.

heroin A powerfully addictive opiate drug, also called "junk," "smack," or "horse." It causes nausea, panic, and insomnia; withdrawal symptoms are very severe. Overdoses and contaminated supplies can trigger convulsions, coma, even death.

inhalants These include many substances found in the home, including glue, lighter fluid, and aerosols. Sniffing these substances may cause loss of consciousness or suffocation. Prolonged use can damage the brain, kidneys, or liver.

LSD (lysergic acid diethylamide) Known as "acid." Produces hallucinations – visions and distortions in sound. For some users LSD brings a temporary feeling of happiness and relaxation; for others it leads to feelings of anxiety and fear. Heavy users may develop brain damage.

marijuana Also called "pot," "grass," or "hash." The marijuana now available is far more powerful and dangerous than that smoked in the 1960s. Even small doses can damage the memory, and prolonged use is far more likely to cause cancer than smoking ordinary cigarettes.

nicotine The addictive drug in tobacco. Besides tending to cause cancer, it contracts the blood vessels and causes increased blood pressure, putting a strain on the heart.

PCP (phencyclidine) Also called "angel dust," this drug alters perception and may cause hallucinations and bizarre, dangerous behavior, similar to that of schizophrenics. Long-term use can cause permanent brain damage.

HUMAN BODY GLOSSARY

abscess A painful, swollen area inside the body, caused by bacteria and filled with pus. A gumboil is a type of abscess caused by an infected tooth.

acne Blackheads or whiteheads caused by overactivity and inflammation of the oil glands in the skin. Four out of five teenagers suffer from it.

Adam's apple The piece of cartilage that sticks out over the front of the larynx. It is more prominent in men than in women.

adenoids Small glands made of lymph tissue at the back of the nasal passages. They help to protect the lungs from infection.

adolescence Development from a child to an adult.

adrenaline A hormone that stimulates the heart and increases muscular strength and endurance.

allergy A reaction, such as a running nose, rash, or wheezing, caused when a person is sensitive to certain substances. Hay fever is an allergy to pollen.

amino acids The chemical substances that make up proteins. When protein in food is digested (broken down), the amino acids are transported around the body and assembled into new proteins in the cells.

antibiotics Drugs that can kill bacteria by preventing them from growing or reproducing.

antibodies Substances produced by the body's immune system. They destroy harmful bacteria and viruses.

antiseptics Substances that kill certain micro-organisms or slow down their growth.

arteries Any blood vessels that carry oxygen-rich blood away from the heart to the rest of the body.

bacteria Microscopic one-celled organisms found everywhere – in water, in soil, and on and in our bodies. Most are harmless; some are essential, such as those in the intestines; a few cause disease.

benign Word used to describe a tumor or growth that is harmless and not likely to become worse.

bile Greenish liquid produced by the liver. It is stored in a sac called the gall bladder and helps to digest fat in the small intestine.

blood vessel Any of the many tubes – arteries, veins, and capillaries – that carry blood around the body.

bronchus One of the branches of the windpipe, leading to the lungs.

capillaries The smallest type of blood vessel.

cardiac Referring to the heart.

cartilage Soft, elastic tissue, often called gristle.

cells The basic living units of the body, sometimes called the "building blocks" of life. Every part of the body is made up of cells – one million million of them in an average man.

central nervous system The brain and spinal cord.

chromosome One of 46 structures found in the nucleus of every human cell. Chromosomes carry the genes which determine inherited characteristics, such as sex, hair color, and height.

colon Lower part of the large intestine.

coronary Referring to the blood vessels that supply the heart. Coronary arteries over the surface of the heart provide oxygen for its cells.

diaphragm Flat muscle that separates the chest from the abdomen.

DNA (Deoxyribonucleic Acid) Complicated chemical that makes up genes and chromosomes.

enzymes Chemical substances that speed up chemical reactions within the body and control processes such as digestion.

epiglottis Small flap at the back of the tongue that blocks the windpipe when you swallow and so prevents food from "going down the wrong way."

esophagus Gullet leading from the throat to the stomach.

Esophagus

follicle Small pocket in the skin from which a single hair grows.
gall bladder Small sac, about 3–4 in (80–100 mm) long, that stores bile.
genes Combinations of DNA that make up the chromosomes in each cell.

The lymphatic system

The main endocrine glands of the body

glands Organs in the body, such as the salivary glands, kidneys, and liver, that produce or work on chemical substances.
hormones Sometimes called the body's chemical messengers; produced in certain glands and released into the blood. They control many body processes, such as growth and the amount of sugar in the blood.
immune system The body's own defenses against infection.
intestines The long tube, beginning at the stomach and ending at the anus, in which food is digested.
keratin The hard substance found in hair, nails, and skin.
kidneys Two organs that filter waste from the blood and produce urine, which collects in the bladder. They lie on each side of the spine.
larynx The voice box, located at the top of the trachea and containing the vocal cords.
ligaments Tough elastic bands of tissue that hold bones together at a joint.
liver The body's largest gland; it stores iron and some glucose, processes amino acids, and produces bile.
lymph Clear liquid that contains white blood cells. It flows through a set of vessels (tubes) called the "lymphatic system."
marrow Soft, jelly-like substance found in the center of bones; blood cells are made in some bone marrow.
membrane Thin layer of cells which lines or covers various parts of the body.
micro-organisms Tiny living things such as bacteria and viruses; often called germs.
organ Group of tissues that work together, for example the heart or the liver.
pancreas Gland that produces the hormone insulin, that controls the level of glucose in the blood.
plasma Liquid part of blood.
proteins Body-building chemicals, made of amino acids.
pulse Rhythmic throbbing which can be felt in the arteries as your heart beats.
pus Whitish-yellow liquid produced in certain infections.
reflex actions Actions that are automatic and cannot be controlled by thinking about them.
renal Referring to the kidneys.
respiration Breathing; also the use of oxygen in the cells to release energy from glucose and the release of carbon dioxide.

saliva Liquid released by three pairs of glands in the mouth; it starts digestion.

sebaceous gland Oil-producing gland in the skin.

sinuses Four sets of cavities in the skull, where the air you breathe in is warmed.

spinal cord Thick cord of nerves which begins at the base of the brain and extends to the bottom of the back.

spleen Organ that helps to fight infection.

tendons Very strong bands of tissue which connect muscles to bones.

thymus Gland in the lower neck, which helps in the immune process.

thyroid Gland in the neck that produces a hormone, thyroxine, which controls growth rate and the speed of chemical processes.

tissues Groups of similar cells which form various parts of the body, such as nerves and muscles.

trachea Windpipe, leading from the larynx to the lungs.

tumor Swelling caused by abnormal growth of cells. It may be benign (unharmful) or cancerous.

ulcer Open sore on the skin, or on a membrane inside the body.

ureters Tubes that carry urine from the kidneys to the bladder.

urethra Tube that leads from the bladder to the outside of the body.

veins Blood vessels that carry used blood back to the heart.

viruses Micro-organisms that cause disease if they invade the body.

vitamins Group of about 15 substances found in food. They are needed for health.

vocal cords Two ligaments stretched across the larynx. They vibrate as air passes over them, enabling speech.

AIDS

AIDS stands for Acquired Immune Deficiency Syndrome. It is a serious disorder brought about by a virus called Human Immunodeficiency Virus. It attacks the white blood cells which form part of the body's immune system guarding the body against disease.

Cause is one of two viruses in the group called retroviruses.

Symptoms include diarrhea, fever, tiredness, night sweats, loss of appetite and weight, and enlarged lymph glands.

Transmission is by intimate sexual contact, or by exposure to infected blood (for example, by sharing hypodermic needles with an infected person). An infected woman can pass the virus to her fetus.

Treatment is still a matter of experiment; no cure has yet been found.

▷ The AIDS virus prevents the white blood cells, the body's natural defense mechanism, from working. 1. The virus attaches itself to and 2. moves into a white blood cell. Once inside 3., the core of the virus breaks open and releases DNA to match that of the white blood cell. The blood cell makes copies of the virus and dies (4.). When the body has lost a large number of white blood cells it is not protected from even minor infections.

AIDS virus
1
White blood cells
Nucleus with chromosomes
Outer coat of virus
2
3
Core
4
Virus DNA

Animals

The last dinosaur died 65 million years ago, the dodo is dead, and other animals are in danger of extinction, yet there are still over two million species left on this planet, from the speedy cheetah to the tardy snail, and from the egg-laying platypus to the remarkably skilled termite.

Animals dominate the Earth today. They have done so for only about 500 million years, a fraction of the Earth's 4,600-million-year existence. The number of species (kinds) is probably at least two million, and nobody can calculate how many different individuals there are.

Animal life became possible when the Earth built up a sufficient stock of oxygen, which all animals must breathe in order to live. Some, such as fish, extract oxygen from the waters of the oceans and rivers. Others draw it from the atmosphere. Animals also depend on plants for their food, either directly, as cows do, or indirectly, as flesh-eating animals such as lions and wolves do.

The easiest way to divide the many species of animals is into the vertebrates – those with backbones – and the invertebrates – those without.

The vertebrates are the "higher" animals, those with the most developed brains. They are, in ascending order of development, fishes, amphibians, reptiles, birds, and mammals. They include all the large animals which appear to rule the world. But they are not necessarily the most successful.

The invertebrates – all the rest – are much simpler creatures. Some, such as amoebas and sponges, are very simple indeed. Others, especially the insects, are more complex and very successful. There are more kinds and total numbers of insects than of any other land-based creature. They make their

△ Fossils are the preserved remains of plants and animals that died millions of years ago. This spider has been preserved in amber, the hardened resin from pine trees.

▽ This fossil is a trilobite. I lived on the sea bed before even dinosaurs were around.

▷ The English naturalist, Charles Darwin (1809–1882), put forward the theory that all living things have evolved (developed) over millions of years from primitive forms of life.

homes almost everywhere on land, and if something can be eaten, an insect has evolved that can eat it. Most insects themselves are in danger of being eaten by some other creature.

Large numbers of animals live in the seas, which cover almost three-quarters of the Earth's surface. There are fish, and countless millions of invertebrates such as krill, squid, jellyfish, and other smaller creatures. These animals take their oxygen from water. There are also a few mammals – whales, seals, and their relatives – that have moved from land to live in water. They still breathe air.

One of the big differences between animals and plants is that animals are free to move about. A number of animals move regularly from one place to another, in the process we call migration.

The most obvious migration is that of birds. Many species spend the winter months in the warmer parts of the world, nearer the Equator, and fly north or south to temperate climates to lay their eggs and rear their young. Some insects migrate, notably the monarch butterflies of North America, which fly south to hibernate.

Some mammals also migrate. For example, in East Africa grazing animals – antelopes, zebras, giraffes, and others – move from place to place in a huge circle to graze on fresh vegetation. In the north, caribou and reindeer move south in the winter and north in the summer.

At sea, shoals of fish and smaller creatures swim from place to place in search of their food, and they are followed by larger fish, such as sharks, and by whales.

▷ Darwin noticed differences in the finches that lived on several islands in the Pacific, and this led him to his theory of evolution, which he called "natural selection." It took him another 20 years to work out all the implications.

THE ANIMAL KINGDOM

▽ The main groups in the animal kingdom. The principal stem includes the lower, but very numerous, groups such as brachiopods, molluscs, and arthropods. The vertebrate animals (mammals, birds, and reptiles, for instance) include the most advanced animals. Some of the classes of worm and other small groups have been omitted.

◁ An Arctic tern on its nest.

▽ The swifts include the world's fastest flyer in level flight. Swifts may spend weeks in the air, catching insects and even sleeping on the wing. Their small feet render them virtually helpless on level ground.

MIGRATION

Longest bird migration is by the Arctic tern (*Sterna paradisaea*), which leads a life of perpetual summer. It breeds in the Arctic, but leaves as summer ends and flies 11,000 miles (18,000 km) to Antarctica. At the end of the Antarctic summer it flies back to its breeding ground – so making a round trip of 22,000 miles (36,000 km).
Longest mammal migration is by the Alaska seal (*Callorhinus ursinus*), which does a round trip of 6,000 miles (9,600 km).
Most traveled butterfly is the monarch butterfly (*Danaus plexippus*) of North America, which migrates 2,500 miles (4,000 km) from Hudson Bay to Florida and back. Occasionally, individuals reach Europe.

◁ The tortoise lives longer than any other animal.

▽ The great ram's horn is a water-dwelling mollusc.

ANIMAL SPEED RECORDS

	mph	km/h		mph	km/h
Spine-tailed			Greyhound	39	63
swift	106	170	Rabbit	35	56
Cheetah	70	112	Giraffe	32	51
Sailfish	68	109	Grizzly bear	30	48
Pronghorn			Cat	30	48
antelope	61	98	Elephant	25	40
Racing			Sea lion	25	40
pigeon	60	97	Black mamba	20	32
Lion	50	80	Bee	11	18
Gazelle	50	80	Pig	11	18
Hare	45	72	Chicken	9	14
Zebra	40	64	Spider	1.17	1.88
Racehorse	40	64	Giant tortoise	.17	.27
Shark	40	64	Snail	0.03	0.05

Spider

Woodlouse

Lugworm

Dahlia Anemone

Starfish

Animals without Backbones

Animals without backbones are called *invertebrates*. Most of them do not have any form of internal skeleton, though some, such as the cuttlefish, have internal shells. Many have *exoskeletons* (external skeletons). Invertebrates range from simple sponges and worms to snails and insects. Many of them live in water.

There are more than 20 *phyla* (groups) of invertebrates. Several of them are particularly important. The coelenterates include jellyfish, sea anemones, and corals. Most molluscs have shells. They include winkles, oysters, limpets, snails, octopuses, and squids.

Annelids are worms of various kinds, including the familiar earthworms. Arthropods (the name means "joint-footed") are very diverse indeed. They include insects, spiders, centipedes, millipedes, and crustaceans such as crabs, lobsters, and woodlice. Echinoderms are star-like animals with five limbs. They include starfish and sea urchins.

The chordates are a very mixed bunch. They have some kind of internal rod to support the body, although some lose it when they are adults. There are about 1,300 species that rank as invertebrates, including seasquirts and salps. The most important chordates are the vertebrates, or animals with true backbones.

INVERTEBRATE RECORDS

Largest spiders are some of the bird-eating spiders (family Theraphosidae) of South America, whose bodies are more than 3 inches (75 mm) long with a leg span of about 10 inches (250 mm).

Largest centipede is the giant scolpender (*Scolpendra giganta*) of Central America. Its body is up to 12 inches (300 mm) long and 1 inch (25 mm) wide. It is large enough to feed on mice and lizards, as well as insects.

Centipedes with most legs are those in the order Geophilomorpha. Adults may have up to 177 pairs of legs, or 354 legs altogether.

Millipedes with most legs are generally the oldest. Several species are known to have almost 750 legs.

ANIMALS

175

INVERTEBRATE CLASSIFICATION

Phylum	Common name, if any	Number of species
Mesozoa	None	About 50
Porifera	Sponges	About 5,000
Coelenterata	Jellyfish and relatives	About 9,500
Ctenophora	Comb jellies	About 100
Platyhelminthes	Flatworms	About 5,500
Nemertina	Ribbonworms	750
Aschelminthes	Roundworms and others	11,800
Gastrotricha	Hairy backs	175
Kinorhyncha	None	100
Acanthocephala	Thorny-headed worms	300
Entoprocta	None	60
Ectoprocta	Moss animals or bryozoans	4,000
Brachiopoda	Lamp shells	260
Annelida	Earthworms and relatives	About 7,000
Arthropoda	Spiders, insects, crustaceans	About 1,150,000
Sipunculoidea	Peanut worms	250
Echiuroidea	Echiurid worms	60
Pentastomida	Tongue worms	70
Tardigrada	Water bears	180
Mollusca	Molluscs	More than 46,000
Chaetognatha	Arrow worms	50
Pogohophora	Beard worms	About 80
Echinodermata	Starfish and relatives	About 5,500
Hemichordata	Acorn worms and relatives	90
Chordata	Chordates	About 1,300 plus back-boned animals

Cockle

Portuguese man of war

Millipede

Edible crab

△ The western marbled white butterfly is found in central and southern Europe and in North Africa.

△ Wood ants make their nests in wooded areas, covering the mounds with leaves and twigs.

△ The common pond skater lives on the surface of still water.

▽ The white-tailed bumblebee often nests in old mouse holes.

INSECTS

Of all forms of life, the most varied are the insects. More than 1,000,000 species are known, and more are being discovered and classified every year. There are more species of insects than all of the rest of the animal kingdom put together. The number of individual insects is beyond calculation.

An adult insect has six legs and a body in three sections with a hard outer casing. Most adult insects have wings. They have what are called compound eyes, which may have as many as 30,000 tiny lenses called facets. Each facet conveys a very small part of the whole picture to the insect's brain.

Insects have senses of smell and taste, and many kinds can hear, too. They have cold blood, which may be colorless, green, or yellow.

Insects are grouped into 33 orders, each containing many families, genera, and species. Some orders of insects are little known, and have no common name.

Apterygote insects are the simplest kinds. They have no wings, and the young are similar in appearance to the adults, except in size. They include the familiar silverfish, which is often found in houses.

Exopterygote insects mostly have wings. They pass through three stages of development – egg, nymph, and adult. They include dragonflies, mayflies, and stoneflies, which pass their pre-adult life in water; grasshoppers; stick insects; cockroaches; termites; earwigs; lice; and the true bugs, including cicadas and aphids.

Endopterygote insects are also winged. They go through four stages of development: egg, larva, pupa, and adult. They include beetles, the most numerous of the lot; butterflies and moths; true flies; bees, wasps, and ants, which, with termites, are called the "social insects"; and caddis flies, whose larvae live in water.

△ The housefly is a pest that carries disease.

△ The great diving beetle is found mainly by ponds and streams.

△ The common wasp builds its nest with paper, which it makes by chewing wood.

▽ The caddis fly is usually seen only at night. Its wings are covered with hairs.

INSECT RECORDS

Largest insects are several forms of beetle (order Coleoptera). They include the goliath beetles (genus *Goliathus*), the rhinoceros beetle (*Dyastes hercules*) and the longhorned beetle (*Titanus giganteus*), which have all been found at sizes between 5 and 7 inches (125–175 mm) long.

Longest insects are varieties of stick insect (genera *Palophus* and *Pharnacia*), known to grow more than 12 inches (300 mm) long.

Smallest insects are the feather-winged beetles (family Ptiliidae), which are less than 1/100 inch (0.2 mm) long.

Most remarkable builders are various species of termite (order Isoptera). They build nests of soil that may be as much as 23 ft (7 m) tall, with deep cellars as well. Many species build their nests with "air conditioning," while the compass termites of Australia (*Amitermes meridionalis*) build wedge-shaped mounds with the two short sides facing north-south, so the noonday heat strikes as small a surface as possible.

Animals with Backbones

FISH

Fish form the largest group of vertebrates. There are altogether about 13,000 species. They fall into three groups: jawless fish, fish with skeletons of cartilage (gristle), and bony fish.

There are two main kinds of jawless fish – hagfish and lampreys. Instead of jaws they have circular mouths with rasping teeth. The cartilaginous fish, of which there are about 575 species, include chimeras (also known as ratfish or, sometimes, elephantfish), sharks, and rays.

The bony fishes are the most numerous. They include well-known species such as eels, herring, and salmon, as well as a large and bewildering variety of lesser-known species.

FISH RECORDS

Longest bony fish is the beluga (*Huso huso*), a kind of sturgeon found in the Caspian Sea. It has been known to grow up to 23½ ft (7.2 mm) in length, and to reach a weight of 3,000 lb (1,360 kg).

Heaviest bony fish is the ocean sunfish (*Mola mola*), which can weigh up to 2 tons.

Smallest fish and also the smallest vertebrate is the dwarf goby (*Pandaka pygmaea*), found in fresh water in the Philippines and the Marshall Islands. The maximum size for these fish is ½ inch (12 mm).

Largest shark (and largest fish) is the whale shark (*Rhincodon typhus*), which can reach a length of 50–60 ft (15–18 m), and weigh 15 tons or more.

Largest rays are the devil rays, in the family Mobulidae, which measure up to 20 ft (6 m) across. They "fly" through the water by flapping their pectoral fins like wings. Some can even leap quite high into the air.

△ The sea horse, despite its name, is a fish.

▽ Lampreys and hagfishes fasten onto other fishes with their sucker mouths.

▽ The South American piranha is small but a ferocious feeder.

FISH CLASSIFICATION

Order	Common name	No. of species	Order	Common name	No. of species
Class Agnatha: jawless fish			Cypriniformes	Carp and relatives	350
Cyclostomata	Lampreys and hagfish	45	Siluriformes	Catfish	200
			Percopsiformes	Pirate perch	10
Class Chondrichthyes: fish with a cartilage skeleton			Batrachoidi-formes	Toadfish	10
Selachii	Sharks	200	Gobiesociformes	Clingfish	100
Batoidea	Rays and skates	350	Lophiiformes	Angler fish	150
Chimeriformes	Chimeras	25	Gadiformes	Cod and relatives	450
Class Osteichthyes: fish with a bony skeleton			Beryciformes	Whalefish, squirrelfish	150
Polypteriformes	Bichirs	12	Atheriniformes	Flying fish, killifish	600
Acipenseriformes	Sturgeons	22	Zeiformes	John Dory	60
Amiiformes	Bowfin	1	Lampridiformes	Ribbonfish	50
Semionotiformes	Garpikes	7	Gasterostei-formes	Seahorses and relatives	150
Crossopterygii	Coelacanth	1	Channiformes	Snakeheads	5
Dipnoi	Lungfishes	5	Synbranchi-formes	Swamp eels and cuchias	7
Elopiformes	Tarpons	12	Scorpaeniformes	Gurnards and relatives	700
Anguilliformes	Eels	300			
Notacanthi-formes	Spiny eels	20	Dactylopteri-formes	Flying gurnards	6
Clupeiformes	Herring and relatives	350	Pegasiformes	Sea moths, dragonflies	4
Osteoglossi-formes	Bony tongues	16	Tetraodonti-formes	Triggerfish, puffer fish	250
Mormyriformes	Mormyrids	150	Pleuronecti-formes	Flatfish	500
Salmoniformes	Salmon, trout	500	Perciformes	Perch and relatives, e.g. tuna, mackerel, sea bass	6,500
Myctophiformes	Lantern fish	300			
Ctenothrissi-formes	Macristid fish	1			
Gonorhynchi formes	Milk fish	15			

△ Flatfish, such as plaice, are important commercial food fish. Young flatfish flip over on their sides during development, the mouth twisting and one eye moving across to adapt to a bottom-dwelling existence.

△ Stingrays have whip-like tails armed with poisoned spines.

Life Cycle of a Frog
1. Eggs (spawn) are laid in springtime.
2. The tadpole hatches out in two weeks.
3. Front and back legs have grown after nine weeks.
4. The frog is fully formed in about eleven weeks.

AMPHIBIANS AND REPTILES

Amphibians – animals with backbones that can live both in water and air – are the last survivors of the first true land vertebrates that ever existed. They have cold blood – that is, they take their body temperatures from their surroundings.

There are three orders of amphibians, with a total of about 3,000 species. They are caecilians (simple wormlike creatures); newts and salamanders; and toads and frogs. Most amphibians lay their eggs in water. The eggs hatch into a larval form called a tadpole.

Reptiles are animals with backbones that live by breathing air. They, too, have cold blood. The 5,000 species alive today are all that remain of a group of animals that once dominated the Earth, including dinosaurs and other giant forms.

Reptiles vary in size from 2 inches (50 mm) long to more than 30 feet (9 m). They usually have scaly skins, and most of them lay eggs. A few give birth to live young. They have lungs, like mammals, and most of them are carnivores.

There are four living orders of reptiles: alligators and crocodiles; tuataras (of which only one species exists); tortoises, terrapins, and turtles; and lizards and snakes.

△ The puff adder's poisonous fangs fold back when not in use, but swing forward when in attack (*right*).

'Hinges' of bone

Fang

Upper jaw

Lower jaw

SNAKE NOTES

Skin is changed several times a year by a process known as molting. The snake slips out of its old skin, leaving it lying like a dummy. The new skin is underneath.

Breathing for most snakes is done on one lung only. The left lung is either greatly reduced in size or missing completely.

Pit vipers have sense organs that can detect heat. These organs help them detect their prey.

Gastric juices in a snake can digest bones and teeth – but not hair and fur.

Burrowing snakes burrow into the ground. They feed largely on ants and termites.

◁ The adder has a zigzag pattern along its back.

AMPHIBIAN AND REPTILE RECORDS

Largest amphibians are the giant salamanders (genus *Megalobatrachus*) of China and Japan, specimens of which have been known to grow up to 5 ft (1.5 m).

Longest-lived amphibians are probably Japanese giant salamanders (*Megalobatrachus japonicus*), specimens of which have lived up to 60 years in captivity.

Largest frog is the goliath frog (*Gigantorana goliath*) of Africa. This amphibian habitually grows to a body length of 12 inches (300 mm) but many considerably larger specimens have been reported.

Largest reptile is the estuarine crocodile (*Crocodylus porosus*), which can grow up to 20 ft (6 m).

Largest marine turtle is the leathery or leatherback turtle (*Dermochelys coriacea*), whose shell may be 6 ft (1.8 m) long, with a flipper-to-flipper stretch of 12 ft (3.6 m), and a weight of more than 1,600 lb (725 kg).

Largest land tortoise is the giant tortoise (*Testudo gigantea*), which may have a shell 6 ft (1.8 m) long, and a weight of 500 lb (225 kg) or more.

Largest lizard is the Komodo dragon (*Varanus komodoensis*), which can grow up to 10 ft (3 m) long and weigh 250 lb (113 kg).

Largest snakes are the anaconda (*Eunectes murinus*) and the reticulated python (*Python reticulatus*), both of which are reported to grow up to 30 ft (9 m) long.

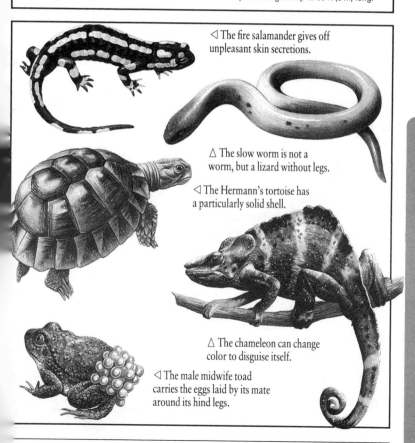

◁ The fire salamander gives off unpleasant skin secretions.

△ The slow worm is not a worm, but a lizard without legs.

◁ The Hermann's tortoise has a particularly solid shell.

△ The chameleon can change color to disguise itself.

◁ The male midwife toad carries the eggs laid by its mate around its hind legs.

△ Contour feathers, like the one shown here, cover the outer body of the bird and give it a smooth shape.

BIRDS

Birds are animals with feathers, wings, and beaks. Nearly all of them can fly. They are warm-blooded – they make their heat from the food they eat.

There are nearly 11,000 species of bird, and they are grouped into 27 orders. Birds can be classified in many different ways. Water birds spend their lives on or near water. They include wildfowl – ducks, geese, and swans – waders, gulls, albatrosses, and penguins.

Perching birds are land-based birds that spend their lives in trees or other high places when they are not flying. Game birds include chicken, guinea fowl, partridges, and turkeys. Birds of prey hunt other birds and small mammals. They include eagles, hawks, and vultures. Owls, which are mostly night-flying, also hunt game.

Birds are directly descended from reptiles. They have some links with their ancestors: many birds have scales on their legs, like those of reptiles, while their feathers are made of the same substance – keratin – as scales.

A bird makes full use of its wings in flight. On takeoff the wings and feet are used to lift the bird off the ground. On landing, the fully-spread flight feathers act like a brake; the tail is kept low, and the feet are pushed out to check speed.

Feathers grow unevenly on a bird's body. Some parts are well covered, others are lightly protected. Flight feathers grow on the wings, contour feathers cover the body, and downy feathers are found on the breast. A bird may have between 1,300 and 12,000 feathers. The skeleton is very light; this makes flight easier.

BIRD RECORDS

Largest bird is the male African ostrich (*Struthio camelus*), which grows to a height of about 8 ft (2.5 m). Specimens weighing as much as 340 lb (155 kg) have been found.

Heaviest flying bird is the Kori bustard (*Choriotis kori*) of eastern and southern Africa, which may weigh as much as 40 lb (18 kg).

Smallest bird is the bee hummingbird (*Calyptae helenae*) of Cuba. It is about 2¼ in (60 mm) long and weighs only about 0,07 oz (2 g). Its nest would fit into half a walnut shell.

Greatest wingspan belongs to the male wandering albatross (*Diomedea exulans*) which has an average wingspan of 10 ft (3 m). It can stay in the air for days.

Fastest fliers are various species of spine-tailed swifts (family Apodidae), which fly at about 60 mph (100 km/h). Duck hawks and golden eagles dive at speeds estimated at up to 180 mph (290 km/h).

Fastest runner is the ostrich, which can maintain a speed of 34 mph (55 km/h), with bursts up to 50 mph (80 km/h).

▽ The ostrich is the world's largest living bird. Although it cannot fly, it is faster on land than any other bird, and its height enables it to see danger approaching from a long way off.

The broad wings of an eagle allow it to soar high up in the sky.

The narrow, pointed wings of a swift enable it to fly and turn quickly.

Albatrosses can glide for days with the help of their long wings.

The short, wide, and powerful wings of a duck give it plenty of lift, so it can leave the water quickly if disturbed.

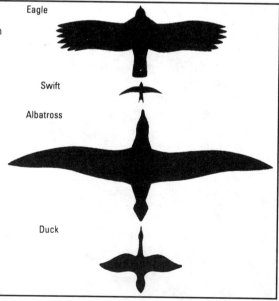

Eagle

Swift

Albatross

Duck

BIRD CLASSIFICATION

Order	Common name	No. of species	Order	Common name	No. of species
Passeriformes	Perching birds; passerines	5,000	Gruiformes	Cranes and relatives	197
Piciformes	Woodpeckers and relatives	400	Galliformes	Game birds	151
Coraciformes	Kingfishers and relatives	190	Falconiformes	Birds of prey	271
Coliformes	Mousebirds	6	Anseriformes	Ducks and relatives	148
Trogoniformes	Trogons	36	Ciconiiformes	Storks and relatives	120
Apodiformes	Swifts and relatives	387	Pelecaniformes	Pelicans and relatives	59
Caprimulgiformes	Nightjars and relatives	94	Procellariiformes	Albatrosses and relatives	91
Strigiformes	Owls	130	Sphenisciformes	Penguins	18
Cuculiformes	Cuckoos and relatives	147	Gaviformes	Divers	5
Psittaciformes	Parrot family	315	Podicipediformes	Grebes	21
Columbiformes	Pigeons and relatives	305	Tinamiformes	Tinamous	50
Charadriformes	Gulls and relatives (mainly waders)	295	Cassuariiformes	Emu and cassowaries	4
			Rheiformes	Rheas	2
			Struthioniformes	Ostrich	1
			Apterygiformes	Kiwis	3

△ Bills for various purposes. The eagle's hooked bill is for plucking and tearing the flesh of prey. The blue tit (*above*) feeds on seeds and fruit. The heron is a fish-eater, while the wading avocet skims the mud for small creatures. Blackbirds catch worms and insects. The tree creeper uses its bill to extract insects and spiders from the bark.

▽ The pelican uses the pouch beneath its large bill to store fish caught at sea.

△ The kingfisher dives into ponds and rivers to catch small fish.

Small perching bird

Eagle

Duck

Woodpecker

Grebe

△ Different birds' feet. From top, clockwise – perching, hunting, partly webbed (grebes and divers), climbing, fully webbed for swimming.

△ A gentoo penguin. Penguins are flightless, but excellent swimmers.

▽ The owl is a nocturnal hunter, with superb hearing and night vision.

△ The sparrow is found worldwide, usually close to human settlement.

Mammals

Mammals are animals whose females feed their young on milk from their *mammary glands* (breasts). Most mammals retain their young inside their bodies for a period of development. A few, called the monotremes – platypuses, and echidnas – lay eggs. Some, known as the marsupials, such as kangaroos and wombats, give birth to young that are only partly developed and have to crawl into a pouch on the mother's belly to continue growing.

Even among the other mammals, the young vary in how developed they are when they are born. Some newly-born animals, such as antelopes and horses, can get to their feet and walk within an hour or so of being born. Others, such as puppies and kittens, can do nothing for themselves for some days.

The basic mammal type is an animal with four legs, breathing air, and having warm blood. But there are exceptions. Besides the monotremes and the marsupials, there are two groups of sea mammals. Seals have four flippers instead of legs, while whales and porpoises have just one pair of flippers.

△ Bats are the only mammals that truly fly. Their wings are delicate membranes stretched between the "fingers" of their forelimbs. This horseshoe bat flies within 3 ft (1 m) of the ground, and its flight is slow, almost like that of a butterfly.

Curiosity

Happiness

Fear

Excitement

△ Chimpanzees are highly developed social animals. Each individual has a personality, and a chimp's facial expression reveals its emotions. Four typical expressions are shown here.

MAMMAL RECORDS

Largest mammal is the blue whale (*Balaenoptera musculus*), which can be up to 100 ft (30 m) in length.

Largest land mammal is the African elephant (*Loxodonta africana*) it can be up to 11½ ft (3.5 m) tall and weigh 7 tons.

Smallest mammal is Savi's pygmy shrew (*Suncus etruscus*), which has a head and body length of 1½ inches (38 mm) and a tail about 1 inch (25 mm) long. Its weight is less than 1/10 oz (2.8 gm).

Tallest mammal is the giraffe (*Giraffa camelopardis*), which can be as much as 18 ft (5.5 m) tall, and can weigh up to 1 ton.

△ Wild rabbit. Hares and rabbits belong to the order Lagomorpha.

△ Unlike most rodents, squirrels build their nests or dreys in trees.

CLASSIFICATION OF MAMMALS

There are about 4,000 species of mammal, grouped into 19 orders and about 120 families.

Order	Animals	No. of species
Monotremata	Egg-laying mammals – the platypus and echidnas	6
Marsupialia	Pouched mammals, including kangaroos, opossums, koalas	238
Insectivora	Insect-eating animals including hedgehogs, moles, and shrews	293
Chiroptera	Bats, the only mammals that can really fly	690
Primates	Lemurs, monkeys, apes, humans	171
Edentata	Anteaters, armadillos, sloths	30
Pholidota	Pangolins (scaly anteaters)	7
Dermoptera	Flying lemurs	2
Rodentia	Rodents, gnawing animals, including beavers, capybara, hamsters, mice, porcupines, rats, squirrels	1,792
Lagomorpha	Hares, pikas, rabbits	64
Cetacea	Whales, dolphins, porpoises	82
Carnivora	Flesh-eating animals such as bears, cats, dogs, pandas, raccoons	245
Pinnepedia	Seals, sea lions, walrus	32
Artiodactyla	Hoofed mammals with an even number of toes, including antelopes, camels, cattle, deer, giraffe, hippopotamuses, pigs	377
Perissodactyla	Hoofed mammals with an odd number of toes – rhinoceroses, horses and zebras, tapirs	15
Sirenia	Water mammals – dugong, manatees	4
Tubulidentata	The aardvark	1
Hyracoidea	Hyraxes	6
Proboscidea	Elephants	2

15   10   3   1   Birth

▽ Elephants grow slowly and are among the longest-lived of animals. They are classed in an order of their own.

DOGS

The dog is probably the favorite companion of human beings. For thousands of years dogs have guarded people's homes, herded their cattle and sheep, helped with hunting for food, and played with their children.

All the members of the dog family, Canidae, belong to the carnivores, the flesh-eaters. They tend to hunt in packs. The domestic dog, *Canis familiaris*, is the best known member of the family. There are more than 100 breeds of domestic dog.

Wild dogs are found in India, Siberia, southeastern Asia, southern and eastern Africa, Brazil, and the Guianas. The Australian dingo is a semi-wild dog, which may have been domesticated a long time ago. Other members of the dog family include the North American coyote, fennecs, foxes, jackals, and wolves.

Domestic dogs are divided into sporting and non-sporting groups. Sporting groups include gundogs, such as pointers, retrievers, setters, and spaniels; and hounds, such as Afghans, beagles, and bloodhounds; and terriers. Non-sporting dogs include working dogs such as collies and German shepherds; and utility dogs include all the others.

△ The red fox is an adaptable animal and is found in both the town and the countryside.

▽ Wolves live in open country and forests. They work closely together when hunting for food.

DOG RECORDS

Heaviest domestic dog is the St. Bernard, which weighs up to 220 lb (100 kg) and stands 27 in (700 mm) high at the shoulders.

Tallest domestic dog is the Irish wolfhound, which is 31 inches (800 mm) high at the shoulders, and well over 6 ft (1.8 m) when standing on its hind legs.

Smallest domestic dogs are miniature breeds of the chihuahua, poodle, and Yorkshire terrier, which weigh 1 lb (0.45 kg) or less.

Largest wild dogs are timber wolves (*Canis lupus*), which stand 31 inches (800 mm) high at the shoulders and weigh up to 125 lb (56 kg).

Fastest domestic dogs are the saluki, timed at speeds up to 43 mph (69 km/h) and the greyhound 37 mph (60 km/h).

▽ West highland terriers were traditionally used for hunting.

◁ Wild cape dogs stand by their prey.

▷ Greyhounds are the fastest dogs on flat ground.

▽ The toy poodle is the smallest breed of poodle.

◁ The dog Laika was the first living creature in space, sent by the Soviets in Sputnik 2 in 1957.

THE CAT FAMILY

Cats are the most purely carnivorous carnivores. They have teeth for stabbing and slicing, but not for chewing. Their lithe bodies are built for speed, and their sharp claws are further formidable weapons. Except for differences in size, all kinds of cat are very similar animals. The lioness roaming through the African shrubland is only a larger version of the small domestic cat. Because of these similarities all cats belong to one family, Felidae.

The cat family also includes tigers, jaguars, leopards, cheetahs, pumas, caracals, lynxes, servals, ocelots, and several small wild cats.

Domestic cats fall into two main groups – short-haired and long-haired. Short-haired cats include Burmese, Manx, Abyssinian, and Siamese. Siamese were originally bred in Thailand, where they were royal sacred cats. The penalty for stealing one was death. Long-haired cats include the different kinds of Persian and Angora cats.

△ Cats are unique among carnivores in having retracting claws. The claws are shown above retracted and (*lower picture*) extended.

▽ Members of the cat family: lion, domestic cat, wild cat, caracal, black leopard, snow leopard, and tiger.

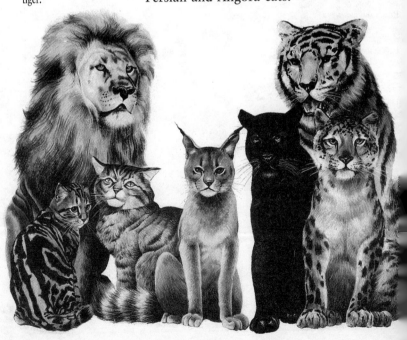

The Americas are particularly rich in cat species, some of which are found nowhere else in the world. The jaguar (*Panthera onca*) of South America is the largest and fiercest of the American cats. It is quite untamable and may attack humans. The puma (*Felis concolor*), also called cougar or mountain lion, is another cat found only in America. Smaller than these two is the ocelot (*Felis pardalis*) of South America.

Cats cannot see in total darkness, but they can see far better in the dark than people. At the back of their eyes there is a reflecting layer which sends light back through the sensitive cells, so increasing the effect of minute amounts of light on the brain.

Iris closed

Iris opened

CAT RECORDS

Largest member of the cat family is the Siberian tiger (all tigers are *Panthera tigris*). Males have been found up to 10½ ft (3.2 m) long, standing 3 ft (900 mm) tall at the shoulder.

Smallest wild cat is probably the rusty-spotted cat (*Felis rubiginosa*) that lives in Sri Lanka and southern India. Males have a body length that may be as little as 16 inches (400 mm), plus a tail of 9 inches (230 mm).

Rarest of the cats is probably the Java tiger, now found in only two areas of the Indonesian island of Java. About a dozen are thought to survive.

Longest lived of the big cats is probably the lion (*Panthera leo*), which is known to live more than 25 years in captivity.

▷ The European wild cat is larger and heavier than its domestic cousin, and considerably more fierce.

Nictitating membrane

△ Cats' eyes are adapted for night vision, with pupils that expand or contract to slits, according to whether the incoming light is weak or strong. Cats also have a third eyelid, called the nictitating membrane.

◁ The extinct saber tooth cat *Smilodon* had enlarged teeth used for hunting large prey.

△ The long-eared bat has large ears to make its sonar system very efficient. Bats do not interfere with each other's signals, even when many are flying at the same time.

Miscellany
BATS

Bats (order Chiroptera) are the only mammals that have mastered the art of powered flight, though several other animals, such as flying squirrels and flying phalangers, can glide. Bats' hands have greatly lengthened fingers, connected with thin membranes of skin to form wings. There are two main kinds of bats. Fruit bats are the largest bats; they fly by day. Insect-eating bats are mostly small and feed at night, catching insects in flight. They use a form of sonar to detect and catch their prey.

▷ The physical structure of a bat. The wings are membranes of skin which stretch from the tips of the bat's "fingers" down to its feet. The wings are supported by the bat's legs and tail.

3rd 4th Finger-tips 5th Shin Tail membrane Calcar
2nd finger Thumb Forearm

BAT RECORDS

Largest bat is the kalong or Malay fruit bat (*Pteropus vampyrus*), which has a wingspan of up to 5 ft (1.5 m). Its weight is about 2 lb (900 g). It is also called the flying fox.

Smallest bats are the pipistrelles, several species of which are 3 inches (80 mm) or less in length; they include the European pipistrelle (*Pipistrellus pipistrellus*) and the Eastern pipistrelle (*Pipistrellus subflavus*).

Most dangerous bats are the blood-sucking vampires (family Desmodontidae) of tropical America, because they can transmit rabies and possibly other diseases.

▽ Bats use "echo-location" to navigate and find flying insects. They emit an ultrasonic signal which bounces off objects in their path. Some species of moth can send out their own signals to "block" the bats' sonar.

ANIMALS

BEARS

Bears may look friendly and cuddly; in fact, they are among the most ferocious of animals. Although they do not usually attack people, they can be dangerous if provoked.

Brown bears live in Europe and Asia. Their close relatives are the large grizzly bears (*Ursus horribilis*) and Kodiak bears (*Ursus middendorffi*) of North America. Polar bears (*Thalarctos maritimus*) live around the coasts of the Arctic Ocean. The American black bears belong to the species *Euarctos americanus*. Spectacled bears (*Tremarctos ornatus*) live in the Andes, while the Himalayan, Malay, and sloth bears (*Selenarctos thibetanus*, *Helarctos malayanus*, and *Melursus ursinus*) live in Asia.

△ Brown bears are true omnivores: they enjoy a varied diet that includes roots and berries, small animals, and fish.

▷ Polar bears are excellent swimmers and often travel far out to sea. They eat seals, fish, and birds and will even attack walruses. Males move southward in winter, but the females build dens in the snow where they give birth to their cubs.

▽ Kodiak bears live on Kodiak Island, off Alaska. When standing on their hind legs, Kodiak bears may reach a height of 13 ft (4 m).

BEAR RECORDS

Largest bears are the Kodiak and Kenai bears of Alaska. They stand more than 9 ft (2.7 m) and may weigh up to 1,650 lb (750 kg).

Smallest bears are the Malay bears, some of which stand only 3¼ ft (1 m) tall.

Best swimmer is the polar bear, which is often found several miles out to sea.

CUD-CHEWING ANIMALS

Most of the hoofed animals with even numbers of toes belong to the group known as the ruminants, or cud-chewers. They have a digestive system with a four-part stomach, which can cope with such difficult foodstuffs as grass. They include antelopes, cattle, deer, giraffes, goats, sheep, and yaks.

▽ The giraffe is the world's tallest animal, and can measure up to 18 ft (5.5 m) in height.

RUMINANT RECORDS

Largest deer is the Alaskan bull moose (*Alces americana*), which stands about 8 ft (2.4 m) tall at the shoulder and weighs 1,800 lb (800 kg).

Largest antelope is the giant eland, or Lord Derby's eland (*Taurotragus oryx*), which is about 6 ft (1.8 m) tall at the shoulder and weighs a ton.

Largest wild ox is the gaur (*Bibos gaurus*) of India and southeastern Asia. It stands 6½ ft (2 m) at the shoulder.

Largest wild sheep is the argali (*Ovis ammon*) of central Asia. It stands 4 ft (1.2 m) tall and weighs over 300 lb (140 kg).

Largest wild goat is the markhor (*Capra falconeri*) of Afghanistan, which stands about 40 inches (1 m) tall at the shoulders and weighs more than 200 lb (90 kg).

Smallest ruminants are the hornless little chevrotains (genus Tragulus) which hide in the forests of India and Indonesia. Some species are only 8 inches (200 mm) tall at the shoulder.

△ The moose is the largest living deer. It can have an antler spread of up to 6½ ft (2 m). The moose is found in the forests of North America, northern Europe, and Asia.

ELEPHANTS

The largest of all animals that live on land is the elephant. Fully grown it may be as much as 11½ ft (3.5 m) tall and weigh up to 7 tons. There are two kinds of elephant – the Asian elephant (*Elephas maximus*) and the larger African elephant (*Loxodonta africana*). Elephants live in herds of about ten to fifty and move quietly through the forests in single file, traveling at about 6 mph (10 km/h). Elephants are vegetarian – an adult male may eat about 600 lb (270 kg) of fodder a day.

▽ The elephant's closest relative is the tiny hyrax, which is about 1 ft (30 cm) long. Like an elephant, it has hoofed toes and a two-chambered stomach for digesting a vegetable diet. It is found in the Middle East and Africa.

ELEPHANT RECORDS

Largest elephant recorded stood about 12½ ft (3.8 m) tall.

Heaviest known tusk weighs 226½ lb (102.7 kg).

Smallest elephant is the Pygmy elephant (*Loxodonta africana cyclotis*), a variety of African elephant. The males are only about 6½ ft (2 m) tall at the shoulder.

▽ Indian elephants can be used for transportation.

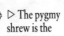

△ The largest and most aggressive hyena is the spotted hyena. It grows up to 5 ft (1.5 m) long. Besides eating carrion, hyenas also hunt for food, chasing their prey at speeds up to 37 mph (60 km/h).

HYENAS

Hyenas (family Hyaenidae) have a bad reputation as cowardly, ugly animals. This is partly because they eat the leftovers of bigger predators such as lions. However, like all scavengers, hyenas perform a useful function, helping to clear up meat that would otherwise turn rotten. There are four species. The spotted hyena is known for its strange laughing cry.

HYENA RECORD

Largest hyena is the spotted or laughing hyena (*Crocuta crocuta*), which may have a body length of 4½ ft (1.4 m), with a short tail.

▷ The pygmy shrew is the smallest mammal of all.

△ The mole spends most of its life underground. It feeds mainly on earthworms.

▽ Tenrecs live on the island of Madagascar. The common tenrec may be the most prolific of all mammals, having up to 25 babies in a litter.

INSECT-EATERS

Insectivores are mostly small animals and include such familiar types as shrews and hedgehogs.

Hedgehogs (family Erinaceidae) are animals with a forest of prickly spines all over their backs and sides.

True shrews (family Soricidae) are small animals that work and rest on a three-hour shift pattern, day and night.

Moles (family Talpidae) are the master burrowers of the insectivores. The mole weighs from 1½ to 5 oz (40–140 g) and eats about its own weight each day. A mole can dig through 45 ft (14 m) of soil in an hour.

INSECTIVORE RECORDS

Largest insectivore is the Common tenrec (*Centetes ecaudatus*), which may be as much as 16 inches (40 cm) in body length.
Smallest insectivore is Savi's pygmy shrew (*Suncus etruscus*), the smallest mammal, which has a head and body length of 1½ inch (38 mm).

THE POUCHED MAMMALS

Marsupials are mammals whose females have a *marsupium*, a pouch in which to carry their young while they finish developing. They are found only in Australia, New Guinea, and South America, with a few – the Virginia opossums – in North America. They include bandicoots, kangaroos and wallabies, koalas, numbats, and wombats.

MARSUPIAL RECORDS

Largest marsupial is the red kangaroo (*Macropus rufus*). Its body is about 5 ft (1.5 m) long, and its tail may be up to 3½ ft (1.07 m) long. It is also the fastest and can bound along at more than 30 mph (48 km/h) for short distances.

Smallest marsupial is the planigale, a kind of marsupial mouse. It is about 3½ inches (90 mm) long, including the tail.

Most fussy eater is the koala. It lives only on the leaves of eucalyptus trees – and only on the leaves of five out of the 350 species of eucalyptus at that.

Least thirsty marsupial is the mulgara, or crest-tailed marsupial mouse. It gets all its moisture from the insects it eats and needs no drinking water.

△ A young koala bear will ride on its mother's back after leaving the pouch.

THE WEASEL FAMILY

The weasel family (Mustiladae) contains not only weasels and stoats, but also badgers, ferrets, martens, otters, polecats, skunks, and gluttons (wolverines). The family includes animals with beautiful furs such as mink and sable. Most of its members have a strong and unpleasant smell.

▽ When threatened, the skunk raises its tail to disclose a pair of musk glands which can squirt foul-smelling liquid a distance of about 10 ft (3 m). This spray can cause temporary blindness.

WEASEL RECORDS

Largest member of the weasel family is the glutton or wolverine (*Gulo luscus*), which is 4 ft (1.2 m) long, including a 12 inch (300 mm) tail.

Smallest weasel is the Least weasel (*Mustela rixosa*) of North America, which is less than 7½ inches (200 mm) long.

▷ The marten is a carnivore that preys on squirrels and birds.

▷ The hummingbird makes a delicate, round nest.

Names and Homes

Over the centuries, hunters have developed specialized terms for animals – their males, females, and young – and the groups in which they are found. Here is a selection. There are also names for animal tracks (such as a fox's *print* and a fallow deer's *view*); beds (a badger's *earth*, a hare's *form*); and cries (a bittern's *boom*, a panther's *saw*).

Many animals are extremely skilled in making homes for themselves and their young to live in. They weave, build, and dig. The remarkable thing is that all this work is done by instinct – the animals can do it even if they have never seen other animals constructing their homes.

▷ The oven bird builds a mud nest.

▷ A hornet's paper nest is made from chewed wood pulp.

▽ The beaver builds a dam to raise the water level in its lodge.

△ Swallows often nest in farm buildings and sheds.

ANIMALS: LONGEVITY AND SPECIALIZED NAMES

	Average life span (years)	Male	Female	Young	Group
Antelope	10	buck	doe	fawn	herd
Bear	18–20	boar	sow	cub	sleuth
Cat	15	tom	queen	kitten	cluster
Cattle	20	bull	cow	calf	herd
Deer	10–20	buck, hart, stag	doe, hind	fawn	herd
Dog	12	dog	bitch	puppy	kennel
Donkey	20	jack	jenny	foal	herd
Duck	10	drake	duck	duckling	team
Elephant	60	bull	cow	calf	herd
Fox	7	dog-fox	vixen	cub	skulk
Giraffe	10	bull	cow	calf	herd
Goat	10	billy-goat	nanny-goat	kid	herd
Goose	25	gander	goose	gosling	skein, gaggle
Hippopotamus	30–40	bull	cow	calf	herd
Horse	20–30	stallion	mare	foal	herd
Kangaroo	7	buck	doe	joey	mob
Lion	20–25	lion	lioness	cub	pride
Ostrich	50	cock	hen	chick	flock
Pig	10	boar	sow	piglet	drove
Rabbit	5–8	buck	doe	kit	warren
Rhinoceros	15–20	bull	cow	calf	crash
Sheep	12	ram	ewe	lamb	flock
Tiger	16	tiger	tigress	cub	
Whale	20	bull	cow	calf	school, pod
Zebra	20–25	stallion	mare	foal	herd

A DICTIONARY OF ANIMAL LIFE

adaptation Any characteristic that a species of plant or animal has developed which helps it to survive in its environment. The thick coats, small ears, and short tails of Arctic mammals are adaptations to cold living conditions.

aging Process by which an adult animal or plant wears out. An aging animal cannot make enough new body cells to replace all the old ones that die off. Also wastes collect in the body and affect it.

amoeba Group of one-celled jelly-like animals that constantly change shape. They reproduce by simply splitting into two.

amphibians Cold-blooded vertebrates usually with four limbs and soft moist skins. Their shell-less unprotected eggs are generally laid in water, and when the young larvae hatch out they usually spend some time in water before they become adults and live on land. Frogs, toads, salamanders, and newts are amphibians.

antelopes Cud-chewing mammals with bony horns. Among them are the eland, the springbok, the hartebeeste, and the gnu. Most species are found in Africa.

arachnids Class of arthropods which includes spiders, scorpions, ticks, and mites. Most have four pairs of legs.

arthropods Largest phylum of all the many-celled animals. The phylum consists of invertebrates with jointed legs and an external skeleton. All insects and spiders are arthropods; so are shrimps, crabs, and lobsters.

birds Warm-blooded feathered vertebrates with light, hollow bones and with their two forelimbs developed as wings. Most of them can fly, but a few, such as penguins and ostriches, are flightless.

carnivores Animals that feed wholly or mainly on flesh. Dogs, lions, tigers, and sharks are typical carnivores.

crustaceans Class of arthropods with hard shells. Most of them, such as crabs, lobsters, shrimps, and water-fleas, live in water.

ecology Study of all the plants and animals in any particular habitat, and the relationships between them.

family An order of animals is divided into groups called families. The members of a family are all closely related and usually quite alike. All cats, for example, belong to one family in the order Carnivora.

genus Many families of animals are divided into a number of genera. The cat family, for example, contains several genera, but all the small cats, including the domestic cat, belong to the genus *Felis*. Each genus is made up of very similar animals.

habitat A creature's natural environment. Four very different habitats are seashores; hot, sandy deserts; coniferous forests; and grasslands.

herbivores Animals that feed entirely on plants. Cows, giraffes, and sheep are herbivores.

hibernation Animals' winter sleep. When an animal hibernates, its body temperature falls, slowing down all the chemical changes that go on in the body and making the animal sleepy and inactive.

insects Largest class of arthropods. Adults have three pairs of legs, and three distinct parts of the body (head, thorax, and abdomen). Many of them have wings. Earwigs, bees, ants, fleas, and butterflies are insects.

invertebrates Animals without even a rudimentary backbone. Cockles, mussels, snails, insects, spiders, starfish, and worms are all invertebrates.

kingdom Major division of living things. Most biologists recognize three kingdoms: Protista, single-celled organisms; Metaphyta or Plantae, plants; and Metazoa or Animalia, animals. Some zoologists add two more: Monera, bacteria; and Mycota, fungi.

larva Stage that many animals pass through between hatching from an egg and becoming adult. The larva is very different from the adult, as a tadpole is from a frog, or a caterpillar from a butterfly.

△ The cockchafer, or May bug and its larva.

lizards Reptiles that have long, slender, scaly bodies, a tail, and usually four five-toed limbs.

mammals Warm-blooded vertebrates with hair and a well-developed brain. All feed their young with their own milk. They range in size from the tiny shrew to the giant blue whale.

marsupials Mammals such as kangaroos and koalas whose young are very underdeveloped when born. They spend a period of development in a pouch on the mother's body. Most of the world's marsupials live in Australia, but opossums live in North and South America.

metamorphosis Drastic change that many animals undergo between the stages of being a larva and being an adult, as when a tadpole becomes a frog or a caterpillar becomes a butterfly.

mimicry Device by which many harmless and otherwise defenseless animals are shaped and colored very much like poisonous or dangerous ones. This makes it more likely that predators will be confused and will therefore not attack them.

molluscs Soft-bodied invertebrates, most of which have a hard shell. They include snails, oysters, and octopuses.

monotremes Primitive mammals that do not give birth to live young ones but lay eggs instead. The duck-billed platypus and the two species of echidna (spiny anteater) are the only monotremes.

mutualism An association between two different kinds of living creature that brings advantages to both. Mutualism is another word for *symbiosis*.

nematodes Eel-worms, roundworms, and thread-worms. Some nematodes live as parasites in plants or on other animals but other nematodes live independent lives. There are millions in the soil.

nocturnal animals Animals that are active by night and rest during the day. Owls and bats are almost all nocturnal, and so are most moths.

parasites Creatures that live on or in the bodies of other creatures (called their "hosts"). A parasite obtains food from its host but gives nothing in return. Parasites are not always dangerous to their hosts but are often a nuisance to them. It is not in the parasite's interest to kill its host, for by doing so it would lose its home and its food supply.

phylum Biologists divide the Animal Kingdom into major groups called phyla. All the animals in the same phylum have important features in common. Among the phyla of the Animal Kingdom are coelenterates, rotifers, molluscs, arthropods, echinoderms, and chordates.

placental mammals The largest group of mammals. Their young ones become well-developed inside the mother's body before they are born. They are nourished by an organ in the womb called a placenta.

predators Animals that live by preying on other animals. Many birds are predators of caterpillars; sharks are predators of various fish.

△ The predator's weapons. The teeth of a shark are arranged in overlapping rows. As the outer row wears out, it is replaced by the next row. The rows of teeth are renewed throughout the shark's life.

primates The order of mammals that includes monkeys and apes, and also human beings. They have large brains, good eye-sight, usually nails instead of claws, and fingers, thumbs, and toes that are especially useful for grasping things.

protozoans Organisms that consist of only a single cell with a nucleus. They are found in the Kingdom Protista.

reptiles Class of cold-blooded vertebrates with tough, horny, or scaly skins. Most lay eggs protected by a shell. They include turtles, tortoises, snakes, lizards, and crocodiles. Most of them live on land, though some, such as crocodiles, turtles, and sea snakes, live in water.

rodents Gnawing mammals, such as rats, mice, beavers, and squirrels. Rodents have chisel-like front teeth that grow continually, so that they are never worn down.

roundworms Large group of simple worms that have no sign of rings or segments on their bodies. Many are parasites, living inside other animals.

scavengers Animals that feed on dead plants, dead animals, or animal droppings. By doing so they help to keep a habitat clean. Vultures are useful and important scavengers in many tropical countries.

snakes Long, cylindrical limbless reptiles with scaly skins which they shed from time to time. Snakes can swallow prey larger than their own heads. They do this by "unhinging" their jaws. Many snakes secrete poison in their salivary glands. The bite of some species can swiftly kill a person.

△ Bees are social insects. No individual can survive alone outside the organization of the hive.

social insects Insects that live in communities, with different individuals doing different jobs to help the rest. Honeybees are typical. The queen's only job is to lay eggs. The worker bees have many tasks – gathering food, feeding the larvae, tidying the hive, and beating their wings to fan and ventilate it. Other social insects are wasps, ants, and termites.

species Every genus of animal consists of one or more species. For example, the genus *Equus* includes the horse, three species of zebra, and two kinds of wild ass. These six species are alike in their basic structure, but they differ in certain details. Only male and female animals of the same species can produce young capable of breeding.

symbiosis "Living together." Used mainly to describe an association between two different kinds of living creature that brings advantages to both – for example the relationship between oxpeckers and buffalo. Symbiosis is another word for *mutualism*.

tadpole Fish-like larva of an amphibian such as a frog or toad. Having no legs or lungs, a tadpole swims in water and breathes through gills. In time it develops legs and lungs; it then loses its tail and gills, and lives on land.

territory Specific area that an animal has marked out as its own home and that it is prepared to defend against other animals of its own kind. For example, a dog may bark at another dog that sniffs at the garden gate, but ignore a hedgehog that ambles across the lawn. A robin may chase other robins away from a wide area around its nest, but pay little or no attention to sparrows.

warm-blooded animals Animals that control their own body temperatures, so that they do not become too hot in hot surroundings or too cold in cold surroundings.

ungulates Herbivorous (plant-eating) hoofed mammals. Horses, camels, and cows are ungulates.

△ Modern sheep have been selectively bred for wool and meat.

vertebrates Animals with true backbones and skulls. Fish, amphibians, reptiles, birds, and mammals are all vertebrates.

womb Organ in a female mammal in which baby develops.

zooplankton All the tiny animals, larvae, and eggs that drift along on or near the surface of the world's seas and lakes.

Classifying Animals

Names for animals differ widely from one language to another. For example, the English *bear* is the French *ours*, the German *Bär*, the Italian *orso* and the Spanish *osa*. For this reason, zoologists use Latin names for describing animals in order to be quite sure what animal they are talking about. For example, scientists all over the world know exactly what is meant by the family name for bears, *Ursidae*.

Another reason for having an international Latin "code" is that the same common name is often used for different animals. To an American, a robin is a songbird, *Turdus migratorius*. To a Briton, a robin is a smaller bird in the same family, *Erithacus rubecula*, while to an Australian, a robin is a kind of flycatcher, genus *Petroica*.

Equally, the same name is used for several similar creatures. For example, there are about 2,500 different species of horsefly.

Zoologists classify animals in seven ranks. Kingdom is the highest, followed by Phylum (plural phyla), Class, Order, Family, Genus, and finally Species. Species is a group of animals of the same kind that can breed together. By convention, the names for the genus and species are always printed in *italics* with a capital letter for the genus but not for the species.

△ The Swedish naturalist Karl von Linné (1707–1778), known as Linnaeus, developed the Latin-name system of animal nomenclature that is now generally used.

▽ Wolves are members of the dog family. The varieties of wolf belong to the same species (*lupus*), differing only in color, size, and geographical location.

CLASSIFYING WOLVES

The American timber wolf and the European wolf are varieties of the same species of animal. A complete classification of the animal is as follows:

Kingdom: Animalia
Phylum: Chordata
Subphylum: Vertebrata
Class: Mammalia
Order: Carnivora
Family: Canidae
Genus: *Canis*
Species: *lupus*

▽ Dinosaurs came in all shapes and sizes, from the horned *Triceratops*, to giant sauropods such as *Diplodocus*, about 88 ft (27 m) long. *Tyrannosaurus*, a fierce meat-eater, stood up to 20 ft (6 m) tall.

Dinosaurs

In the long course of evolution, many more species of animals have come and gone than are alive today. The most fascinating were the dinosaurs, the huge reptiles that dominated the Earth for about 135 million years, until they all died out about 65 million years ago.

A GLOSSARY OF DINOSAURS

Allosaurus Huge meat-eating dinosaur over 30 ft (9 m) long which ran on powerful hind legs.

Ankylosaurus One of the most heavily armored dinosaurs, with bony plates and spikes.

Brachiosaurus Dinosaur that resembled Brontosaurus but was even larger. It was the biggest land animal ever to live on Earth.

Brontosaurus Huge plant-eating dinosaur.

Camptosaurus Ornithopod about 20 ft (6 m) long which fed mainly on juicy leaves of trees.

Diplodocus The longest of the dinosaurs. It measured 100 ft (30 m) from head to tail.

Hadrosaurs A group of dinosaurs with broad, toothless beaks which have earned them the name "Duckbills."

Iguanodon A plant-eating ornithopod about 30 ft (9 m) long which ran on its hind legs.

Ornithischians formed one of the two great groups of dinosaurs. All were plant-eaters.

Ornithomimus was the shape and size of an ostrich. It was a nimble reptile which probably stole eggs from the nests of other reptiles.

Ornithopods A group of plant-eating dinosaurs that walked on their hind legs.

Saurischians formed one of the two great groups of dinosaurs. They included the gigantic sauropods, such as Brachiosaurus, and the fearsome flesh-eaters, such as Tyrannosaurus.

Sauropods A group of gigantic plant-eating dinosaurs with huge bodies, long necks, and tiny heads, such as Brontosaurus and Diplodocus.

Stegosaurus Armored dinosaur about 23 ft (7 m) long. It had bony plates on its back and spikes on its tail.

Triceratops Armored dinosaur with three long horns on its head and a bony frill around its neck.

Tyrannosaurus Largest of the fearsome flesh-eating dinosaurs. It stood 20 ft (6 m) tall on its powerful hind legs.

Animals in Danger

One of the big problems facing the world today is the number of species of animals that are in danger of becoming extinct. A number have already died out over the past few hundred years. There are many reasons for such losses, but human activities are mainly to blame.

The most obvious cause of extinction is hunting, which brought about the end of animals such as the dodo and the passenger pigeon. The dodo was found on just one small island, Mauritius, where it flourished happily for hundreds of years until Europeans discovered the island in the 1500s. Seamen killed the birds for food. By 1681 there were no dodos left.

It is not only comparatively rare animals that can be extinguished in this way. The passenger pigeon existed in huge numbers in North America when Europeans first went there. Some of the flocks are said to have been two billion strong. Hunters began killing them for food on a large scale in the 1800s, and the last passenger pigeon died in a zoo in 1914.

Today, animals are being threatened by the destruction of their habitats, such as the felling of tropical rain forests. However, zoos are saving many animals that are already extinct in the wild.

△ Moas were hunted for food by early Polynesian settlers until they became extinct. They were flightless birds but very fast runners.

▽ The American bison nearly became extinct in the 19th century, when they were hunted for their meat and skins. They have since been protected, and there are today several thousand in the United States alone.

△ The dodo, of Mauritius, became extinct in the late 17th century.

ANIMALS RECENTLY EXTINCT

Animal	Where last seen	When last seen
Great Auk	N. Atlantic coasts	1840s
Aurochs (wild ox)	Europe	1627
Burchell's Zebra	South Africa	1910
Dodo	Mauritius	1681
Elephant Bird	Madagascar	c.1600
Heath Hen	Martha's Vineyard, U.S.A.	1932
Moa (flightless bird)	New Zealand	1600s
Carolina Parakeet	United States	1904
Passenger Pigeon	North America	1914
Quagga (zebra)	South Africa	1883
Schomburk's Deer	Thailand	1932
Tasmanian wolf	Tasmania	1930*

Paw marks have been seen since.

◁ Przewalski's horse nearly became extinct, but is now protected.

SOME ANIMALS IN DANGER

Animal	Where last seen	Estimated numbers
Asiatic Buffalo	India, Nepal	2,200
Blue Whale	World oceans	7,500
Bontebok (antelope)	South Africa	800
Crested Ibis (wading bird)	Japan	Under 12
European Bison	Poland	Over 1,000*
Everglades Kite	Florida	100
Florida Panther	Florida	Under 300
Giant Panda	China	200
Imperial Eagle	Spain	100
Indian Rhinoceros	India, Nepal	Under 600
Java Rhinoceros	Indonesia	Under 100
Kakapo (parrot)	New Zealand	Under 100
Key Deer	North America	600
Mediterranean Monk Seal	Mediterranean Sea	500
Orang-utan	Borneo, Sumatra	5,000
Père David's Deer	China	600*
Polar Bear	Arctic	8,000
Przewalski's Horse	Central Asia	40–60*
Siberian Tiger	U.S.S.R., China, Korea	Under 200
Southern Bald Eagle	North America	600
Whooping Cranes	North America	About 50

Saved from extinction by zoos.

△ The giant panda is a protected species, and is the symbol of the World Wildlife Fund, a leading conservation organization

Plants

The plant kingdom extends all over the Earth, in steaming jungles, lush pastures, and the surface waters of the oceans; there are plants that survive in parched deserts and on bleak mountaintops. Plants play a vital part in the ecosystem of the Earth. They protect the land from erosion by wind and water; they give cover to wildlife; and they provide people and animals with food and oxygen. Trees are one of the most valuable assets of this planet, yet we are cutting down tropical rain forests at the rate of 30 acres (12 hectares) a minute, day and night.

Plants belong to the plant kingdom, called either *Plantae* or *Metaphyta*. Plant life is found on all parts of the Earth – even in the sea. Floating about in the upper layers of the oceans is a mass of tiny plants and animals, together known as plankton (from a Greek word meaning "floating"). These plants and animals are so small they are like dust. The plants of the plankton are eaten by the animals of the plankton, and both provide food for larger sea creatures, such as fish.

When biologists discuss the "who eats whom" of wildlife, they refer to food chains. The reason that plants always come at the beginning of all food chains is that, unlike animals, green plants can make their own food. They draw in carbon dioxide from the air, and water and minerals from the ground, and convert them into fats, proteins, starches, and oxygen.

△ In dicotyledon plants such as this sunflower, the stem thickens with each year's growth. In monocotyledon plants, such as grasses, the stem lengthens with age but does not thicken.

◁ The leaf cells of green plants make food from sunlight by photosynthesis.

ade cell

Vein

Chloroplast

Oxygen out

Stomata (pores)

Carbon dioxide in

▽ The main branches of the plant kingdom. The dicotyledons are flowering plants with broad leaves and seedlings having two tiny leaves. Monocotyledons have narrower leaves and seedlings with a single leaf. Bacteria, shown here with the simplest plants, are sometimes classified as animals.

For this work plants need energy. They draw their energy from light. The light is absorbed and processed by *chlorophyll*, a pigment that colors plants green. Fungi – such as mushrooms and toadstools – which do not have chlorophyll, have to draw their food from other plants.

DICOTYLEDONS

Elm
Foxglove
Rhododendron
Sweet pea
Rose
Daisy
Cowslip
Carrot
Cucumber
Chestnut
Grapes

MONOCOTYLEDONS

Palm
Iris
Lily
Orchid
Barley
Bulrush
Daffodil
Onion
Oats
Banana
Pineapple

Conifers
Cycads
Horsetails
Club mosses
Ferns
Liverworts
Mosses
Algae
Fungi
Bacteria

THALLOPHYTA
BRYOPHYTA
PTERIDOPHYTA
SPERMATOPHYTA
GYMNOSPERMS
ANGIOSPERMS

▽ Plants use various ingenious methods of seed dispersal, including the wind, animals, and birds. The poppy has a "sprinkler" system. The ripe ovary swells into a hollow container with holes around the lip. The wind shakes the seeds out through the holes.

When plants have finished making their food they release oxygen into the atmosphere. In this way they perform a valuable service to animal life, because animals must have oxygen to live. In turn, animals perform an essential service for flowering plants (and some other plants too) by pollinating them — that is, transferring *pollen*, the male cells of flowers, to the *stigmas*, the female parts of flowers. Most pollination is done by insects.

Besides emitting oxygen into the atmosphere, plants release a great deal of water. They draw this water from the ground through their roots and pump it up through their stems to the leaves, where it is given off in a process called transpiration.

Plants also help to keep the soil together. Their roots bind it and help to hold water in the ground. Without plant cover, exposed land is at the mercy of wind and water. The wind blows loose dry soil away, and water washes the soil downhill. Ignorant or wasteful farming practices and the removal of the

Ash seeds

Thistle seeds

Burdock

Poppy

Bird

Mouse

Blackberries

Dandelion seeds

210

△ Uncontrolled forest
clearance can lead to
ecological disaster. Rains
can wash away fragile
forest soil.

▽ The world's tallest trees
dwarf most human
constructions.

Coast redwood

Average-sized
house to scale

natural plant cover created the Dust Bowl of
America's Great Plains area during the
1930s. In a similar way, clearing large areas
of Amazonian rain forest in Brazil in the
1980s has damaged the soil of the region.

Diversity of plant life
Plants include the largest and oldest living
things on Earth. The largest is a huge tree, a
giant sequoia known as "General Sherman"
which stands in Sequoia National Park,
California. It has been estimated that this tree
contains about 1,800 cubic yards (1,400
cubic meters) of timber.

By contrast, the plants of the plankton are
so small that one drop of water can hold as
many as 500 of them. Some land plants are
also very tiny.

The "General Sherman" is thought to be
about 3,500 years old, but it is barely middle-
aged compared with the oldest known living
tree. That is a bristlecone pine, called
"Methuselah," which is also growing in
California. "Methuselah" is 4,600 years old.

Plants can flourish in all sorts of extreme

conditions. There are plants growing in the cold of the Arctic, in Antarctica, and high in the Himalayas of central Asia. Other plants can survive in all but the hottest deserts. Most desert plants are small or medium-sized, but the saguaro cactus of the California and Arizona deserts can reach a height of more than 50 feet (15 meters).

Plants can survive even when they seem to be dead. For example, when the apparently bare deserts of Israel receive a welcome shower of rain, plants spring up overnight from seeds lying in the soil, and soon provide the land with a rare carpet of flowers. Every year the frozen tundra of northern Canada and Siberia thaws out for a few weeks in the summer sunshine, and plants have a brief period of life.

The richest plant life is in the warm, wet tropical regions of Africa, Central and South America, and southeast Asia. The rain forests that flourish there contain more diverse species of plants than any other parts of the world. Some of these forests have flourished for more than 40 million years.

△ Cacti are desert plants that store water. Some have swollen stems, others extra-long roots.

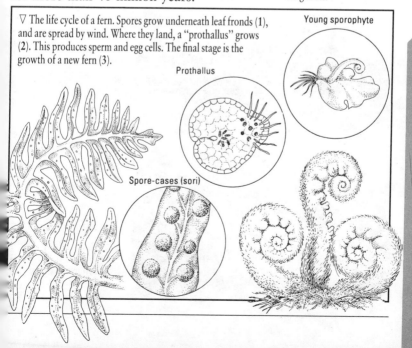

▽ The life cycle of a fern. Spores grow underneath leaf fronds (1), and are spread by wind. Where they land, a "prothallus" grows (2). This produces sperm and egg cells. The final stage is the growth of a new fern (3).

Young sporophyte

Prothallus

Spore-cases (sori)

Plants and people

Earth's plant life is the most valuable asset that the human race possesses. Just over 10,000 years ago people found out how to grow plants. As a result of this discovery, they no longer had to move about from place to place, gathering fruit and seeds and hunting animals, but could settle down. This was the beginning of civilization (literally "living in cities") and the start of life as we know it today.

It also marked the beginning of human changes to the plants they grew. By selecting the best seeds and plants, people were able to grow larger crops. In recent years they have produced some amazing changes. The so-called "Green Revolution," which started in the 1960s, produced some very high-yielding crops, especially of corn, rice, and wheat. The new crops greatly reduced food shortages, especially in southern Asia.

But human influence on plant life has not always been good. People need huge quantities of wood for fuel, to build furniture, houses, and boats, and to make paper. As a

△ Corn and sugar beets are two important food crops. The world's chief cereal crops are wheat, oats, barley, and rye (cooler climates); and rice, millet, and corn (warm climates).

◁ The world consumes vast quantities of timber and wood pulp, produced from temperate and tropical forests. Most softwoods come from the cool coniferous forests of temperate lands.

△ A tea-picker at work.

▽ Rubber is made from the latex oozing from cuts in the rubber trees.

result there has been wholesale destruction of the forests that once covered the Earth.

Europe and North America were the first continents to lose large areas of forest. But people in South America and Africa are now cutting down their trees at a great rate – 30 acres (12 hectares) a minute, day and night. Since 1945 more than 40 percent of the world's great tropical forests have been destroyed.

Apart from the loss of trees, cutting down forests also destroys the habitats (living places) of many animals and some humans. The tropical rain forests in particular are a serious loss, because they contain many valuable plants. Some of these plants have been discovered and turned to good use, for food and for medicines. Although there are many more to be discovered and exploited, some species have already become extinct because of the destruction of their forest habitats.

Flowering Plants

Flowering plants are not only the most beautiful plants; they are the most important. They provide food for herbivores – plant-eating animals – and for humans. There are about 285,000 species of flowering plant, compared to 148,000 for all other plants. Flowering plants form two groups. *Monocotyledons* produce a single seed leaf when they begin to grow; *dicotyledons* start with two seed leaves.

When a flower has been fertilized it produces a fruit. Some fruits dry out as they ripen. Examples of these are peas, beans, and nuts. Others are fleshy fruits, such as bananas, grapes, squashes, and tomatoes.

The scientific name for flowering plants is *angiosperms*, meaning "cased seeds," because their seeds are enclosed in the fruits. Some seeds are small, such as those of apples and oranges. These fruits are pomes or berries, according to how they are formed.

Cherries, peaches, and plums have a hard inner stone, inside which is the seed. Fruits of this type are called drupes. Many fruits that are known as berries, such as blackberries and raspberries, are actually several small drupes joined together.

△ A dicotyledon seedling (*top*) with two seed-leaves, and a monocotyledon. Examples of these two kinds of plant are shown on the facing page.

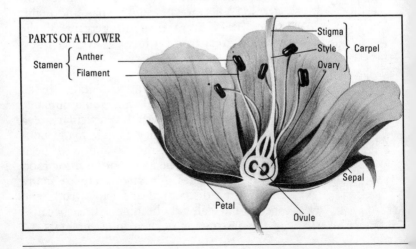

PARTS OF A FLOWER

Stamen { Anther
         Filament

Stigma
Style   } Carpel
Ovary

Petal

Ovule

Sepal

Barley

Rushes

Daffodil

Grasses

Wood lily

Monocotyledon Plants

Dicotyledon Plants

Deadnettle

Black-eyed Susan

Poppy

Rose

Potato

216

△ Prickly juniper.

SECTION THROUGH A TREE

The annual rings seen in the cross-section of the trunk of a tree each mark a year's growth.

Sapwood Heartwood Outer bark

Annual ring

FAMILIES OF FLOWERING PLANTS

There are more than 140 families (related groups) of flowering plants. Some families have only one or two species in them. Others have dozens. Often quite dissimilar plants are found to be related – for example, the rose and the raspberry, and the cabbage and the wallflower. Here are some of the more important families, with examples of the plants in them:

Amaryllis family: daffodil, onion, snowdrop, narcissus.
Arum family: arum, jack-in-the-pulpit.
Banana family: banana, Bird-of-Paradise flower.
Beech family: beech, chestnut, oak.
Birch family: alder, birch, hazel.
Borage family: Virginia cowslip, forget-me-not.
Buckwheat family: dock, rhubarb, sorrel.
Cactus family: cactus, prickly pear.
Cashew family: mango, pistachio nut, sumac.
Composite family: artichoke, chrysanthemum, daisy, dandelion, lettuce, sneezewort, thistle.
Crowfoot family: anemone, larkspur, peony.
Ebony family: ebony, persimmon.
Figwort family: foxglove, toadflax.
Ginger family: cardamom, turmeric.

Grass family: bamboo, rice, rye, wheat.
Heath family: azalea, briar, heath, rhododendron.
Laurel family: avocado, baytree, laurel.
Lily family: asparagus, crocus, lily, tulip.
Madder family: bedstraw, coffee.
Mallow family: cotton, hollyhock.
Mint family: basil, lavender, rosemary.
Morning-glory family: bindweed, dodder.
Mulberry family: fig, hop, mulberry.
Mustard family: cabbage, sweet alyssum, turnip, wallflower.
Myrtle family: clove, eucalyptus, pimento.
Nightshade family: eggplant, henbane, nightshade, potato, tobacco, tomato.
Olive family: ash, jasmine, privet.
Palm family: coconut palm, date palm.
Parsley family: carrot, dill, parsnip.
Pea family: bean, brazilwood, clover, peanut, laburnum, licorice, soya bean.
Pink family: carnation, pink.
Primrose family: European cowslip, pimpernel.
Rose family: rose, apple, blackberry, nectarine, plum, raspberry, strawberry.
Rue family: grapefruit, lemon, lime, orange.
Saxifrage family: currant, gooseberry, hydrangea.
Spurge family: cassava, rubber, teak.
Tea family: camellia, tea.
Willow family: aspen, osier, poplar.

Trees and Shrubs

Trees and shrubs differ from other plants in having woody stems. These stems support the plants and enable them to grow tall. A few plants, such as lianas and other creepers, have woody stems which are not strong enough to allow them to stand alone.

There are two main kinds of trees. Conifers are trees with needle-like leaves. They produce their seeds in cones. Most of them are evergreens – that is, they do not lose their leaves in the autumn, but shed and renew a few all the year round.

Broadleaved trees have wide leaves. They have flowers and produce their seeds in fruits. Most of them are deciduous – that is, they shed their leaves in the fall and grow new ones in the spring. But some, such as holly, rhododendron, and many trees of the rain forests, are evergreens.

△ Sequoia

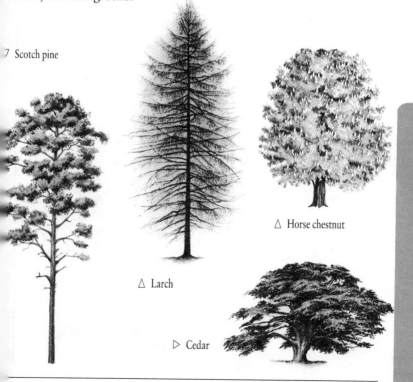

▷ Scotch pine

△ Larch

△ Horse chestnut

▷ Cedar

△ The South American bromeliads are epiphytic plants, growing on other plants but able to make their own food.

▷ The Amazon rain forest supports different animal life within each layer.

THE MULTISTORY RAINFOREST

The Amazon rain forest has five main layers as shown in the diagram (right). The layers and their characteristics are:

Emergent layer: A few trees grow high above the others.

Canopy layer: A thick mass of treetops which break the heavy rain into fine spray. Many plants and animals live here on nuts and fruit.

Middle layer: This layer, sometimes called the understory, is dark. Lianas (creepers) and climbing plants grow and young trees struggle toward the light.

Lower layer: Some shrubs and young trees. Tall trees have buttress roots. Dark.

Ground layer: Little light but very damp. Seedlings, herbs, and fungi grow in the fragile soil.

Emergent layer 50 m
Canopy layer
30 m
Middle layer
10 r
Lower layer
Ground layer 0

Chlamydomonas

Chloroplast

Nucleus

Chloroplast

Nucleus

The Protists

Some living things are difficult to classify as
animals or plants. Today many biologists put
them into a third kingdom, the "Protista."
The name Protista comes from a Greek word
meaning "the very first."

The protists include all the organisms that
consist of one cell only, such as bacteria,
some of the smaller algae, amoebas, and sea-
dwelling creatures in the plankton such as
diatoms, radiolarians, and sun animals.
Many single-celled animals live in colonies.

Some biologists include the fungi in the
Protista. Others list them with plants or give
them their own kingdom, the Mycota. A few
biologists put the bacteria and the blue-green
algae in yet another kingdom, the Monera.

Simple plants such as
chlamydomonas and spirogyra
reproduce either by cell division
or sexually (producing separate
male and female cells which
combine to make a new part).

Bladderwrack is a seaweed
growing on rocky shores. These
plants cling tightly to rocks, and
have rubbery exteriors to
prevent them from drying out
when exposed at low tide.

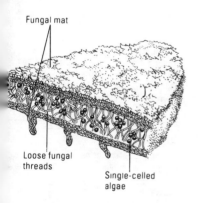

Fungal mat

Loose fungal
threads

Single-celled
algae

Cross-section through a crusty lichen. The
fungal threads make a dense mat on the outside,
while inside the threads are looser, with green
algal cells making food.

Two edible fungi: field mushroom and
shaggy ink cap.

DICTIONARY OF PLANTS

annual A plant that completes its life cycle in one season and then dies.

anther The part of the stamen that contains the pollen.

asexual reproduction Any form of reproduction that does not involve the fusing of male and female sex cells (gametes).

bark The outer layer of a woody stem.

berry A fleshy fruit with no hard inner layer and usually with several seeds, for example orange, blueberry.

biennial A plant that completes its life cycle in two seasons and then dies.

bud An undeveloped shoot.

bulb An enlarged underground bud with fleshy leaves in which food is stored.

calyx The name for the sepals of a flower.

carbohydrate A food – for example sugar and starch – made up of carbon, hydrogen, and oxygen, produced in a plant by photosynthesis. Carbohydrate is "burned" to provide energy.

carpel The female reproductive organ of a flower; it is made up of stigma, style and ovary.

cell Minute living unit. All living matter is made up of cells.

chlorophyll The green pigment that enables green plants to use the energy from light to make food (photosynthesis).

chromosome Minute thread-like structure in the nucleus of a cell containing the genes.

clone A group of plants with identical chromosomes and features, produced by vegetative reproduction – for example clusters of bulbs.

compound leaf One in which the blade is divided into separate leaflets.

corm A short fleshy underground stem in which food is stored.

cotyledon A seed leaf. The first leaf or pair of leaves of the embryo plant in a seed often providing a food store.

deciduous Shedding all leaves at the end of each growing season.

dicotyledon (or dicot). A flowering plant with two cotyledons in each seed.

drupe A fruit with a fleshy outer layer and a hard inner layer – for example peach, cherry.

ecology The study of the relations between living things and their environment.

embryo The young plant in the seed.

fertilization The combining of the male reproductive cell with the ovule to form a seed.

fruit A ripened carpel or group of carpels. It protects and helps in the dispersal of seeds.

gene Part of a chromosome, containing the coded hereditary information for a particular characteristic. Most characteristics involve many genes.

germination The beginning of growth of a seed or spore.

glucose The simple sugar produced in photosynthesis and stored as a food reserve by some plants.

herb A non-woody seed plant in which the aerial parts (those exposed to the air) die (or die down) at the end of each growing season. Also a scented plant used in cooking or medicine.

humus Decaying organic matter in the soil.

hybrid A plant produced when pollen from one species fertilizes the flower of different, but usually very closely related, species. Hybrids are usually sterile.

PLANT RECORDS

Oldest surviving species of tree is the ginkgo or maidenhair tree of China. It first appeared about 160 million years ago.

Largest seeds are those of the coco-de-mer, a palm growing in the Seychelles. The nuts may weigh as much as 50 lb (23 kg).

Longest seaweed is the Pacific giant kelp, which can grow nearly 200 ft (61 m) long.

Tallest grasses are the thorney bamboos of India, which reach a height of 120 ft (37 m).

Largest flowers are those of the southeast Asian plant *Rafflesia*, which reach more than 3 ft (90 cm) across. Their smell give them the popular name of stinking corps lily.

Tallest trees are the coast redwoods California. The tallest living specimen is ov 364 ft (111 m) tall.

Earliest fossil land plants were of a primiti type called *Cooksonia*, which flourished Ireland about 415 million years ago.

Earliest fossil flowers so far known we found at Scania, Sweden, in 1981 in d posits more than 65 million years old.

legume (or pod) A type of dry fruit formed from a single ovary, which splits down two sides when ripe – for example, pea.

monocotyledon A member of the class of flowering plants with only one cotyledon (seed leaf) in each seed.

nectar The sweet liquid, produced in glands called nectaries, that attracts insects to a flower.

nucleus The part of a cell containing the chromosomes.

nut A one-seeded fruit with a hard woody wall.

organic Living; also used of material that was once part of a living thing.

osmosis The process in which a solvent such as water diffuses through a semi-permeable membrane, tending to equalize the strengths of the solutions on each side of the membrane.

ovary The hollow part of the carpel which contains the ovules. It may also be formed from the cavities of several carpels joined together.

ovule A structure inside the ovary which contains the female reproductive cell and which, after fertilization, develops into the seed.

parasite A living thing that lives on or in another living thing (the host), and which obtains all its food from the host.

perennial A plant that lives on from year to year.

photosynthesis The process by which green plants use the energy of light to make glucose from carbon dioxide and water.

pistil Another word for the female part of the flower – the carpel or group of carpels.

pollen Mass of grains produced in the stamens of a flower, carrying the male reproductive cells.

pollination The transfer of pollen from stamen to stigma.

rhizoid Hair-like structure which anchors mosses in the ground.

rhizome A horizontal underground stem, sometimes containing stored food.

runner A creeping stem by which plants such as the strawberry reproduce.

self-pollination Transfer of pollen from the stamens to the stigma of the same flower.

sepals The outermost parts of a flower. They are usually green and protect the petals before the flower opens.

shrub A fairly short woody plant with many branches and no main trunk.

spore A single-celled reproductive body which grows into a new plant; found in algae, fungi, ferns, and mosses.

stamen Male reproductive part of a flower, made up of the pollen-producing anther and its supporting filament (stalk).

starch A type of carbohydrate food often stored in plants.

stigma The tip of the carpel which receives the pollen.

style Stalk-like part of the carpel with the stigma at its tip.

symbiosis A close association between two organisms in which both organisms benefit.

taproot The main root of the plant.

tendril A modified stem, leaf, or leaflet used by some climbing plants. It is very thin and coils round any support that it meets.

tuber A swollen stem (such as a potato) or root (for example a dahlia) used to store food.

◁ Plant fossils, like these of an ancient *Segillaria* discovered in South Wales, reveal much about the ecology of the prehistoric Earth. Plants are the planet's oldest life-forms.

Science

The study of science is a quest for knowledge and the origins of life. By observation, measurement, and assessment of facts, scientists aim to discover answers to the questions "How?" and "Why?" Their research penetrates back into time, down into the depths of the ocean, and even beyond the reaches of our planet into outer space.

Science is the study of the physical side of the universe. It is based on observation, measurement, and experiment. It is concerned with facts and with the methodical study of them.

Science may be divided into two disciplines: pure science, the study of things for their own sake; and applied science, using science for practical purposes. One aspect of applied science is technology, which is discussed in more detail on pages 242–243.

The story of science began long ago, before people could read and write. One of the earliest scientific discoveries was how to make and use fire. Even something as simple as the discovery that a sloping roof throws off the rain better than a flat one ranks as an early scientific advance.

When people began to settle down and build themselves cities to live in, science progressed by leaps and bounds. More than 5,000 years ago the ancient Babylonians developed early mathematics and a calendar, and studied the stars. The Egyptians added geometry and surgery. A little later the Chinese made similar advances in science, but there was no exchange of scientific knowledge between China and the Middle East.

The biggest advances in science in ancient times were made by the Greeks, who also had developed an alphabet in which to write it down. The philosopher Aristotle, developed the skills of observation and classifying

△ Sumerian cuneiform writing. Writing enabled knowledge to be permanently recorded.

△ Aristotle (384–322 B.C.) laid the foundations of many of the modern sciences. He defined and classified the branches of knowledge.

knowledge in the 300s B.C.; a century later, Archimedes established the principle of conducting experiments.

The Romans did not advance science much, and during the early Middle Ages people in Europe studied it hardly at all. However, the Arabs preserved much of the ancient Greek knowledge. In the Americas, the Aztec, Inca, and Maya Indians developed their own independent scientific knowledge, but their discoveries, like those of the Chinese, were unknown in Europe.

The revival of science came in the 1500s, during the period that we call the Renaissance – "rebirth" – because there was a renewed interest in learning. The Greek books preserved by the Arabs were revived and studied. Since then science has progressed very fast.

We are now living at a most exciting time in the story of science. Modern methods of research have enabled us to understand many things that were mysteries to our ancestors. With the aid of telescopes and space probes we are increasing our understanding of the universe. Special deep-sea submarines are enabling us to penetrate the secrets of the oceans and so add to our knowledge of our own planet and the origin of life.

But the more we find out, the more we realize how much there is still to learn. The main branches of science today are listed on the next page.

△ A model of an early reflecting telescope. Invented in the 1600s, it was an enormous advance in scientific instrumentation. For the first time, scientists could study the stars and planets in detail.

▽ Ancient stone circles, such as Stonehenge, may have been used to observe movements of the stars and planets. These observations might then have been used to work out calendars.

Focusing knob
Eyepiece lens
Turret
Objective lens
Condenser lens
Mirror
Specimen table

△ An optical microscope, with three lenses – each magnifying to a different degree. The microscope revolutionized the life sciences from the 1600s.

▽ A lead-acid accumulator battery, with six wet cells connected in series. The accumulator can be recharged and reused repeatedly.

BRANCHES OF SCIENCE

Science	*Study of*
Earth Sciences	(See section 2, Planet Earth)
geology	Rocks, earthquakes, volcanoes, and fossils
meteorology	The atmosphere and weather
oceanography	Waves, tides, currents, trenches, and ocean life
paleontology	Plant and animal fossils
Life Sciences	
anatomy	Structure, form, and arrangement of the body
bacteriology	Bacteria; their growth and behavior
biology	Animals and plants; origin, morphology, and environment
botany	The plant world
ecology	Relationship between living things and environment
medicine	Cause, prevention, and cure of disease
nutrition	Supply of adequate and correct foods to satisfy the body's requirements
pharmacology	Drugs; their preparation, use, and effects
physiology	The function of living things
psychology	Behavior of humans and animals; working of the brain
zoology	Animal life
Mathematical Sciences	
computing	The use of computers in mathematics and statistics
logic	Reasoning by mathematics; used by computers
mathematics	The application of geometry, algebra, and arithmetic to concrete data
statistics	Numerical information and its analysis
Physical Sciences	
astronomy	Heavenly bodies and their motions
chemistry	Properties and behavior of substances
electronics	Behavior of electrons in a vacuum, in gases and in semiconductors
engineering	Application of scientific principles to industry
mechanics	The invention and construction of machines; their operation, and the calculation of their efficiency
metallurgy	The working of metals; smelting and refining
physics	Nature and behavior of matter and energy
Social Sciences	
anthropology	Origin, culture, development, and distribution of human beings
archaeology	Remains and monuments left by earlier people
economics	Use of natural resources to the best advantage
geography	Location of Earth's features and our relation to them
linguistics	Languages and their relationship to each other
political science	Function of states and governments
sociology	Relationship between groups and individuals

KEY DATES IN SCIENCE

*c.*400 B.C. Hippocrates devises the code of medical ethics – now the "Hippocratic oath."

1543 Nicolaus Copernicus argues that the Sun is at the center of the solar system.

*c.*1600 Galileo Galilei develops and uses the scientific method.

1687 Sir Isaac Newton publishes his book, *Principia*, setting out the laws of mechanics.

1789 Antoine Lavoisier writes *Elements of Chemistry*, the first modern textbook of chemistry.

1839 Matthias Schleiden and Theodor Schwann suggest that living things are made up of cells.

1858 Charles Darwin and Alfred Russel Wallace set out their theory of evolution.

1869 Dmitri Mendeleyev classifies the elements into the Periodic Table.

1900 Max Planck puts forward the quantum theory.

1905 Albert Einstein advances his Special Theory of Relativity.

1911 Ernest Rutherford discovers the nucleus and formulates the atomic theory.

1942 Enrico Fermi and others achieve the first successful nuclear chain reaction.

1953 Francis Crick and James Watson discover that DNA – "the molecule of life" – is a double helix, resembling a twisted ladder.

1957 Arthur Kornberg grows DNA in a test tube.

1963 F.J. Vine and D.H. Matthews revolutionize geology by proving that the sea-floor spreads, so confirming the theory of continental drift.

1969 Neil Armstrong and Edwin Aldrin become the first men to explore the Moon.

1986 Spacecraft *Voyager 2* flies past Uranus, the planet seventh from the Sun, and takes the first close-up pictures of it.

1989 *Voyager 2*, the American space probe takes pictures of Neptune.

▽ Much of the equipment used in a modern chemistry laboratory has changed little over the years, though computers are now used widely to store the results of experiments. Some of the more common items found in a chemistry laboratory are shown here. They are 1. Chemical balance; 2. Bottles with ground glass stoppers; 3. Centrifuge; 4. Microscope; 5. Burette; 6. Conical flask; 7. Filter funnel; 8. Measuring cylinder; 9. Long-necked flask; 10. Pipette; 11. Flat-bottomed flask; 12. Beaker; 13. Test tube and holder; 14. Bunsen burner; 15. Mortar and pestle; 16. Condenser; 17. Tripod stand.

△ Many heavy atoms have unstable nuclei, which break down spontaneously in radioactive decay. As it breaks down, this heavy nucleus is emitting an alpha particle, which comprises two protons and two neutrons.

△ Here the heavy unstable nucleus, in breaking down, emits a beta particle, identical to an electron. This form of radiation is more penetrating than alpha-particle radiation. More penetrating still is gamma radiation.

Chemistry

Chemistry is the study of matter. Matter is made up of chemical elements – substances that differ from one another. The elements are made up of atoms, and the atoms of each element are different, too.

Each atom has a nucleus, or center, containing a number of protons – particles carrying a positive electrical charge. The atomic number of each element in the periodic table on pages 228–229 is the number of protons in the nucleus. Whirling around the nucleus are as many electrons (negatively charged particles) as there are protons.

In addition, the periodic table shows the elements arranged in periods (rows) according to their atomic numbers. The vertical columns contain elements that have similar characteristics; for example, the end column on the right contains a group of inert gases which are called the "noble gases."

Two groups of elements appear at the bottom of the table: the "Lanthanides" or rare-earth elements, and the "Actinides," which are all radioactive. Elements 1 (hydrogen) to 92 (uranium) are found in nature. Those from 93 onward are called trans uranium elements, which have been made i laboratories.

HOW TO READ A CHEMICAL FORMULA

Chemists use a form of shorthand whe writing out the formula of a chemical com pound. It is very precise, and tells the exactly what is in each molecule (unit) of th compound. It is based on standard abbrevi ations, which you will find in the periodi table.

A simple example is the formula for wate H_2O. H stands for hydrogen and O stands fo oxygen. The subscript (lower) number aft the letter H shows how many atoms of tha element there are in each water molecule. So we know that each molecule of water contains two atoms of hydrogen and one of oxygen. Many compounds consist of chains or webs of atoms. For example, ethanoic acid, better known in its dilute form as vinegar, has the formula CH_3COOH.

▽ The arrangement of ions in a crystal of sodium chloride (common salt). Chlorine and sodium ions are held together by electric attraction.

CHEMICAL NAMES OF EVERYDAY SUBSTANCES

Many chemical substances have common names such as we use every day. However, chemists have more precise names for them which describe exactly what they are. Here is a selection:

Substance	Chemical name
Baking soda	Sodium bicarbonate
Blue vitriol	Copper sulphate
Borax	Sodium borate
Caustic soda	Sodium hydroxide
Chalk	Calcium carbonate
Common salt	Sodium chloride
Corrosive sublimate	Mercuric chloride
Epsom salts	Magnesium sulphate
Glauber's salt	Sodium sulphate
Hydrochloric acid	Hydrogen chloride
Lime	Calcium oxide
Magnesia	Magnesium oxide
Plaster of Paris	Calcium sulphate
Prussian blue	Ferric ferrocyanide
Red lead	Triplumbic tetroxide
Saltpeter	Potassium nitrate
Sal volatile	Ammonium carbonate
Vinegar	Dilute ethanoic (acetic) acid
Washing soda	Crystalline sodium carbonate
Water glass	Sodium silicate

CHEMICAL INDICATORS

Indicators are chemicals that show how a chemical change is progressing, or whether a substance is an acid or a base (alkali). Two examples are litmus and methyl orange:

	Litmus	Methyl Orange
Acid	Turns red	Turns red
Base	Turns blue	Turns yellow

CHEMICAL RECORDS

Lightest element is the gas hydrogen.
Lightest metal is lithium, which is half the weight of an equal volume of water.
Hardest element is carbon when it occurs in the form of diamond.
Commonest element in the universe as a whole is hydrogen; in the atmosphere, nitrogen; and in the Earth's crust, oxygen.

Periodic table of elements

The elements, listed with their symbols and atomic numbers, lie horizontally in order of their atomic numbers. Those with chemically similar properties fall under one another in the columns. Elements with atomic numbers of 93 and over are man-made.

1 Hydrogen H								
3 Lithium Li	4 Beryllium Be							
11 Sodium Na	12 Magnesium Mg							
19 Potassium K	20 Calcium Ca	21 Scandium Sc	22 Titanium Ti	23 Vanadium V	24 Chromium Cr	25 Manganese Mn	26 Iron Fe	27 Cobalt Co
37 Rubidium Rb	38 Strontium Sr	39 Yttrium Y	40 Zirconium Zr	41 Niobium Nb	42 Molybdenum Mo	43 Technetium Tc	44 Ruthenium Ru	45 Rhodium Rh
55 Caesium Cs	56 Barium Ba	57–71 Lanthanide series	72 Hafnium Hf	73 Tantalum Ta	74 Wolfram W	75 Rhenium Re	76 Osmium Os	77 Iridium Ir
87 Francium Fr	88 Radium Ra	89–103 Actinide series	104 Rutherfordium Rf					

57 Lanthanum La	58 Cerium Ce	59 Praseodymium Pr	60 Neodymium Nd	61 Prometheum Pm	62 Samarium Sm	63 Europium Eu
89 Actinium Ac	90 Thorium Th	91 Protactinium Pa	92 Uranium U	93 Neptunium Np	94 Plutonium Pu	95 Americium Am

◁ Dalton's chart of elements, their atomic weights, and models of their atoms.

								2 Helium He
			5 Boron B	6 Carbon C	7 Nitrogen N	8 Oxygen O	9 Fluorine F	10 Neon Ne
			13 Aluminum Al	14 Silicon Si	15 Phosphorus P	16 Sulfur S	17 Chlorine Cl	18 Argon Ar
28 ...ckel Ni	29 Copper Cu	30 Zinc Zn	31 Gallium Ga	32 Germanium Ge	33 Arsenic As	34 Selenium Se	35 Bromine Br	36 Krypton Kr
46 ...adium Pd	47 Silver Ag	48 Cadmium Cd	49 Indium In	50 Tin Sn	51 Antimony Sb	52 Tellurium Te	53 Iodine I	54 Xenon Xe
78 ...inum Pt	79 Gold Au	80 Mercury Hg	81 Thallium Tl	82 Lead Pb	83 Bismuth Bi	84 Polonium Po	85 Astatine At	86 Radon Rn
...4 ...inium ...d	65 Terbium Tb	66 Dysprosium Dy	67 Holmium Ho	68 Erbium Er	69 Thulium Tm	70 Ytterbium Yb	71 Lutecium Lu	
...6 ...ium ...m	97 Berkelium Bk	98 Californium Cf	99 Einsteinium Es	100 Fermium Fm	101 Mendelevium Md	102 Nobelium No	103 Lawrencium Lr	

> Albert Einstein, one of the greatest scientists, put forward the theory of relativity, which was a new way of looking at time, space, matter, and energy. His explanations made possible many developments, one of which was nuclear energy and, through it, the atomic bomb. Despite this, he also campaigned passionately for world peace.

Russian chemist Dmitri Mendeleyev (1834–1907) laid the foundation for the modern periodic classification of the chemical elements, shown above. He allowed gaps in the table to represent undiscovered elements.

Physics

Physics is the study of matter and energy. It is basic to the study of many other branches of science, including chemistry and the Earth sciences. Knowledge of its laws has enabled people to put satellites into orbit around the Earth, land men on the Moon, and send space probes to the most distant planets.

△ Boyle's law describes the behavior of gases under pressure.

LAWS AFFECTING GASES

Boyle's Law At a constant temperature, the volume of a gas is inversely proportional to its pressure – that is, the higher the pressure, the smaller the space occupied by the gas (described by the Irish physicist Robert Boyle in 1662).

Charles's Law At a constant pressure, the volume of a gas is proportional to its absolute temperature - that is, the higher the temperature, the greater the volume (described by the French chemist Jacques Charles in 1787).

Avogadro's Law states that equal volumes of different gases, at the same pressure and temperature, all contain the same number of molecules (described by the Italian scientist Amedeo Avogadro in 1811).

△ Sir Isaac Newton (1642–1727).

NEWTON'S LAWS OF MOTION

The movement of all objects, both in space and on Earth, was explained by the English scientist Sir Isaac Newton in 1687, in the following three laws of motion:

The first law states that a stationary object remains still, and a moving object continues to move in a straight line, unless some external force acts on them.

The second law states that how much a force makes an object accelerate depends on the mass of the object and the strength of the force. The same force will move an object of twice the mass at half the acceleration.

The third law states that for every action there is an equal and opposite reaction. This is the law that governs rocket motors: when the burning gases escape from the back end of the rocket, they press against the rocket, driving it forward.

THE LAWS OF THERMODYNAMICS

The study of the relationship between heat and work, and how one can be transformed into the other, is called "thermodynamics." There are four laws, numbered from 0 to 3:

Law 0 states that no heat will flow between two bodies at the same temperature.

Law 1 states that energy cannot be created or destroyed. So energy, in the form of heat, may be transformed into another form of energy, such as motion, as in an automobile engine, but the amount of energy stays the same.

Law 2 says that heat can never pass spontaneously from a colder body to a hotter one.

Law 3 states that it is impossible to cool anything down to absolute zero, the lowest possible temperature, because heat from it would have to be transferred to an even colder body.

▽ By bending light rays, refraction causes images to be displaced. This paintbrush seems to bend because light from it is refracted as it passes from the air into water. The brush also looks enlarged, since the glass gives the water a curved shape, like a magnifying lens.

A coin invisible in a dish becomes visible when the dish is filled with water – because the light from it bends.

BRANCHES OF PHYSICS

acoustics The study of sound and sound waves

atomic physics The study of the behavior, properties, and structure of atoms

biophysics The physics of biological processes

crystallography The study of the formation, structure, and properties of crystals

cryogenics The study of very low temperatures

electrodynamics The study of the relation between electrical and mechanical forces

fluid physics The study of gases and liquids

geophysics The study of the physical properties of the Earth

mechanics The study of bodies in motion and at rest

nuclear physics The study of the atomic nucleus and nuclear reactions

optics The study of light

rheology The study of the flow of matter

solid-state physics The study of the effect of such things as temperature and pressure on properties of solid materials

thermodynamics The study of work and energy

tribology The study of friction and lubrication

232

Electricity and Electronics

△ Electronically controlled robots that duplicate human actions are now widely used in industrial processes.

Electricity is a form of energy. We are familiar with it as the power that operates electrical appliances; but in fact, it is found throughout the world of matter. Each atom contains electrically-charged particles, including protons, which have a positive charge, and electrons, with a negative charge.

Electronics is an important part of the study of electricity. It deals with the way in which electrons control the flow of electricity. It is largely a matter of pulses of current. The current is controlled by devices such as semiconducting transistors.

These days electronics is involved in many of our daily activities. It is found in factories controlling robot machines; in the home, in the form of radio and TV sets, and controlling dishwashers and washing machines; in transportation, controlling railroad signals and electric trains, regulating car engines and controlling the engines of airplanes. An important application of electronics is the production of new and increasingly powerful calculators and computers.

MODERN TRENDS IN ELECTRONICS

1982 Capacity of the most powerful memory chips is increased to 256 kilobits (256,000 bits).
1983 Compact discs (CDs) come onto the market.
1984 Capacity of memory chips is increased to 1 megabit (a million bits).
1986 A two-way wrist radio weighing only 2 oz (57 g) is developed in Japan.
An electronic pacemaker that can vary the heartbeat rate to suit a patient who is taking exercise is developed in the United States.
1987 Memory chips with capacities of 4 megabits and 16 megabits are developed in Japan.
"Smart cards" – credit cards with built-in computers to prevent forgery and overspending – are tested in the U.S.
First 3-D video systems are introduced.
1988 First pocket-sized color television sets are marketed.

Signs Used in Electrical DC Circuits

Cell Resistance Capacitor

Conventional current flow Galvanometer

Variable resistance

Switch Lamp

Computers

The first working electronic computer was built at the University of Pennsylvania in 1945. It was called ENIAC (Electronic Numeral Integrator And Calculator). It weighed 30 tons and occupied a large hall of 1,500 square feet (140 square meters). It contained more than 18,000 valves. Today's personal computers occupy just a small amount of desk space, and have as much power as ENIAC.

COMPUTER LANGUAGE

access To connect to a remote computer database (usually by telephone line).

A.I. Artificial Intelligence; used of software, but true artificial intelligence has yet to be attained.

ALGOL A mathematically-oriented programming language; short for ALGOrithmic Language.

analog A representation of numerical or physical quantities by means of physical variables such as voltage or resistance.

ASCII Short for American Standard Code for Information Interchange, a system of codes used by most computers to represent the alphabet, the numbers 0 to 9, and some punctuation.

assembler A program that translates an assembly language into machine language.

assembly language A computer language that uses symbols as well as words, more difficult to use than a high-level language.

backup A copy of a program or file, made for safety.

BASIC Beginner's All-purpose Symbolic Instruction Code: a computer programming language using common English terms.

binary A number system with a base of 2, using the symbols 0 and 1; it can be represented electronically by a current on or off in a computer.

bit Binary DigiT: A numeral in binary notation – that is 0 or 1.

bug An error in a program, causing it to fail.

byte A space in a computer's memory occupied by one character.

COBOL COmmon Business Oriented Language: a programming language designed for business and commercial use.

△ A daisywheel printer has letters and symbols at the end of the wheel's spokes.

compatible Used to describe a computer or program able to work with another computer.

compiler A program that translates a high-level language into machine language.

continuous stationery A continuous sheet of paper folded into pages.

CP/M Control Program for Microcomputers: an operating system used by some computers.

cursor An area of highlighting on screen which picks out the character or block which is being worked on.

daisywheel A kind of printer that has the characters arranged on a daisy-like wheel.

data General term for information processed by a computer.

debug To remove the bugs from a program.

default The drive, program, or other material that is entered automatically if there is no other command.

desk-top publishing Producing material for commercial printing using a micro-computer.

disk The most commonly used means of storing programs and data; a hard disk is rigid, a floppy disk is not.

dot matrix A kind of printer in which the characters are built up from a system of dots.

draft quality Low-quality text produced at high speed by a dot-matrix printer, using only a relatively few dots.

drive Part of a computer that accepts disks, writes to them, and reads from them.

field A specific set of characters treated as a whole, or the recording area used for some particular kind of data.

file A collection of data or the contents of a document, as stored in memory or on disk.

file-name A collection of characters which an operating system identifies as the file.

format Electronically marking up a disk so that it will receive data, and erasing any previously entered data.

FORTRAN FORmula TRANslation: a programming language for scientific use.

graphics Pictures or diagrams on screen and printed out; as distinct from text.

hacker A person who does programming as a hobby, often breaking into other people's programs and computer systems.

hard copy A print-out of a document held in a computer.

hardware The physical working units of a computer system.

high-level language Any computer language that enables the user to write instructions in everyday terms, such as "read" or "stop."

highlighting Also called reverse video: a method of reversing light and dark areas of a screen to show something up.

high quality The best quality of print produced by a dot matrix printer, using more dots at a slower speed than draft quality.

K Short for kilobytes: 1 K = 1,024 bytes.

language A defined set of characters for communication with a computer.

loop Repeated execution of a series of commands.

▽ These children are using a computer to draw. Graphics are used to make designs, maps, and graphs.

△ Microminiaturization has made the silicon chip smaller and smaller, as this comparison with an ant demonstrates. Now chips may be as small as 1 mm square.

machine language The language of binary digits – representing codes and symbols – which a computer works with.
mainframe computer A powerful high-speed computer, usually with a large storage capacity, to which one or more work stations have access.
memory Storage of data or programs within the computer.
micro Abbreviation for micro-computer, a small computer for individual use.
micro chip A small silicon chip which provides memory for a computer.
modem A device that enables one computer to communicate with another over a telephone line; from MOdulator-DEModulator.
monitor A cathode ray tube similar to a television set, on which data are displayed.
mouse A small pointing device which, when rolled across the desktop, causes a pointer to move across the computer screen.
MSDOS An operating system for business micro-computers.
NLQ Near Letter Quality: another term for high quality on dot matrix printers.
printer A typewriter-like machine that produces printed copy from a computer.
print-out The output of a printer.

program A complete sequence of instructions for a task to be carried out by a computer.
programming Writing a program to carry out a specific task.
RAM Random Access Memory, the computer's memory, in which both a program and data are held ready for processing. Whatever is stored in it is lost when the computer is switched off.
ROM Read Only Memory: permanent instructions or programs kept in the computer's memory, retained when the computer is switched off.
screen The visible part of a monitor.
software Programs for use in a computer to simplify programming and operations, usually available on disk.
string A sequence of zero or more characters.
terminal Another name for a work station.
VDU Visual Display Unit: a monitor for use with a computer.
window Small section of the screen that has a separate display from the main section.
word processor A program to store and edit text typed on a computer's keyboard, effectively a superior form of typewriter; also the machine itself.
work station A set-up of screen, keyboard, and printer linked to a mainframe computer.
zero suppression Elimination of non-significant zeros either on screen or in a print-out.

236

△ The abacus has been used in calculation since ancient times and is still in use today.

Mathematics

Mathematics is the science of numbers. It plays an important part in all the other sciences. There are three basic branches of mathematics.

Pure mathematics studies what mathematics can do without any particular practical use.

Applied mathematics relates mathematics to other activities.

Statistics deals with collecting large numbers of figures and analyzing them – for example, taking the United States census every ten years and looking at what its figures tell us about our country.

NUMERATION

The three types of numbers in common use today are the decimal or Arabic system, with the base 10 and using the symbols 0–9; the Roman system, based on the letters I, V, X, L, C, D, and M; and the binary system used by computers, with the base two and using just two symbols, 0 and 1.

In the Roman system I stands for 1, and is repeated to make 2 (II) and 3 (III). V stands for 5, X for 10, L for 50, C for 100, D for 500, and M for 1,000. These letters are combined to make other numbers. A lower symbol before a higher one subtracts from it; a lower symbol after a higher one adds to it; for example XL is 40, while LX is 60. Lines over the top are used for higher figures in the thousands.

In binary, the base of the system is two (written as 10). And, just as 10 to the power of three is written as 1 followed by three zeros (1,000), so two to the power of three (8 in decimal) is written 1000 in binary. In other words, to write any number in binary, using just the symbols 0 and 1, you break it up into powers of two. Computers can read binary numbers very quickly indeed because they contain just the two symbols.

△ Computers work on information in binary code form using only 1s and 0s, indicated by electrical pulses: 0 = no pulse, 1 = a pulse. This table shows the binary forms for 0 to 8.

0	Ø	Ø	Ø	Ø
1	Ø	Ø	Ø	1
2	Ø	Ø	1	Ø
3	Ø	Ø	1	1
4	Ø	1	Ø	Ø
5	Ø	1	Ø	1
6	Ø	1	1	Ø
7	Ø	1	1	1
8	1	Ø	Ø	Ø

EQUIVALENT NUMBERS

Arabic	Roman	Binary	Arabic	Roman	Binary
1	I	1	50	L	110010
2	II	10	60	LX	111100
3	III	11	64	LXIV	1000000
4	IV	100	90	XC	1011010
5	V	101	99	XCIX	1100011
6	VI	110	100	C	1100100
7	VII	111	128	CXXVIII	10000000
8	VIII	1000	200	CC	11001000
9	IX	1001	256	CCLVI	100000000
10	X	1010	300	CCC	100101100
11	XI	1011	400	CD	110010000
12	XII	1100	500	D	111110100
13	XIII	1101	512	DXII	1000000000
14	XIV	1110	600	DC	1001011000
15	XV	1111	900	CM	1110000100
16	XVI	10000	1,000	M	1111101000
17	XVII	10001	1,024	MXXIV	10000000000
18	XVIII	10010	1,500	MD	10111011100
19	XIX	10011	2,000	MM	11111010000
20	XX	10100	4,000	M$\bar{V}$	111110100000
21	XXI	10101	5,000	$\bar{V}$	1001110001000
30	XXX	11110	10,000	$\bar{X}$	10011100010000
32	XXXII	100000	20,000	$\bar{X}\bar{X}$	100111000100000
40	XL	101000	100,000	$\bar{C}$	11000011010100000

DECIMAL MULTIPLES

Prefix	Symbol	Multiplication factor	
tera	T	10^{12}	1,000,000,000,000
giga	G	10^{9}	1,000,000,000
mega	M	10^{6}	1,000,000
kilo	k	10^{3}	1,000
hecto	h	10^{2}	100
deca	da	10	10
deci	d	10^{-1}	0.1
centi	c	10^{-2}	0.01
milli	m	10^{-3}	0.001
micro	μ	10^{-6}	0.000001
nano	n	10^{-9}	0.000000001
pico	p	10^{-12}	0.000000000001
femto	f	10^{-15}	0.000000000000001
atto	a	10^{-18}	0.000000000000000001

ANGLES

second (″)
60″ = 1 minute (′)
60′ = 1 degree (°)
90° = 1 quadrant, or right-angle
4 quadrants = 1 circle = 360°
1 radian = 57.2958° = 57°17′44.8″
2π radians = 1 circle = 360°
1° = 0.017453 radian

	2	3	4	5	6	7	8	9	10	
	ΥΥ	ΥΥΥ	ΥΥΥ Υ	ΥΥΥ ΥΥ	ΥΥΥ ΥΥΥ	ΥΥΥ ΥΥΥΥ	ΥΥΥ ΥΥΥΥΥ	ΥΥΥ ΥΥΥΥΥΥ	◄	Babylonian
	B	Γ	Δ	E	Z	H	Θ	I	K	Greek
	II	III	IV	V	VI	VII	VIII	IX	X	Roman
=	=	≡	四	五	六	七	八	九	十	Chinese
	••	•••	••••	▬	•	••	•••	••••	≡ ◡	Mayan
	۲	۳	۴	۵	۶	۷	۸	۹	۹۰	Indian

◁ The Romans had no zero, so their numbers were difficult to work with. The zero was introduced in India some 1,500 years ago.

238

<table>
<tr><td colspan="2">MATHEMATICAL FORMULAS</td></tr>
</table>

Note: r = radius, h = height; π = 3.14159

Circumference

Circle	$2\pi r$

Area

Circle	πr^2
Surface of sphere	$4\pi r^2$
Ellipse, semi-axes a, b	πab
Triangle, base b	$\frac{1}{2}bh$
Rectangle, sides a, b	ab
Trapezoid, parallel sides a, c	$\frac{1}{2}h(a+c)$
Regular pentagon, side a	$1.721a^2$
Regular hexagon, side a	$2.598a^2$
Regular octagon, side a	$4.828a^2$

Volume

Sphere	$\frac{4}{3}\pi r^3$
Cylinder	$h\pi r^2$
Cone	$\frac{1}{3}h\pi r^2$
Rectangular prism, sides a, b, c	abc
Pyramid, base area b	$\frac{1}{3}hb$

Algebraic

$$a^2 - b^2 = (a+b)(a-b)$$
$$a^2 + 2ab + b^2 = (a+b)^2$$
$$a^2 - 2ab + b^2 = (a-b)^2$$

For quadratic equation $ax^2 + bx + c = 0$,
$$x = \frac{-b \pm \sqrt{b^2 - 4ac}}{2a}$$

Weights and Measures

△ The kitchen measuring jug is customarily marked in fluid ounces/pints and cu. cm/liters.

The system of measurement used in the United States is called "customary." It is based on the British "imperial" system, and most measurements in the two systems are identical. One important difference is that the U.S. pint contains 16 fluid ounces, whereas the imperial pint contains 20.

The metric system, used in most other countries and by scientists everywhere, is easier to use than the customary/imperial system because it is based on multiples of 10, like decimal currency.

LENGTH

Metric units
millimeter (mm)
10 mm = 1 centimeter (cm)
100 cm = 1 meter (m)
1,000 cm = 1 kilometer (km)

1 micron (µ) = 10^{-6}m (i.e. 1 micrometer)
1 millimicron (mµ) = 10^{-9}m (i.e. 1 nanometer)

Customary units
inch (in. or ")
12 in. = 1 foot (ft. or ')
3 ft. = 1 yard (yd.)
1,760 yd. = 1 mile = 5,280 ft.
1 link = 7.92 in.
100 links = 1 surveyor's chain = 22 yd.
1 rod or pole = 5½ yd.
4 rods = 1 chain
10 chains = 1 furlong = 220 yd.
8 furlongs = 1 mile

AREA

Metric units
square millimeter (sq mm)
100 sq mm = 1 square centimeter (sq cm)
10,000 sq cm = 1 square meter (sq m)
100 sq m = 1 are (a) = 1 square decameter
100 a = 1 hectare (ha) = 1 square hectometer
100 ha = 1 square kilometer (sq km)

Customary units
square inch (sq. in.)
144 sq. in. = 1 square foot (sq. ft.)
9 sq. ft. = 1 square yard (sq. yd.)
4,840 sq. yd. = 1 acre
640 acres = 1 square mile (sq. mile)

625 square links = 1 square rod
16 square rods = 1 square chain
10 square chains = 1 acre
36 square miles = 1 township

WEIGHT

Metric units
milligram (mg)
1,000 mg = 1 gram (g)
1,000 g = 1 kilogram (kg)
100 kg = 1 quintal (q)
1,000 kg = 1 metric ton, or tonne (t)

Customary units (Avoirdupois)
grain (gr.); dram (dr.)
7,000 gr. = 1 pound (lb.)
16 dr. = 1 ounce (oz.)
16 oz. = 1 lb.
25 lb. = 1 quarter
100 lb. = 1 hundredweight (cwt.)
20 cwt. = 1 ton (short) = 2,000 lb.
2,240 lb. = 1 ton (long)

Troy weight
24 gr. = 1 pennyweight (dwt.)
20 dwt. = 1 (troy) ounce = 480 gr.
12 oz. = 1lb.

Apothecaries' weight
20 gr. = 1 scruple
3 scruples = 1 dram
8 drams = 1 (apoth.) ounce = 480 gr.

CAPACITY

Metric units
milliliter (ml)
1,000 ml = 1 liter (l)
100 l = 1 hectoliter (hl)

Customary units
fluid ounce (fl. oz.)
4 fl. oz. = 1 gill
16 fl. oz. = 1 pint
2 pints = 1 quart
4 quarts = 1 gallon = 231 cu. in.

Dry
2 gallons = 1 peck
4 pecks = 1 bushel

Apothecaries' fluid
minim (min.)
60 min. = 1 fluid dram (fl. dr.)
8 fl. dr. = 1 fluid ounce (fl. oz.)

British units
5 fl. oz. = 1 gill
20 fl. oz. = 1 pint

VOLUME

Metric units
cubic millimeter (cu. mm)
1,000 cu. mm = 1 cubic centimeter (cu. cm)
1,000 cu. cm = 1 cubic decimeter (cu. dm)
    = 1 liter
1,000 cu. dm = 1 cubic meter (cu. m)
1,000,000,000 cu. m = 1 cubic kilometer (cu. km)

Customary units
cubic inch (cu. in.)
1,728 cu. in. = 1 cubic foot (cu. ft.)
27 cu. ft. = 1 cubic yard (cu. yd.)
5,451,776,000 cu. yd. = 1 cubic mile (cu. mile)

HISTORICAL UNITS

Where used	Current equivalent	Where used	Current equivalent
Cubit (elbow to finger tip)		**Foot** (length of foot)	
Egypt (2650 B.C.)	20.6 in. (52.4 cm)	Athens	12.44 in. (31.6 cm)
Babylon (1500 B.C.)	20.9 in. (53.0 cm)	Rome	11.66 in. (29.6 cm)
Hebrew	17.7 in. (45 cm)	Northern	13.19 in. (33.5 cm)
Black Cubit		England (Medieval)	13.19 in. (33.5 cm)
(Arabia A.D. 800s)	21.3 in. (54.1 cm)	France	12.79 in. (32.5 cm)
Mexico (Aztec)	20.7 in. (52.5 cm)	**Ancient Roman units**	
Ancient China	20.9 in. (53.2 cm)	1 digitus	0.73 in. (1.85 cm)
Ancient Greece	18.2 in. (46.3 cm)	4 digiti = 1 palmus	2.9 in. (7.4 cm)
Ancient Rome	17.4 in. (44.4 cm)	4 palmi = 1 pes	11.7 in. (29.6 cm)
England	18.0 in. (45.7 cm)	5 pes = 1 passus	4.86 ft. (1.48 m)
Northern Cubit	26.6 in. (67.6 cm)	125 passus = 1 stadium	202.3 yd. (185 m)
(c.3000 B.C.–A.D.1800s)		8 stadia = 1 milliar	0.92 mi. (1,480 m)

CONVERSION FACTORS

If measurements are in customary (or imperial), multiply by the conversion factors given below to find the metric equivalent; if they are in metric, divide by the conversion factors to find the customary.

1 **acre** = 0.4047 hectares
1 **bushel (U.S.)** = 35.238 liters
1 **centimeter** = 0.3937 inch
1 **chain** = 20.1168 meters
1 **cord** = 3.62456 cubic meters
1 **cubic centimeter** = 0.0610 cubic inch
1 **cubic decimeter** = 61.024 cubic inches
1 **cubic foot** = 0.0283 cubic meter
1 **cubic inch** = 16.387 cubic centimeters
1 **cubic meter** = 35.3146 cubic feet = 1.3079 cubic yards
1 **cubic yard** = 0.7646 cubic meter
1 **fathom** = 1.8288 meters
1 **fluid oz** = 28.4 milliliters
1 **foot** = 0.3048 meter = 30.48 centimeters
1 **foot per second** = 0.6818 mph = 1.097 km/h
1 **gallon (imperial)** = 4.5461 liters
1 **gallon (U.S. liquid)** = 3.7854 liters
1 **gill (imperial)** = 0.142 liter
1 **gill (U.S.)** = 0.118 liter
1 **gram** = 0.0353 ounce = 0.002205 pound = 15.43 grains = 0.0321 ounce (Troy)
1 **hectare** = 2.4710 acres
1 **hundredweight** = 45.36 kilograms
1 **inch** = 2.54 centimeters
1 **kilogram** = 2.2046 pounds
1 **kilometre** = 0.6214 mile = 1093.6 yards
1 **knot (international)** = 0.5144 meters/ sec = 1.852 km/h
1 **liter** = 0.220 gallon (imperial) = 0.2642 gallon (U.S.) = 2.11 pints (U.S.) = 1.057 quarts (U.S.)
1 **meter** = 39.3701 in. = 3.2808 ft. = 1.0936 yd.
1 **metric tonne** = 0.9842 ton (long) = 1.102 tons (short)
1 **mile (statute)** = 1.6093 kilometers
1 **mile (nautical)** = 1.852 kilometers
1 **millimeter** = 0.03937 inch
1 **ounce** = 28.350 grams
1 **peck (U.S.)** = 8.810 liters
1 **pennyweight** = 1.555 grams
1 **pica (printer's)** = 4.2175 millimeters
1 **pint (U.S.)** = 0.551 liter
1 **pound** = 0.4536 kilogram
1 **quart (U.S.)** = 1.102 liters
1 **square centimeter** = 0.1550 square inch
1 **square foot** = 0.0929 square meter
1 **square inch** = 6.4516 square centimeters
1 **square kilometer** = 0.3860 square mile
1 **square meter** = 10.7639 square feet = 1.1960 square yards
1 **square mile** = 2.5900 square kilometers
1 **square yard** = 0.8361 square meter
1 **yard** = 0.9144 metre

TIME

Second (s. or sec.)
60 s. = 1 minute (min.)
60 min. = 1 hour (h. or hr.)
24 h. = 1 day (d.)
7 days = 1 week
365¼ days = 1 year
10 years = 1 decade
100 years = 1 century
1,000 years = 1 millennium
1 mean solar day = 24 h. 3 min. 56.555 s.
1 sidereal day = 23 h. 56 min. 4.091 s.
1 solar, tropical, or equinoctial year = 365.2422 d. (365 d. 5 h. 48 min. 46 s.)
1 sidereal year = 365.2564 d. (365 d. 6 h. 9 min. 9.5 s.)
1 synodic (lunar) month = 29.5306 d.
1 sidereal month = 27.3217 d.
1 lunar year = 354.3672 d. = 12 synodic months

INTERNATIONAL PAPER SIZES*

	mm	inches
A0	841 × 1189	33.11 × 46.81
A1	594 × 841	23.39 × 33.11
A2	420 × 594	16.54 × 23.39
A3	297 × 420	11.69 × 16.54
A4	210 × 297	8.27 × 11.69
A5	148 × 210	5.83 × 8.27
A6	105 × 148	4.13 × 5.83
A7	74 × 105	2.91 × 4.13
A8	52 × 74	2.05 × 2.91
A9	37 × 52	1.46 × 2.05
A10	26 × 37	1.02 × 1.46

*The sizes are based on a rectangle of area 1 sq. meter (A0), with sides in the ratio 1: $\sqrt{2}$.

MISCELLANEOUS MEASURES

Nautical
1 span = 9 in. = 23 cm
8 spans = 1 fathom = 6 ft.
1 cable's length = ¹⁄₁₀ nautical mile
1 nautical mile (old) = 6,080 ft.
1 nautical mile (international) =
   6076.1 ft. = 1.151 statute miles
   (= 1852 meters)
60 nautical miles = 1 degree
3 nautical miles = 1 league (nautical)
1 knot = 1 nautical mile per hour
1 ton (shipping) = 42 cubic feet
1 ton (displacement) = 35 cubic feet
1 ton (register) = 100 cubic feet

Crude oil (petroleum)
1 barrel = 35 imperial gallons
        = 42 U.S. gallons

Paper (writing)
24 sheets = 1 quire
20 quires = 1 ream = 480 sheets

Printing
1 point = ¹⁄₇₂ in
1 pica = ⅙ in = 12 points

Timber
1,000 millisteres = 1 stere = 1 cu. m
1 board foot = 144 cu. in. (12 × 12 × 1 in.)
1 cord foot = 16 cu. ft.
1 cord = 8 cord feet

Horses (height)
1 hand = 4 in. = 10 cm

Knitting needle sizes

metric	American
2 mm	0
2¼ mm	1
2¾–3 mm	2
3¼ mm	3
—	4
3¾	5
4 mm	6
4½ mm	7
5 mm	8
5½ mm	9
6 mm	10
6½–7 mm	10½
7½–8 mm	11
9 mm	13
10 mm	15

TEMPERATURES

The following table shows comparative temperatures in the Celsius (Centigrade) scale and in the Fahrenheit scale. Note that freezing point in Celsius is 0°, and in Fahrenheit is 32°, while boiling point in the two scales is respectively 100° and 212°. The scales coincide on just one temperature – minus 40°.

Maximum and minimum thermometers (*right*) are of the alcohol type, with metal markers. The bimetal thermometer (*below*) relies on the different expansion rates of two metals.

°Celsius	°Fahrenheit
100	212
90	194
80	176
70	158
60	140
50	122
40	104
30	86
20	68
10	50
0	32
−10	14
−20	−4
−30	−22
−40	−40
−50	−58

△ James Watt's steam engine (1761) was more efficient than earlier designs. It was quickly adopted in factories to drive machinery, such as looms in textile mills.

Technology

Technology is defined as the application of practical science to industry. We live in the age of technology. Its benefits are everywhere – in the home, the factory, the office, at school, in the hospital.

The most obvious benefits of modern technology are the public services – suppliers of water, gas, and electricity; modern sewage and refuse disposal; telephone, radio and television services. To travel from home to school or work, there are cars, trains, and buses – even the humble bicycle is a technological achievement.

Modern factories are equipped with a range of machines, many of them controlled by computers. Offices have such business machines as typewriters, photocopiers, word-processors, and computers. Schools are equipped with laboratories, computers, television, and video. Hospitals have a range of equipment to detect disorders and treat them, ranging from electrocardiographs, which monitor heart conditions, to X-ray machines and ultrasonic scanners which can peer inside a person's body.

Most of this technology is very recent. It all began in the 1700s, in what is known as the Industrial Revolution – a peaceful revolution which is still going on. The revolution began in Britain, where conditions were right – a period of internal peace and prosperity.

The start was in the textile industry, with machines to spin thread and weave cloth. Early factories were set up beside rivers, which provided power through waterwheels to drive the new machines. At the same time the steam engine was being developed and by the end of the 1700s, steam was driving much of the machinery. It became easier to build machines because iron was now freely available.

Although the Industrial Revolution began in Britain, it spread almost at once to the res of Europe and to North America. Inventors in these lands were quick to help the revolution along.

The French contributed new ways of bleaching cotton cloth and of weaving intricate patterns; cheaper supplies of cotton for the busy textile mills came about through the genius of an American inventor, Eli Whitney. Other American inventors contributed harvesting machines to make farming easier.

The combination of steam and iron made railroads and fast steamships possible in the 1800s, thus speeding up communications. During that century the electric telegraph, the telephone, and the radio made their appearance; airplanes followed early in the 1900s. The latest revolution has been brought about by the computer, which has speeded up work in offices and factories since the 1950s.

But all these technological advances have been bought at a price: damage to the environment in which we live by pollution of air, water, and soil – especially from factories and cars. Chemicals released into the atmosphere are even damaging the layer of ozone high above us which protects us from the more harmful rays of the Sun. Now we are having to harness the resources of technology to preserve the Earth we live on, before it is too late.

▽ Wave power is one projected answer to future "clean energy" requirements. Each "beak" of the nodding boom, or "duck," contains a small generator. As the waves move the "beak" up and down (*inset*) the generator turns to produce electricity.

Beam

Arch

Suspension

△ Three common bridge designs. The beam is the simplest, with the weight borne on vertical piers. Suspension bridges have the longest individual spans.

Engineering

Engineering is the term used to cover construction of all kinds. There are several branches of it.

Mechanical engineering is concerned with the making of machines, from airplanes to power plants.

Civil engineering covers the construction of buildings, canals, dams, highways, railroads and tunnels.

Mining engineering and metallurgy includes the construction of mines, the extraction of minerals, and the refining of metals.

Chemical engineering includes all the manufacturing processes that involve chemicals, such as making medicines, plastics, and soap.

Electrical and electronic engineering is concerned with any processes using electricity and, more and more, those using electronic equipment, such as computers, radio, and television.

△ Oil-based chemicals are used in the manufacture of thousands of products – among them, the items illustrated here. Plastics, (vinyl, polyester, polyurethane, and polyethylene for example) are all by-products of the petro-chemical industry, which relies on oil (and to a lesser extent coal) as its raw material.

HOW TUNNELS ARE BUILT

Many tunnels are dug with special machines called moles, which are like huge drills that push slowly through the ground. At the head of the mole, rotating cutters dig out the rock or soil, which is carried away along a conveyor belt.

Powerful jacks act like springs to force the mole forward as it digs away the rock and soil. As the mole advances, engineers fix lining panels in place to form the walls of the tunnel. For both power and safety, the mole is driven by electric motors and hydraulic jacks, which are supplied with high-pressure fluid along lines from the surface.

In good conditions, a mole can burrow through the ground at 16 ft. (5 m) an hour for a train-sized tunnel. To prevent waterlogged soil from slowing down the rate of progress, the head of the mole is contained in a sealed compartment.

ENGINEERING RECORDS

First successful solar furnace was built in the 1960s at Odeillo, in the French Pyrenees. It produces a heat of 6,300°F (3,500°C) – enough to melt a steel plate in one minute.

World's biggest hydroelectric plant is the Itaipu power plant, on the Paraná River between Brazil and Paraguay. It produces enough power to supply a city nearly twice the size of Los Angeles.

Largest man-made hole is the open-cast Bingham Canyon Copper Mine near Salt Lake City, Utah. It is 2,543 ft (775 m) deep and covers more than 2¾ sq miles (7.2 sq km).

Deepest mine is the Western Deep Levels gold mine at Carletonville, South Africa. It is 12,390 ft (3,777 m) deep.

Largest movable flood barrier is the Thames Barrier, London, England, completed in 1983. It is 1,706 ft (520 m) wide.

Biggest vehicles are the two Marion "Crawler" transporters used to carry U.S. space shuttles to their launch pads. They measure 131 ft × 114 ft (40 m × 34.7 m) and travel at 1 mph (1.6 km/h).

Largest radio telescope is the V.L.A. (Very Large Array) at Socorro, New Mexico. It consists of 27 dish aerials, each 82 ft (25 m) across, spaced out on a Y-shaped track 13 miles (21 km) long.

LONGEST TUNNELS

Railroad*

Seikan (Japan)	33 miles 862 yds	53.9 km	Opened 1988
Eurotunnel (England/France)	31 miles 53 yds	49.94 km	Due to open 1993
Oshimizu (Japan)	13 miles 1,397 yds	22.2 km	**
Simplon II (Switz/Italy)	12 miles 559 yds	19.823 km	Opened 1922

Road

St. Gotthard (Switzerland)	10 miles 246 yds	16.32 km	Opened 1980
Arlberg (Austria)	8 miles 1,232 yds	14.0 km	Opened 1978
Mont Blanc (France/Italy)	7 miles 350 yds	11.59 km	Opened 1965

Underwater

Seikan (Japan)†	14 miles 880 yds	23.3 km	Opened 1988
Shin Kanmon (Japan)	11 miles 1,073 yds	18.7 km	Opened 1974

Longest continuous rail tunnel is the Belyaevo-Medvedkovo stretch of the Moscow Metro subway, opened in 1979: it is 19 miles 123 yds (30.7 km) long.
** *Under construction.*
† *Length of the underwater section of the tunnel.*

LONGEST BRIDGE SPANS

	Location	Longest span		Opened
		(ft)	(m)	
Suspension				
Akashi-Kaiko	Japan	6,496	1,980	*
Humber Estuary	England	4,626	1,410	1980
Verrazano Narrows	New York	4,260	1,298	1964
Golden Gate	California	4,200	1,280	1937
Cantilever				
Quebec Railway	Canada	1,800	549	1917
Forth Rail	Scotland	1,710	521	1890
Steel Arch				
New River Gorge	W. Virginia	1,700	518	1977
Bayonne	New Jersey	1,652	504	1931
Sydney Harbour	Australia	1,650	503	1932
Cable-Stayed				
Vancouver	Canada	1,526	465	1986
St. Nazaire	France	1,325	404	1975
Sunshine Valley	Florida	1,200	366	1986
Continuous Truss				
Astoria	Oregon	1,232	376	1966
Concrete Arch				
Gladesville	Australia	1,000	305	1964
Longest bridge (total length)				
Pontchartrain Causeway	Louisiana	23.9 miles	38.4 km	1969

* *Under construction.*

TALLEST TOWERS

Name	Location	Height (ft)	Height (m)	Date
Warszawa Radio Mast	Konstantynow, Poland	2,120	646	1974
KTHI-TV Mast	Fargo, North Dakota	2,063	628	1963

There are many other TV masts in excess of 1,000 ft (305 m) tall.

TALLEST BUILDINGS

Name	Location	Height (ft)	Height (m)	Date
CN Tower	Toronto, Canada	1,815	553	1976
Sears Tower	Chicago	1,454	443	1974
World Trade Center	New York City	1,350	411	1973
Empire State Building	New York City	1,250	381	1931
Chrysler Building	New York City	1,046	319	1930
Woolworth Building	New York City	792	241	1913

DAMS: HIGHEST AND LARGEST

Highest	Location	Type	(ft)	(m)	Completed
Nurek	U.S.S.R.	earthfill	1,040	317	1980
Grande Dixence	Switzerland	gravity	932	284	1962
Inguri	U.S.S.R.	arch	892	272	*
Vaiont	Italy	multi-arch	858	262	1961
Mica	Canada	rockfill	794	242	1973
Mauvoisin	Switzerland	arch	777	237	1958

Largest	Location	(cu yd)	(cu m)	Completed
Syncrude Tailings	Canada	706,000,000	540,000,000	*
Chapetón	Argentina	387,400,000	296,200,000	*
Pati	Argentina	311,527,000	238,180,000	*
New Cornelia Tailings	Arizona	274,026,000	209,506,000	1973
Tarbela	Pakistan	138,100,000	105,570,000	1979
Fort Peck	Montana	125,630,000	96,050,000	1940
Lower Usuma	Nigeria	121,650,000	93,000,000	*

*Under construction.

△ An arch dam curves, so the weight of water pushes against the sides of the valley.

▽ Earth embankment dams are triangular in section with a skin of concrete.

▽ A gravity dam of concrete or stone is usually massive.

△ Buttress dams have relatively thin walls strengthened by buttress supports.

INVENTIONS

7000 B.C. **Pottery** – in Iran
6000 B.C. **Bricks** – at Jericho, Palestine
4000 B.C. **Writing** – in Mesopotamia
3750 B.C. **Cosmetics** – in Egypt
3200 B.C. **The wheel** – in Mesopotamia
3000 B.C. **Glass** – in Egypt
2600 B.C. **Geometry** – in Egypt
747 B.C. **Calendar** – by the Babylonians
700 B.C. **Dentures** – by the Etruscans (Italy)
100s B.C. **Paper** – in China
A.D. 767 **Printing** – in Japan
950 **Gunpowder** – in China
1280 **Cannon** – in China
1280s **Spectacles** – in Italy
1440s **Printing press and metal type** –
Johann Gutenberg (Ger.)

△ Gutenberg's printing press. A wine press provided the first screw mechanism.

1589 **Knitting machine** – William Lee (Eng.)
1590 **Microscope** – Hans and Zacharias Janssen (Neth.)
1592 **Thermometer** – Galileo (It.)
1608 **Telescope** – Hans Lippershey (Neth.)
1620 **Submarine** – Cornelius van Drebbel (Neth.)
1644 **Barometer** – Evangelista Torricelli (It.)
1679 **Pressure cooker** – Denis Papin (Fr.)
1698 **Steam pump** – Thomas Savery (Eng.)
1712 **Steam engine** – Thomas Newcomen (Eng.)
1733 **Flying shuttle** – John Kay (Eng.)
1752 **Lightning conductor** – Benjamin Franklin (U.S.)
1767 **Spinning jenny** – James Hargreaves (Eng.)
1783 **Parachute** – Louis Lenormand (Fr.)
1785 **Power loom** – Edmund Cartwright (Eng.)
1792 **Cotton gin** – Eli Whitney (U.S.)
1800 **Battery** – Alessandro Volta (It.)
1816 **Camera** – Nicéphore Niépce (Fr.)

△ Pressure cooker, 1930. The device was first tried in the late 1600s.

1823 **Electromagnet** – William Sturgeon (Eng.)
1827 **Friction matches** – John Walker (Eng.)
1831 **Dynamo** – Michael Faraday (Eng.)
1834 **Reaping machine** – Cyrus McCormick (U.S.)
1838 **Single-wire telegraph** – Samuel F. B. Morse (U.S.)
1839 **Bicycle** – Kirkpatrick Macmillan (Scot.)
1841 **Vulcanization** – Charles Goodyear (U.S.)
1845 **Sewing machine** – Elias Howe (U.S.)
1849 **Safety pin** – Walter Hunt (U.S.)
1852 **Gyroscope** – Léon Foucault (Fr.)
1852 **Elevator** – Elisha Otis (U.S.)
1858 **Washing machine** – Hamilton Smith (U.S.)
1862 **Machine gun** – Richard Gatling (U.S.)
1866 **Dynamite** – Alfred Nobel (Swe.)

▽ Hargreaves's spinning jenny was hand-operated but spun eight threads simultaneously.

1868 **Motorcycle** – Michaux brothers (Fr.)
1872 **Typewriter** – Christopher Scholes (U.S.)
1873 **Barbed wire** – Joseph Glidden (U.S.)

△ Bell's first telephone.

1876 **Telephone** – Alexander Bell (Scot./U.S.)
1876 **Carpet sweeper** – Melville Bissell (U.S.)
1877 **Phonograph** – Thomas Edison (U.S.)

△ Baird's televisor.

1898 **Tape recorder** – Valdemar Poulson (Den.)
1901 **Vacuum cleaner** – Herbert Booth (Eng.)
1903 **Airplane** – Wright brothers (U.S.)
1924 **Frozen food process** – Clarence Birdseye (U.S.)
1925 **TV** – John L. Baird (Scot.) and others
1928 **Electric shaver** – Jacob Schick (U.S.)
1930 **Jet engine** – Frank Whittle (Eng.)
1935 **Nylon** – Wallace Carothers (U.S.)
1938 **Ballpoint pen** – Ladislao Biro (Hung.)
1945 **Electronic computer** – J. Presper Eckert (U.S.) and John W. Mauchly (U.S.)
1947 **Polaroid camera** – Edwin Land (U.S.)
1948 **Transistor** – John Bardeen (U.S.), Walter Brattain (U.S.), and William Schockley (U.S.)
1960 **Laser** – Theodore Maiman (U.S.)
1961 **Silicon chip** – Texas Instruments (U.S.)
1971 **Microprocessor** – Intel Corp (U.S.)
1973 **Teletext** – BBC and ITA (U.K.)
1981 **Space shuttle** – NASA (U.S.)

▽ The Polaroid camera.

△ Edison's original phonograph played cylindrical records.

1878 **Microphone** – David Hughes (Eng./U.S.)
1879 **Incandescent lamp** – Thomas Edison (U.S.)
1884 **Fountain pen** – Lewis Waterman (U.S.)
1885 **Automobile engine** – Karl Benz (Ger.) and Gottlieb Daimler (Ger.), independently
1885 **Transformer** – William Stanley (U.S.)
1891 **Zipper** – Whitcomb Judson (U.S.)
1892 **Vacuum flask** – James Dewar (Scot.)
1892 **Diesel engine** – Rudolf Diesel (Ger.)
1895 **Radio** – Guglielmo Marconi (It.)
1895 **Safety razor** – King C. Gillette (U.S.)

SCIENCE GLOSSARY

absolute zero Lowest temperature possible in theory; zero on absolute scale is $-459.67°F\ (-273.15°C)$.

acceleration Rate of change of velocity; measured in distance per second per second.

acid Chemical substance that when dissolved in water produces hydrogen ions, which may be replaced by metals to form salts.

alkali Base consisting of a soluble metal hydroxide.

alloy Metal composed of more than one element; e.g. brass (copper and zinc).

△ Bronze, an alloy of tin and copper, was widely used in the ancient world. These bronze-tipped spears are nearly 2,000 years old, and the bronze vessel was made in China in about 1100 B.C.

alternating current Electric current that rapidly goes from maximum in one direction through zero to maximum in the other direction.

ampere (A) Unit of electric current equivalent to flow of 6×10^{18} electrons per sec (i.e. 6 million million million electrons).

anode Positive electrode through which current enters an electrolytic cell or a vacuum tube.

Archimedes' principle When a body is immersed or partly immersed in a fluid, the apparent loss in weight is equal to the weight of the fluid displaced.

atom Smallest fragment of an element that can take part in a chemical reaction. See also isotope.

base Substance that reacts chemically with an acid to form a salt and water.

battery Device that converts chemical energy into electrical energy.

boiling point Temperature at which liquid turns into vapor throughout its bulk.

calorie Unit of heat equal to amount needed to raise the temperature of one gram of water through one degree C.

catalyst Substance that markedly alters the speed of a chemical reaction without appearing to take part in it.

cathode Negative electrode through which an electric current leaves an electrolytic cell or a vacuum tube.

Celsius Temperature scale on which 0°C is the melting point of ice and 100°C is boiling point of water; often called centigrade.

circuit, electrical The complete path taken by an electric current.

combustion (burning) Chemical reaction in which a substance combines with oxygen and gives off heat and light.

compound Substance consisting of two or more elements in chemical combination in definite proportions.

condensation Change of vapor into liquid that takes place when pressure is applied to it or the temperature is lowered.

conductor, electric Substance that permits the flow of electricity; e.g. metal.

crystal Substance that has been solidified in a definite geometrical form. Some solids do not form crystals.

current Flow of electrons along a conductor.

decibel Unit for comparing power levels or sound intensities.

△ A dry battery wired to a bulb makes a simple electrical circuit.

△ All snowflakes are hexagonal crystals.

diffraction The spreading out of light by passing it through a narrow slit or past the edge of an obstacle.

direct current Current that always flows in the same direction.

elasticity Property of a material that makes it go back to its original shape after a force deforming it is removed.

electrode Metal plate through which electric current enters or leaves an electrolysis cell, battery, or vacuum tube. See anode and cathode.

electron Negatively charged subatomic particle.

element Substance made up entirely of exactly similar atoms (all with the same atomic number).

energy Capacity for doing work.

evaporation Phenomenon in which liquid turns into vapor without necessarily reaching the boiling point.

△ In a flowing current, all the electrons in the wire move in the same direction – from negative terminal to positive terminal.

fission (splitting) In atomic or nuclear fission, the nuclei of heavy atoms split and release vast quantities of energy.

fluid Substance (liquid or gas) that takes the shape of part or all of the vessel that contains it.

focus The point at which converging rays of light meet.

force Anything that can act on a stationary body and make it move, or make a moving body change speed or direction.

frequency Of a wave motion, the number of oscillations, cycles, vibrations, or waves per second.

friction Force that resists sliding or rolling of one surface in contact with another.

△ The tread on a tire increases friction, and so reduces slipping or skidding.

fulcrum The point of support of a lever when it is lifting something.

fusion, nuclear The joining of nuclei of light atoms together with the release of vast amounts of energy; this is the process that occurs in stars.

gas A fluid that, no matter how little there is, always takes up the whole of the vessel containing it.

gravitation Force of attraction between any two objects because of their masses.

inclined plane Simple machine consisting of smooth plane sloping upward; used for moving heavy loads with a relatively small force.

inertia Property of an object that makes it resist being moved or its motion being changed.

infra-red rays Electromagnetic radiation of wavelengths just longer than those of visible light; invisible heat radiation.

insulator Substance that does not conduct electricity.

ion Atom or group of atoms carrying an electrical charge.

isotope One of two or more forms of an element with the same atomic number (i.e. number of protons in the nucleus), but different relative atomic masses (due to different numbers of neutrons in the nucleus).

joule Unit of work or energy.

laser Device that produces an intense, thin beam of light; abbreviation for **l**ight **a**mplification by **s**timulated **e**mission of **r**adiation.

Light bounces to and fro and gains energy

Crystal or gas

Mirror — Energy source | Beam of laser light

△ A laser consists of a crystal or a tube of gas. The laser absorbs incoming energy, amplifies it, and releases a beam of laser light.

latent heat Heat absorbed, without a rise in temperature, when a substance is changed from solid to liquid or liquid to gas.

lens Device that affects light passing through it by converging (bringing together) or diverging (spreading apart) the rays.

lever Simple machine consisting of a rigid beam pivoted at one point, called the fulcrum; effort applied at one point on the beam can lift a load at another point.

liquid Substance that, without changing its volume, takes up the shape of all, or the lower part of, the vessel containing it.

mass Amount of matter in an object.

melting point Temperature at which solid turns to liquid; equal to freezing point of the liquid.

metal Element or alloy that is a good conductor of heat and electricity and has a high density.

△ The lever (*top*) and pulley are two of the most important simple machines.

mixture More than one element or compound together, but not in chemical combination.

molecule Smallest amount of chemical substance that can exist alone; it is made up of two or more atoms.

momentum The product of the mass and velocity of a moving body.

motion, Newton's laws of (1) A stationary object remains still or a moving object continues to move in a straight line unless acted on by an external force. (2) The force producing acceleration in an object is proportional to the product of the object's mass and its acceleration. (3) Every action has an equal and opposite reaction.

neutron Uncharged atomic particle found in the nuclei of all atoms except hydrogen.

nucleus, atomic The positively charged center of an atom; consists of one or more protons and, except for hydrogen, one or more neutrons. See also atom.

ozone Form of oxygen containing three atoms in each molecule; O_3.

proton Positively charged atomic particle found in the nuclei of all atoms.

radiation, heat Transfer of heat by means of waves; infra-red rays.

radioactivity Emission of radiation, such as alpha-particles, beta-particles, and gamma-rays, from unstable elements by the spontaneous splitting of their atomic nuclei.

refraction Bending of a light ray as it crosses the boundary between two media of different optical density.

salt Chemical compound formed, with water, when a base reacts with an acid; a salt is also formed, often with the production of hydrogen, when a metal reacts with an acid.

surface tension Property of the surface of a liquid that makes it behave as though it were covered with a thin elastic skin.

ultrasonic waves "Sound" waves beyond the range of human hearing.

ultraviolet rays Electromagnetic radiation of wavelengths just shorter than those of visible light. The Sun's radiation is rich in ultraviolet rays.

vacuum In practice, a region in which pressure is considerably less than atmospheric pressure.

vapor Gas that can be turned into a liquid by compressing it without cooling.

velocity Rate of change of position equal to speed in a particular direction.

volt (V) Unit of electromotive force; (emf).

volume Measurement of the space occupied by an object.

watt (W) Unit of electrical power, defined as the rate of work done in joules per second; equal to the product of current in amperes (A) and potential difference in volts (V). $W = AV$.

wavelength Of a wave motion, the distance between crests (or troughs) of two consecutive waves.

waves Regular disturbances that carry energy. Light and radio travel as electromagnetic waves.

X-rays Very short wavelength electromagnetic waves.

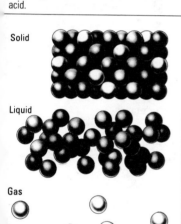

△ The three states of matter. In each state, molecules are arranged differently.

solid State of matter that has a definite shape and resists having it changed; a crystalline solid melts to a liquid on heating above its melting point.

solubility Quantity of a substance (solute) that will dissolve in a solvent to form a solution.

speed Distance traveled by a moving object divided by the time taken. Speed in a particular direction is velocity.

static electricity Electricity at rest (not flowing), in contrast to current.

superconductor Material that conducts current at very low temperatures with virtually no resistance.

△ Ultraviolet rays from the Sun will tan pale skin. Most UV light is absorbed by the atmosphere.

Transportation

One of the world's greatest inventions is the wheel – most likely developed from the notion of transporting heavy loads on rolling logs. Logs floating downstream probably provided inspiration for the first rafts and boats. A man watching steam lift the lid off a kettle got the idea for a steam engine, which revolutionized transportation in the 1700s. Since then, people have discovered how to fly and have penetrated the ocean depths and outer space, but in many parts of the world we still rely on faithful beasts of burden to get us and our belongings from one place to the next.

Transportation and the need for it have grown up together over the centuries. At first, people had to rely on their own two feet for moving from place to place, and had to carry any loads themselves.

Water was probably the first means of transportation that people used. Logs floating in rivers would have put the idea into their heads. It seems likely that river transportation has been used for hundreds of thousands of years because, when migrating over the land, people must have had to cross streams many times.

The first craft to be used were undoubtedly rafts – logs lashed together with vines, or bundles of reeds tied together. By 6,000 years ago, people were building boats and had invented sails.

▽ Ancient Egyptian boat made from bundles of reeds.

The big change in land transportation came with the domestication of animals, which began less than 10,000 years ago. The most important animal for carrying loads and riders was the horse, in use in the Middle East more than 5,000 years ago. Horses remained the chief means of transportation until the development of railroads in the 1800s.

Important as horses were for carrying people and loads, oxen of various kinds were preferred as draught animals – that is, animals used for pulling loads – because with the primitive harness then in use they could draw larger and heavier weights.

The harness consisted of a wooden yoke attached to the shoulders and neck of the ox. An ox pulls with its head, whereas a horse uses the base of its neck. Therefore, the yoke tended to throttle horses. When the horse collar came into use in Europe, from about ?00 B.C. onward, the full power of the horse for pulling heavy loads could be exploited.

Horses are not suited to desert conditions. There the camel is the most important beast of burden. It can travel for days without water and can feed on plants that other animals reject, such as thorn trees. Its feet are large and do not sink into soft sand. The main disadvantage is that camels seem to have a grudge against everything, even other camels, and especially against work!

In the 1980s researchers in Egypt, Israel, Pakistan, Saudi Arabia, and Syria were studying camels with the idea of extending their use in areas of Africa and Asia where severe drought and famine are common and where other animals such as horses and cattle do not manage well.

The Industrial Revolution

The Industrial Revolution, which began in Britain in the 1700s, changed the methods and speed of transportation. In the 1700s people began constructing networks of

△ An early submarine: David Bushnell's *Turtle* of 1776. This tiny one-man craft tried to sink a British warship during the American Revolutionary War.

△ Leonardo da Vinci sketched this helicopter-like flying machine in the early 1500s. It never flew, for there was no engine able to power it.

▽ An ordinary bicycle of the 1880s.

256

Liner Lengths

Great Western (1837)

Great Eastern (1858)

Mauretania (1906)

Normandie (1932)

United States (1952)

France (1962)

Queen Elizabeth 2 (1968)

△ The evolution of the ocean liner: as engine power increased, so did the size, speed, and luxury of passenger ships.

canals, especially in Britain and continental Europe; in the early 1800s many were built in the United States. Canal travel was cheap and ideal for shipping heavy loads.

However, the development of the steam engine led quickly to the development of railroads. Canals became less important in Britain, although they are still a major means of transportation in continental Europe and the Soviet Union, where they link with the extensive system of rivers.

Railroads dominated land travel until the advent of the car, in the early 1900s. Today, cars and trucks form the main means of transportation for millions of people.

At sea, steam, and later diesel, engines made sea travel faster. For the first 50 years of the 20th century, the oceans were dominated by the giant passenger liners, such as Britain's *Queen Mary* and *Queen Elizabeth*, which made regular journeys across the Atlantic and other oceans. The great liners have had their day. Giant ships still ply the seas, but now they are bulk freight carriers.

Air transportation developed rapidly after World War II, and now most long-distance passenger traffic and some freight is carried by air.

Modern transportation

Transportation today is a combination of many means of travel and freighting. On land, roads provide the basic means of transportation, because they run from door to door. All over North America and Europe trucks carry freight, while cars and buses carry passengers.

Other means of transportation provide service only to and from certain places — seaports, airports, railroad stations — and depend on road vehicles to carry people and loads to their final destinations. The modern transportation network is a highly complex organization.

MILESTONES IN TRANSPORTATION

B.C.

4000 Earliest known canals were constructed in Mesopotamia (modern Iraq).
c. **3200** First wheeled vehicles, with solid disc wheels, are used in Mesopotamia.
c. **2000** Spoked wheels come into use.
1800 Hittites develop war chariots.
540 Chinese begin the Grand Canal, from Beijing to Hangzhou (completed A.D. 1327).
312 Roman engineers build the Appian Way from Rome to Capua.
c. **200** China develops a system of roads.

A.D.

c. **1100** Magnetic compass comes into use.
1400s The first three-masted ships are built.
1474 Four-wheeled coaches are built in Germany.
1662 Blaise Pascal (France) invents the first (horse-drawn) omnibus.
1783 Marquis Jouffroy d'Abbans (France) builds the first successful steamboat.
1802 First paddle steamer, the *Charlotte Dundas*, on the Forth and Clyde Canal (U.K.).

△ Cugnot's steam carriage of 1769 had a top speed of 3¹⁄₁₀ mph (5 km/h).

1831 First passenger railroad opens (U.K.).
1835 Screw propeller invented.
1839 First pedal-driven bicycle.
1852 Henri Giffard (France) flies first airship.
1863 First subway (or "underground") opens in London.
1869 Suez Canal opens.
1869 U.S. transcontinental railroad finished.

△ Last of its line: Atlantic 4-4-2 steam locomotive of U.S. railroads.

1890 First electric-powered tube railroad.
1897 First diesel engine built.
1903 First power flight in heavier-than-air craft.
1914 Panama Canal is opened.
1925 First diesel locomotive goes into regular service in the U.S.
1936 Prototype helicopter successfully tested.
1939 First jet aircraft.
1954 First nuclear-powered submarine (U.S.).
1961 First man in space.
1968 First supersonic airliner (U.S.S.R.).
1987 Work begins on the Channel Tunnel.

▽ A nuclear submarine.

△ An early raft constructed from logs tied together with reeds.

1807 Robert Fulton launches first American steamboat on Hudson River.
1815 John L. McAdam (Scotland) develops macadam paving for roads.
1819 First iron passenger vessel, the barge *Vulcan*, goes into service (U.K.).
1821 First iron-hulled merchant ship, the *Aaron Manby* (U.K.).
1825 Erie Canal links New York City with Great Lakes.

Conning tower

Stabilizers

Turbines Nuclear reactor

Navigation room

Living quarters Missile

△ The modern automobile is manufactured in various shapes. Among them are the sedan, hatchback (European) and station wagon.

▷ How a gasoline engine works. *Induction*: Piston moves downward and gas/air mixture is drawn into cylinder. *Compression*: Piston rises, compressing mixture. *Ignition*: Spark plug sparks, igniting compressed mixture. Gases force piston downward. *Exhaust*: Piston moves upwards, forcing out burned gases.

△ Electric streetcars (1890) provided cheap urban transportation.

Travel by Road

In 1769 the *Fardier*, the world's first horse-less carriage, rumbled onto the road. The brainchild of Capitaine Nicolas Cugnot of the French army, it was a steam cart designed to haul guns. Its top speed was 3 mph (5 km/h), and it had to stop every 15 minutes to take in water and raise steam pressure. It was not a success.

From such unlikely beginnings came the modern automobile and truck. Steam proved unreliable, and it was not until nearly a century later, after the invention of the internal combustion engine, that Benz, in 1885, and Daimler, in 1886, produced the first successful cars. Mass production of cars was begun in the United States by Eli Ransom Olds, whose Oldsmobiles began rolling off the production lines in 1901.

Today, there are more than 411 million vehicles on the world's roads. The United States has about 40 percent of them.

DATES IN ROAD TRAVEL HISTORY

1888 First successful electric streetcars run in Richmond, Virginia.
1901 A car with front-wheel drive, the Korn and Latil Voiturette, is built in France.
1901 A new model Daimler is named the Mercedes, after the daughter of one of the agents. The name has persisted to this day.
1902 A nine-horsepower Napier car is built in Britain with an all-steel body.
1902 Belgium's Dechamps cars are built with an electric starter as standard.
1902 Renault of France introduces drum brakes, and Frederick Lanchester of Britain experiments with disk brakes.
1903 First coast-to-coast automobile trip, San Francisco–New York, 10 weeks.
1903 A Dutch Spyker is the first car to be fitted with four-wheel drive and brakes.
1904 Charles Rolls and Henry Royce found the firm of Rolls-Royce in Britain.
1904 First car with a muffler is built in the United States.
1905 Gasoline-driven buses are introduced in London.
1908 Henry Ford produces his first Model T; over the next 19 years he sells 15,007,033 of them.
1916 First automatic windshield wipers are fitted to a Willys Knight in the United States.

▽ The Ford Model T, known as the "Tin Lizzie."

△ Lead-free gas and catalytic converters reduce pollution from car exhausts.

1919 The world's first traffic lights are installed in Detroit.
1921 The first hydraulic brakes are fitted to an American Duesenberg.
1924 The world's first divided highway is opened, an *autostrada* between Milan and Varese, Italy.
1926 The Soviet Union builds its first car, the "Nami 1."
1928 The first transcontinental bus service in the United States begins a San Francisco–New York service.
1929 An American Cadillac is the first production car to be fitted with a synchromesh gearbox.
1934 Citroën of France introduces monocoque construction – building body and chassis in one.
1934 Percy Shaw invents "Cat's eyes" – reflecting road studs – in England.
1938 Automatic direction signaling is introduced.
1948 Tubeless tires are introduced.
1967 First car with a Wankel rotary engine is built in Germany.
1980 General Motors begins fitting computers in some cars to reduce fuel consumption.
1988 Lead-free gasoline is introduced in the European Community.

HOOD ORNAMENTS

Hood ornaments are not so common as they used to be. Projecting ornaments on the top of car hoods are now considered dangerous, as they can cause additional injury in an accident. Manufacturers do not always put a badge-type ornament on every car they build, though there are sometimes badges for special models. Here are a few of the best-known ornaments, with something about the famous makers to whom they belong.

Alfa-Romeo

Alfa-Romeo uses a heraldic badge, of which the serpent on the right comes from the coat-of-arms of Milan, Italy, where the cars are made.

Cadillac, named after Antoine de la Mothe Cadillac, founder of Detroit where the cars are made, also has a heraldic badge.

Fiat's badge stands for Fabbrica Italiana Automobile Torino, the name of the Italian manufacturer.

Ford has always used a script badge; older Fords bore it on their radiators.

Peugeot's lion comes from the arms of the Peugeot family's home city, Belfort, France.

Renault has used a diamond badge since 1924; before that its cars carried the firm's name on a round badge.

Rolls-Royce uses two capital Rs, the initials of the firm's founders. For many years the lettering was red, but it was changed to black in 1933 on the death of Sir Henry Royce.

Chevrolet has a simple design incorporating the name. The firm was founded by Louis Chevrolet in 1911, but was sold to General Motors in 1917.

Mercedes-Benz's three-pointed star in a circle was the house emblem of the automobile pioneer Gottlieb Daimler, whose Mercedes company merged with Benz in 1926.

Volkswagen's distinctive "VW" badge stands for the initials of the name, which means "People's Car." The first VW, the "Beetle," was designed to the order of the German dictator Adolf Hitler just before World War II.

Volvo uses a symbol for iron, for which Sweden, where the cars are made, is famous.

Cadillac

Renault

Mercedes

Volkswagen

Peugot

MOTORCYCLES

The motorcycle was actually made before the car, because Gottlieb Daimler built one of hickory wood to serve as a test bed for the gasoline engine he was planning to use for his first car. After 1903 motorcycles developed into useful machines, prized for their low purchase and running costs and for their ease in maneuvering.

Between the world wars the United States and Britain led the world in the production of motorcycles, with the American Harley-Davidson and Indian, and the British BSA and Norton among the leading makes. After World War II the American and British motorcycle industries collapsed, and Japan became the leading manufacturer, with Honda, Suzuki, Yamaha, and Kawasaki the chief firms.

△ Streamlining of motorcycles reduces wind resistance and increases stability.

MOTORCYCLING MILESTONES

1868 Ernest and Pierre Michaux of Paris, France, make the first motorcycle, powered by steam.
1885 Daimler of Germany builds his first motorcycle, with a four-stroke engine.
1887 James Butler of Britain builds a motorcycle with a two-stroke engine.
1894 Hildebrand and Wolfmüller of Munich, Germany, manufacture the first commercially-produced motorcycle.
1895 The French firm of De Dion-Bouton makes a high-speed, lightweight engine for motorcycles.

△ The 1885 Daimler was the first motorcycle. It had no brakes and no gears.

△ Honda's VFR 750F machine has a powerful 750cc engine.

1896 Car Club de France holds the first motorcycle race, from Paris to Nantes.
1901 The Indian Motorcycle Company is formed.
1903 Harley-Davidson machines are first made.
1914 Georges Gauthier of France makes the first motor scooter.
1915 Britain's Post Office begins using motorcycles to deliver mail.
1926 Front-wheel brakes are introduced.
1929 The Golden Helmet, the oldest surviving speedway race, is founded in Czechoslovakia.
1948 Honda begins making motorcycles in Japan.

INTERNATIONAL IDENTIFICATION LETTERS

A	Austria	GCA	Guatemala	RC	Taiwan
ADN	Yemen P.D.R.	GH	Ghana	RCA	Central African Rep.
AFG	Afghanistan	GR	Greece	RCB	Congo
AL	Albania	GUY	Guyana	RCH	Chile
AND	Andorra	H	Hungary	RH	Haiti
AUS	Australia	HK	Hong Kong	RI	Indonesia
B	Belgium	HKJ	Jordan	RIM	Mauritania
BD	Bangladesh	I	Italy	RL	Lebanon
BDS	Barbados	IL	Israel	RM	Malagasy Rep.
BG	Bulgaria	IND	India	RMM	Mali
BH	Belize	IR	Iran	RO	Romania
BR	Brazil	IRL	Ireland,	ROK	South Korea
BRN	Bahrain		Republic of	ROU	Uruguay
BRU	Brunei	IRQ	Iraq	RP	Philippines
BS	Bahamas	IS	Iceland	RSM	San Marino
C	Cuba	J	Japan	RU	Burundi
CDN	Canada	JA	Jamaica	RWA	Rwanda
CH	Switzerland	KWT	Kuwait	S	Sweden
CI	Côte d'Ivoire	L	Luxembourg	SCV	Vatican
CL	Sri Lanka	LAO	Laos	SD	Swaziland
CO	Colombia	LAR	Libya	SF	Finland
CR	Costa Rica	LB	Liberia	SGP	Singapore
CS	Czechoslovakia	LS	Lesotho	SME	Surinam
CY	Cyprus	M	Malta	SN	Senegal
D	West Germany	MA	Morocco	SU	U.S.S.R.
DDR	East Germany	MAL	Malaysia	SWA	Namibia
DK	Denmark	MC	Monaco	SY	Seychelles
DOM	Dominican Rep.	MEX	Mexico	SYR	Syria
DY	Benin	MS	Mauritius	T	Thailand
DZ	Algeria	MW	Malawi	TG	Togo
E	Spain	N	Norway	TN	Tunisia
EAK	Kenya	NA	Netherlands	TR	Turkey
EAT	Tanzania		Antilles	TT	Trinidad and
EAU	Uganda	NIC	Nicaragua		Tobago
EC	Ecuador	NIG	Niger	USA	United States
ES	El Salvador	NL	Netherlands	VN	Vietnam
ET	Egypt	NZ	New Zealand	WAG	Gambia
F	France	P	Portugal	WAL	Sierra Leone
FJI	Fiji	PA	Panama	WAN	Nigeria
FL	Liechtenstein	PE	Peru	WD	Dominica
FR	Faroe Islands	PK	Pakistan	WL	St. Lucia
GB	United Kingdom	PL	Poland	WS	Western Samoa
GBA	Alderney C.I.	PNG	Papua	WV	St. Vincent
GBG	Guernsey C.I.		New Guinea	YU	Yugoslavia
GBJ	Jersey C.I.	PY	Paraguay	YV	Venezuela
GBM	Isle of Man	RA	Argentina	Z	Zambia
GBZ	Gibraltar	RB	Botswana	ZA	South Africa
				ZRE	Zaïre
				ZW	Zimbabwe

◁ A U.S. license plate publicizes the owner's home state.

THE MIGHTY ENGINE

The heart of the car is the internal combustion engine, whose development in the 19th century made the car possible. Here are some of the terms used in describing the working of an engine.

accelerator Pedal that regulates engine speed by controlling the flow of fuel.

air-cooled engine Engine cooled by air drawn into the engine compartment by a fan.

choke Means of enriching the fuel/air mixture going to the cylinder.

crankshaft Shaft that is turned by the connecting rods from the pistons. The up-and-down motion of the pistons is converted into rotary motion.

cylinder Broad tube in the engine in which each piston moves up and down.

dipstick Rod for measuring the amount of oil in the sump or gearbox.

distributor Unit that distributes high-voltage current from the coil to each of the spark plugs in turn.

exhaust system Pipes that carry exhaust gases away from the engine.

fan belt Belt that drives the cooling fan from a pulley on the crankshaft.

four-stroke cycle Operating cycle of the internal combustion engine. The strokes (up or down movements of the piston) are induction, compression, power, and exhaust.

ignition Firing of the fuel/air mixture in the cylinders.

radiator Device for cooling the water in the car's cooling system.

spark plug Device that, using high-voltage current from the distributor, generates a spark to ignite the fuel/air mixture in the cylinder.

Air filter

Flywheel: heavy wheel fixed to the crankshaft to help the engine run smoothly

Carburetor

Oil filter

Sump, full of oil

Dipstick, to check the oil level

Pump to pump gasoline from the tank to the carburetor

△ Cutaway of a car engine. The engine may have as many as 150 moving parts. The fly-wheel insures that the engine runs smoothly throughout the cylinder-firing sequence.

Travel by Rail

Railroads first came into use in the 1500s in Britain and other parts of Europe, where they were used to haul coal from underground mines. The wagons were drawn by horses or people, women as well as men.

The steam locomotive was developed in Britain in the 18th and 19th centuries. The first practical steam railroad was built by Richard Trevithick, a Cornish inventor and professional wrestler.

The first public railroad, the Stockton and Darlington Railway, opened in the north of England in 1825. It was engineered by George Stephenson and carried coal and freight, hauled by the engine *Locomotion No 1*. The first passenger line ran between Liverpool and Manchester; it opened in 1830. It was also engineered by Stephenson, whose locomotive, the *Rocket*, won trials at Rainhill, near Liverpool, the year before, in a contest with four other locomotives.

▽ The *Rocket*, victor in the 1829 Rainhill trials for steam locomotives. It had a multitube boiler, enabling steam to be raised more quickly with less fuel, and was a rugged, reliable design.

Chimney

Connecting rod

Multitube boiler

Safety valve

Cylinder

Valve controls

Firebox

Footplate

ROCKET

Driving wheel

Trailing wheel

RAILROAD TERMS

arrester Trackside device to slow or stop shunted vehicles.

brake van Van manned by a guard and containing a screw brake, marshaled at the rear of a goods train.

buffers Sprung metal "studs" at the ends of a vehicle to absorb the shocks of minor collisions in shunting.

bufferstop Set of buffers mounted at the end of a length of track.

chair U-shaped metal casting that holds rail to sleepers.

coupling Hooking device for joining railroad vehicles to a train.

double-heading Using two locomotives to pull one train.

fishplate Metal plate used to join rails end to end.

freight train Train of closed or gondola cars for carrying freight.

frog X-shaped casting that allows rails to "cross" at points.

gauge Width of track, measured between the inside edges of the rails.

gondola car Open-topped shallow car for carrying coal and similar freight.

hump shunting Using a downgrade after a hump in the track to move railroad vehicles.

light engine Locomotive traveling without pulling a train.

loading gauge Maximum permitted height of a railroad vehicle.

marshaling Sorting vehicles into the correct order for a train.

point Tip of the angle formed by the intersection of rails at a frog or switch.

shoe Steel collector on electric train for collecting electricity from a third rail.

shunting Pushing uncoupled vehicles along the track.

siding Branch track for holding stationary vehicles.

sleeper Wood or concrete tie across and beneath the rails to form the track.

standard gauge In North America and most of Europe 4 ft 8½ in (1.44 m).

vacuum brake Type of railroad vehicle brake held *off* by low air pressure (vacuum).

welded rail Rail made continuous by welding together shorter lengths.

Fishplate

Spikes

T-rail section

Baseplate or 'chair'

Sleeper

Chipped-stone ballast

△ Most of the world's railroads use track laid in the traditional way.

GOING UNDER

The New York City Subway has more stations – 458 – than any other underground railroad in the world. It runs for a total of 232 miles (373 km), and it carries approximately 1.1 billion passengers a year.

The London Underground (often called the "Tube" because of the tunnels that make up so much of the system), has the longest route in the world: 254 miles (408 km), serving 272 stations. The Tube carries about 770 million passengers a year.

The Paris Métro includes 119 miles (192 km) of track in its 15 lines and has 360 stations. It carries more than 1.16 billion people every year. In rush hours trains run about every 1½ minutes.

The Moscow Metro carries about 2 billion passengers a year, which makes it the world's busiest. It has 234 miles (198 km) of track and 123 spacious stations finished in black and white marble.

Travel by Sea

Today, when people fly everywhere, it is hard to realize that until recently it was necessary to travel by ship for any journey overseas. Before the days of rail it was often quicker, if you were near the coast, to sail along it than to travel overland.

It is still often easier to send freight along the coast, and for all except perishable freight, which must be transported quickly, the sea is still the most economical means of transporting goods long distances across the world.

▽ A supertanker (*foreground*) and a container ship, loaded with containers destined for onward movement by road or rail.

SHIP'S LOG

A ship's logbook is a day-by-day account of everything that happens during a voyage, including her course, speed, and weather encountered. This "log" is a chronology of the sea.

pre-8000B.C. Old Stone Age people use form of dugout canoe.
c. 7250B.C. Earliest form of seafaring – trade in Mediterranean between Melos and Greek mainland.
c. 3000B.C. First known ships – Egyptian galleys.

c. 1000B.C. Phoenicians develop bireme, galley with two rows of oars on each side.
c. 200B.C. Romans build huge galleys, with as many as 200 oars.
c. A.D.1100 Sailors in the Mediterranean and in the China Seas navigating by means of magnetic compass.
1400s Portuguese develop three-masted ship; facilitates sailing against wind.
1620 Dutch scientist Cornelius van Drebbel demonstrates "submarine," a leather-covered rowing boat, in England.

△ A Viking longship of around 900.

1783 Steam propulsion first achieved, by the Marquis Jouffroy d'Abbans (France), with 180-ton paddle-steamer *Pyroscaphe*.
1790s Sailing ships built with iron hulls.
1801 Robert Fulton (U.S.) builds 21 ft (6.4 m) submarine *Nautilus*.
1801 First successful power-driven vessel, the *Charlotte Dundas*, built by William Symington (U.K.).
1807 Robert Fulton (U.S.) builds the *Clermont*, first regular passenger steamer.

1822 First iron-built steamship, the *Aaron Manby*; also first prefabricated ship.
1839 British steamer *Archimedes* first to use screw propeller successfully.
1845 *Rainbow* (U.S.), first true clipper ship.
1897 Charles Parsons (U.K.) demonstrates first turbine-driven ship, *Turbinia*.
1912 First ocean-going diesel-driven ships.
1955 First nuclear-powered submarine, *Nautilus* (U.S.).
1959 First hovercraft, SR-N1, invented by Christopher Cockerell (U.K.).
1959 First nuclear-powered surface ship, Russian ice-breaker *Lenin*.
1962 *Savannah* (U.S.) goes into service as first nuclear-powered merchant ship.
1962 First public hovercraft service, inaugurated in Britain.
1979 First helicopter-carrying patrol vessel in operation with Danish Fisheries Protection.
1986 World's largest dry cargo ship, the Norwegian *Berge Stahl*, launched.
1988 Catamaran *Jet Services 5* makes fastest Atlantic crossing under sail.

△ The SR-N4 hovercraft's four propellers give the ferry a speed of up to 60 knots as it skims over the sea on its cushion of air.

SAILING TERMS

The great days of sailing ships began thousands of years ago and came to an end only in the 19th century. Over that time sailors built up a language all their own. Some of its terms have passed into everyday use ashore. For example, the phrase "by and large," meaning "generally speaking," originally meant sailing just off the wind when a vessel was sailing as near as possible into the wind. These are some common sailing terms.

aft Toward the rear of a vessel.
amidships Near the middle of a vessel.
barque Sailing vessel with three or more masts, all but the last square-rigged; the third mast is rigged fore-and-aft.
beam Width of vessel's hull.
bow The front of a vessel.

△ Early Egyptian seagoing vessel, with steering oars and a single sail.

foresail Lowermost sail on the foremast.
jib Triangular sail between the foremast and the bowsprit.
keel The main structural member running lengthwise along the bottom of a ship's hull.
knot Unit of speed for boats and ships. One knot equals one nautical mile per hour.
lateen A triangular sail suspended from a sloping yard attached to a mast.
mainmast Mast second from the front; the middle mast on a three-masted vessel.
mainsail Lowermost sail on mainmast.
mizzen Lateen sail on mizzen mast.
mizzen mast Third mast toward the rear of a vessel.
overall length Length of a vessel's hull.
poop Raised deck toward the stern of a vessel.

△ A paddle steamer of the 1800s. Early steamships had sails as well as engines.

bowsprit Long projection from the bow that supports rigging and possibly a jib or spritsail.
crow's nest Look-out position near the top of a mast.
deck The planked or plated-over "floor" across a ship's hull. A small vessel has only one deck.
displacement Weight of water (generally expressed in tons) displaced by a floating vessel.
draft Amount of a ship's hull below the waterline, i.e. the minimum depth of water in which a vessel will float.
fo'c'sle (forecastle) Raised deck at the front of a vessel.
fore (or for'ard) Toward the front of a vessel.
foremast Mast at the front of a vessel.

△ The carrack of the 1400s retained the raised stern and forecastle, originally used as fighting platforms.

△ An example of the popular sternwheelers that plied the Mississippi River.

rudder Vertical control surface in the water at the rear of a vessel, by means of which it is steered.
royal Sail above the topgallant.
schooner Two-masted sailing vessel with mainly fore-and-aft sails.
sheet Rope or cable attached to the end of a yard for controlling the angle of the sail to the mast.
spanker Fore-and-aft sail on the rearmost mast.
spritsail Square sail on yard suspended from the bowsprit.
stay Thick cable sloping down from a mast, generally to the base of the mast in front of it.
staysail Triangular sail between two masts.
stern The rear of a vessel.
topgallant Sail above the topsail.
topsail Sail above the foresail or mainsail, etc.
yard A spar, generally horizontal and pivoted to a mast, from which a sail is suspended.

△ A three-masted schooner, with a combination of sails. Such vessels were common trading ships into the early 1900s.

▷ The square-rigged windjammer *Herzogin Cecilie*, 1902. Originally designed for the Atlantic passenger trade, she ended her days in 1936 carrying cargo.

△ *Sirius* (*left center*) was the first ship to cross the Atlantic under steam, followed into New York harbor in April 1838 by Brunel's *Great Western* (*center*).

VOYAGES AND DISASTERS

Many of the most exciting voyages were those made by the explorers. They needed courage, too, because they were often setting off into the unknown. When Bartholomeu Dias and Vasco da Gama sailed south down the coast of Africa, many of their crews had a real fear that they would fall off the edge of a flat Earth.

SEA DISASTERS

Date	Ship and nature of accident	Deaths
1852	**Birkenhead,** British troopship, ran aground off Port Elizabeth, South Africa, and broke in two on the rocks	455
1865	**Sultana,** Mississippi River steamer, blew up (boiler explosion)	1,450
1872	**Mary Celeste,** American half-brig, found abandoned in Atlantic with no sign of life; great mystery of the sea	
1904	**General Slocum,** an excursion steamer, burned in New York harbor	1,021
1912	**Titanic,** British liner, struck iceberg in Atlantic	1,500
1914	**Empress of Ireland,** Canadian steamer, sank after collision in St. Lawrence River	1,204
1915	**Lusitania,** British liner, torpedoed by German submarine off Ireland	1,198
1934	**Morro Castle,** U.S. steamer, burned off N.J. coast	134
1942	**Curaçao,** British cruiser, sank after collision with liner *Queen Mary*	335
1945	**Wilhelm Gustloff,** German liner, torpedoed by Russian submarine off Danzig	700
1954	**Toya Maru,** Japanese ferry, sank in Tsugaru Strait	1,172
1963	**Thresher,** American nuclear submarine, sank in Atlantic	129
1987	**Herald of Free Enterprise,** cross-Channel ferry, capsized off Zeebrugge, Belgium	193
1987	**Doña Paz,** Philippines ferry, collided with tanker, *Victor,* off Marinduque Island	1,500

FAMOUS VOYAGES

1487 Bartolomeu Dias of Portugal sailed south in search of a route to India and discovered the Cape of Good Hope.

1492 Christopher Columbus sailed from Spain hoping to find a westward route to the Indies, but landed instead on a Caribbean island.

△ Columbus's first voyage to the New World, 1492. He landed on a Caribbean island.

△ Columbus's *Santa Maria* may have looked like this.

1497–1499 Vasco da Gama of Portugal found the sea route to India around the Cape of Good Hope. The round trip took him two years and two months.

1519–1521 Ferdinand Magellan of Portugal, sailing with Spanish backing, found the way westward into the Pacific Ocean by sailing through the Magellan Strait. He died on the voyage, but 18 members of his expedition led by Sebastián Del Cano completed the first voyage round the world.

1577–1580 Francis Drake of England made the second voyage around the world, leaving with five ships and returning with one.

1642 Abel Janszoon Tasman of the Netherlands sailed southward from Java and discovered Tasmania and New Zealand.

1768–1779 James Cook of Britain made three voyages to explore the Pacific and discovered Hawaii.

1895–1898 Joshua Slocum of the United States made the first single-handed voyage around the world.

1947 Thor Heyerdahl of Norway, with five companions, sailed a balsa wood raft, the *Kon-Tiki*, from Peru to the Tuamoto Islands in Polynesia, to prove that some Pacific Islands could have been settled by people from America.

△ Vasco da Gama was the first European to sail around Africa to India, 1497–99.

△ Magellan's voyage (1519–21) ended with his death in the Philippines. One ship completed the circumnavigation.

Travel by Air

People have been trying to fly for thousands of years. The ancient legend of Daedalus and his son Icarus, who set out to fly from Crete to Sicily, may well have a foundation in experiments with artificial wings and gliding. The 16th-century artist Leonardo da Vinci designed several flying machines, which were never built.

People first sailed through the skies in 1783 when two French brothers, the Montgolfiers, made a balloon. Balloons are at the mercy of the wind, and it was not until the Wright brothers made their historic flight in 1903 that people conquered the air. And man-powered flight came in the 1970s. *Gossamer Albatross*, with a pedal-driven propeller powered by biologist and cyclist Bryan Allen, made the first flight across the English Channel.

△ Blanchard and Jeffries flew across the English Channel in 1785. Their balloon was fitted with "oars" in a vain attempt at aerial steering.

Wings covered with unbleached muslin

Pilot operates warp control wires by moving his body from side to side

Two propellers rotating in opposite directions push plane through air

Wire trailing edge

Ash ribs

Spru brac

Twin rudders for steering

Elevator control lever

Laced seam

Warp control wire

Stitched seam

△ The Wright *Flyer* of 1903 was developed from earlier glider designs. It had a wingspan of 39 ft (12.3 m) and weighed about 745 lb (340 kg). The pilot lay on the wing, just left of center, to balance the tiny engine. He controlled the machine in flight by "warping" (twisting) the wings.

FIRSTS IN FLIGHT

1783 First human ascent, in a Montgolfier hot air balloon, by J. F. Pilâtre in Paris.
1783 First flight in a hydrogen balloon, made by J. A. C. Charles and M. Roberts.
1785 First balloon crossing of the English Channel, by J. P. Blanchard and J. Jeffries.
1852 First (steam) powered airship, flown by Henri Giffard (France).
1853 First successful airplane (glider), built by Sir George Cayley (U.K.).
1890s First successful glider flights, made by Otto Lilienthal (Germany).
1903 First controlled flights in a heavier-than-air machine, made by Wilbur and Orville Wright (U.S.).
1909 First flight across the English Channel, by Louis Blériot (France).
1919 First transatlantic flight by flying-boat by Albert C. Read (U.S.).
1919 First non-stop transatlantic airplane flight, by J. Alcock and A. W. Brown (U.K.).
1923 First autogiro, flown by Juan de la Cierva (Spain).
1927 First non-stop transatlantic solo flight, by Charles Lindbergh (U.S.).
1928 First transatlantic flight by a woman, Amelia Earhart (U.S.).

△ Alcock and Brown after their first non-stop transatlantic flight.

1928 First transatlantic passenger flight, by a German airship.
1930 First patented design for jet aircraft engine, by Frank Whittle (U.K.).
1930 Amy Johnson (U.K.) becomes first woman to fly solo from England to Australia.
1933 First solo round-the-world flight, made by Wiley Post (U.S.).
1939 First transatlantic passenger service begun by Pan American Airways.
1939 First jet-propelled plane, built by Heinkel (Germany).
1939 First flight of a single-rotor helicopter, made by Russian-American Igor Sikorsky.
1947 First supersonic flight by Charles Yeager (U.S.).
1949 First non-stop round-the-world flight, in a Boeing *Superfortress* bomber.
1979 Bryan Allen (U.S.) in *Gossamer Albatross* makes first man-powered cross-Channel flight.
1986 Richard Rutan and Jeana Yeager (U.S.) make first non-stop round-the-world flight without refueling.

▽ The round-the-world aircraft *Voyager* of Rutan and Yeager.

MILITARY AIRCRAFT

△ British Sopwith Camel fighter of World War I (1914–18).

▽ German Fokker D.VIII (1918). With a top speed of 117 mph (189 km/h) it was one of the finest World War I warplanes.

△ German Messerschmitt Me 109 fighter of World War II (1939–45).

△ Supermarine Spitfire, probably the most famous British fighter plane.

△ U.S. Boeing B-17 Flying Fortress bomber.

▷ The F-86 Sabre, first U.S. warplane to break the sound barrier. Some 700 F-86s were built between 1947 and 1958.

▷ The U.S. F-111 was the first swing-wing combat aircraft (1964). The F(B)-111 variant (illustrated) is a strategic bomber.

◁ The Soviet Tupolev TU-28 (NATO code-named Fiddler) is the world's largest fighter, 85 ft (26 m) long with a 65 ft (20 m) wingspan.

▷ Israel's Kfir (Lion Cub) is based on the French Mirage 5, but is faster, with a top speed of 1,516 mph (2,440 km/h).

▽ The Harrier was the first V/STOL warplane in service. This is the RAF GR3 variant.

INTERNATIONAL MARKINGS

All civil aircraft must be entered on the International Aeronautical Register, which was begun in 1926. Each country has a two-letter (sometimes more) prefix which precedes the aircraft's own code.

A2-	Botswana	EP-	Iran
A40-	Oman	ET-	Ethiopia
A7-	Qatar	F-	France, colonies and
AN-	Nicaragua		protectorates
AP-	Pakistan	G-	Great Britain,
B-	Taiwan (Formosa)		Gibraltar,
C-	Canada	HA-	Hungary
C2-	Nauru	HB-	Switzerland,
CC-	Chile		Liechtenstein
CCCP-	U.S.S.R.	HC-	Ecuador
CF-	Canada	HH-	Haiti
CN-	Morocco	HI-	Dominican Republic
CP-	Bolivia	HK-	Colombia
CR-	Portuguese overseas	HL-	South Korea
	provinces	HP-	Panama
CS-	Portugal	HR-	Honduras
CU-	Cuba	HS-	Thailand
CX-	Uruguay	HZ-	Saudi Arabia
D-	West Germany	I-	Italy
DM-	East Germany	JA-	Japan
DQ-	Fiji	JY-	Jordan
EC-	Spain	LN-	Norway
EI-, EJ-	Republic of Ireland	LQ-, LV-	Argentina
EL-	Liberia	LX-	Luxembourg

LZ-	Bulgaria
N-	United States
OB-	Peru
OD-	Lebanon
OE-	Austria
OH-	Finland
OK-	Czechoslovakia
OO-	Belgium
OY-	Denmark
PH-	Netherlands
PI-	Philippines
PJ-	Netherlands Antilles
PK-	Indonesia
PP-, PT-	Brazil
PZ-	Surinam
S2-	Bangladesh
SE-	Sweden
SP-	Poland
ST-	Sudan
SU-	Egypt
SX-	Greece
TC-	Turkey
TF-	Iceland
TG-	Guatemala
TI-	Costa Rica
TJ-	Cameroon
TL-	Central African Republic
TN-	Congo
TR-	Gabon

STRANGE AIRCRAFT

These illustrations show some very unusual experiments; not all of them were disasters. For example, in 1954 the Lockheed/Rolls-Royce Thrust Measuring Rig (below) was an early machine capable of flying forward and backward. This facility was built into the Harrier combat aircraft.

▽ The curious *Safety* airplane of 1909 probably never flew. It had a sturdy frame, circular biplane wings, and three propellers.

TS-	Tunisia	XT-	Upper Volta	5H-	Tanzania
TT-	Chad	XU-	Cambodia	5N-	Nigeria
TU-	Côte d'Ivoire	XV-	Vietnam	5R-	Madagascar
TY-	Benin	XW-	Laos	5T-	Mauritania
TZ-	Mali	XY-, XZ-	Union of	5U-	Niger
VH-	Australia		Myanmar	5V-	Togo
VP-B	Bahamas	YA-	Afghanistan	5W-	Western Samoa
VP-F	Falkland Islands	YI-	Iraq	5X-	Uganda
VP-H	Belize	YJ-	New Hebrides	5Y-	Kenya
VP-L	Antigua	YK-	Syria	6O-	Somalia
VP-P	Western Pacific	YR-	Romania	6V-, 6W-	Senegal
	High Commission	YS-	El Salvador	6Y-	Jamaica
VP-V	St. Vincent	YU-	Yugoslavia	7O-	Yemen P.D.R.
VP-X	Gambia	YV-	Venezuela	7P-	Lesotho
VP-Y,		ZA-	Albania	7QY-	Malawi
VP-W	Malawi,	ZK-, ZL-,		7T-	Algeria
	Zimbabwe	ZM-	New Zealand	8P-	Barbados
VQ-G	Grenada	ZP-	Paraguay	8R-	Guyana
VQ-H	St. Helena	ZS-, ZT-,		9G-	Ghana
VQ-L	St. Lucia	ZU-	South Africa	9H-	Malta
VQ-S	Seychelles	3A-	Monaco	9J-	Zambia
VR-B	Bermuda	3B-	Mauritius	9K-	Kuwait
VR-H	Hong Kong	3C-	Equatorial Guinea	9L-	Sierra Leone
VR-O	Sabah (Malaysia)	3D-	Swaziland	9M-	Malaysia
VR-U	Brunei	3X-	Guinea	9N-	Nepal
VR-W	Sarawak (Malaysia)	4R	Sri Lanka	9Q-	Zaïre
VT-	India	4W-	Yemen	9U-	Burundi
XA-,		4X-	Israel	9V-	Singapore
XB-,		5A-	Libya	9XR-	Rwanda
XC-	Mexico	5B-	Cyprus	9Y-	Trinidad and Tobago

◁ Northrop's futuristic Flying Wing of the 1940s.

△ The "Flying Mattress" (1956) had an inflatable wing.

▽ The Italian Caproni Ca-60 multi-wing seaplane of 1919.

AIR DISASTERS

Date	Aircraft and nature of accident	Deaths
8.24.21	ZR-2 dirigible (U.K.) broke in two, near Hull, England	62
9.3.25	*Shenandoah* dirigible (U.S.) broke up, Caldwell, Ohio	14
4.4.33	*Akron* dirigible (U.S.) crashed, New Jersey coast	73
5.6.37	*Hindenburg* zeppelin (Ger.) burned at mooring, Lakehurst, N.J.	36
8.23.44	U.S. Air Force B-24 hit school, Freckelton, England	76*
7.28.45	U.S. Army B-25 hit Empire State Building N.Y., in fog	19*
11.1.49	DC-4 airliner (U.S.) rammed by Bolivian P-38 fighter, Washington, D.C.	55
12.20.52	U.S. Air Force C-124 fell and burned, Washington	87
6.18.53	U.S. Air-Force C-124 crashed and burned near Tokyo	129
6.30.56	Super-Constellation and DC-7 airliners collided over Grand Canyon	128
2.6.58	Elizabethan airliner (U.K.) crashed on take-off at Munich, W. Germany	23‡
12.16.60	DC-8 and Super-Constellation airliners collided over New York	134*
2.15.61	Boeing 707 (Belgian) crashed near Brussels	73§
6.3.62	Boeing 707 (French) crashed on takeoff, Paris	130
6.22.62	Boeing 707 (French) crashed in storm, Guadeloupe	113
5.20.65	Boeing 720B (Pakistani) crashed at Cairo airport	121
1.24.66	Boeing 707 (Indian) crashed on Mont Blanc, France	117
2.4.66	Boeing 727 (Jap.) plunged into Tokyo Bay	133
3.5.66	Boeing 707 (U.K.) crashed on Mt. Fuji, Japan	124
4.20.67	Britannia turboprop (Swiss) crashed at Nicosia, Cyprus	126
3.16.69	DC-9 (Venezuelan) crashed on takeoff, Maracaibo	155*
7.30.71	Boeing 727 (Jap.) collided with F-86 fighter, Japan	162
8.14.72	Ilyushin-62 (E. Ger.) crashed on takeoff, Berlin	156
10.13.72	Ilyushin-62 (U.S.S.R.) crashed near Moscow	176
12.4.72	Spanish charter jet airliner crashed on takeoff, Canary Is.	155
1.22.73	Boeing 707 (chartered) crashed on landing at Kano, Nigeria	176

△ The airship *Hindenburg* was completed in 1936 and was hailed as a turning point in passenger transportation, Its fiery crash in May 1937 ended an era in aviation.

Date	Aircraft and nature of accident	Deaths
6.3.73	TU-144 (U.S.S.R.) exploded in air, Goussainville, France	14¶
3.3.74	DC-10 (Turk.) crashed in forest, Ermenonville, France	346
9.10.76	British Trident 3 and Yugoslavian DC-9 collided in mid-air near Zagreb, Yugoslavia	176
3.27.77	Two Boeing 747s (American and Dutch) collided on ground at Tenerife's Los Rodeos airport, Canary Islands	582
1.1.78	Boeing 747 (Indian) crashed into the sea off Bombay, India	
15.11.78	DC-8 (Iceland) crashed while attempting to land, Sri Lanka	262
14.3.79	Trident (China) crashed near Beijing	200
28.11.79	DC-10 (NZ) crashed into Mount Erebus, Antarctica	257
19.8.80	Lockheed Tristar (Saudi) destroyed by fire after emergency landing, Riyadh	301
13.1.82	Boeing 737 (US) struck bridge over Potomac River, Washington DC	78*
9.7.82	Boeing 727 (US) crashed in strong winds into a housing estate, Kenner, Louisiana	153*
7.12.83	Two jet liners (Spain) collided in fog on the runway at Madrid airport	93
28.10.84	Soviet military aircraft crashed after take-off from Kabul	240
23.6.85	Boeing 747 (Indian) blown up by bomb over Atlantic	329
2.8.85	Delta Airlines jumbo crashed on landing at Fort Worth, Texas	140
12.8.85	Boeing 747 (Japan) crashed into Mt Otusaka, Japan	520
22.8.85	Boeing 737 (UK) caught fire on take-off at Manchester	54
12.12.85	Charter jet (US) crashed at Gander, Canada	256
6.11.86	Helicopter (UK) crashed into North Sea	45
28.11.87	South African jumbo jet crashed into Indian Ocean	159
21.12.88	Boeing 747 (US) blown up by bomb over Scotland	258
9.1.89	Boeing 737 (UK) crashed on motorway in England	46

*Total includes deaths on ground or in buildings.
‡Mostly players (8) and officials (3) of England football champions Manchester United and 8 journalists.
§Including skaters (17) and officials of US world championships team.
¶First supersonic airliner crash.

Communications

All living creatures communicate with one another – whales sing, bees dance, and cats scent-mark their territory. People communicate by speech, laughter, gesture, and touch. They advanced further by inventing the written word, and this has formed the basis of our civilization. Today's technology means that words and pictures, in the form of electronic signals, can be transmitted across continents and bounced from satellites in outer space. The method is there – the message is up to us!

All animals communicate in one way or another – dogs bark, birds sing to mark out their territories, female moths emit phero-mones (scent-like chemical messages) to lure males from many miles away. But human beings have developed the art of communica-tion far beyond that of animals.

△ Written Chinese uses 80,000 characters, traditionally painted with a brush.

We can communicate with one another not only from city to city, but across the oceans and out into space. Communications can be instant: someone in Boston can chat by telephone to a friend in California as readily as to a friend in the next street. Interesting events such as a royal wedding, the Olympic Games or a spacecraft launch can be seen as they happen on television in every country in the world.

Perhaps the most important way in which we communicate is by storing and sharing knowledge. If you go into a big library, you will find books containing the knowledge and experience collected over thousands of years.

People invented writing about 5,500 years ago. They had accumulated knowledge and passed it on to others long before that. They passed on their news and knowledge orally – that is, by word of mouth. Bards used to memorize and chant stories of bygone days. The great poems the *Iliad* and the

Odyssey, attributed to the Greek minstrel Homer, who lived around 2,800 years ago, were undoubtedly passed on in this way for a long time before they were written down.

The earliest visual form of communication that has survived is the paintings we see on the walls of caves, particularly those in France and Spain. Some of those paintings are more than 30,000 years old. Writing gradually evolved from just such paintings.

People have always been travelers. From their beginnings in Africa they spread first through Europe and Asia, and then to the Americas and across the ocean to the islands of the Pacific. Wherever they went, they carried with them their knowledge and the ability to communicate it.

Modern methods of communication developed only in the past 500 years or so. The first real breakthrough was the invention of printing in the 1400s. Books and, later, newspapers, have poured off the presses ever since. The next breakthrough came less than 200 years ago, when the discovery of electricity enabled people to send messages instantly over long distances. The telegraph and the telephone made possible quick communication between distant places.

The importance of sending news quickly is shown by the War of 1812 between Britain and the United States. The cause of the quarrel was British interference with U.S. shipping during war with France. The British agreed on June 16, 1812, to end this interference, but because Congress did not know this it declared war on Britain on June 18. The peace treaty ending that war was signed on December 24, 1814. The news took so long to reach America that another battle, the Battle of New Orleans, took place 15 days after the treaty was signed.

Now, thanks to radio, television and satellite link-ups, it would be much more difficult for this kind of tragic error to happen.

▽ Two electric wires are needed for each telephone conversation, whereas one glass fiber can transmit nearly 1 million calls at the same time.

Electric cable

Laser transmitter

Glass fiber cable

Repeater

Decoder

Electric cable

Writing

△ In the Middle Ages, before the invention of printing, books were written by hand. Many hours of painstaking work went into the elaborate decoration of illuminated manuscripts.

The earliest way in which people tried to write was by drawing pictures. The cave paintings of the Stone Age showed the animals the men were hunting, possibly as an indication to the gods that the hunters needed help to find their prey.

Soon people started using drawings to describe not just things but ideas, such as "front" and "God." From there it was a step to make the drawings stylized – symbols or signs rather than pictures. People used signs for words, as in written Chinese. Then they used them to stand for syllables. Finally our alphabet, in which the signs stand for sounds, came into being.

TERMS IN THE HISTORY OF WRITING

alphabet A set of letters used in writing; the name comes from the first two letters of the Greek alphabet, alpha and beta.

cuneiform Wedge-shaped writing inscribed with a stylus on clay tablets. It was invented by the Sumerians about 3000 B.C.

Cyrillic Form of alphabet used in Russian and Bulgarian, derived from the Greek alphabet.

Greek Form of alphabet was adapted about 1000 B.C. from the writing systems of the Middle East. Modern alphabets are derived from it.

hieroglyphics Picture writing, especially the picture writing used by the ancient Egyptians and by early American Indians, such as the Aztecs.

letter A symbol representing a sound.

logogram A symbol representing a complete word or phrase; the sign $, dollar, is a logogram.

pictographs Pictures of objects; used in the ancient Middle East and by the Aztec and Maya Indians of North America.

quipu Knotted strings used by the Inca of Peru, mainly for keeping accounts.

rebus A mixture of words and pictures, the pictures representing syllables or words.

runes Letters of an alphabet used by the Teutonic peoples of northern Europe before A.D. 1000.

stylus Tool made from a reed for impressing cuneiform characters into clay tablets.

syllabary A set of symbols representing syllables, as in Japanese writing.

tally Split stick used for keeping accounts, according to the number of notches cut in it.

▷ A Sumerian clay table with cuneiform writing, about 2800 B.C., and a reed "pen."

▷ The first pencil, 1565, contained a lead of pure graphite.

Greek				Hebrew				Russian		
Letter	Name	Transliteration		Letter	Name	Transliteration		Letter		Transliteration
A α	alpha	a		א	aleph	'		А а	a
B β	beta	b		בּ	beth	b		Б б	b
Γ γ	gamma	g		גּ	gimel	g		В в	v
								Г г	g
Δ δ	delta	d		ד	daleth	d		Д д	d
E ε	epsilon	e		ה	heh	h		Е е	e, ye
Z ζ	zeta	z		ו	waw	w		Ж ж	zh
H η	eta	ē		ז	zayin	z		З з	z
Θ θ	theta	th		ח	heth	ḥ		И и	i
I ι	iota	i		ט	teth	ṭ		Й й	ĭ
K κ	kappa	k		י	yod	y		К к	k
Λ λ	lambda	l		כך*	kaph	k, kh		Л л	l
M μ	mu	m		ל	lamed	l		М м	m
N ν	nu	n		מם*	mem	m		Н н	n
Ξ ξ	xi	x (ks)		נן*	nun	n		О о	o
								П п	p
O o	omicron	o		ס	samekh	s		Р р	r
Π π	pi	p		ע	ayin	'		С с	s
P ρ	rho	r		פף*	peh	p, ph		Т т	t
Σ σ, ς*	sigma	s		צץ*	sadhe	ṣ		У у	u
T τ	tau	t		ק	qoph	q		Ф ф	f
Υ υ	upsilon	u, y		ר	resh	r		Х х	kh
Φ φ	phi	ph		שׁ	shin	sh		Ц ц	ts
X χ	chi	kh, ch		שׂ	sin	ś		Ч ч	ch
Ψ ψ	psi	ps		ת	taw	t		Ш ш	sh
Ω ω	omega	o						Щ щ	shch
								ы	ĭ
								ь	'
								Э э	e
								Ю ю	yu
								Я я	ya

Steel nib
n, 1800s.

Ballpoint
n, mid-1900s.

△ Fountain pen,
late 1800s.

△ Printing by letterpress using inked, raised type.

Printing

Printing was one of the world's impor tant inventions because it brought knowledg within the reach of ordinary people. Fo thousands of years before printing, book were made by scribes laboriously writing ou each copy by hand. Such books were rare and expensive. Modern printing began in Europ in the 1440s.

▷ In offset lithography, inked rollers transfer ink to the large cylinder holding the printing plate. Ink is then transferred or "offset" from the plate to a rubber blanket and onto the paper.

PRINTING GLOSSARY

electrotype A copy of engravings and type made by an electroplating process.
engraving A plate engraved for printing, or a printed illustration.
halftone A printing process in which a picture is made up of tiny dots; varying sizes of black dots create an illusion of different shades of gray.
intaglio Printing from a design cut into a metal plate; ink stays in the cut-away part when the rest of the plate is wiped clean.
lithography A form of planographic printing.
photogravure A form of intaglio printing from a plate made photographically.
planographic printing Printing from a flat surface with the design in a greasy medium; the ink clings only to the greasy part.

relief printing Printing from an inked design which is raised above the background.
stereotype A copy of a page of type made with the aid of a mold.

△ The collation process of a modern newspaper press.

CHRONOLOGY OF PRINTING

c. 1320 B.C. The Chinese use inked engraved seals to stamp documents.

A.D. 868 The earliest known printed book is produced in China, using a carved wood block.

c. 1040 The Chinese alchemist Pi Sheng invents movable type made of pottery.

1403 T'ai Tsung, king of Korea, establishes a foundry for casting metal type.

1423 The earliest known European printed picture is produced from a wood block.

c. 1440 Johannes Gutenberg, a goldsmith of Mainz, Germany, invents a system of casting type, a printing press, and suitable ink.

1451 Gutenberg prints his first book, a Latin grammar, using a black-letter (Gothic) type.

1457 First book printed in two colors, black and red, is produced in Mainz.

1470 Nicolas Jensen, a French printer working in Venice, invents Roman type.

1475 William Caxton sets up the first English printing press.

1477 Intaglio printing from engraved metal plates is introduced.

1501 Francesco Griffo of Bologna, Italy, invents *italic* type.

1719 Full color printing is pioneered in Frankfurt, Germany.

1727 William Ged invents stereotyping in Scotland.

1798 Bavarian actor Alois Senefelder invents lithography.

1800 Earl Stanhope, an English amateur printer, makes the first iron-framed press.

1810 German printer Friedrich König, working in London, makes a steam-powered press.

1839 Electrotyping is invented in the United States, Britain, and Russia.

Keyboard

Computer

Phototypesetter

△ Computerized phototypesetting system.

▽ Linotype composing machine, 1886.

1845 Richard Hoe of New York makes the first high-speed rotary press.

1880 The first halftone picture is printed in the New York *Daily Graphic*.

1886–7 Linotype and Monotype machines speed up typesetting, hitherto done by hand.

1895 Photogravure comes into use.

1939 American William C. Huebner invents the first photocomposition machine.

1965 Computer typesetting is introduced in Germany.

1980s Complete pages are produced by computers, transferred to paper by laser, and then photographed onto a printing plate.

△ Daguerreotype camera, 1839.

△ Powell's stereoscopic camera, 1858, produced 3-D photographs.

△ The cheap Brownie camera, 1900, made the snapshot universal.

△ Leitz camera, 1925, was the first reliable hand-held camera using fast film.

Photography

There is an old Chinese saying that a picture is worth a thousand words; but before the advent of photography pictures were expensive and not always accurate. Pictures depended on the ability of the artist – and only a few people can draw and paint well.

Since the first photograph was taken in 1826 that has changed. Anyone can take a photograph. Communication by pictures has proved of immense importance in science and education as well as in everyday life.

Photography has many applications in industry, including the production of the miniature circuits needed for the silicon chips in computers and pocket calculators. In medicine it has enabled doctors to examine the interior of the body from the outside by means of X-ray photography, and to photograph inside by inserting long tubes incorporating fiber optics.

▽ How a camera works. Opening the shutter lets light from the object through a lens, which directs the light through an aperture (the iris). The light is focused onto the film by a second set of lenses, forming an inverted (upside-down) image.

Film advance

Shutter release

Rewind lever

Film

Lenses

Aperture

Iris

Inverted image

Object

GLOSSARY

aperture Opening of variable size made by the diaphragm. It helps to control the amount of light entering the camera.

exposure The amount of light reaching the film, controlled by the aperture size and the shutter speed.

f-number (or f-stop) One of a collection of numbers on a camera showing the aperture size after adjusting the diaphragm.

focus To make an image clear and sharp on the viewing screen and the film.

image The upside-down picture captured on the film when the shutter is released.

lens Several specially shaped pieces of glass focusing the image.

negative An image fixed on a film. Light tones appear dark; dark tones appear light.

reflex camera Camera with a mirror or mirrors inside to reflect light entering through the lens onto a viewing screen.

transparency A true-to-life color picture made on transparent film.

▽ Inside a twin-lens reflex camera.

▽ Inside a single-lens reflex camera.

KEY DATES IN PHOTOGRAPHY

c.1000 Arab astronomers use the camera obscura, a tiny aperture in a darkened room.

1725 Johann Schulze of Germany discovers that some silver compounds darken on exposure to light.

1826 Joseph Nicéphore Niépce, a French inventor, takes the earliest known surviving photograph.

1839 Louis Jacques Daguerre, a French artist, invents a process of making photographs on copper plates.

1839 William Henry Fox Talbot, an English scientist, produces the Calotype negative, from which prints can be made.

1851 Frederick Scott Archer, an English sculptor, invents the wet glass plate.

1855 Roger Fenton of England photographs the Crimean War.

1858 First aerial photograph is taken from a captive balloon.

1860s Experiments in color photography in England and France prove unsuccessful.

1861 Matthew Brady begins photographing the American Civil War.

1873 Bromide printing paper is introduced.

1888 George Eastman, an American, introduces flexible paper roll film and the Kodak camera in which to use it.

1889 Eastman replaces the paper film with celluloid.

1895 X-ray photography is introduced.

1903 French brothers Louis and Auguste Lumière invent the first practical three-color process.

1914 Panchromatic black and white film, sensitive to all colors, comes into use.

1925 A German firm, Leitz, produces the first miniature camera, the Leica.

1931 Harold Edgerton of the United States invents electronic flash.

1935 Kodak introduces the Kodachrome process.

1942 Agfa in Germany and Kodak in the United States introduce color prints.

1945 The zoom lens is introduced.

1947 Edwin Land of the United States invents the Polaroid camera, producing instant black and white prints.

1963 Polaroid produces instant color film.

1963 Holography – three-dimensional photography – is introduced in the United States.

1970s Automatic focusing is introduced.

1989 Ultra high speed flash, producing an output of 40 joules in 1/250,000 second, becomes commercially available.

△ Carrier pigeons were used to carry the news of the Battle of Waterloo to London in 1815. Pigeons were still useful message-carriers during World War II.

▽ Many letters are still sorted by hand (*below*). Automatic sorting machines scan coded phosphorescent dots on envelopes and direct each letter to the correct destination box.

Postal Services

The world's earliest postal services were set up by kings to send messages to distant parts of their lands. One of the most efficient was that of the Persian ruler Darius the Great in the 500s B.C. He had couriers galloping along specially built post roads, carrying his orders. Similar services were organized by the Mongol emperors of China, Genghis Khan and his grandson Kublai Khan.

In Europe the first Roman emperor, Augustus, organized an efficient postal system during the first century A.D. After the end of the Roman empire, postal services lapsed. They were revived in Russia in the 1200s, and in England and France in the 1400s. England's post office, as a service available to the public, began in the 1600s. The first American postal service was started in Massachusetts in 1639.

Today every country has a postal service, linked by the Universal Postal Union, which is now an agency of the United Nations.

MILESTONES IN POSTAL SERVICES

1635 Charles I sets up England's first public postal service.

1680 English merchant William Dockwra sets up a short-lived penny postal service in London.

1775 Benjamin Franklin sets up the United States federal postal service.

1784 First British mail coaches run.

1809 Australia's first postal service begins in New South Wales.

1838 First traveling post office runs on British railroads.

1840 First adhesive postage stamp (the "Penny Black") is issued in Britain, with the introduction of a universal penny post.

△ A collection of British stamps, from Queen Victoria to Queen Elizabeth II.

1847 First adhesive postage stamps in the United States.

1848 France introduces adhesive stamps and universal postal rates.

1860 Pony Express mail service between St. Joseph, Missouri, and Sacramento, California, is started; it lasts only 17 months, killed by the telegraph.

△ A U.S. mailbox. Postal services have become an indispensable part of modern life.

1869 First postcard is introduced in Austria.

1874 Universal Postal Union formed.

1911 First experimental British airmail service.

1919 First regular airmail service between London and Paris begins.

1929 England–India airmail service begins.

1935 Transpacific airmail service is started between San Francisco, California, and the Philippines.

1939 Transatlantic airmail service starts.

1959 British Post Office introduces experimental post codes in Norwich.

1960 Mechanized sorting office opens at Providence, Rhode Island.

SPECIAL POSTAL SERVICES

C.O.D. (collect on delivery) enables a person to pay the postman for goods when they are delivered.

Express mail provides a guaranteed service, between major U.S. cities, either same day or next day, for important items.

Metered post Large users can rent franking machines which print the postage directly on envelopes or on adhesive labels.

Postal order A form of check that can be bought at a post office and mailed to a named person, who must prove identity when cashing it.

Poste restante Mail may be sent to a post office to be called for—particularly useful for travelers.

Prepaid international reply coupons These can be purchased at U.S. post offices and then exchanged for stamps in the recipient's country.

Registered letters or packages are charged extra: the receiver must sign for them; compensation is paid if they are lost.

Special delivery Packages and letters sent special delivery are delivered to their destinations the next day.

Long-distance Signaling

For thousands of years, people have sent pre-arranged signals by means of hilltop beacon fires. But detailed long-distance communications began only in the 1790s when Claude Chappé, a French engineer, built a semaphore telegraph. Moving mechanical arms on a tall tower signaled messages in code, and, following the same principle, signals are still sometimes sent by flag-waving today. A series of such towers sent messages swiftly from one to the next down the line over hundreds of miles.

Modern electronic communications began a few years later with the invention of the electric telegraph, perfected in 1838 by an American portrait painter, Samuel F.B Morse, and his colleagues Professor Leonard D. Gale and Alfred Vail.

▽ Samuel Morse's electric telegraph, 1882. The key (C) was used to send messages in Morse code. The recorder (A) registered incoming signals as dots and dashes on a paper tape.

A ·–	G ––·	M ––	S ···	Y –·––	5 ·····
B –···	H ····	N –·	T –	Z ––··	6 –····
C –·–·	I ··	O –––	U ··–	1 ·––––	7 ––···
D –··	J ·–––	P ·––·	V ···–	2 ··–––	8 –––··
E ·	K –·–	Q ––·–	W ·––	3 ···––	9 ––––·
F ··–·	L ·–··	R ·–·	X –··–	4 ····–	0 –––––

IMPORTANT DATES IN TELEGRAPHY

△ Chappé's semaphore used relay stations like this.

1794 First semaphore telegraph, 140 miles (225 km) from Lille to Paris, is built by Claude Chappé.

1804 Francisco Salva of Barcelona sends messages up to 900 yards (1 km) by electric telegraph, using one wire for each letter of the alphabet.

1837 William Cooke and Charles Wheatstone of Britain patent a five-wire telegraph system.

1838 Samuel Morse perfects his single-wire telegraph system and the Morse code.

1844 Morse sends the first long-distance message, "What hath God wrought!" from Washington D.C. to Baltimore, Maryland.

1845 A railroad telegraph message sent over 20 miles (32 km) from Slough to London, leads to the arrest of a murderer.

1851 Submarine cable is laid under the English Channel between Britain and France.

1855 British professor David E. Hughes, working in the United States, invents a printing telegraph machine.

1856 Formation of Western Union Telegraph Company leads to unified telegraph service in the United States.

1858 Wheatstone patents a punched-tape system for faster transmission.

1861 Telegraph service is extended from the east to the west coast of America.

1866 First successful transatlantic cable is laid.

1872 Duplex telegraphy is invented in the United States and multiplex telegraphy is invented in France.

1927 Teleprinter services come into general use.

1935 First facsimile telegraph service opens in the United States.

△ Optical fiber and conventional electric cables. The smaller optical cable has much greater capacity.

LONG-DISTANCE SIGNALING GLOSSARY

cablegram A telegram sent by an undersea cable.

duplex system A method of sending two messages simultaneously in opposite directions over the same cable.

flag-hoist signaling Signaling between ships by displaying different-colored flags on ships' masts.

hand-signal flags Two flags used in a simple method of semaphore signaling (see diagram on p.281).

heliograph A system of sending signals by flashing sunlight from a mirror, used by the British and other armies in the 1800s.

international flag code The code used for flag-hoist signaling at sea.

multiplex system Sending several messages simultaneously over the same cable.

pyrotechnic signals Signals made with rockets, flares, and smoke.

semaphore Signaling by means of two flags or mechanical arms, held in various positions to represent letters.

telegram A message transmitted by telegraph.

wireless telegraphy Telegraphy by means of signals transmitted by radio.

Radio and Television

Radio and television are the two quickest means of communication. They depend on electromagnetic waves, which travel through space as fast as light. There are several kinds of electromagnetic waves, including radio waves (the longest), infrared rays, visible light, ultraviolet light, X-rays, and gamma rays (the shortest). Radio and television both use radio waves. These were discovered by the German physicist Heinrich Hertz in 1887, though their existence had been predicted by James Clerk Maxwell, a Scottish scientist, 23 years earlier.

△ Radio pioneer Guglielmo Marconi with his 1901-style transmitter.
▽ An early radio receiver.

The first radio signals for communications were transmitted in 1895 by the Italian inventor Guglielmo Marconi. Radio was used for communicating to ships at sea from 1903 onward, and first saved lives in 1909 when two ships collided in the Atlantic.

Radio telephones came into use in the 1920s to cross the Atlantic Ocean, before the first permanent cable was laid in 1956. From 1962 radio signals relayed by satellites carried phone calls and radio programs all over the world. Soon after, licensed amateur, or "ham," radio began, first in North America and then in Europe. In the 1980s, radio came into use for mobile telephones.

Television received its first practical demonstration in 1926 from a Scottish inventor, John Logie Baird, though Baird's system

Antenna

▷ A huge radio telescope reflecting dish. Dishes like this one are used to pick up signals from distant stars. They developed from research by the American Karl Jansky into the way in which the atmosphere affects radio reception.

◁ A VCR records the incoming signal in a diagonal pattern of strips across the tape.

Video cassette recorder

Videotape

John Logie Baird pioneered TV with a mechanical system that produced flickering images. Light from the object (a doll's head) passed through holes in a spinning disk and was turned into electrical signals. These signals were then turned back into a light beam projected onto a screen to produce pictures.

was not the one finally adopted. Regular broadcasting began in the 1930s. Television's main use in communications is in bringing into people's homes news and pictures of events as they happen. It is also used for surveillance purposes by police and shop-keepers.

Both radio and television have an important role in communicating what is loosely called "entertainment" direct to people's homes. This ranges from popular music to comedy shows, drama, and informative talks. They also have an important part in education, beaming learning material to schools, colleges and people's homes. In Britain, for example, television and radio programs are used in college-level courses given by the Open University for part-time students.

RADIO AND TV FACTS

Biggest TV manufacturer is Japan, producing around 13 million sets a year.

Biggest radio manufacturer is Hong Kong, making about 42 million sets a year.

The coronation of Queen Elizabeth II in 1953 was the first major international TV broadcast.

Earliest transatlantic radio transmission was the Morse signal for "S," sent in 1901.

Earliest transatlantic TV transmission was made in 1928 by Baird to a liner; it was picked up in Hartsdale, New York.

First public radio broadcast was by Professor Reginald A. Fessenden in Massachusetts in 1906.

First stereo broadcasts on radio were made in the United States in 1961.

Geostationary satellites – those that orbit the Earth in step with Earth's rotation – came into use in 1963, making constant radio links possible.

The ionosphere, a region of electrified air between 80 and 100 miles (130–160 km) above the Earth, "bounces" radio waves around the world.

Most TV sets in use – China claimed 600 million sets in use in 1988.

Ninety-eight per cent of United States households owned at least one TV set in 1988.

Satellite TV began in Europe in 1989, with signals beamed via the Astra satellite to home receivers.

Teletext, transmission of pages of information by television using spare lines not normally seen, was pioneered in Britain in 1973.

Telstar, launched in 1962, was the first successful communications satellite.

Videotape recording was first demonstrated in 1956.

△ A teletext machine.

Diaphragm

Electromagnet

Earpiece

Mouthpiece

Diaphragm

Carbon granules

△ How a telephone works.
As the caller speaks, a
microphone vibrates and
the vibrations are turned
into electrical signals which
travel along cables. At the
earpiece, these signals set up
vibrations in the
diaphragm, which
reproduces the sound-
patterns of the caller's
voice.

Business Communications

The main advances in communications have
come in the realm of business, which can
increasingly be carried on at a distance.

Electronic mail is an international series of
computer networks, through which a subscriber can send messages to other subscrib-
ers by addressing them to mailboxes. A
mailbox is an electronic store with a code
number. Messages can be sent and stored, or
retrieved, at any time.

Electronic offices enable staff of a company
to work at home or in small branch offices.
The basis of the system is either a computer
terminal linked to a mainframe (see p.235) at
the head office, or personal computers linked
by fax or another form of electronic mail.

Electronic paging is a radio system which
enables key workers to be contacted quickly.
It is used extensively in factories and hospitals. Each person on the system carries a
small pocket "beeper" which can be acti-
vated, calling them to the nearest telephone.

Fax – short for "facsimile" – machines
enable people to send copies of documents or
pictures over telephone lines or radio links.
The document to be transmitted is scanned
by a photoelectric cell, which turns tones of
black and white into electronic signals.

Telephones have come a long way since
their invention in 1876, and business as we
know it would be impossible without them.
Mobile telephones allow people to be contacted while traveling. One kind operates
within a building, enabling the user to move
about freely carrying a small telephone receiver. Many countries now have networks of
transmitters and receivers enabling people to
use telephones in their cars, on trains, and
even on airplanes.

Photocopying is a method of making quick copies of documents. It was invented in 1938. An image of the document is recorded temporarily on an electrically charged plate, which prints it onto paper by means of powder. The image is fixed by heat.

Telex is an older system of quick communication, and is an advance on simple telegraph systems. Each subscriber has a teleprinter machine, like a large typewriter. Any message is typed on the machine and recorded on a punched tape. When the tape is fed through the machine it transmits the message to a similar machine at the receiving end at about 100 words a minute. This system is used by newspapers and agencies for transmitting "copy" quickly.

Teletext is a faster form of telex that links word processors through a telephone line. It was developed in Europe in the 1980s. The message is encoded on a floppy disk and is transmitted electronically to the receiving station.

Videotex is a system by which information can be stored at a central point and retrieved by means of a telephone line, linked to word processors. A subscriber to the system can call up thousands of pages of information, ranging from the latest stock market prices to encyclopedia-style reference data.

▽ A photocopier reproduces images electrostatically. Light is reflected from the original onto a light-sensitive material charged with static electricity. An image forms, and is fixed when dusted with powdered ink and heat-transferred onto paper.

Page being copied   Mirrors

Finished copies

Lens

Plain copying paper

Copy being made   Drum

Arts and Entertainment

Since the dawn of civilization, people have been moved to express their feelings and relate their experiences in pictures, words, music, and dance. Twenty thousand years ago Stone Age people painted on the walls of caves scenes of life at that time; they also made primitive musical instruments. Literature began when stories were told around the hunters' fire; dance was born in rituals to appease or thank the gods. All art is a celebration of life, in sorrow and in happiness. Today we can enjoy art and entertainment in our homes through television, video, radio and recordings.

Throughout the history of mankind, people have been involved in those activities that we now call "the arts." Having met their basic needs for food, warmth, and shelter, they have used their creative skills and imagination to satisfy a need for decoration, color and entertainment in their lives.

The earliest carvings and paintings we know of were produced by Stone Age people over 20,000 years ago. Archaeologists have discovered primitive musical instruments made during the Stone Age. Decorated pottery of baked clay has been found dating from the Neolithic period (6000–3000 B.C.). The Greeks and Romans had theaters where plays were performed, and the plays and poetry of ancient Greece are considered to be the world's first important literature.

Some 4,500 years ago, the Egyptians built huge stone temples for their gods and tombs (pyramids) for their kings and queens. These are among the first major works of architecture, and many can still be seen today.

Across the Atlantic, in Central and South America, Indian civilizations had developed their own types of art, architecture, pottery,

△ Roman theater at Orange, France. Actors wore large masks denoting the character they were playing.

▽ The lute was a popular early stringed instrument. Its name comes from the Arabic *al-'ud*.

and stone carving by about 1000 B.C.

This section covers the traditional arts of painting and sculpture, pottery and porcelain, architecture, classical music, opera and ballet, the theater, and literature. It also includes a new range of media which the scientific advances of the 20th century have brought into being. These are the movies, radio and television, and the recording industry. They can be seen as arts in their own right, especially the movies. The use of satellites in space to relay television signals means that events happening in one country can be shown on TV, as they happen, on the other side of the world.

The movies were developed in the early years of this century, and the first film with a soundtrack came out only in 1927. The development of radio and television came even more recently. The first public radio broadcasting services did not begin until the 1920s, and the world's first television service began in Britain in 1936. Few people had television sets until the 1950s.

In the 1970s video became popular. Video is a way of recording pictures and sounds on magnetic tape, which is simpler to use than film. Many people now have video cassette recorders (VCRs), which enable them to record television programs and to play video cassettes. In the mid-1980s nearly one-third of American homes had VCRs. Easy-to-use video cameras make it simple for people to make their own home movies.

Toward the end of the nineteenth century, the phonograph (gramophone) was invented by an American, Thomas A. Edison. Soon afterwards the wax-coated, grooved disk that we call "a record" was invented. The development of the phonograph record and the coming of radio brought about the growth of the huge popular music industry. Now records are being replaced by tapes and, latest of all, by compact discs.

△ *Figure of a Standing Woman* by the Swiss sculptor Alberto Giacometti (1901–66).

▽ A modern hand-held video camera. Video technology has revolutionized visual entertainment in the 20th century.

Painting

The earliest paintings we know of are cave paintings in France and Spain. Some beautiful wall paintings still survive from ancient Egypt, Greece, and Rome. In western Europe, the subjects of medieval paintings were religious. They were followed by the real flowering of art which came with the Renaissance. Painters such as Leonardo da Vinci began to make their subjects more lifelike. Later Dutch painters such as Rembrandt and Vermeer began to portray everyday scenes. In the late 19th century an important new style of painting called "Impressionism" developed. Artists such as Monet and Renoir painted from nature, studying the effects of different lights on a subject. Painting in the 20th century became even freer, and styles included "Cubism" and then "abstract" art.

△ Egyptian tomb paintings preserve echoes of a vanished civilization.

SOME PAINTING TERMS

abstract art Art form that represents ideas (by means of geometric and other designs) instead of natural forms.

airbrush Device used by artist to spray paint, varnish, or fix, worked by compressed air.

aquarelle A watercolor painting.

cave paintings Pictures painted by prehistoric artists on the walls of caves.

chiaroscuro ("light-dark") Balance of light and shade in a picture; also an especially dramatic use of light and shade.

▽ Picasso's *Guernica* (1937) was inspired by the horrors of war.

Cubism Important movement in modern French painting started by Picasso and Braque in 1907. Cubists aimed to reduce objects to basic shapes of cubes, spheres, cylinders, and cones.

distemper Cheap and impermanent method of painting in which powdered colors are mixed with glue.

Dutch School Art and artists of Netherlands in 1600s. Leaders were Rembrandt, Hals, Van der Velde.

egg tempera A painting medium in which the colors are ground with pure egg yolk; one of the most permanent media available.

Expressionism Movement that aims at expressing the artist's inner feelings and experiences. It began in late 1800s.

Fauves ("wild beasts") Group of Parisian painters of early 1900s (Dufy, Matisse, Rouault, Vlaminck, etc.) who shocked the critics by their brilliant use of color.

finger painting Chinese watercolor technique using finger instead of a brush.

fresco Method of great antiquity but perfected during Italian Renaissance; uses pigments ground in water applied to a fresh lime-plaster wall or ceiling.

gouache Non-transparent watercolor paint that provides easy way of obtaining oil-painting effects.

icon Religious picture (usually painted on wood or ivory) associated with Eastern Orthodox Church.

Impressionism Important movement that developed among French painters just after mid-1800s. Impressionists were concerned with light and its effects. They included Renoir, Manet, Degas, Monet, Pissarro, Morisot, and Sisley.

landscape painting Picture whose main subject is pure landscape without human figures; rare before 1600s.

miniature Tiny painting (less than 6 in [15 cm] across), usually a portrait.

mural Wall-painting, usually executed in fresco, oil, or tempera.

narrative painting One that tells a story; popular in Victorian England.

oil painting Technique of covering a slightly absorbent surface with pigment ground in an oil-based medium.

op art (optical art) Modern technique with which painter creates optical illusions by means of dazzling patterns.

palette Range of colors available to a painter; usually arranged on little board for easy mixing, with thumb-hole for holding.

pastel Painter's coloring medium consisting of a crayon of pure pigment or pigment mixed with chalk and other materials.

pigments Dry paints or dyes that are mixed with oil, water, or other material.

portrait painting Representation in painting of a human being. First portraits were usually of kings and other leaders.

post-impressionism Work of French painters that followed Impressionism between 1885 and 1905. Typified by Cezanne, Gauguin, Van Gogh, and Seurat.

△ *The Scream*, lithograph by Edvard Munch (1893).

Renaissance Rebirth in arts and learning that took place in Europe (initially in Italy) from 1300s to 1500s. Among the masters of this period were Botticelli, Leonardo da Vinci, Michelangelo, Titian, and Raphael.

representational art Type of painting that shows objects as nearly as possible as they actually are; the opposite of abstract art.

rococo European art style (about 1735–1765) characterized in painting by lavish decoration and extravagant ornament.

still life Art form in which subject of picture is made up of inanimate objects; a favorite form of Dutch School.

tempera Binding medium for powder colors, made up of egg yolk, sometimes thinned with water. Tempera mixtures last longer than oil colors.

Venetian School Painters who worked in Venice during High Renaissance. They included Titian, Veronese, Tintoretto, and Giorgione.

watercolor Technique of painting with colors that have been mixed with water-soluble gum; paints are applied to paper with soft, moistened brush. The English painter J.M.W. Turner was supreme at the art; some noted American artists who worked in watercolor are Charles Burchfield and John Marin.

GREAT ARTISTS

Botticelli, Sandro (1444–1510) Italian painter who spent most of his life in Florence. Most of his subject matter is religious and mythological.

Braque, Georges (1882–1963) French painter and sculptor; one of the founders of Cubism.

Brueghel, Pieter (1520?–1569) Flemish artist renowned for lively pictures of village life.

Cézanne, Paul (1839–1906) French painter famous for his landscapes and still lifes.

Constable, John (1776–1837). One of the greatest English landscape painters.

Degas, Edgar (1834–1917) French artist of the Impressionist period, noted for his pictures of ballet dancers.

△ Degas is famous for his paintings of the ballet.

Dürer, Albrecht (1471–1528) German artist who made many fine woodcuts and engravings for book illustrations.

Gauguin, Paul (1848–1903) French painter who escaped from European civilization to paint in the peaceful Pacific island of Tahiti.

Giotto (1266?–1337) Italian painter who greatly influenced Renaissance art. His style was more realistic than that of the formal painters of his time.

Goya, Francisco (1746–1828) Spanish court painter who represented people realistically rather than in a flattering light.

Greco, El (1541–1614) Nickname meaning "The Greek," born in Crete, but worked in Venice and Spain. His pictures often contain strange, thin, brightly colored figures.

Hogarth, William (1697–1764) English artist who satirized the cruelty and vice which he saw around him in London.

△ Giotto's *The Madonna in Majesty* (early 1300s).

Holbein, Hans, the Younger (1497?–1564) German portrait painter who created realistic likenesses of his subjects.

Leonardo da Vinci (1452–1519) Italian painter, architect, sculptor, and musician – also a brilliant inventor and scientist.

Michelangelo Buonarroti (1475–1564) Italian painter, sculptor, and architect. Possibly his finest work was painted on the ceiling of the Sistine Chapel, in the Vatican.

Monet, Claude (1840–1926) French artist who developed the Impressionist technique of using small dabs of intense colors to create a luminous effect.

Picasso, Pablo (1881–1973) Spanish painter whose early paintings were dominated by the color blue. In 1907 he introduced the style known as Cubism, which changed the whole course of art.

△ Dürer's woodcut *Praying Hands*.

Raphael (1483–1520) Italian artist whose pictures are notable for their peaceful beauty and perfect composition.

Rembrandt van Rijn (1606–1669) One of the finest Dutch portrait painters; a master at capturing the character of his subjects, and in the dramatic use of light and shade (chiaroscuro).

Renoir, Pierre Auguste (1841–1919) French Impressionist painter who used rich colors; particularly known for his nudes.

Rubens, Peter Paul (1577–1640) Flemish artist who became court painter in Antwerp after spending eight years in Italy.

Titian (1477–1576) One of the greatest Venetian painters. He painted many religious works for churches.

△ Self-portrait, Van Gogh.

Toulouse-Lautrec, Henri de (1864–1901) French artist, best remembered for his Parisian cabaret posters and his pictures of music-hall performers.

Turner, Joseph Mallord William (1775–1851) English painter especially noted for his watercolors and his magnificent sunsets.

Van Gogh, Vincent (1853–1890) Dutch painter; early pictures were somber, but in his later work he used bright, swirling colors. His later paintings reflect his growing insanity.

Velázquez, Diego Rodríguez de Silva (1599–1660) Spanish court painter; renowned for his portraits of Philip IV and the courtiers.

△ Self-portrait, Rembrandt.

▽ *Chain Pier, Brighton* by Constable.

△ Mysterious stone carved heads stand on Easter Island in the Pacific Ocean. More than 600 statues have been discovered.

Sculpture

The earliest pieces of sculpture we know of were carved by Stone Age people some 30,000 years ago. The ancient Egyptians made fine sculptures between 2,000 and 4,000 years ago – many were huge statues of their kings and queens. Some of the world's most beautiful carvings were done by the sculptors of ancient Greece and Rome. All over the world, in China, India, Africa, and many other countries, people have made three-dimensional images. During the Renaissance, especially in Italy, the art of sculpture advanced rapidly. Michelangelo carved superb statues, such as his *David*. Today, sculptors work in stone, marble, wood, metal, even fiberglass. They often carve sculptures in which the general shape is more important than the likeness of the figure or object.

SOME SCULPTURAL TERMS

armature Wood or metal framework used to support sculptor's model.

bronze Alloy of copper and tin used by sculptors in ancient Greece. Rome, China, and Africa; revived in modern times.

bust Sculpture of the upper part of the human body.

cast Figure made from mold of original model. See cire perdue; plaster cast; sand cast.

cire perdue (French, "lost wax") Traditional method for casting bronze sculptures: model with wax surface is enclosed in mold; wax is melted and runs out through holes at bottom; molten metal is poured through holes at top, filling up space left by wax.

figurine Miniature figure.

free-stone An easily worked fine-grained limestone or sandstone.

genre sculpture Style that reflects everyday or rustic life; hallmark of Etruscan art and of biblical subjects in Middle Ages.

heroic Any figure or group of figures carved larger than life.

maquette (French, "small model") Small wax or clay model made by sculptor in preparation for larger work.

marble Popular stone for sculpture because of its extreme durability; found in many colors ranging from nearly pure white to nearly pure black.

mobile Movable sculpture of shapes cut out of wood or sheet metal, linked by wires or rods in order to revolve easily or move up and down; invented by American sculptor Alexander Calder (1932).

modeling Building-up of forms in three dimensions by means of plastic material such as clay or wax.

plaster cast Intermediate stage in bronze sculpture from which final mold is made.

polychromatic sculpture Sculpture painted in naturalistic colors to make it more lifelike; mostly pre-1500s.

relief Sculpture not free-standing from background; various degrees, from *bas-relief* (low relief) to *alto-relievo* (high relief).

sand cast Mold of special sand made from plaster model and from which bronze cast is made.

sculpture-in-the-round Sculpture that can be seen from all sides.

stabile Abstract, stationary sculpture, usually of metal.

FAMOUS SCULPTORS

Bernini, Gianlorenzo (1598–1680) Italian Renaissance sculptor and architect. Besides owing much to classical tradition, his figures appear almost to be living people.

Brancusi, Constantin (1876–1957) Romanian sculptor, most famous for a series of bird sculptures made of different materials, but also for bronzes such as the powerful Prodigal Son.

Calder, Alexander (1898–1976) American sculptor, known particularly for his moving sculptures made from flat metal disks suspended from wires. These were given the name "mobiles."

Donatello (1386–1466) Italian Renaissance sculptor who carved realistic figures. He developed a new form of relief sculpture in which the feeling of depth is created without cutting deep into the surface of the marble.

Epstein, Sir Jacob (1880–1959) English sculptor influenced by primitive art. At the beginning of his career, people were shocked by the directness of his work.

△ *The Kiss*, by Constantin Brancusi.

Gabo, Naum (1890–1977) Russian sculptor who made new use of industrial materials such as glass, metal, plastics, and wire.

Giacometti, Alberto (1901–1966) Swiss sculptor and painter, best-known for his tall, spindly figures cast in bronze.

Hepworth, Barbara (1903–1975) British sculptor, created abstract carvings in wood and stone, huge shapes broken by holes with wires stretched across them.

Lipschitz, Jacques (1891–1973) Cubist Lithuanian sculptor, most famous for his powerful, angular animals and figures.

Michelangelo Buonarroti (1475–1564) Italian Renaissance sculptor, painter, and architect, famous for many fine carvings including the Pietà, David, and a series of slaves who seem to be trying to escape from the rock from which they are carved.

Modigliani, Amedeo (1884–1920) Italian sculptor and painter. Influenced by Cézanne and by African art, he carved elongated faces from wood.

Moore, Henry (1898–1986) British sculptor best known for his large reclining nudes and for groups of figures. He was influenced by both primitive African and Mexican art.

Phidias (c. 490–c. 417 B.C.) Influential Greek sculptor. He designed and supervised the Parthenon sculptures, as well as a sculpture of Zeus at Olympia.

Rodin, Auguste (1840–1917) French sculptor who worked in bronze and marble. His work includes The Thinker, The Kiss, and The Burghers of Calais.

◁ *The Prodigal Son*, by Rodin.

▽ The art of making fine porcelain reached Europe from China in the 18th century.

Pottery and Porcelain

Objects made from baked clay are called pottery. They include cups, saucers, plates, bowls, pots, jugs, vases, and many other useful items. People have made pottery for thousands of years and have gradually learned to make it more efficient and more beautiful. Porcelain is fine pottery made with white china clay – the art of making it was perfected in China – and Chinese porcelain is some of the most beautiful ever produced. Stoneware (also called earthenware) is often made of blue, brown, gray, red, or yellow clay. It is thicker and heavier than porcelain, but less hard.

▽ The Ancient Greeks are known for their finely decorated vases, wine cups, and jars.

CHINESE DYNASTIES

Chinese pottery and porcelain is dated by the dynasty (royal family) or individual emperor in whose time it was made. Some of the most important are:

Dynasty	Dates
Han	206 B.C.–A.D. 220
Three Kingdoms	220–265
Six Dynasties	265–588
Sui	589–618
T'ang	618–906
Five Dynasties	906–959
Sung	960–1279
Yüan (Mongol)	1280–1368
Ming	1368–1644
Ch'ing (Manchu)	1644–1912
	(Emperor Chi'en Lung 1736–1795)

▽ The T'ang dynasty is noted for its superb ceramics, like this decorated jar.

SOME POTTERY AND PORCELAIN TERMS

biscuit ware Pottery fired but not glazed.
bone china Type of porcelain made in England today, for high-quality tableware.
ceramics Term for anything made of baked clay; the potter's art.
china (originally "Chinaware") Chinese porcelain of 16th century; now any Chinese porcelain or Western version of it.
chinoiserie Decoration on 18th-century European porcelain, depicting Chinese scenes.
clay The potter's basic material, found just beneath the topsoil, formed by decomposition of rock; *kaolin*, or *china clay*, a pure white coarse clay; *ball clay*, a highly plastic, fine pure clay; *fireclay*, a dark rough clay, able to stand high temperatures, but not plastic; *buff*, or *stoneware clay*, a smooth plastic clay hardening at high temperatures.
crackle Effect of finely cracked or crazed glaze, produced for decoration.
creamware High-quality earthenware perfected by Josiah Wedgwood in Staffordshire (18th century).
delftware Tin-enameled earthenware, mostly blue-and-white, originally made in Delft (Holland) in 17th and 18th centuries.
earthenware Pottery fired to relatively low temperature (about 2,000°F [1,100°C]), easy to work and having dull finish.
enamel Colored glaze used to decorate pottery already glazed.
firing Process of hardening shaped clay by heating it.
glazing Process for producing smooth, waterproof finish to pottery; *glaze* is liquid clay-like mixture applied before or after first firing.
kiln Chamber in which clay is fired.

△ A potter's wheel.

paste Tern for mixture from which porcelain is made; *hard-paste* porcelain made from kaolin and petuntse, the true porcelain originating in China and rediscovered at Meissen (Germany) in 18th century, fired at very high temperatures; *soft-paste* porcelain made from white clay and fusible silicate, more translucent than hard paste but with softer whiteness.
porcelain The finest kind of pottery, white all through and translucent. See *paste*.
pottery Strictly, all baked-clay ware except stoneware and porcelain.
slip Clay in liquid form, used for casting, joining or decoration.
stoneware Hard, strong type of pottery fired at about 2,280°F (1,250°C) and able to hold liquid without glazing. Used for items such as pots and heavy dishes.
terracotta Brownish-red burnt-clay pottery, baked in molds and used for architectural moldings.
throwing Shaping wet clay by hand on potter's wheel.
turning Final trimming of partially dried pottery on wheel or lathe.

▽ How a pot is made in a factory: molten clay is poured into a mold and water is allowed to seep out until the required thickness of clay has hardened.

Hollow mould Slip Layer of clay

Doric

Ionic

△ The style of Greek capitals (carved column tops) helps to identify a building's architectural style.

Architecture

Architecture is the art of designing buildings. It began about 4,500 years ago in ancient Egypt, and many of the Egyptians' huge pyramids and tombs still stand. Greek architecture began to take shape about 600 B.C. Its beauty is typified by the Acropolis in Athens. The Romans copied Greek architecture, but also discovered how to make an arch, enabling them to construct much stronger buildings. During the Middle Ages many of Europe's most beautiful cathedrals were built in the Gothic style. Then came the Renaissance, which brought new ideas in architecture as it did in the other arts. Later, famous architects such as Sir Christopher Wren (1632–1723) built grander churches, colleges, and houses. Today, people still build with brick and stone, but architects are also using new materials such as concrete and steel, tinted glass, and plastics.

SOME ARCHITECTURAL TERMS AND STYLES

apse Semicircular (or polygonal) area projecting from far (altar) end of church.

arcade Row of arches supported by columns and carrying roof.

arch Curved structure spanning an opening.

architrave Lowest section of entablature.

Art Nouveau Style (1890–1910) characterized by use of, for example, colored materials, molded stonework, tapered wrought-iron brackets, and curving motifs of flowers and leaves.

Baroque Heavily decorated European style (1600s–1700s) involving flamboyant use of classical forms.

basilica Huge vaulted civic hall (Roman) or early Christian church following same open rectangular plan.

Brutalism Reforming movement in modern architecture that emerged in Britain in 1950s; based on the work of Le Corbusier and Mies van der Rohe.

buttress Projecting support (mass of masonry) built on outside of wall; in *flying-buttress*, masonry is free-standing with half-arch transferring thrust from wall.

Byzantine Style that flourished in Eastern Roman Empire (A.D. 400s to 1453), characterized by ornately domed and vaulted churches, rounded arches, minarets, spires, and frequent use of mosaics.

cantilever horizontal beam weighted at one end so it will support a weight at the other.

capital Broad top part of column, supporting entablature.

classical Style of ancient Greece or Rome, or any style based on these.

cloisters Quadrangle surrounded by roofed passages connecting parts of monastery.

cornice Top, projecting section of entablature, supporting roof.

dome Roof in shape of semi-sphere, usually built over square base.

dormer Small gabled window projecting from sloping roof.

Elizabethan English style of 1500s marking change from Gothic to Renaissance and featuring sturdy, squared buildings with large windows and ornamentation in Flemish and German styles.

entablature Part of building in classical architecture between top of columns and roof; consists of architrave, frieze, and cornice.

façade Main face of building.

fluting Longitudinal grooves in a column.

frieze Middle section of entablature.

Functionalism Theory that the shape of a building should be decided by its proposed use.

gable Triangular end of roof with two sloping sides.

gargoyles Projecting stone spouts (usually grotesquely carved) acting as outlets for gutter water on medieval buildings.

Georgian English style (1700s), a quiet and dignified classical style; called Colonial in U.S.

Gothic Style developed in France in 1100s. Characterized by pointed arches, elaborate vaulting, flying-buttresses, slender pillars, large stained-glass windows, and intricate tracery.

Greek Beautifully proportioned classical style lasting from about 700 B.C. until conquest by Romans in mid-100s B.C. Graceful buildings, with three orders of columns: *Doric* (stubby columns), the later (from about 400 B.C) *Ionic* (slimmer columns on molded bases with intricately carved capitals), and *Corinthian* (more elaborate, with foliage on capital).

International Style Term given to modern style of architecture that evolved in Western Europe in 1920s, spread internationally in 1930s, and flourished in United States.

keystone Locking stone at top of arch.

lantern Small decorative turret on dome.

lintel Horizontal beam or stone above doorway or window, supporting wall above.

minaret Tower of mosque, with gallery for muezzin to call Muslims to prayer.

molding Decorative edging on architectural surface.

nave Main body of church, west of crossing, flanked by aisles.

pagoda Tower, of Chinese origin, partitioned horizontally with balconies or cornices.

△ Roman: Arch of Constantine in Rome. The Romans invented the arch.

pediment Triangular end of sloping roof in classical architecture.

Perpendicular Last phase of English Gothic (mid-1300s to 1500s); characterized by strong vertical lines and conical "fan" vaulting.

piazza Open square surrounded by buildings.

pier Free-standing vertical support for arch, beam, etc.

pilaster Flat, rectangular column attached to or built into wall.

portico Area with roof supported by rows of columns.

post-and-lintel Construction using vertical elements (posts) and horizontal beams (lintels).

Post-Modernism Style that developed in the 1970s. It uses freely adapted motifs from earlier styles, often, brightly colored.

Renaissance Style emerging in Italy in 1400s, based on classical style of Ancient Greece and Rome.

Rococo Light, airy version of baroque style that developed in the 1700s.

Roman Style at its height from about 100 B.C. to A.D. 300s. Characterized by vaults and semicircular arches.

Romanesque Style that preceded Gothic; features include thick walls, massive pillars, and round arches; called Norman in England.

rotunda Circular building, usually domed.

steel-frame Skeleton of steel girders that provides framework for tall buildings.

tracery Elaborately patterned openwork in Gothic architecture, originally framework of light stone bars dividing large window.

transept In church, hall running north-south and crossing nave at right angles.

Tudor English late-Gothic period (1500s).

vault Brick or stone ceiling built on arch principle.

△ Ancient Greek: Temple of Artemis.

FAMOUS ARCHITECTS

Aalto, Alvar (1898–1976) Finnish architect whose buildings include the Hall of Residence, at the Massachusetts Institute of Technology, and the church at Imatra, in Finland. He made wide use of timber.

Adam, Robert (1728–1792) British architect, decorator, and furniture designer. He used ancient Greek and Roman styles, making them lighter and more romantic.

Alberti, Leon Battista (1404–1472) Italian Renaissance architect who built influential churches using classical features in an experimental approach.

Bernini, Gianlorenzo (1598–1680) Italian architect responsible for the completion of the rebuilding of St. Peter's, Rome, designing the piazza in the baroque style.

Bramante, Donato (1444–1514) First of the Italian High Renaissance architects. Sticking closely to severe classical design, he had a great influence on later architects.

Brunelleschi, Filippo (1377–1446) Italian Renaissance architect, most famous for designing and building the dome of Florence Cathedral. This was used as a model for St. Peter's, Rome.

Gaudí, Antoni (1852–1926) Spanish architect of the Art Nouveau style. The Casa Milá in Barcelona has a wavy roof line, and the apartment rooms have no straight walls or right angles.

Gropius, Walter (1883–1969) Great modern German architect known for functional factory and office designs and for refounding the "Bauhaus" (House of Building) to teach arts and crafts.

Hardouin-Mansart, Jules (1646–1708) French architect known for his use of baroque designs in the Palace of Versailles.

△ Wren's masterpiece, St. Paul's Cathedral, London.

Johnson, Philip (1906–) American architect who once worked in International style, is now a leading Post-Modernist. His AT&T Building, New York, resembles a giant piece of 18th-century furniture.

Jones, Inigo (1573–1652) Influential English architect who introduced Palladian style to Britain.

Le Corbusier (1887–1965, Charles Edouard Jeanneret) Swiss architect who worked in France. Best-known for designing apartments and houses and for his wide use of reinforced concrete.

Lutyens, Sir Edwin (1869–1944) English architect who built country houses.

△ Church of the Holy Family, Barcelona, designed by Gaudí in 1905.

Mackintosh, Charles Rennie (1868–1928) Scottish Art Nouveau architect, and designer of interiors and furniture. Used effects of simplicity and curved lines.

Michelangelo Buonarroti (1475–1564) Italian Renaissance architect, painter, and sculptor, who rejected the rigid classical rules and introduced novel designs. Best-known for his work on St. Peter's, Rome.

Mies van der Rohe, Ludwig (1886–1969) German architect and planner. Director of the Bauhaus from 1930 to 1933. His designs were suited to the use of the buildings.

Nash, John (1752–1835) English architect, known particularly for his work on the Royal Pavilion at Brighton, where he used Gothic, Hindu, and Chinese forms.

Nervi, Pier Luigi (1891–1978) Italian engineer and architect known for his inventive use of reinforced concrete. He built two sports halls for the Olympic Games held in Rome in 1960.

Niemeyer, Oscar (1907–) Inventive Brazilian architect responsible for many buildings in the new capital, Brasilia.

△ Drawing of a mansion by Palladio.

Palladio, Andrea (1508–1580) Probably the most influential Italian architect; he returned to classical Roman forms with symmetrical planning and fine proportions.
Pugin, Augustus (1812–1852) English architect who promoted Gothic Revival style; worked on the Houses of Parliament.
Rogers, Richard (1933–) English architect who worked on designs for Beaubourg (Georges Pompidou Center) in Paris and the Lloyds Building in London.
Saarinen, Eero (1910–1961) American architect who used interesting new designs on industrial buildings.
Sullivan, Louis (1856–1924) Chicago-based architect who pioneered the development of the multistory office building.
Utzon, Jørn (1918–) Famous for his design for the Sydney Opera House, whose roof looks like the sails of ships.

△ Lloyd's of London, by Richard Rogers.

Wren, Sir Christopher (1632–1723) English architect and scientist, responsible for much of the rebuilding of London after the Great Fire in 1666. Also famous for his work on St. Paul's Cathedral and Greenwich Hospital.
Wright, Frank Lloyd (1869–1959) Considered the greatest American architect. His work ranged from prairie houses to plans for a skyscraper 1 mile high. Among the most original works from his 60-year-long career are the Johnson Wax Building (Racine, Wisconsin), and the top-shaped Guggenheim Museum (New York).

PERIODS OF ARCHITECTURE

Greek 600s–100s B.C.
Roman 100s B.C.–A.D. 400s
Byzantine A.D. 400s–1453
Romanesque late 800s–late 1100s
Norman (England) late 1000s–1100s
Gothic (France) mid-1100s–1400s
Renaissance (Italy) 1400s–1500s
French Renaissance 1500s
Elizabethan (England) 1500s–1600
Baroque (Europe) 1600–1750
Georgian (England, U.S.) 1725–1800
Rococo (Europe) mid-1700s
Greek Revival late 1700s–early 1800s
Gothic Revival (Europe, U.S.) 1800s
Art Nouveau (Europe) 1890–1910
Expressionism (Germany) 1910–1930s
International Style (Modernism) 1920s–
Brutalism (Britain) 1950s–
Post-Modernism 1970s–

△ One of George
Cruikshank's illustrations
from Dickens's novel *Oliver
Twist*.

Literature

Literature – the art of the written word – has existed as long as people have been able to express themselves in writing. In Europe the first great ages of literature were those of ancient Greece and Rome. The works of Homer, Virgil, and others, which became known as "the classics," have influenced writers up to the present day. The first great writer in English was Geoffrey Chaucer, in the 14th century; perhaps the greatest of all time was William Shakespeare. Poems and plays are both very ancient forms of literature, but the novel is relatively new. It was fully developed only at the end of the 18th century and reached a peak of popularity in the 19th century.

SOME LITERARY TERMS

allegory A story in which the obvious meaning symbolizes a hidden meaning.

ballad A poem describing a historical or legendary event or deed. Ballads were very popular in the late Middle Ages.

blank verse A form of poetry based on unrhyming ten-syllable lines with alternate syllables stressed.

couplet Two successive lines of verse that rhyme with one another.

drama A story written as a dialogue, in conversational form, so that it can be spoken and acted.

elegy A poem mourning a death or treating some other solemn theme.

epic A long narrative poem about heroic, historical, or legendary events and people. An example is Homer's *Odyssey*.

fable A short tale with a moral lesson in which animals act and talk like people.

limerick A kind of comic, nonsense poem in five lines, usually rhyming *a a b b a*. Edward Lear wrote many limericks.

ode A medium-length poem, usually in praise of something. It has various forms.

rhyme Agreement in sound of two syllables, but with differing preceding consonants.

romantic Belonging to the Romantic period, the early 1800s, when writers stressed liberty and chose exotic themes and settings.

satire A style using sarcasm or irony to

△ An illustration from *Don Quixote*, one of the earliest novels, by the Spanish writer Cervantes.

attack some form of human behavior.

sonnet A 14-lined poem with various rhyming schemes. Italian sonnets rhyme *abba abba cde cde*. Elizabethan sonnets rhyme *abab cdcd efef gg*.

SOME GREAT WRITERS

Andersen, Hans Christian (1805–1875), Danish writer, best known for his fairy tales. Some of the most loved are *The Tinder Box, The Emperor's New Clothes,* and *The Snow Queen.*

Austen, Jane (1775–1817), English novelist, wrote about comfortably-off country people, who led lives bound by strict rules of behavior. Her books include *Sense and Sensibility, Pride and Prejudice*, and *Emma.*

△ Jane Austen, drawn by her sister.

Balzac, Honoré de (1799–1850), French novelist, wrote a series of 90 realistic stories about everyday life in France called the *Human Comedy.*

Blake, William (1757–1827), English poet and artist. His *Songs of Innocence* and *Songs of Experience* show the same world from the viewpoints of innocence and disillusioned experience.

Brontë Family name of English novelist sisters: **Charlotte** (1816–1855), **Emily Jane** (1818–1848), and **Anne** (1820–1849). Charlotte included many personal experiences in her most famous novel, *Jane Eyre. Wuthering Heights*, a dramatic love story, is probaby Emily's best work.

Burns, Robert (1759–1796), Scottish poet who wrote poems in Scottish dialect and composed songs, including *Auld Lang Syne.*

Byron, Lord George (1788–1824), English Romantic poet, wrote several long narrative poems. Probably the finest is *Don Juan.*

Carroll, Lewis (Charles Lutwidge Dodgson 1832–1898), best remembered for his stories *Alice's Adventures in Wonderland* and *Through the Looking Glass.*

△ Danish storyteller Hans Christian Andersen.

Cervantes, Miguel de (1547–1616), Spanish novelist, playwright, and poet, author of the novel *Don Quixote*, story of a gentleman who imagines he can put right all the evil in the world.

Chaucer, Geoffrey (1340?–1400), English poet, famous for his *Canterbury Tales*, a collection of stories told by travelers on a journey.

Coleridge, Samuel Taylor (1772–1834), English Romantic poet and friend of Wordsworth, wrote the famous poem *The Rime of the Ancient Mariner.*

△ Illustration of pilgrims from Chaucer's *Canterbury Tales.*

Dante Alighieri (1265–1321), Italian poet, wrote the *Divine Comedy*, a poem in three parts about the poet's imagined journey through Hell, Purgatory, and Heaven.

Dickens, Charles (1812–1870), English novelist, wrote stories about the harsh lives of people in industrial England including *David Copperfield* and *Oliver Twist*.

Dostoevsky, Fyodor (1821–1881), Russian novelist, wrote powerful stories. Among the finest *Crime and Punishment*, *The Idiot*, and *The Brothers Karamazov*.

Eliot, George (Marian Evans 1819–1880), English novelist, wrote *The Mill on the Floss*, *Middlemarch* and *Silas Marner*.

Eliot, T. S. (Thomas Stearns 1888–1965), American-born British poet, dramatist, and critic, wrote *The Waste Land*.

Faulkner, William (1897–1962) American novelist and shot story writer known especially for his depiction of life in the rural South, with its racial and social conflicts. Among his works are *Absalom, Absalom!* and *The Sound and the Fury*.

△ Dante, painted amid scenes from the *Divine Comedy*.

△ Charles Dickens, one of Britain's greatest novelists.

Hemingway, Ernest (1898–1961), American novelist, wrote stories about adventurous and violent lives. Best-known include *A Farewell to Arms* and *For Whom the Bell Tolls*.

Homer (700s B.C.), great and influential Greek poet, wrote the *Iliad* which tells the story of the siege of Troy, whereas the *Odyssey* describes the wanderings of the hero Odysseus after the war.

Johnson, Dr. Samuel (1709–1784), English poet and essayist; compiled a *Dictionary of the English Language*.

Joyce, James (1882–1941), Irish novelist, wrote stories about people in conflict with their surroundings.

Keats, John (1795–1821), English Romantic poet, composed narrative poems. The finest include *Ode to Autumn* and *Ode to a Nightingale*.

▷ Portrait of John Keats by Benjamin Haydon.

Kipling, Rudyard (1865–1936), an Indian-born English novelist, wrote of the British Empire, and adventure stories for children which include *Kim* and *The Jungle Book*.

Lawrence, D. H. (David Herbert 1885–1930), English novelist; much of his work is about working-class life, including growing up and natural love. He wrote *Sons and Lovers* and *Lady Chatterley's Lover*.

Milton, John (1608–1674), English poet and religious and political writer. His most important works are the long poems *Paradise Lost* and *Paradise Regained*.

Poe, Edgar Allan (1809–1849), American short-story writer, poet, and critic, is best known for his tales of mystery.

Rabelais, François (1494?–1553?), French priest and doctor, poked fun at life in his day.

Scott, Sir Walter (1771–1832), Scottish novelist and poet, author of romantic adventures often set in the Middle Ages. They include *Waverley* and *Ivanhoe*.

Shelley, Percy Bysshe (1792–1822), English Romantic poet, wrote idealistic poems including *Ode to a Skylark*.

Stevenson, Robert Louis (1850–1894), Scottish novelist, wrote *Treasure Island* and *Kidnapped*, both adventure stories, and *Dr. Jekyll and Mr. Hyde*, a mystery.

Swift, Jonathan (1667–1745), Irish clergyman, wrote satirical pamphlets, but is best known for his story *Gulliver's Travels*.

Tennyson, Alfred, Lord (1809–1892), English poet, wrote *The Charge of the Light Brigade*.

Tolstoy, Leo, Count (1828–1910), Russian novelist and playwright, wrote one of the world's greatest novels, *War and Peace*. It traces the lives of several families during Napoleon's invasion of Russia.

Twain, Mark (Samuel Langhorne Clemens 1835–1910), American novelist, wrote many books about American life. His best-known, *The Adventures of Huckleberry Finn*, describes life along the Mississippi River.

Virgil (Publius Vergilius Maro 70–19 B.C.), a Roman poet, wrote the *Aeneid*, a long epic poem about the founding of Rome.

Wolfe, Thomas (1900–1938) American novelist whose often autobiographical books, are written in an extravagant, expansive style.

Wordsworth, William (1770–1850), an English poet, expressed his deep love of nature in poems often written in beautiful, simple language.

▽ William Wordsworth, pioneer of the Romantic Movement in English poetry.

Music

We know that people have been making some kind of music all through history – for example, paintings of musicians have been found in Egyptian tombs – but we do not know what early music sounded like because there was no way of writing it down. As instruments improved through the centuries, something resembling a modern orchestra began to take shape. Bach and Handel, both born in 1685, wrote for orchestras consisting mainly of stringed instruments such as violins, but they also had flutes, oboes, trumpets, and horns. In the 18th century, the symphony was developed, especially by Franz Joseph Haydn. The piano as we know it today did not evolve until the early 19th century. Early in this century new kinds of music were produced by composers such as Stravinsky. Recently, composers have used electronic systems to produce sounds which are often strange to our ears.

△ J. S. Bach, the greatest of his distinguished musical family.

▽ The Emperor Maximilian I of Germany traveled with an impressive entourage of court musicians.

▷ Illustration of string family of instruments, 1618.

SOME MUSICAL TERMS

accelerando Gradually faster.

adagio At a slow pace.

allegro At a fast pace.

alto Short for "contralto"; also highest adult male voice (falsetto)

andante At a quiet, peaceful pace.

arpeggio Notes of chord played in rapid succession.

bar Metrical division of music bounded by vertical bar lines.

baritone Male voice higher than bass and lower than tenor.

bass Lowest male voice.

brass instruments Metal instruments sounded by blowing through mouthpiece and altering tension of lips (French horn, trumpet, euphonium, trombone, tuba).

choir A body of singers.

chord Three or more notes sounded together.

chorus Main body of singers in choir; words and music repeated after stanzas of song.

classical music Music that aims at perfection of structure and design (period of Bach to Brahms).

clef Sign in musical notation that fixes pitch of each note written on the stave.

concerto Substantial work for one or more solo instruments and orchestra.

contralto Lowest female voice.

counterpoint Two or more melodies combined to form a satisfying harmony.

crescendo Increasing in loudness.

descant The addition of a second melody above a given melody, form of counterpoint.

diminuendo Gradually softer.

flat Conventional sign showing that pitch of a certain note has been lowered by a semitone.

forte Played or sung loudly.

fortissimo Very loud (loudest).

harmony Combining of chords to make musical sense.

key Classification of the notes of a scale.

largo At a slow pace.

lied German word for "song" (plural lieder).

major One of the two main scales, with semitones between 3rd and 4th and 7th and 8th notes.

measure Another term for bar.

melody A tune; series of musical sounds following each other, as distinct from harmony.

mezzo Half or medium.

mezzo-soprano Female voice between contralto and soprano.

minor One of the two main scales. Harmonic minor scales have a semitone between 2nd and 3rd, 5th and 6th, and 7th and 8th notes.

movement Complete section of larger work (such as symphony).

SYMBOLS AND NOTATION

Stave or staff

Semibreves

Quavers (eighth notes)

Semibreve rest

Quaver rest

Treble clef

Minims

Semiquavers

Minim rest

♯ A sharp raises the note that follows by a semitone

♭ A flat lowers the note that follows by a semitone

Bass clef

Crotchets

Demisemiquavers

Crotchet rest

♮ A natural cancels a sharp or flat

316

nocturne A "night-piece," tuneful but sad.

octave Interval made up of eight successive notes of scale, from one note to note of same name, above or below.

oratorio Religious musical composition for soloists, chorus, and orchestra.

percussion instruments Instruments that are struck; they include drums, tambourine, cymbals, bells, glockenspiel, xylophone, vibraphone, marimba, triangle, gong, and castanets.

piano Played or sung softly; the stringed keyboard instrument of this name was originally called a *piano-forte*, meaning that it could be played softly or loudly.

pitch Highness or lowness in sound of one note compared with another.

plainsong Unaccompanied vocal melody used in medieval church music.

presto At a fast pace.

scale Progression of successive notes ascending or descending.

score Written music showing all parts (vocal and instrumental) of composition on separate staves.

semitone A half-tone; smallest interval commonly used in western music.

▽ Tuba (brass family).

△ Throughout history, drums have often been regarded as sacred instruments.

sharp Conventional sign indicating that note referred to has been raised in pitch by a semitone.

sonata Musical piece, usually for one or two players, and usually containing three or four movements.

soprano Highest female voice.

staff or **stave** Framework of lines and spaces on which music is usually written.

stringed instruments Instruments that are played with a bow (violins, violas, cellos, double basses).

symphony Large orchestral piece of music of a serious nature, usually in four movements.

tempo Pace or speed of piece of music.

tenor Highest natural male voice.

treble Upper part of a composition; a high voice, usually of children.

virtuoso Musician of outstanding skill.

woodwind instruments Instruments that are blown and are traditionally, but not always, made of wood; they include flute, oboe, clarinet, piccolo, recorder, saxophone, bassoon, and English horn (cor anglais).

THE TONIC SOL-FA

The tonic sol-fa is a method of musical notation using letters and syllables instead of notes on a stave. It was devised by the English musician John Curwen (1816–1880), who based it on the system known as solmization used in the Middle Ages. Curwen's aim was to teach a sense of the relationship of notes to each other.

The eight notes of a major scale are denoted by the syllables do, re, mi, fa, sol, la, ti, do. It works for any scale by just changing the note that represents do. Sharpened and flatted notes are indicated by changing the vowel sounds (for example, sol sharp is se, and ti flat is taw).

ARTS AND ENTERTAINMENT

SOME GREAT COMPOSERS

Bach, Johann Sebastian (1685–1750) German composer born at Eisenach; the most distinguished in a long line of musicians. Bach's vast output can be divided into three groups: organ works; instrumental and orchestral works; and religious choral works.

Beethoven, Ludwig van (1770–1827) German composer, one of the outstanding figures of Western music. His symphonies, overtures, concertos, piano sonatas, and string quartets are considered some of the world's greatest.

▽ Beethoven's early music was influenced by Mozart and Haydn.

Brahms, Johannes (1833–1897) German composer. His works include four symphonies, two piano concertos, a violin concerto, a double concerto (violin and cello), chamber music, piano music, and many songs and choral compositions.

Britten, Benjamin (1913–1976) One of the outstanding 20th-century British composers, and a brilliant pianist, Britten is especially noted for his operas, choral music, and songs.

Chopin, Frédéric (1810–1849) Polish piano virtuoso and composer, known almost entirely for piano music.

Dvořák, Antonín (1841–1904) Czech composer. From 1892–1895 was in the United States as Director of the National Conservatory in New York, where he wrote the symphony *From the New World*.

Gershwin, George (1898–1937) American composer and pianist whose combination of American styles (jazz and blues) with impressionist harmony was a major influence on 20th century American music.

▽ German composer, George Frideric Handel (1685–1759).

Handel, George Frideric (1685–1759) German-born composer of Italian operas and, later, oratorios (music dramas) mainly on religious themes; *Messiah* is the most famous. Handel also wrote many instrumental compositions.

Haydn, Franz Joseph (1732–1809) Prolific Austrian composer whose development of the sonata-symphony form and style earned him the title "Father of the Symphony."

Mahler, Gustav (1860–1911) Bohemian-born composer noted for his symphonies, written in late German-Romantic style.

Mozart, Wolfgang Amadeus (1756–1791) Austrian composer who produced, in a short life, more than 600 works, including many piano concertos (a form he virtually invented) and several operas, notably *Don Giovanni*, and *The Magic Flute*. His music embodies classical ideals of perfection.

Schubert, Franz Peter (1797–1828) Austrian composer. In a career even shorter than Mozart's, Schubert achieved a large output ranging from symphonies to chamber music and over 500 songs.

Stravinsky, Igor (1882–1971) Russian-born composer and one of the key figures of 20th-century music. Made his reputation with a series of remarkable ballets, including *The Firebird*, *Petrushka*, and *The Rite of Spring*.

Tchaikovsky, Peter Ilyich (1840–1893) Russian composer, the first to become widely popular outside his country. His work is notable for its melodic flair, emotional content, and vivid orchestration.

318

△ Dame Kiri Te Kanawa

OPERA

An opera is a play with music. The actors are singers, who sing all or many of their words. An orchestra accompanies them. The first operas were performed in Italy nearly 400 years ago. Famous composers of serious operas include Mozart (*The Marriage of Figaro, The Magic Flute*); Verdi (*Aida, La Traviata*); Puccini (*Tosca, Madame Butterfly*); Wagner (*The Ring of the Nibelung*).

SOME OPERATIC TERMS

aria (Italian, "air") A solo.

ballad opera Simple kind of opera, made up of popular tunes interspersed with spoken dialogue.

comic opera Opera with a farcical plot.

finale Closing portion of act or opera; usually whole company sings together.

folk opera Opera based on folk music and folk tales.

grand opera Opera with libretto entirely set to music.

intermezzo Instrumental piece interposed between scenes or acts of opera, also called interlude.

Leitmotiv (German, "leading motive") Short theme in opera that emphasizes by repetition an individual character, object, or idea.

libretto Text of opera.

opera buffa Humorous opera, but not farcical like comic opera; typical is Rossini's *Barber of Seville*.

opera seria Serious opera, as distinct from opera buffa. Also, a very formal style of 18th-century Italian opera, usually based on mythology.

operetta Light opera based on amusing subjects and implying some spoken dialogue.

patter song Comical song made up of string of words and sung at high speed; Gilbert and Sullivan's operas include many songs of this type.

prima donna (Italian, "first lady") Principal female singer in cast; or, more often, most famous or most highly paid; also called diva.

▽ The Opera House, Paris.

BALLET

The ballet as it is danced today began in France, and during the reign of King Louis XIV (1600s) it was officially recognized as a form of art. Traditional or classical ballet follows strict rules – the five basic ballet positions were devised over 300 years ago. Some of the most famous classical ballets have been danced for many years. *Giselle*, for example, was first performed in 1841. Other long-time favorites are *Swan Lake* and *Sleeping Beauty*. Modern ballets include freer dance steps and often illustrate a mood or theme rather than telling a story.

△ Vaslav Nijinsky in *Le Spectre de la Rose* (1911).

◁ Modern classical ballet enjoys worldwide popularity, despite the high cost of production.

SOME BALLET TERMS

arabesque Position in which dancer stands on one leg with arms extended, body bent forward from hips, while other leg is stretched out backward.

attitude Position in which dancer stretches one leg backward, bending it a little at the knee so that lower part of leg is parallel to floor.

ballerina Female solo ballet dancer.

barre Exercise bar fixed to classroom wall at hip level; dancers grasp it when exercising.

battement Beating movement made by raising and lowering leg, sideways, backward or forward.

choreography Art of dance composition.

corps de ballet Main body of ballet dancers, as distinct from soloists.

entrechat Leap in which dancer rapidly crosses and uncrosses feet in air.

fouetté Turn in which dancer whips free leg around.

glissade Gliding movement.

jeté Leap from one foot to another.

pas Any dance step.

pas de deux Dance for two.

pas seule Solo dance.

pirouette Movement in which dancer spins completely around on one foot.

pointes Tips of female dancer's toes, on which many movements are executed.

positions Five positions of feet on which ballet is based.

tutu Short, stiff, spreading skirt worn in some classical ballets.

POPULAR MUSIC

Early popular music was what we now call "folk music," but "pop music" as we know it today developed largely from jazz. This was the music that grew mainly from work songs, religious songs, and blues songs sung in the United States by Black slaves, who came originally from Africa. During the 1940s popular music was "swing," the music of the big bands. Then, in the 1950s, came "rock and roll." Performers such as Elvis Presley and, after him, the Beatles – at their peak from 1962 to 1970 – have influenced the course of popular music ever since.

▽ Jazz developed from marching band music and work songs. Originally played by Blacks, jazz rapidly became popular with Whites and developed into various styles including traditional Dixieland, big band or swing, mainstream, and modern.

SOME POPULAR MUSIC TERMS

a cappella In the world of popular music, singing unaccompanied, especially in groups.
acoustic Not electrically amplified.
backing group Group of singers who sing in support of a soloist.
big bands Dance bands of swing era (late 1930s and early 1940s), featuring many musicians and one or more vocalists.
bluegrass American country music played with a distinctive beat; line-up includes some or all of following: acoustic guitar, banjo, mandolin, fiddle, string bass.
blues Originally Black American folk music using 12-bar melodic section; usually vocal, the music is often slow and sad but it can be fast and exciting.

calypso Folk music of West Indies, usually sung, in 4/4 time.
country and western, country Topical and traditional rural music, mainly vocal and American, evolved from folk, blues, and hillbilly music.
cover version Re-issue of a number, often to compete with the original.
folk music, folk song Music and ballads of the people, usually handed down from one generation to another.
gig One-night musical engagement.
gospel music Black American religious music, first sung in the churches of the southern states.
jitterbugging Improvised, all-in, athletic dancing, originating in late 1930s.

jive A later form of jitterbugging.
mainstream jazz Middle-of-the-road jazz that avoids extremes.
New Wave Movement beginning in the 1970s which included punk influences, offbeat arrangements, and also heavy rock.
pop Currently popular music or song, generally launched and performed with maximum publicity and with an eye to record sales.
punk rock Rock music with outrageous, often obscene, words, accompanied by equally outrageous behavior by its performers.
ragtime Essentially Black American piano music based on rigidly syncopated pattern; had some influence on jazz.
reggae A West Indian type of rock jazz with simple 2-beat rhythm.
rhythm and blues Urban blues performed mainly by Black American musicians.
rock, rock and roll, rock 'n' roll Mixture of rhythm and blues with country and western, originating in 1950s with emphasis on the beat and body movements of dancers.
soul music Popular, often religious music written and performed by Blacks; used for dancing.
spiritual Religious folk song, usually of Black American origin (also White spirituals); generally superseded by gospel music.

△ A pop concert in support of South African black nationalist leader Nelson Mandela.

steel bands West Indian percussion bands, originating in Trinidad, that use as instruments the tops of oil drums, tuned to various pitches.
swing Commercialized jazz featured by the big bands.
Tin Pan Alley Originally 28th Street in New York City, where most of commercial song hits were published; today, term describes any well-known area of the pop publishing business.
traditional jazz, trad Jazz that adheres to traditional New Orleans style of highly improvised melodies.

△ The Beatles had 30 million-selling records between 1962 and 1970.

ROCK & ROLL STARS

The following singers and groups have made an impact on popular music in the past few decades. Each name is followed by one of their hit singles or albums.

The Animals "House of the Rising Sun"
The Beach Boys "Surfin' U.S.A."
The Beastie Boys "(You've Got to) Fight for Your Right to Party"
The Beatles "Hey Jude"
The Bee Gees "Stayin' Alive"
Pat Benatar "Hit Me With Your Best Shot"
Chuck Berry "Johnny B. Goode"
Black Sabbath "Paranoid"
Blondie "Heart of Glass"
Bon Jovi "Slippery When Wet"
Booker T. and the MGs "Green Onions"
David Bowie "Let's Dance"
James Brown "Papa's Got a Brand New Bag"
Jackson Browne "Doctor My Eyes"
The Byrds "Turn! Turn! Turn!"
Ray Charles "Georgia on My Mind"
Chubby Checker "The Twist"
Eric Clapton "Layla"
Eddie Cochran "Summertime Blues"
Phil Collins "Against All Odds"
Sam Cooke "You Send Me"
Alice Cooper "School's Out"
Elvis Costello "Oliver's Army"
Cream "Sunshine of Your Love"
Crosby, Stills, Nash and Young "Suite: Judy Blue Eyes"
The Crystals "Da Doo Ron Ron"
Culture Club "Colour by Numbers"
The Cure "Boy's Don't Cry"
Spencer Davis Group "Gimme Some Lovin' "
Dire Straits "Brothers in Arms"
Fats Domino "Blueberry Hill"
The Doors "Light My Fire"
Duran Duran "Hungry Like the Wolf"
Bob Dylan "Like a Rolling Stone"
The Eagles "Hotel California"
Earth, Wind and Fire "Shining Star"
The Eurythmics "Sweet Dreams"
Fleetwood Mac "Rumours"
The Four Tops "I Can't Help Myself"
Aretha Franklin "Respect"
Marvin Gaye "I Heard it through the Grapevine"
Genesis "Land of Confusion"
The Grateful Dead "Truckin' "
Bill Haley and the Comets "Rock Around the Clock"
Jimi Hendrix "Are You Experienced?"
Buddy Holly "That'll Be the Day"
Whitney Houston "The Greatest Love"
The Isley Brothers "It's Your Thing"
The Jam "Going Underground"

Michael Jackson "Beat It"
Billy Joel "Uptown Girl"
Elton John "Sad Songs"
Janis Joplin "Me and Bobby McGee"
Chaka Khan "I Feel for You"
B.B. King "The Thrill is Gone"
The Kinks "You Really Got Me"
Cyndi Lauper "Girls Just Want to Have Fun"
Led Zeppelin "Stairway to Heaven"
Huey Lewis and the News "Sports"
Little Richard "Tutti Frutti"
Madonna "Material Girl"
Bob Marley "Jamming"
Joni Mitchell "Big Yellow Taxi"
The Monkees "I'm a Believer"
Moody Blues "Nights in White Satin"
The Osmonds "Puppy Love"
Pink Floyd "Dark Side of the Moon"
The Police "Every Breath You Take"
Iggy Pop "Lust for Life"
Elvis Presley "Love Me Tender"
The Pretenders "Learning to Crawl"
Prince "Purple Rain"
Queen "Bohemian Rhapsody"
Otis Redding "The Dock of the Bay"
Lou Reed "Walk on the Wild Side"
Cliff Richard "The Young Ones"
Smokey Robinson and the Miracles "Ooh Baby Baby"
The Rolling Stones "Satisfaction"
The Sex Pistols "Anarchy in the U.K."
Simon and Garfunkel "Sound of Silence"
Carly Simon "You're So Vain"
Patti Smith "Because the Night"
The Specials "Too Much Too Young"
Bruce Springsteen "Born in the U.S.A."
Cat Stevens "Wild World"
Rod Stewart "Maggie May"
The Supremes "Stop! in the Name of Love"
T. Rex "Ride A White Swan"
Talking Heads "Wild Wild Life"
James Taylor "You've Got a Friend"
The Temptations "My Girl"
Tina Turner "What's Love Got to Do with It?"
U2 "With or Without You"
Dionne Warwick "Heartbreaker"
Wham "Young Guns"
The Who "My Generation"
Stevie Wonder "Master Blaster"
Yes "Owner of a Lonely Heart"
Neil Young "After the Goldrush"
Frank Zappa "Sheik Yerbouti"

Radio and Television

Television and radio broadcasting has developed even more recently than the movies. The first advertised radio broadcast in the United States came in 1906, and in Great Britain in 1920. The world's first television service (from London's Alexandra Palace) did not begin until 1936. Now, nearly every home in the U.S. and Britain has both TV and radio, and for many people they are the main source of both news and entertainment.

Television programs that combine entertainment with education have always been very popular. Special film-making techniques make it possible for us to see things, such as right inside a living colony of ants, that we are unlikely to observe in everyday life.

Most of us enjoy fantasy as entertainment, and absurd antics in cartoon films, such as those featuring Mickey Mouse or Tom and Jerry, are old favorites. In addition, as technology improved rapidly after World

Did you know?

The final episode of *M*A*S*H*, shown in February 1983, was watched by 125 million viewers – the largest-ever American TV audience.

In Britain the most popular television event was the wedding of Prince Charles and Lady Diana Spencer on July 29th, 1981. The total number of people who tuned in was 39 million.

▽ Three of the stars from TV's ever-popular show M*A*S*H. From left to right: Alan Alda, Loretta Swit, and Harry Morgan. Filming finished in 1983.

War II, it became possible to make TV programs with special effects – for example, *Star Trek* and *Dr. Who*, so that impossible things seem to happen, transporting us to make-believe worlds.

The use of satellites in space to transmit TV pictures even allows us to receive pictures of events on the other side of the world as they happen. The widespread use of video also means that many more people can make their own recordings to show on the television screen. A series of channels devoted to different subjects is now offered by cable television. Music, sport, and natural history programs are just three of the specialties that we can see on cable TV at any time.

With the advent of television, people probably listen to radio less nowadays. Radio remains, however, very important to people wanting frequent news broadcasts or background listening while doing something at home, or the top 40 records in the charts.

▷ Radio disc jockeys often do much more than just spin pop records. Interviews with performers, commentary on the records, and light-hearted banter all form part of their repertoire.

Theater

Actors have been performing plays in theaters since the time of the ancient Greeks, and some of the most famous plays are the tragedies by the Greek writers Aeschylus, Sophocles, and Euripides. In Britain there were no theaters as such until the 1500s. Before then, troupes of actors traveled around the countryside performing plays outside churches or in market places. William Shakespeare (1564–1616) is probably England's greatest playwright, and the Elizabethan and Jacobean period in which he lived can be seen as the great age of the theater in Britain.

△ William Shakespeare, probably the greatest playwright in English. Surprisingly little is known about his life.

SOME GREAT DRAMATISTS

Beckett, Samuel (born 1906), Irish dramatist whose plays express the absurdity of human existence. The most important are *Waiting for Godot* and *Endgame*.

Chekhov, Anton (1860–1904), Russian dramatist, whose plays include *Uncle Vanya, The Three Sisters*, and *The Cherry Orchard*.

Goethe, Johann Wolfgang von (1749–1832), German poet, dramatist, and novelist. His most famous work is *Faust*, a long poetic drama in two parts. It tells the legendary story of a man who sells his soul to the Devil.

Ibsen, Henrik (1828–1906), Norwegian dramatist, known for his realistic, poetic, and increasingly symbolic plays about problems of modern life. They include *Ghosts, A Doll's House*, and *Hedda Gabler*.

Molière (Jean Baptiste Poquelin, 1622–1673), French writer of comedies and actor,

ran a theater company. His best plays include *The Bourgeois Gentleman, Tartuffe, The Misanthrope*.

O'Neill, Eugene (1888–1953), American dramatist, wrote a series of successful plays between 1920 and 1934, of which *Mourning Becomes Electra* is the best-known.

Shakespeare, William (1564–1616), Probably Britain's greatest dramatist, also an actor and a writer of beautiful sonnets. His 36 plays include historical dramas, such as *Henry V* and *Julius Caesar;* comedies, *A Midsummer Night's Dream* and *The Taming of the Shrew;* tragedies, *Hamlet, King Lear,* and *Romeo and Juliet;* and fantasy romances, *The Tempest*.

Williams, Tennessee (1911–1983), American writer noted for his psychological insights and portrayal of southern decadence.

△ A scene from *Le Bourgeois Gentilhomme*, by Molière.

△ The Globe Theatre, London, about 1600.

SOME THEATRICAL TERMS

cabaret Entertainment performed while audience dines.

epilogue Speech made at the end of a play by one of the characters or by an actor representing the author.

farce Kind of comic play based on a series of hilariously improbable events. For example the farces of Georges Feydeau and Arthur Wing Pinero.

kitchen-sink drama Realistic plays of the mid-1950s about the lives of working-class people. For example Arnold Wesker's *Chicken Soup with Barley*.

melodrama Play with a sensational plot and exaggerated emotion. For example *East Lynne* by Mrs. Henry Wood.

mime Art of acting without words. Marcel Marceau is a famous mime artist.

mystery play Religious play of the 1300s and 1400s presenting a scene from the Bible. Also called a miracle play.

passion play Play about the Crucifixion performed on Good Friday in Middle Ages. A passion play is still performed every ten years at Oberammergau, in Germany.

prologue Speech made at the beginning of a play by one of the characters or by an actor representing the author.

props, or **properties** Small objects needed on the stage to make a play realistic, such as cups, flowers, and newspapers, but not furniture or scenery.

repertory Collection of plays that a company performs in a season.

revue Theater entertainment popular since the 1890s and consisting of a series of songs, short acted scenes, and dances. These are often topical or satirical.

son et lumière ("sound and light") Open-air entertainment at a place of historical interest. The history of the place is told over loudspeakers while relevant features are lit up.

theater-in-the-round Theater in which the stage is surrounded by the audience.

theater of the absurd Kind of drama of the 1950s portraying the absurdity of human existence on Earth, such as plays by Samuel Beckett, Harold Pinter, and Eugène Ionesco.

thriller Play with an exciting plot, usually including crime with murder.

tragedy Play in which the main character(s), or protagonist, is engaged in a great struggle which ends with his/her death or downfall.

vaudeville Kind of theater from the 1850s to World War I, which presented variety entertainment consisting of comic acts, acrobats, songs and dances.

▽ Cutaway view of a large modern theater.

Films

The first moving pictures came from an invention called the kinetoscope, built by Thomas Edison, in 1891. Shortly afterward, the French inventors Auguste and Louis Lumière built their cinematographe, which projected pictures from a piece of film onto a screen. Early films were black and white, movements were jerky, and they had no sound. At first they showed only real events, but soon filmmakers began to invent their own stories and use actors. By the end of World War I (1914–1918), Hollywood had become the filmmaking capital of the world, as it still is today. The first moving picture with sound was the *Jazz Singer* (1927).

△ Charlie Chaplin made film clowning an art.

SOME FILMMAKING TERMS

close-up Picture taken near the subject.
dolly Mobile carriage to carry a camera.
dubbing Adding sound to a film.
editing Cutting or rearranging recorded material.
freeze A shot held so that the action seems to stop.
flashback Interruption in the story of a film to recall a past event.
intercut shots Two related series of shots shown alternately, such as the heroine tied to the railroad tracks and the train approaching.
library shot Film taken from material already made and in stock.
long shot A shot taken from a distance.
pan Short for panoramic shot – a sideways sweep by the camera.

prop Short for property – an object used by an actor, such as a gun or a telephone.
rushes The day's shots, before editing.
scenario Scene-by-scene outline of a film script.
set Area prepared for a film scene, either in a studio or outside.
shooting Filming a scene.
take Part of a scene shot without interruption.
track in, track back Move a camera on its dolly toward or away from the subject.
zooming Using a variable lens to give the effect of tracking in or back.

▽ *Gone with the Wind*, starring Clark Gable and Vivien Leigh, broke all box-office records.

ACADEMY AWARDS

Year	Best film	Best actor	Best actress	Best director
1927–28	Wings	Emil Jannings (The Way of All Flesh and The Last Command)	Janet Gaynor (Seventh Heaven; Street Angel; and Sunrise)	Frank Borzage (Seventh Heaven) Lewis Milestone (Two Arabian Knights)
1928–29	The Broadway Melody	Warner Baxter (In Old Arizona)	Mary Pickford (Coquette)	Frank Lloyd (The Divine Lady)
1929–30	All Quiet on the Western Front	George Arliss (Disraeli)	Norma Shearer (The Divorcee)	Lewis Milestone (All Quiet on the Western Front)
1930–31	Cimarron	Lionel Barrymore (A Free Soul)	Marie Dressler (Min and Bull)	Norman Taurog (Skippy)
1931–32	Grand Hotel	Frederic March (Dr. Jekyll and Mr. Hyde), Wallace Beery (The Champ)	Helen Hayes (The Sin of Madelon Claudet)	Frank Borzage (Bad Girl)
1932–33	Cavalcade	Charles Laughton (The Private Life of Henry VIII)	Katharine Hepburn (Morning Glory)	Frank Lloyd (Cavalcade)
1934	It Happened One Night	Clark Gable (It Happened One Night)	Claudette Colbert (It Happened One Night)	Frank Capra (It Happened One Night)
1935	Mutiny on the Bounty	Victor McLaglen (The Informer)	Bette Davis (Dangerous)	John Ford (The Informer)
1936	The Great Ziegfeld	Paul Muni (The Story of Louis Pasteur)	Luise Rainer (The Great Ziegfeld)	Frank Capra (Mr. Deeds Goes to Town)
1937	The Life of Émile Zola	Spencer Tracy (Captains Courageous)	Luise Rainer (The Good Earth)	Leo McCarey (The Awful Truth)
1938	You Can't Take It With You	Spencer Tracy (Boys' Town)	Bette Davis (Jezebel)	Frank Capra (You Can't Take It with You)
1939	Gone With the Wind	Robert Donat (Goodbye Mr. Chips)	Vivien Leigh (Gone with the Wind)	Victor Fleming (Gone with the Wind)
1940	Rebecca	James Stewart (The Philadelphia Story)	Ginger Rogers (Kitty Foyle)	John Ford (The Grapes of Wrath)
1941	How Green Was My Valley	Gary Cooper (Sergeant York)	Joan Fontaine (Suspicion)	John Ford (How Green Was My Valley)
1942	Mrs. Miniver	James Cagney (Yankee Doodle Dandy)	Greer Garson (Mrs. Miniver)	William Wyler (Mrs. Miniver)
1943	Casablanca	Paul Lukas (Watch on the Rhine)	Jennifer Jones (The Song of Bernadette)	Michael Curtiz (Casablanca)
1944	Going My Way	Bing Crosby (Going My Way)	Ingrid Bergman (Gaslight)	Leo McCarey (Going My Way)
1945	The Lost Weekend	Ray Milland (The Lost Weekend)	Joan Crawford (Mildred Pierce)	Billy Wilder (The Lost Weekend)

Year	Best film	Best actor	Best actress	Best director
1946	The Best Years of Our Lives	Frederic March (The Best Years of Our Lives)	Olivia de Havilland (To Each His Own)	William Wyler (The Best Years of Our Lives)
1947	Gentleman's Agreement	Ronald Colman (A Double Life)	Loretta Young (The Farmer's Daughter)	Elia Kazan (Gentleman's Agreement)
1948	Hamlet	Laurence Olivier (Hamlet)	Jane Wyman (Johnny Belinda)	John Huston (The Treasure of Sierra Madre)
1949	All the King's Men	Broderick Crawford (All the King's Men)	Olivia de Havilland (The Heiress)	Joseph L. Mankiewicz (A Letter to Three Wives)
1950	All About Eve	José Ferrer (Cyrano de Bergerac)	Judy Holliday (Born Yesterday)	Joseph L. Mankiewicz (All About Eve)
1951	An American in Paris	Humphrey Bogart (The African Queen)	Vivien Leigh (A Streetcar Named Desire)	George Stevens (A Place in the Sun)
1952	The Greatest Show on Earth	Gary Cooper (High Noon)	Shirley Booth (Come Back, Little Sheba)	John Ford (The Quiet Man)
1953	From Here to Eternity	William Holden (Stalag 17)	Audrey Hepburn (Roman Holiday)	Fred Zinnemann (From Here to Eternity)
1954	On the Waterfront	Marlon Brando (On the Waterfront)	Grace Kelly (The Country Girl)	Elia Kazan (On the Waterfront)
1955	Marty	Ernest Borgnine (Marty)	Anna Magnani (The Rose Tattoo)	Delbert Mann (Marty)

▽ Marlon Brando, in *On the Waterfront*, or which he won an Oscar.

▽ Katherine Hepburn, in *The Philadelphia Story*.

330

△ The hit musical *My Fair Lady* transferred from the stage to the screen in the 1960s.

Year	Best film	Best actor	Best actress	Best director
1956	Around the World in 80 Days	Yul Brynner (The King and I)	Ingrid Bergman (Anastasia)	George Stevens (Giant)
1957	The Bridge on the River Kwai	Alec Guinness (The Bridge on the River Kwai)	Joanne Woodward (The Three Faces of Eve)	David Lean (The Bridge on the River Kwai)
1958	Gigi	David Niven (Separate Tables)	Susan Hayward (I Want to Live)	Vincente Minnelli (Gigi)
1959	Ben-Hur	Charlton Heston (Ben-Hur)	Simone Signoret (Room at the Top)	William Wyler (Ben-Hur)
1960	The Apartment	Burt Lancaster (Elmer Gantry)	Elizabeth Taylor (Butterfield 8)	Billy Wilder (The Apartment)
1961	West Side Story	Maximilian Schell (Judgment at Nuremberg)	Sophia Loren (Two Women)	Robert Wise and Jerome Robbins (West Side Story)
1962	Lawrence of Arabia	Gregory Peck (To Kill a Mockingbird)	Anne Bancroft (The Miracle Worker)	David Lean (Lawrence of Arabia)
1963	Tom Jones	Sidney Poitier (Lilies of the Field)	Patricia Neal (Hud)	Tony Richardson (Tom Jones)
1964	My Fair Lady	Rex Harrison (My Fair Lady)	Julie Andrews (Mary Poppins)	George Cukor (My Fair Lady)
1965	The Sound of Music	Lee Marvin (Cat Ballou)	Julie Christie (Darling)	Robert Wise (The Sound of Music)
1966	A Man for All Seasons	Paul Scofield (A Man for All Seasons)	Elizabeth Taylor (Who's Afraid of Virginia Woolf?)	Fred Zinnemann (A Man for All Seasons)

△ A scene from the 1979 Oscar-winning movie *Cabaret*.

Year	Best film	Best actor	Best actress	Best director
1967	*In the Heat of the Night*	Rod Steiger *(In the Heat of the Night)*	Katharine Hepburn *(Guess Who's Coming to Dinner)*	Mike Nichols *(The Graduate)*
1968	*Oliver*	Cliff Robertson *(Charly)*	Katharine Hepburn *(A Lion in Winter)*, Barbra Streisand *(Funny Girl)*	Sir Carol Reed *(Oliver)*
1969	*Midnight Cowboy*	John Wayne *(True Grit)*	Maggie Smith *(The Prime of Miss Jean Brodie)*	John Schlesinger *(Midnight Cowboy)*
1970	*Patton*	George C. Scott *(Patton)*	Glenda Jackson *(Women in Love)*	Franklin J. Schaffner *(Patton)*
1971	*The French Connection*	Gene Hackman *(The French Connection)*	Jane Fonda *(Klute)*	William Friedkin *(The French Connection)*
1972	*The Godfather*	Marlon Brando *(The Godfather)*	Liza Minnelli *(Cabaret)*	Robert Fosse *(Cabaret)*
1973	*The Sting*	Jack Lemon *(Save the Tiger)*	Glenda Jackson *(A Touch of Class)*	George Roy Hill *(The Sting)*
1974	*The Godfather Part II*	Art Carney *(Harry and Tonto)*	Ellen Burstyn *(Alice Doesn't Live Here Anymore)*	Francis Ford Coppola *(The Godfather Part II)*
1975	*One Flew Over the Cuckoo's Nest*	Jack Nicholson *(One Flew Over the Cuckoo's Nest)*	Louise Fletcher *(One Flew Over the Cuckoo's Nest)*	Milos Forman *(One Flew Over the Cuckoo's Nest)*
1976	*Rocky*	Peter Finch *(Network)*	Faye Dunaway *(Network)*	John G. Avildsen *(Rocky)*
1977	*Annie Hall*	Richard Dreyfuss *(The Goodbye Girl)*	Diane Keaton *(Annie Hall)*	Woody Allen *(Annie Hall)*

Year	Best film	Best actor	Best actress	Best director
1978	*The Deer Hunter*	John Voight (*Coming Home*)	Jane Fonda (*Coming Home*)	Michael Cimino (*The Deer Hunter*)
1979	*Kramer vs. Kramer*	Dustin Hoffman (*Kramer vs. Kramer*)	Sally Field (*Norma Rae*)	Robert Benton (*Kramer vs. Kramer*)
1980	*Ordinary People*	Robert De Niro (*Raging Bull*)	Sissy Spacek (*Coalminer's Daughter*)	Robert Redford (*Ordinary People*)
1981	*Chariots of Fire*	Henry Fonda (*On Golden Pond*)	Katharine Hepburn (*On Golden Pond*)	Warren Beatty (*Reds*)
1982	*Gandhi*	Ben Kingsley (*Gandhi*)	Meryl Streep (*Sophie's Choice*)	Sir Richard Attenborough (*Gandhi*)
1983	*Terms of Endearment*	Robert Duval (*Tender Mercies*)	Shirley MacLaine (*Terms of Endearment*)	James L. Brooks (*Terms of Endearment*)
1984	*Amadeus*	F. Murray Abraham (*Amadeus*)	Sally Field (*Places in the Heart*)	Milos Forman (*Amadeus*)
1985	*Out of Africa*	William Hurt (*Kiss of the Spider Woman*)	Geraldine Page (*The Trip to Bountiful*)	Sydney Pollack (*Out of Africa*)
1986	*Platoon*	Paul Newman (*The Color of Money*)	Marlee Matlin (*Children of a Lesser God*)	Oliver Stone (*Platoon*)
1987	*The Last Emperor*	Michael Douglas (*Wall Street*)	Cher (*Moonstruck*)	Bernard Bertolucci (*The Last Emperor*)
1988	*Rain Man*	Dustin Hoffman (*Rain Man*)	Jodie Foster (*The Accused*)	Barry Levinson (*Rain Man*)

▽ *The Last Emperor*, spectacularly set in China, was voted best film in 1987.

Sport

Practicing sports gives people a chance to engage in physical or mental combat with one another, to improve their fitness and prowess, or just to exercise and have fun. The first organized sports were the Olympics of ancient Greece, in which athletes competed for crowns of laurels. Today, with huge money prizes and worldwide fame for the champions, sports are taken every bit as seriously as when they were first thought of as a training for warriors.

Sports range from baseball to billiards, from boxing to chess. Dozens of different sports activities can help to make us faster, stronger, more agile, or more skillful. The best athletes compete for money or to break records, but most of us just play for fun. In earlier times, though, sports were not for amusement. More than 2,000 years ago athletic sports trained men for hunting or war.

The ancient Greeks were the first to hold sports festivals for friendly competition. The original Olympic Games began as early as 776 B.C. Athletes raced one another on foot. They also boxed, long-jumped, and hurled

△ Discus-throwing was one of the pentathlon events in the ancient Greek Olympics.

◁ The Olympic flame, carried from Greece, symbolizes the modern Games.

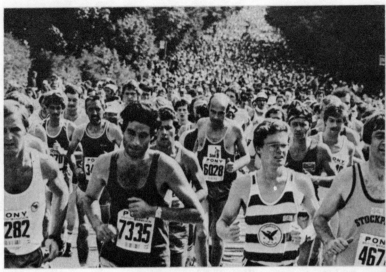

△ A marathon race, traditionally run over 26 miles 385 yards (42.19 km). Major city marathons attract thousands of runners of all levels of ability.

▽ Medieval knights in mock combat. Jousting at tournaments trained soldiers in warlike skills.

the discus and javelin. Ancient Greece was the first home of what we now call track and field athletics. But Rome conquered Greece and in A.D.394 put an end to its Games.

Organized sports stayed almost unknown through Europe's Dark Ages, about A.D.400–1000. Meanwhile, chess was invented, in either India or Persia, and horse racing flourished in the Middle East.

In the Middle Ages, Europe's main sports were archery contests and combat sports between knights fighting on foot or mounted. In the 1400s soccer began as a game in which crowds brawled over a ball, and the Scots played an early form of golf. Germans rolled stones to knock over wooden clubs. The Dutch called the game skittles and took it to North America in the 1600s. In 1841 the original game, played with nine pins, was banned in Connecticut because of the gambling associated with it. To evade the letter of the law, the players added an extra pin, and so created the legal game of "tenpins."

Modern sports truly took shape only in the 1700s and 1800s. In the new Industrial Age, millions of people gained the spare time and money to enjoy organized sports. This fir.

happened in Great Britain, where the Industrial Age started. By the mid-1800s fast steam trains could carry sports teams to play far-off rivals. As sports became popular, organizations laid down rules for them. In 1863 Britain's Football (soccer) Association largely fixed the rules for association football, a sport that has become enormously popular in many countries. No one is quite sure how baseball developed, although it was probably based on an 18th-century English game called rounders. After the Civil War, professional baseball teams were formed, and the National League was established in 1876. By 1900 sports and sports rules invented in North America and Europe had spread to countries around the world.

Some sports were old ones revived. Track and field athletics events reappeared in the modern Olympic Games, first held in Greece in 1896. German schools that taught physical fitness brought back gymnastics. New rules improved many old sports. (Boxers wear gloves and fight rounds with rests in between thanks to rules laid down in 1867.)

Brand new sports appeared, too. In 1823 a boy at Rugby School, England, picked up a football and ran holding it. So rugby football

△ Martial arts, such as judo, karate, and kendo, were originally developed for combat, but have been refined for modern sports competition.

◁ Equestrian sports include horse racing, show jumping, and dressage. Horse and rider are tested equally.

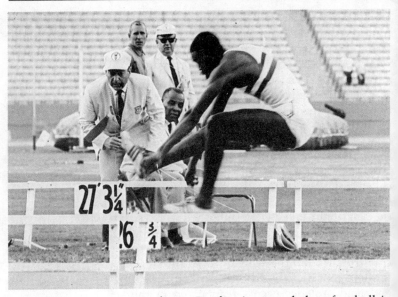

△ American long jumper Ralph Boston jumping over 27 ft (8.2 m) in his bid for the world record at the Los Angeles Olympic Games.

▽ Pole vaulters use fiber glass poles to clear the bar.

was born. Rugby, in turn, led to football in the U.S. In the late 1800s old racket games gave rise to badminton, squash, and lawn tennis. Figure skating dates from the 1860s and basketball from 1891. By 1900 the French were racing the newly developed cars and motorcycles.

Competition grew stronger once airplanes could whisk the world's best athletes to international contests anywhere on Earth. As standards improved, people broke old records again and again. In 1896 the 1,500 meters (Olympic mile) was run in 4 minutes 33.2 seconds. By 1985 more than a minute had been lopped off that time. In 1896 the long jump record stood at under 21 feet (6.4 meters). Since then the distance has increased by nearly half as much again. Year by year old records tumble to new world champions.

Since 1900 sports of all kinds have become ever more popular. Now, millions of people swim, run, skate, ride, row, or play some form of ball game. Millions more watch ball games, contests, and races on television or go to sports events in gymnasiums and stadiums.

Athletics

MEN'S WORLD RECORDS

100 meters	9.83 sec.	Ben Johnson (Canada)	8.30.87
200 meters	19.72 sec.	Pietro Mennea (Italy)	9.12.79
400 meters	43.29 sec.	"Butch" Reynolds (U.S.A.)	8.17.88
800 meters	1 min. 41.73 sec.	Sebastian Coe (G.B.)	6.10.81
1,000 meters	2 min. 12.18 sec.	Sebastian Coe (G.B.)	7.11.81
1,500 meters	3 min. 29.46 sec.	Saïd Aouita (Morocco)	8.23.85
1 mile	3 min. 46.32 sec.	Steven Cram (G.B.)	7.27.85
2,000 meters	4 min. 50.81 sec.	Saïd Aouita (Morocco)	7.16.87
3,000 meters	7 min. 32.1 sec.	Henry Rono (Kenya)	6.27.78
5,000 meters	12 min. 58.39 sec.	Saïd Aouita (Morocco)	7.22.87
10,000 meters	27 min. 13.81 sec.	Fernando Mamede (Portugal)	7.2.84
Marathon*	2 hr. 6 min.50 sec.	Belayneh Dinsamo (Ethiopia)	4.17.88
110 meters hurdles	12.93 sec.	Renaldo Nehemiah (U.S.A.)	8.19.81
400 meters hurdles	47.02 sec.	Ed Moses (U.S.A.)	8.31.83
3,000 m steeplechase	8 min. 5.4 sec.	Henry Rono (Kenya)	5.13.78
4 × 100 meters relay	37.83 sec.	United States	8.11.84
4 × 400 meters relay	2 min. 56.16 sec.	United States	10.20.68
High jump	7 ft. 8¾ in. (2.36 m)	Gerd Wessig (W. Germany)	8.1.80
Pole vault	19 ft. 10½ in. (6.06 m)	Sergey Bubka (U.S.S.R.)	7.10.88
Long jump	29 ft. 2½ in. (8.90 m)	Bob Beamon (U.S.A.)	10.18.68
Triple jump	58 ft. 11 in. (17.97 m)	"Willie" Banks (U.S.A.)	6.16.85
Shot put	75 ft. 8 in. (23.06 m)	Ulf Timmerman (E. Germany)	5.22.88
Discus throw	243 ft. (74.08 m)	Jürgen Schult (E. Germany)	6.6.86
Hammer throw	284 ft. 7 in. (86.74 m)	Yuriy Sedykh (U.S.S.R.)	8.30.86
Javelin throw†	287 ft. 7 in. (87.66 m)	Jan Zelezny (Czech)	5.31.87
Decathlon	8,847 points	"Daley" Thompson (G.B.)	8.8–9.84

WOMEN'S WORLD RECORDS

100 meters	10.49 sec.	Florence Griffith-Joyner (U.S.A.)	7.16.88
200 meters	21.71 sec.	Marita Koch (E. Germany)	6.10.79
400 meters	47.60 sec.	Marita Koch (E. Germany)	10.6.85
800 meters	1 min. 53.28 sec.	Jarmila Kratochvilova (Czech)	7.26.83
1,000 meters	2 min. 30.60 sec.	Tatyana Providokhina (U.S.S.R.)	8.20.78
1,500 meters	3 min. 52.47 sec.	Tatyana Kazankina (U.S.S.R.)	8.13.80
1 mile	4 min. 16.71 sec.	Mary Slaney (U.S.A.)	8.21.85
2,000 meters	5 min. 28.69 sec.	Maricica Puica (Romania)	7.11.86
3,000 meters	8 min. 22.62 sec.	Tatyana Kazankina (U.S.S.R.)	8.26.84
5,000 meters	14 min. 37.33 sec.	Ingrid Kristiansen (Norway)	8.5.86
10,000 meters	30 min. 13.74 sec.	Ingrid Kristiansen (Norway)	7.5.86
Marathon*	2 hr. 21 min. 6 sec.	Ingrid Kristiansen (Norway)	4.21.85
100 meters hurdles	12.29 sec.	Sally Gunnell (G.B.)	8.17.88
400 meters hurdles	52.94 sec.	Marina Styepanova (U.S.S.R.)	9.17.86
4 × 100 meters relay	41.37 sec.	East Germany	10.6.85
4 × 400 meters relay	3 min. 15.17 sec.	U.S.S.R.	10.1.88
High jump	6 ft. 10¼ in. (2.09 m)	Stefka Kostadinova (Bulgaria)	8.30.87
Long jump	24 ft. 8¼ in. (7.52 m)	Galina Chistyakova (U.S.S.R.)	6.11.88
Shot put	74 ft. 3 in. (22.63 m)	Natalya Lisovskaya (U.S.S.R.)	6.7.87
Discus throw	252 ft. (76.80 m)	Gabriele Reinsch (E. Germany)	7.9.88
Javelin throw	258 ft. 10 in. (78.90 m)	Petra Felke (E. Germany)	7.29.87
Heptathlon	7,291 points	Jackie Joyner-Kersee (U.S.A.)	8.16–17.88

* World best time (courses vary)   †New javelin

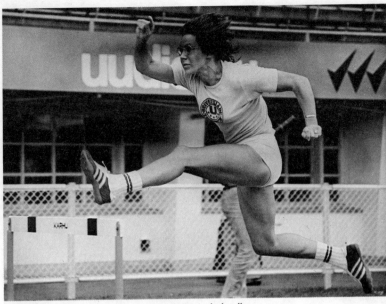

△ Heide Rosendahl (West Germany) competing in the hurdles.

1988 OLYMPICS MEDAL TABLE

	G	S	B	Total		G	S	B	Total
U.S.S.R.	55	31	46	132	Spain	1	1	2	4
East Germany	37	35	30	102	Switzerland	0	2	2	4
United States	36	31	27	94	Morocco	1	0	2	3
West Germany	11	14	15	40	Turkey	1	1	0	2
Bulgaria	10	12	13	35	Jamaica	0	2	0	2
South Korea	12	10	11	33	Argentina	0	1	1	2
China	5	11	12	28	Belgium	0	0	2	2
Romania	7	11	6	24	Mexico	0	0	2	2
Great Britain	5	10	9	24	Austria	1	0	0	1
Hungary	11	6	6	23	Portugal	1	0	0	1
France	6	4	6	16	Surinam	1	0	0	1
Poland	2	5	9	16	Chile	0	1	0	1
Italy	6	4	4	14	Costa Rica	0	1	0	1
Japan	4	3	7	14	Indonesia	0	1	0	1
Australia	3	6	5	14	Iran	0	1	0	1
New Zealand	3	2	8	13	Dutch Antilles	0	1	0	1
Yugoslavia	3	4	5	12	Peru	0	1	0	1
Sweden	0	4	7	11	Senegal	0	1	0	1
Canada	3	2	5	10	U.S. Virgin Islands	0	1	0	1
Kenya	5	2	2	9	Colombia	0	0	1	1
Netherlands	2	2	5	9	Djibouti	0	0	1	1
Czechoslovakia	3	3	2	8	Greece	0	0	1	1
Brazil	1	2	3	6	Mongolia	0	0	1	1
Norway	2	3	0	5	Pakistan	0	0	1	1
Denmark	2	1	1	4	Philippines	0	0	1	1
Finland	1	1	2	4	Thailand	0	0	1	1

Auto Racing

Ruling body Fédération Internationale de l'Automobile (FIA)
Major events and competitions Formula One – World Drivers
   Championship (based on points gained in individual grands prix)
   9, 6, 4, 3, 2, 1 for first 6
   Sports car racing – Le Mans
   Rally driving – Monte Carlo Rally
Other types of auto racing drag racing, karting, hillclimbing,
   trials, autocross, rallycross, autotests, stock-car racing,
   vintage-car racing

Records
World Drivers Championship 5 J.M. Fangio (1951, 1954–57)
Championship Grand Prix wins 39 Alain Prost 1980–
Grand Prix wins in season 8 Ayrton Senna 1988
Land Speed Record 633.5 mph (1019.5 km/h) Richard Noble
   (G.B.) in *Thrust 2*, 1983
Water Speed Record 317.6 mph (511.1 km/h) Ken Warby
   (Australia) in *Spirit of Australia*, 1978

▷ A superkart: its
streamlined body and rear
aerofoils give improved
roadholding and higher
speeds.

	FORMULA ONE WORLD CHAMPIONS		
1950	Giuseppe Farina (Italy)	1969	Jackie Stewart (Scotland)
1951	Juan Manuel Fangio (Argentina)	1970	Jochen Rindt (Austria)
1952	Alberto Ascari (Italy)	1971	Jackie Stewart (Scotland)
1953	Alberto Ascari (Italy)	1972	Emerson Fittipaldi (Brazil)
1954	Juan Manuel Fangio (Argentina)	1973	Jackie Stewart (Scotland)
1955	Juan Manuel Fangio (Argentina)	1974	Emerson Fittipaldi (Brazil)
1956	Juan Manuel Fangio (Argentina)	1975	Niki Lauda (Austria)
1957	Juan Manuel Fangio (Argentina)	1976	James Hunt (England)
1958	Mike Hawthorn (England)	1977	Niki Lauda (Austria)
1959	Jack Brabham (Australia)	1978	Mario Andretti (U.S.A.)
1960	Jack Brabham (Australia)	1979	Jody Scheckter (South Africa)
1961	Phil Hill (U.S.A.)	1980	Alan Jones (Australia)
1962	Graham Hill (England)	1981	Nelson Piquet (Brazil)
1963	Jim Clark (Scotland)	1982	Keke Rosberg (Finland)
1964	John Surtees (England)	1983	Nelson Piquet (Brazil)
1965	Jim Clark (Scotland)	1984	Niki Lauda (Austria)
1966	Jack Brabham (Australia)	1985	Alain Prost (France)
1967	Denis Hulme (New Zealand)	1986	Alain Prost (France)
1968	Graham Hill (England)	1987	Nelson Piquet (Brazil)
		1988	Ayrton Senna (Brazil)
		1989	Alain Prost (France)

GRAND NATIONAL CHAMPIONS (NASCAR)

1955	Buck Baker	1964	Richard Petty	1973	Benny Parsons	1982	Darrell Waltrip
1956	Buck Baker	1965	Ned Jarrett	1974	Richard Petty	1983	Bobby Allison
1957	Buck Baker	1966	David Pearson	1975	Richard Petty	1984	Terry Labonte
1958	Lee Petty	1967	Richard Petty	1976	Cale Yarborough	1985	Darrell Waltrip
1959	Lee Petty	1968	David Pearson	1977	Cale Yarborough	1986	Dale Earnhardt
1960	Rex White	1969	David Pearson	1978	Cale Yarborough	1987	Dale Earnhardt
1961	Ned Jarrett	1970	Bobby Isaac	1979	Richard Petty	1988	Bill Elliot
1962	Joe Weatherly	1971	Richard Petty	1980	Dale Earnhardt	1989	Rusty Wallace
1963	Joe Weatherly	1972	Richard Petty	1981	Darrell Waltrip		

CART CHAMPIONS *(U.S. Auto Club Champions prior to 1979)*

1960	A.J. Foyt	1968	Bobby Unser	1976	Gordon Johncock	1984	Mario Andretti
1961	A.J. Foyt	1969	Mario Andretti	1977	Tom Sneva	1985	Al Unser
1962	Rodger Ward	1970	Al Unser	1978	Tom Sneva	1986	Bobby Rahal
1963	A.J. Foyt	1971	Joe Leonard	1979	Rick Mears	1987	Bobby Rahal
1964	A.J. Foyt	1972	Joe Leonard	1980	Johnny Rutherford	1988	Danny Sullivan
1965	Mario Andretti	1973	Roger McCluskey	1981	Rick Mears	1989	Emerson Fittipaldi
1966	Mario Andretti	1974	Bobby Unser	1982	Rick Mears		
1967	A.J. Foyt	1975	A.J. Foyt	1983	Al Unser		

▽ Three models of sports car.

FORMULA 1 CAR

STOCK CAR

DRAGSTER

Badminton

Court 44 × 20 ft.(13.4 × 6.1 m); *singles* 44 × 17 ft.
(13.4 × 5.2 m)
Height of net 5 ft. 1 in. (1.55 m)
Weight of shuttlecock 4.73–5.50 g (less than ⅕ oz.)
Scoring best of 3 or 5 15-pt. games (men); best of 3 11-pt.
games (women)
Ruling body International Badminton Federation (I.B.F.)
World team championships Thomas Cup (men); Uber Cup
(women)
Major individual competitions World championships; All-
England championships

Baseball

Pitching distance 60 ft. 6 in. (18.4 m)
Side of diamond 90 ft. (27.4 m)
Max. length of bat 3 ft. 6 in. (1.07 m)
Diameter of ball 2¾ in. (7 cm)
Weight of ball 5–5¼ oz. (142–149 g)
Number per side 9 (substitutes allowed)
Number of innings 9 or more (played to finish)
Major organizations American League (A.L.), National League
(N.L.)
Major competition The World Series

△ A baseball bat is
cylindrical, and hitting the
ball keenly demands an
excellent eye.

WORLD SERIES RESULTS	
1939–1988	
1939 New York (AL) 4, Cincinnati (NL) 0	1965 Los Angeles (NL) 4, Minnesota (AL) 3
1940 Cincinnati (NL) 4, Detroit (AL) 3	1966 Baltimore (AL) 4, Los Angeles (NL) 0
1941 New York (AL) 4, Brooklyn (NL) 1	1967 St. Louis (NL) 4, Boston (AL) 3
1942 St. Louis (NL) 4, New York (AL) 1	1968 Detroit (AL) 4, St. Louis (NL) 3
1943 New York (AL) 4, St. Louis (NL) 1	1969 New York (NL) 4, Baltimore (AL) 1
1944 St. Louis (NL) 4, St. Louis (AL) 2	1970 Baltimore (AL) 4, Cincinnati (NL) 1
1945 Detroit (AL) 4, Chicago (NL) 3	1971 Pittsburgh (NL) 4, Baltimore (AL) 3
1946 St. Louis (NL) 4, Boston (AL) 3	1972 Oakland (AL) 4, Cincinnati (NL) 3
1947 New York (AL) 4, Brooklyn (NL) 3	1973 Oakland (AL) 4, New York (NL) 3
1948 Cleveland (AL) 4, Boston (NL) 2	1974 Oakland (AL) 4, Los Angeles (NL) 1
1949 New York AL 4, Brooklyn (NL) 1	1975 Cincinnati (NL) 4, Boston (AL) 3
1950 New York (AL) 4, Philadelphia (NL) 0	1976 Cincinnati (NL) 4, New York (AL) 0
1951 New York (AL) 4, New York (NL) 2	1977 New York (AL) 4, Los Angeles (NL) 2
1952 New York (AL) 4, Brooklyn (NL) 3	1978 New York (AL) 4, Los Angeles (NL) 2
1953 New York (AL) 4, Brooklyn (NL) 2	1979 Pittsburgh (NL) 4, Baltimore (AL) 3
1954 New York (NL) 4, Cleveland (AL) 0	1980 Philadelphia (NL) 4, Kansas City (AL) 2
1955 Brooklyn (NL) 4, New York (AL) 3	1981 Los Angeles (NL) 4, New York (AL) 2
1956 New York (AL) 4, Brooklyn (NL) 3	1982 St. Louis (NL) 4, Milwaukee (AL) 3
1957 Milwaukee (NL) 4, New York (AL) 3	1983 Baltimore (AL) 4, Philadelphia (NL) 1
1958 New York (AL) 4, Milwaukee (NL) 3	1984 Detroit (AL) 4, San Diego (NL) 1
1959 Los Angeles (NL) 4, Chicago (AL) 2	1985 Kansas City (AL) 4, St. Louis (NL) 3
1960 Pittsburgh (NL) 4, New York (AL) 3	1986 New York (NL) 4, Boston (AL) 3
1961 New York (AL) 4, Cincinnati (NL) 1	1987 Minnesota (AL) 4, St. Louis (NL) 3
1962 New York (AL) 4, San Francisco (NL) 3	1988 Los Angeles (NL) 4, Oakland (AL) 1
1963 Los Angeles (NL) 4, New York (AL) 0	1989 Oakland (AL) 4, San Francisco (NL) 0
1964 St. Louis (NL) 4, New York (AL) 3	

▽ The cue used in billiards and snooker. The modern two-piece cue unscrews in the middle.

Ferrule made of brass

Tip made of leather

Basketball

Court 85 × 46 ft. (26 × 14 m)
Height of baskets 10 ft. (3.05 m)
Diameter of baskets 18 in. (46 cm)
Circumference of ball 29½–30½ in. (75–78 cm)
Weight of ball 21–23 oz. (600–650 g)
Duration 40 min. actual play (2 × 20) plus periods of 5 min. until result is obtained
Number per side 5 (usually up to 5 substitutes)
Ruling body Fédération Internationale de Basketball Amateur (F.I.B.A.)
Major competitions World championships (men and women) and Olympic Games

Billiards and Snooker

Table 12 ft. × 6 ft. 1½ in. (3.66 × 1.86 m)
Diameter of balls 2¹⁄₁₆ in. (5.25 cm)
Billiards red, white, spot white
Billiards scoring pot or in-off red 3, white 2; cannon 2
Snooker balls (value) black (7), pink (6), blue (5), brown (4), green (3), yellow (2), 15 reds (1 each), white (cue-ball)
Ruling body Billiards and Snooker Control Council
Major competitions World championships (for both snooker and billiards, professional and amateur)

Bowls (flat green)

Rink (max.) 132 × 19 ft. (40.2 × 5.8 m)
Bowls diam. (max.) 5¾ in. (14.6 cm) biased, weight (max.) 3½ lb. (1.59 kg), made of wood, rubber or composition
Jack diam. 2½ in. (6.35 cm), weight 8–10 oz. (227–284 g)
Ruling body International Bowling Board
Events singles (4 bowls each, 21 *shots* up), pairs (2–4 bowls each, 21 *ends*), triples (2 or 3 bowls each, 18 *ends*), fours (2 bowls each, 21 *ends*)
World championships – every 4 years

Boxing

Professional
Ring 16–20 ft. (4.88–6.1 m) square
Gloves 6 oz. (170 g) fly to welter-weight, 8 oz. (227 g) light-middleweight and above
Duration 6, 8, 10, 12, or 15 (title) 3-min. rounds
Ruling body World Boxing Council (W.B.C.)

Amateur
Ring 12–20 ft. (3.66–6.1 m) square
Gloves 8 oz. (227 g)
Duration three 3-min. rounds (seniors)
Ruling body Amateur International Boxing Association (A.I.B.A.)

WEIGHT LIMITS

Division	WBC lb.	WBC kg	AIBA lb.	AIBA kg
Light-fly	—	—	105	48.0
Fly	112	50.80	112	51.0
Bantam	118	53.52	119	54.0
Feather	126	57.15	126	57.0
Junior light	130	58.97	—	—
Light	135	61.24	133	60.0
Junior welter	140	63.50	140	63.5
Welter	148	66.68	148	67.0
Junior middle	154	69.85	156	71.0
Middle	160	72.58	165	75.0
Light-heavy	175	79.38	178	81.0
Heavy	no limit		199	91.0

△ A boxing glove. The sport is banned in some countries.

▽ A chess board at the start of play

Chess

Ruling body International Chess Federation

WORLD CHAMPIONS

1866–1894	Wilhelm Steinitz (Austria)
1894–1921	Emanuel Lasker (Germany)
1921–1927	José R. Capablanca (Cuba)
1927–1935	Alexander A. Alekhine (U.S.S.R.*)
1935–1937	Max Euwe (Netherlands)
1937–1946	Alexander A. Alekhine (U.S.S.R.*)
1948–1957	Mikhail Botvinnik (U.S.S.R.)
1957–1958	Vassily Smyslov (U.S.S.R.)
1958–1959	Mikhail Botvinnik (U.S.S.R.)
1960–1961	Mikhail Tal (U.S.S.R.)
1961–1963	Mikhail Botvinnik (U.S.S.R.)
1963–1969	Tigran Petrosian (U.S.S.R.)
1969–1972	Boris Spassky (U.S.S.R.)
1972–1975	Bobby Fischer† (U.S.A.)
1975–1985	Anatoli Karpov (U.S.S.R.)
1985–	Gary Kasparov (U.S.S.R.)

*Took French citizenship
†Karpov won title when Fischer defaulted.

▽ Chess pieces: (*from left*) Pawn, Rook, Knight, Bishop, Queen, King.

▽ Croquet was first played in the United States in the 1870s.

Croquet

Court 35 × 28 yd. (32 × 25.6 m)
Players 2 or 4
Balls 4 (blue and black vs. red and yellow), diam. 3⅝ in. (9.2 cm), weight 1 lb. (454 g)
Hoops 6 (twice each) plus *peg* diam. 3¾ in. (9.5 cm)
International team competition MacRobertson Shield

▽ Fencers wear wire mesh masks, thick padded jackets, and gloves. A "hit" is recorded electronically in modern competitions.

Cycling

Ruling body Union Cycliste Internationale
Major competitions ROAD RACING Tour de France, Olympic 100-km (62-mile) race.
  TRACK RACING Olympics and world championships (sprint, pursuit, 1-km time trial, motor-paced)
Other cycle sports six-day racing, cyclo-cross, cycle speedway, bicycle polo, time trials

Equestrian Sports

Ruling body Fédération Equestre Internationale (FEI)
Major competitions SHOW JUMPING world championships (men's and women's) every 4 years, alternating with Olympics; President's Cup (world team championship) based on Nations Cup results; 2-yearly European championships (men's and women's); King George V Gold Cup; Queen Elizabeth II Gold Cup
  THREE-DAY EVENT (1 Dressage, 2 Endurance or Cross-country, 3 Show jumping) 4-yearly world championships and Olympics; 2-yearly European championships; Badminton Horse Trials
  DRESSAGE Olympics and world championships

Fencing

Ruling body Fédération Internationale d'Escrimé (FIE)
Events foil, épée, saber (men); foil (women)
Major competitions annual world championships (including Olympics)
Duration of bout first to 5 hits (or 6 min.) men; 4 hits (or 5 min.) women

Football

Field 360 × 160 ft. (110 × 49 m)
Goals 20 ft. (6 m) high, 18½ ft. (5.6 m) wide, 10 ft. (3 m) off ground, amateur; 30 ft. (9 m), professional
Ball length 11 in. (28 cm), short circum. 21¼ in. (54 cm), weight 14–15 oz. (397–425 g)
Duration 60 min. (4 × 15) playing time
No. per side 11 (unspecified number of substitutes)
Scoring *touchdown* 6 pts, *extra point* 1, *field goal* 3, *safety* 2

NATIONAL FOOTBALL LEAGUE CHAMPIONS

Year	East Winner (W-L-T)	West Winner (W-L-T)	Playoff
1933	New York Giants (11-3-0)	Chicago Bears (10-2-1)	Chicago Bears 23, New York 21
1934	New York Giants (8-5-0)	Chicago Bears (13-0-0)	New York 30, Chicago Bears 13
1935	New York Giants (9-3-0)	Detroit Lions (7-3-2)	Detroit 26, New York 7
1936	Boston Redkins (7-5-0)	Green Bay Packers (10-1-1)	Green Bay 21, Boston 6
1937	Washington Redskins (8-3-0)	Chicago Bears (9-1-1)	Washington 28, Chicago Bears 21
1938	New York Giants (8-2-1)	Green Bay Packers (8-3-0)	New York 23, Green Bay 17
1939	New York Giants (9-1-1)	Green Bay Packers (9-2-0)	Green Bay 27, New York 0

Year	East Winner (W-L-T)	West Winner (W-L-T)	Playoff
1940	Washington Redskins (9-2-0)	Chicago Bears (8-3-0)	Chicago Bears 73, Washington 0
1941	New York Giants (8-3-0)	Chicago Bears (10-1-1)(a)	Chicago Bears 37, New York 9
1942	Wash. Redskins (10-1-1)	Chicago Bears (11-0-0)	Washington 14, Chicago Bears 6
1943	Wash. Redskins (6-3-1)(a)	Chicago Bears (8-1-1)	Chicago Bears 41, Washington 21
1944	New York Giants (8-1-1)	Green Bay Packers (8-2-0)	Green Bay 14, New York 7
1945	Wash. Redskins (8-2-0)	Cleveland Rams (9-1-0)	Cleveland 15, Washington 14
1946	New York Giants (7-3-1)	Chicago Bears (8-2-1)	Chicago Bears 24, New York 14
1947	Philadelphia Eagles (8-4-0)(a)	Chicago Cardinals (9-3-0)	Chicago Cardinals 28, Philadelphia 21
1948	Philadelphia Eagles (9-2-1)	Chicago Cardinals (11-1-0)	Philadelphia 7, Chicago Cardinals 0
1949	Philadelphia Eagles (11-1-0)	Los Angeles Rams (8-2-2)	Philadelphia 14, Los Angeles 0
1950	Cleveland Browns (10-2-0)(a)	Los Angeles Rams (9-3-0)(a)	Cleveland 30, Los Angeles 28
1951	Cleveland Browns (11-1-0)	Los Angeles Rams (8-4-0)	Los Angeles 24, Cleveland 17
1952	Cleveland Browns (8-4-0)	Detroit Lions (9-3-0)(a)	Detroit 17, Cleveland 7
1953	Cleveland Browns (11-1-0)	Detroit Lions (10-2-0)	Detroit 17, Cleveland 16
1954	Cleveland Browns (9-3-0)	Detroit Lions (9-2-1)	Cleveland 56, Detroit 10
1955	Cleveland Browns (9-2-1)	Los Angeles Rams (8-3-1)	Cleveland 38, Los Angeles 14
1956	New York Giants (8-3-1)	Chicago Bears (9-2-1)	New York 47, Chicago Bears 7
1957	Cleveland Browns (9-2-1)	Detroit Lions (8-4-0)(a)	Detroit 59, Cleveland 14
1958	New York Giants (9-3-0)(a)	Baltimore Colts (9-3-0)	Baltimore 23, New York 17(b)
1959	New York Giants (10-2-0)	Baltimore Colts (9-3-0)	Baltimore 31, New York 16
1960	Philadelphia Eagles (10-2-0)	Green Bay Packers (8-4-0)	Philadelphia 17, Green Bay 13
1961	New York Giants (10-3-1)	Green Bay Packers (11-3-0)	Green Bay 37, New York 0
1962	New York Giants (12-2-0)	Green Bay Packers (13-1-0)	Green Bay 16, New York 7
1963	New York Giants (11-3-0)	Chicago Bears (11-1-2)	Chicago 14, New York 10
1964	Cleveland Browns (10-3-1)	Baltimore Colts (12-2-0)	Cleveland 27, Baltimore 0
1965	Cleveland Browns (11-3-0)	Green Bay Packers (10-3-1)(a)	Green Bay 23, Cleveland 12
1966	Dallas Cowboys (10-3-1)	Green Bay Packers(12-2-0)	Green Bay 34, Dallas 27

(a) Won divisional playoff. (b) Won at 8:15 sudden death overtime period.

SUPER BOWL

Year	Winner	Loser
1967	Green Bay Packers, 35	Kansas City Chiefs, 10
1968	Green Bay Packers, 33	Oakland Raiders, 14
1969	New York Jets, 16	Baltimore Colts, 7
1970	Kansas City Chiefs, 23	Minnesota Vikings, 7
1971	Baltimore Colts, 16	Dallas Cowboys, 13
1972	Dallas Cowboys, 24	Miami Dolphins, 3
1973	Miami Dolphins, 14	Washington Redskins, 7
1974	Miami Dolphins, 24	Minnesota Vikings, 7
1975	Pittsburgh Steelers, 16	Minnesota Vikings, 6
1976	Pittsburgh Steelers, 21	Dallas Cowboys, 17
1977	Oakland Raiders, 32	Minnesota Vikings, 14
1978	Dallas Cowboys, 27	Denver Broncos, 10
1979	Pittsburgh Steelers, 35	Dallas Cowboys, 31
1980	Pittsburgh Steelers, 31	Los Angeles Rams, 19
1981	Oakland Raiders, 27	Philadelphia Eagles, 10
1982	San Francisco 49ers, 26	Cincinatti Bengals, 21
1983	Washington Redskins, 27	Miami Dolphins, 17
1984	Los Angeles Raiders, 38	Washington Redskins, 9
1985	San Francisco 49ers, 38	Miami Dolphins, 16
1986	Chicago Bears, 46	New England Patriots, 10
1987	New York Giants, 39	Denver Broncos, 20
1988	Washington Redskins, 42	Denver Broncos, 10
1989	San Francisco 49ers, 20	Cincinatti Bengals, 16

▽ Each team displays its colours and badge on the players' helmets. A helmet normally lasts three-seasons' play before a new one is needed.

△ The three basic types of golf club. A golf driver is called a wood but may be made of metal or plastic.

▽ A gymnast performing an exercise on the rings.

Golf

Ball max. weight 1.62 oz. (46 g), min. diam. U.S. 1.68 in. (4.27 cm) U.K. 1.62 in. (4.11 cm),

Hole diam. 4¼ in. (10.8 cm)

Number of clubs carried 14 maximum

Ruling bodies Royal and Ancient Golf Club of St. Andrews; United States Golf Association

Major competitions Individual – Open, U.S. Open, U.S. Masters, U.S. PGA

Team World Cup (international teams of 2, annual), Eisenhower Trophy (world amateur, teams of 4, 2-yearly), Ryder Cup (U.S. vs. G.B., 2-yearly)

Golf Records

Lowest round 55 A. E. Smith (G.B.) 1936

36 holes 122 Sam Snead (U.S.) 59–63, 1959

72 holes 255 Peter Tupling (G.B.) 1981

Most "Big Four" titles 18 Jack Nicklaus (U.S.)

Most British Opens 6 Harry Vardon (G.B.)

Most U.S. Opens 4 Willie Anderson (U.S.), Bobby Jones (U.S.), Ben Hogan (U.S.), Jack Nicklaus (U.S.)

Most U.S. Masters 6 Jack Nicklaus (U.S.)

Most U.S. PGAs 5 Walter Hagen (U.S.), Jack Nicklaus (U.S.)

Golf Terms

BIG FOUR The major individual tournaments: Open and U.S. Open, Masters, and PGA.

BIRDIE One under par for hole.

BOGEY One over par for hole.

DORMIE In match play, leading by numbers of holes left.

DOUBLE BOGEY Two over par for hole.

EAGLE Two under par for hole.

FAIRWAY Smooth turf between tee and green.

FOURBALL Match in which pairs score their "better ball" at each hole.

FOURSOME Match in which pair play same ball, alternately.

GREEN Specially prepared surface in which hole is situated.

MATCH PLAY In which player or pair play each other and winner is determined by holes won.

MEDAL PLAY In which number of strokes taken determines winner.

PAR Standard score (assessed on first-class play) for hole or holes.

PUTTER Club used to hit ball when on green.

ROUGH Unprepared part of course.

STROKE PLAY Medal play.

TEE Starting place for hole, or peg on which ball is placed.

Gymnastics

Ruling body Fédération Internationale de Gymnastique

Events men's – floor exercises, rings, parallel bars, pommel horse, vault (lengthwise), horizontal bar; overall; team; women's – floor exercises (to music), vault, asymmetrical bars, beam; overall; team

Major competitions World and Olympic championships, alternately every 4 years

Hockey, Field

Goals 12 ft. (3.66 m) wide, 7 ft. (2.13 m) high
Ball circum. 9 in. (23 cm), weight 5½–5¾ oz. (156–163 g), made of cork and twine covered in leather
Duration of game 70 min. (2 × 35)
Number per side 11 (2 substitutes in men's game)
Ruling bodies men's – Fédération Internationale de Hockey (FIH); women's – Women's International Hockey Rules' Board
Major competitions Olympic Games and World Cup (4-yearly)

Horse Racing

Major races
United States Kentucky Derby, Preakness Stakes, Belmont Stakes (Triple Crown); Washington International
England Derby, Oaks, St. Leger, 1,000 and 2,000 Guineas (the 5 Classics), King George VI and Queen Elizabeth Stakes, Ascot Gold Cup; Grand National (steeplechase), Cheltenham Gold Cup (steeplechase), Champion Hurdle
Ireland Irish Sweeps Derby
France Prix de l'Arc de Triomphe
Australia Melbourne Cup, Caulfield Cup
South Africa Durban July Handicap

Lacrosse

Field 110 × 60 yd. (100 × 55 m) men; 120 × 70 yd. (110 × 64 m) preferred for women's international matches
Goals 6 × 6 ft. (1.8 × 1.8 m)
Ball circum. 7¾–8 in. (19.7–20.3 cm), weight 5–5¼ oz. (142–149 g) men; 4¾–5¼ oz. (135–149 g) women
Duration 60 min. (4 × 15) men, 50 min. (2 × 25) women
Number per side 10 (13 substitutes) men, 12 (1 substitute) women

△ The Great Britain hockey team. At the highest level, such as the Olympics, hockey is now played on all-weather surfaces, rather than on grass fields.

▽ A lacrosse stick is strung so that the ball cannot get lodged in it, and may not be made of metal.

348

▷ The bottleneck at the start of a scramble race. Dust and mud fly as riders compete for the lead.

△ The FIFA World Cup, played for every four years, is the leading tournament for national soccer teams.

Motorcycling

Ruling body Fédération Internationale Motocycliste (FIM)
Classes 50 cc, 125 cc, 250 cc, 350 cc (junior), 500 cc (senior), 750 cc, unlimited; sidecar
Major competitions world championships (based on points gained in individual grands prix), including Isle of Man TT
Other motorcycle sports scrambling (motocross), trials, grasstrack racing

Soccer

Pitch (field) 100–130 yd. (91.4–118.9 m) by 50–100 yd. (45.7–91.4 m)
Goals 8 yd. (7.3 m) wide, 8 ft. (2.4 m) high
Ball circum. 27–28 in. (68–71 cm)
weight 14–16 oz. (400–450 gm)
Duration of game 90 min. (2 × 45) plus 2 × 15 min. extra in certain cup games
Number per side 11 (1 or 2 substitutes, depending on competition)
Ruling body Fédération Internationale de Football Association (FIFA)

WORLD CUP FINALS

Year	Venue				
1930	Montevideo, Uruguay (100,000)	Uruguay	4	Argentina	2
1934	Rome, Italy (55,000)	Italy	2	Czechoslovakia	1
1938	Paris, France (65,000)	Italy	4	Hungary	2
1950	Rio de Janeiro, Brazil (199,850)	Uruguay	2	Brazil	1
1954	Bern, Switzerland (55,000)	W. Germany	3	Hungary	2
1958	Stockholm, Sweden (49,700)	Brazil	5	Sweden	2
1962	Santiago, Chile (69,500)	Brazil	3	Czechoslovakia	1
1966	Wembley, England (93,000)	England	4	W. Germany	2
1970	Mexico City, Mexico (110,000)	Brazil	4	Italy	1
1974	Munich, W. Germany (75,000)	W. Germany	2	Netherlands	1
1978	Buenos Aires, Argentina (77,000)	Argentina	3	Netherlands	1
1982	Madrid, Spain (90,000)	Italy	3	W. Germany	1
1986	Mexico City, Mexico (114,580)	Argentina	3	W. Germany	2

Speedway

Track 4 laps of 300–450 yd. (274–411 m) surface – red shale or granite dust
Meeting 20 races, 4 riders in race, each getting 5 rides
Scoring 1st 3 pts., 2nd 2, 3rd 1
Machines Brakeless 500 cc motorcycles
Ruling body Fédération Internationale de Motorcycliste (FIM)
Major competitions World Championship (individual), World Team Cup, World Pairs Championship
Most World Championship wins 6 Ivan Mauger (N.Z.)

▽ Needle-sharp spikes on the tires of ice speedway racers insure grip on the track. The riders wear heavy leg protection.

SPEEDWAY WORLD CHAMPIONS

1936 Lionel Van Praag (Australia)	**1968** Ivan Mauger (New Zealand)
1937 Jack Milne (U.S.A.)	**1969** Ivan Mauger (New Zealand)
1938 Bluey Wilkinson (Australia)	**1970** Ivan Mauger (New Zealand)
1949 Tommy Price (England)	**1971** Ole Olsen (Denmark)
1950 Freddie Williams (Wales)	**1972** Ivan Mauger (New Zealand)
1951 Jack Young (Australia)	**1973** Jerzy Szczakiel (Poland)
1952 Jack Young (Australia)	**1974** Anders Michanek (Sweden)
1953 Freddie Williams (Wales)	**1975** Ole Olsen (Denmark)
1954 Ronnie Moore (New Zealand)	**1976** Peter Collins (England)
1955 Peter Craven (England)	**1977** Ivan Mauger (New Zealand)
1956 Ove Fundin (Sweden)	**1978** Ole Olsen (Denmark)
1957 Barry Briggs (New Zealand)	**1979** Ivan Mauger (New Zealand)
1958 Barry Briggs (New Zealand)	**1980** Michael Lee (England)
1959 Ronnie Moore (New Zealand)	**1981** Bruce Penhall (U.S.A.)
1960 Ove Fundin (Sweden)	**1982** Bruce Penhall (U.S.A.)
1961 Ove Fundin (Sweden)	**1983** Egon Müller (W. Germany)
1962 Peter Craven (England)	**1984** Erik Gundersen (Denmark)
1963 Ove Fundin (Sweden)	**1985** Erik Gundersen (Denmark)
1964 Barry Briggs (New Zealand)	**1986** Hans Nielsen (Denmark)
1965 Bjorn Knuttsson (Sweden)	**1987** Hans Nielsen (Denmark)
1966 Barry Briggs (New Zealand)	**1988** Erik Gundersen (Denmark)
1967 Ove Fundin (Sweden)	**1989** Hans Neilsen (Denmark)

Swimming and Diving

Standard Olympic pool 54.7 yd (50 m) long, 8 lanes
Ruling body Fédération Internationale de Natation Amateur
(FINA)
Competitive strokes freestyle (usually front crawl), backstroke,
breaststroke, butterfly; individual medley (butterfly, backstroke,
breaststroke, freestyle), medley relay (backstroke, breaststroke,
butterfly, freestyle)
Diving events men's and women's springboard at 10 ft. (3 m),
highboard at 33 ft. (10 m) (lower boards also used)
Major competitions Olympics and world championships
Major long-distance swims English Channel, Atlantic City
Marathon (U.S.), Cook Strait (N.Z.)

Swimming

MEN'S WORLD RECORDS

Freestyle
50 meters	22.18 sec.	Peter Williams (South Africa)	4.10.88
100 meters	48.74 sec.	Matthew Biondi (U.S.A.)	6.24.86
200 meters	1 min. 47.44 sec.	Michael Gross (W. Germany)	7.29.84

Breaststroke
100 meters	1 min. 01.65 sec.	Steven Lundquist (U.S.A.)	7.29.84

Butterfly
100 meters	52.84 sec.	Pedro Pablo Morales (U.S.A.)	6.23.86

Backstroke
100 meters	55.00 sec.	Igor Polyanskiy (U.S.S.R.)	7.16.88

WOMEN'S WORLD RECORDS

Freestyle
50 meters	24.98 sec.	Yang Wenyi (China)	4.10.88
100 meters	54.73 sec.	Kristin Otto (E. Germany)	8.19.86
200 meters	1 min. 57.55 sec.	Heike Friedrich (E. Germany)	6.18.84

Breaststroke
100 meters	1 min. 07.91 sec.	Silke Hörner (E. Germany)	8.21.87

Butterfly
100 meters	57.93 sec.	Mary T. Meagher (U.S.A.)	8.16.81

Backstroke
100 meters	1 min. 00.59 sec.	Ina Kleber (E. Germany)	8.24.84

Table Tennis

Table 9 × 5 ft. (2.74 × 1.52 m), 2½ ft. (76 cm) off floor
Net height 6 in. (15.2 cm), length 6 ft. (1.83 m)
Ball diam. 1.46–1.5 in. (37–38 mm), weight 2.4–2.53 g made of
celluloid-type plastic, white or yellow
Bat surface max. thickness 0.08 in. (2 mm) pimpled rubber or
0.16 in. (4 mm) sandwich rubber
Scoring best of 3 or 5 21-pt. games
Ruling body International Table Tennis Federation
Major competitions world championships, Swaythling Cup
(men's team), Corbillon Cup (women's team), all 2-yearly

△ The modern table tennis
bat was introduced in the
1920s.

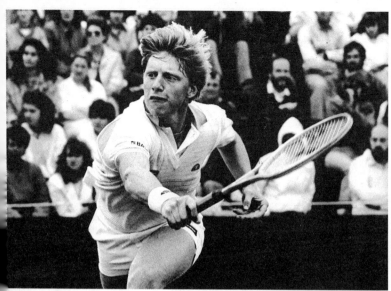

Tennis

Ball diam. 2½–2⅝ in. (6.35–6.67 cm), weight 2–2⅛ oz. (56.7–58.5 g), made of wool-covered rubber, white or yellow

Rackets no limits, wood or metal frames, strung with lamb's gut or nylon

Scoring best of 3 or 5 6-up sets, with tiebreaker at 6–6 (or first to lead by 2); games of 4 pts. (15, 30, 40, game), 40–40 being *deuce* and 2-pt. lead required; tiebreaker game usually first to 7 pts. with 2-pt. lead

Ruling body International Lawn Tennis Federation (ILTF)

Major competitions Wimbledon, Australian Open, U.S. Open, French Open (the four constituting "Grand Slam"), Davis Cup (world team championship), Federation Cup (Women's World Cup), Wightman Cup (U.S. vs. G.B. women)

△ At 17, Boris Becker became Wimbledon's youngest-ever men's singles champion in 1985. He was also the first unseeded champion.

▽ The layout of a tennis court. The inner sidelines are for singles, the outer ones for doubles. The surface may be grass, clay, wood, or one of a variety of synthetic materials.

1980s

1880s   1930s

△ The first tennis rackets were wooden, with offset, pear-shaped heads, strung with natural gut. Most modern rackets use synthetic materials – metal, carbon graphite, fiber glass, or ceramic.

▽ Steffi Graf, likely to dominate women's tennis into the 1990s.

WIMBLEDON CHAMPIONS
(since 1946)

	men	*women*
1946	Yvon Petra (Fr.)	Pauline Betz (U.S.)
1947	Jack Kramer (U.S.)	Margaret Osborne (U.S.)
1948	Bob Falkenburg (U.S.)	Louise Brough (U.S.)
1949	Fred Schroeder (U.S.)	Louise Brough (U.S.)
1950	Budge Patty (U.S.)	Louise Brough (U.S.)
1951	Dick Savitt (U.S.)	Doris Hart (U.S.)
1952	Frank Sedgman (Aus.)	Maureen Connolly (U.S.)
1953	Victor Seixas (U.S.)	Maureen Connolly (U.S.)
1954	Jaroslav Drobny (Cz.)	Maureen Connolly (U.S.)
1955	Tony Trabert (U.S.)	Louise Brough (U.S.)
1956	Lew Hoad (Aus.)	Shirley Fry (U.S.)
1957	Lew Hoad (Aus.)	Althea Gibson (U.S.)
1958	Ashley Cooper (Aus.)	Althea Gibson (U.S.)
1959	Alex Olmedo (Peru)	Maria Bueno (Brazil)
1960	Neale Fraser (Aus.)	Maria Bueno (Brazil)
1961	Rod Laver (Aus.)	Angela Mortimer (G.B.)
1962	Rod Laver (Aus.)	Karen Susman (U.S.)
1963	Chuck McKinley (U.S.)	Margaret Smith (Aus.)
1964	Roy Emerson (Aus.)	Maria Bueno (Brazil)
1965	Roy Emerson (Aus.)	Margaret Smith (Aus.)
1966	Manuel Santana (Sp.)	Billie Jean King (U.S.)
1967	John Newcombe (Aus.)	Billie Jean King (U.S.)
1968	Rod Laver (Aus.)	Billie Jean King (U.S.)
1969	Rod Laver (Aus.)	Ann Jones (G.B.)
1970	John Newcombe (Aus.)	Margaret Court* (Aus.)
1971	John Newcombe (Aus.)	Evonne Goolagong (Aus.)
1972	Stan Smith (U.S.)	Billie Jean King (U.S.)
1973	Jan Kodes (Cz.)	Billie Jean King (U.S.)
1974	Jimmy Connors (U.S.)	Chris Evert (U.S.)
1975	Arthur Ashe (U.S.)	Billie Jean King (U.S.)
1976	Bjorn Borg (Swed.)	Chris Evert (U.S.)
1977	Bjorn Borg (Swed.)	Virginia Wade (G.B.)
1978	Bjorn Borg (Swed.)	Martina Navratilova (Cz.)
1979	Bjorn Borg (Swed.)	Martina Navratilova (Cz.)
1980	Bjorn Borg (Swed.)	Evonne Cawley† (Aus.)
1981	John McEnroe (U.S.)	Chris Evert-Lloyd (U.S.)
1982	Jimmy Connors (U.S.)	Martina Navratilova (U.S.)
1983	John McEnroe (U.S.)	Martina Navratilova (U.S.)
1984	John McEnroe (U.S.)	Martina Navratilova (U.S.)
1985	Boris Becker (W. Ger.)	Martina Navratilova (U.S.)
1986	Boris Becker (W. Ger.)	Martina Navratilova (U.S.)
1987	Pat Cash (Aus.)	Martina Navratilova (U.S.)
1988	Stefan Edberg (Swed.)	Steffi Graf (W. Ger.)
1989	Boris Becker (W. Ger.)	Steffi Graf (W. Ger.)

*Formerly Margaret Smith
†Formerly Evonne Goolagong

Volleyball

Court 59 × 29½ ft. (18 × 9 m)
Net height 7 ft. 11.7 in. (2.43 m) for men, 7 ft. 4 in. (2.24 m) for women
Ball circum. 25.6–26.4 in. (65–67 cm), weight 9–10 oz. (260–280 gm)
Number per side 6 (6 substitutes)
Scoring best of 3 or 5 15-pt. sets
Ruling body Fédération Internationale de Volleyball (FIVB)
Major competitions Olympics and world championships, alternately every 4 years (men and women)

△ *Left*: Volleyball court with standard dimensions and *Right* regulations for a water polo pool.

Water Polo

Pool 22–33 yd. (20–30 m) by 8¾–22 yd. (8–20 m), min. depth 3ft. 3 in. (1 m) (6 ft. [1.8 m] for international competitions)
Goals 9¾ × 3 ft. (3 × 0.9 m) for depths over 4 ft. 11 in. (1.5 m); for shallower pools, crossbar 7 ft. 10 in. (2.4 m) above bottom
Ball circum. 26¾–28 in. (68–71 cm), weight 14–16 oz. (400–450 gm)
Duration of game 28 min. (4 × 7)
Number per side 7 (6 substitutes)
Ruling body FINA (see SWIMMING)
Major competitions as for SWIMMING

Weightlifting

Ruling body International Weightlifting Federation (IWF)
Lifts *snatch* (bar pulled overhead in one movement) and *(clean and) jerk* (bar raised to shoulders first, then driven aloft as legs are straightened); (non-Olympic) *bench press, squat, dead lift*
World championships annual (including Olympics) Classes – flyweight (114½ lb. [52 kg] limit), bantam (123½ lb. [56 kg]), feather (132¼ lb. [60 kg]), light (148¾ lb. [67.5 kg]), middle (165¼ lb. [75 kg]), light-heavy (181¾ lb. [82.5 kg]), middle-heavy (198¼ lb. [90 kg]), heavy (242½ lb. [110 kg]), super-heavy (over 242 lb. [110 kg])

WEIGHTLIFTING RECORDS
(combined snatch and jerk)

Flyweight	595¼ lb. (270 kg)	Sevdalin Marinov	Bulgaria	1988
Bantamweight	661¼ lb. (300 kg)	Neum Shalamanov	Bulgaria	1984
Featherweight	755 lb. (342.5 kg)	Naim Suleimanoglu*	Turkey	1988
Lightweight	782½ lb. (355 kg)	Mikhail Petrov	Bulgaria	1987
Middleweight	843¼ lb. (382.5 kg)	Aleksandr Varbanov	Bulgaria	1988
Light-heavywt.	892½ lb.(405 kg)	Yurik Vardanyan	U.S.S.R.	1984
Middle-heavywt.	931¼ lb. (422.5 kg)	Viktor Solodov	U.S.S.R.	1984
220½ lb. (100 kg)	970 lb. (440 kg)	Yuriy Zakharevich	U.S.S.R.	1983
Heavyweight	1003 lb. (455 kg)	Yuriy Zakharevich	U.S.S.R.	1988
Super-heavywt.	1040½ lb. (472.5 kg)	Aleksandr Kurlovich	U.S.S.R.	1987

Formerly Neum Shalamanov of Bulgaria

Winter Sports

Ice Skating
Ruling body International Skating Union (ISU)
World championships annual (including Olympics)
Figure skating events men's, women's single, pairs, (pairs) dancing (all with compulsory and "free" sections); two sets of marks, for technical merit and artistic impression
Speed skating events (on oval 400-m [436-yd.] circuits) men's 500, 1,500, 5,000, and 10,000 m (545, 1,635, 5,450, and 10,900 yd.); women's 500, 1,000, 1,500 and 3,000 m (545, 1,090, 1,635 and 3,270 yd.); overall titles in world and international events.

△ All ice hockey players, but especially the goal tender, are padded for protection in this fast, rough sport.

Ice Hockey
Rink max. 200 × 100 ft. (61 × 30.5 m)
Surround max. 4 ft. (1.22 m) high boards
Goals 6 × 4 ft. (1.83 × 1.22 m)
Puck diam. 3 in. (7.62 cm), thickness 1 in. (2.54 cm), weight 5½ × 6 oz. (156 × 170 g), made of vulcanized rubber
Duration 60 min (3 × 20) playing time
No. per side 6 (max. 18 on team)
Ruling body International Ice Hockey Federation
Major competitions (amateur) annual world championships (including Olympics)
World championships annual (including Olympics)

Alpine Ski Racing

Events downhill, slalom, giant slalom, combined

Downhill vert. drop 800–1,000 m (2,625–3,281 ft.) men; 500–700 m (1,640–2,297 ft.) women

Slalom 55–75 gates men, 40–60 gates women; alternate gates (pairs of poles 4–5 m, [13–16 ft.] apart) have blue or red flags and are 0.75–15 m (2.5–49 ft.) apart

Giant slalom min. 33 gates 4–8 m (13–26 ft.) wide, at least 10 m (33 ft.) apart

Ruling body Fédération Internationale de Ski (FIS)

Major competitions 2-yearly world championships (including Olympics, which has no combined title), annual World Cup (men's and women's, individuals scoring in 15 of 21 top international events, first 10 scoring 25, 20, 15, 11, 8, 6, 4, 3, 2, 1 pts.), annual Arlberg-Kandahar

Ski-Bob Racing

Events downhill, giant slalom, special slalom, combined

Ruling body Fédération Internationale de Skibob (FISB)

World championships two-yearly (men's and women's)

Nordic Ski Competition

Events 15, 30, 50 km (9.3, 18.6, 31 miles) men's, 5, 10 km (3.1, 6.2 miles) women's; 4 × 10 km (6.2 miles) relay (men), 3 × 5 km (3.1 miles) relay (women); nordic combination (15 km (9.3 miles) cross-country and ski jumping, men's); men's 70 and 90 m (230 and 295 ft.) ski jumping (points awarded for style and distance)

Ruling body Fédération Internationale de Ski (FIS)

Major competitions 2-yearly world championships (including Olympics); 90 m (295 ft.) ski jumping and biathlon, annually

Biathlon

Course 20 km (12.4 miles), with 4 stops for target shooting men; 10 km (6.2 miles), with 3 stops, women

Events men's individual and relay (4 × 7.5 km)

Scoring on time, with 2-min. penalties for shots missing target, 1-min. penalty for hit in outer ring of target

△ Nordic skiing is a test of stamina and, as its name suggests, is most popular in Scandinavia.

▽ In downhill skiing, competitors must descend a given course in the fastest possible time.

▽ Competitors in luge
tobogganing descend the
course feet-first aboard the
lightweight skeleton
toboggan.

Curling
Rink 138 × 14 ft. (42 × 4.27 m)
Houses (targets) diam. 12 ft. (3.66 m), dist. between centers
114 ft. (34.75 cm)
Stones (max.) circum. 36 in. (91.4 cm), thickness 4½ in.
(11.4 cm), weight 44 lb. (20 kg), made of granite or similar
Number per team 4 (2 stones each)
Number of *heads* (or *ends*) 10 or 12 (or time limit)
Ruling body Royal Caledonian Curling Club
World championships Silver Broom Trophy (annual)

Bobsledding
Course min. length 1,640 yd. (1,500 m), with at least 15 banked
turns; aggregate time for 4 descents
Events 2- and 4-man bobs
Ruling body International Bobsleigh Federation
World championships annual (including Olympics)

Luge Tobogganing
Course 1,094–1,640 yd. (1,000–1,500 m); aggregate time for 4
descents
Events 1- and 2-man luge, 1-woman luge; ridden in sitting position
Ruling body International Luge Federation
World Championships annual (including Olympics)

Cresta Run
Course unique to St. Moritz 1,326½ yd. (1,213 m); aggregate
time for 3 descents
Event single seater, ridden face down
Ruling body St. Moritz Tobogganing Club
Major competitions Grand National (full course, from Top),
Curzon Cup (from Junction, 971 yd. or 888 m); Olympic event
(full course) 1928 and 1948

OLYMPIC LOCATIONS

Winter Olympics	*Olympics*	*Olympics*
1924 Chamonix, France	1896 Athens	1976 Montreal
1928 St. Moritz, Switzerland	1900 Paris	1980 Moscow
1932 Lake, Placid, U.S.A.	1904 St. Louis	1984 Los Angeles
1936 Garmisch, Germany	1908 London	1988 Seoul, S. Korea
1948 St. Moritz, Switzerland	1912 Stockholm	
1952 Oslo, Norway	1920 Antwerp	
1956 Cortina, Italy	1924 Paris	
1960 Squaw Valley, U.S.A.	1928 Amsterdam	
1964 Innsbruck, Austria	1932 Los Angeles	
1968 Grenoble, France	1936 Berlin	
1972 Sapporo, Japan	1948 London	
1976 Innsbruck, Austria	1952 Helsinki	
1980 Lake Placid, U.S.A.	1956 Melbourne	
1984 Sarajevo, Yugoslavia	1960 Rome	
1988 Calgary, Canada	1964 Tokyo	
	1968 Mexico City	△ The well-known Olympic flag
	1972 Munich	was not flown until the 1920
		Olympic Games.

Miscellany

Some fact files do not fall readily into a special section. We present a number of them in the next 15 pages.

Nobel Prizes

The Swedish chemist Alfred Nobel invented the explosive dynamite in 1867. It made him a multi-millionaire.

When he realized how much death and destruction his invention was causing, he decided to leave his fortune as a fund to give annual prizes for outstanding work in physics; chemistry; physiology and medicine; literature; and – the one most dear to him – peace. The first prizes were awarded in 1901.

A sixth prize, for economics, was set up by the Swedish Central Bank in 1969.

△ Alfred Nobel (1833–96) endowed the prizes that now bear his name.

PRIZEWINNERS, 1901–1988

Physics

1901	Wilhelm Roentgen (German)
1902	Hendrik Lorentz and Pieter Zeeman (Dutch)
1903	Pierre and Marie Curie and Henri Becquerel (French)
1904	Lord Rayleigh (British)
1905	Philipp Lenard (German)
1906	Sir Joseph Thomson (British)
1907	Albert Michelson (American)
1908	Gabriel Lippmann (French)
1909	Guglielmo Marconi (Italian) and Karl Ferdinand Braun (German)
1910	Johannes van der Waals (Dutch)
1911	Wilhelm Wien (German)
1912	Nils Gustav Dalén (Swedish)
1913	Heike Kamerlingh-Onnes (Dutch)
1914	Max von Laue (German)
1915	Sir William H. Bragg and Sir William L. Bragg (British)
1916	*No award*
1917	Charles Barkla (British)
1918	Max Planck (German)
1919	Johannes Stark (German)
1920	Charles Guillaume (Swiss)
1921	Albert Einstein (German/Swiss)
1922	Niels Bohr (Danish)

△ Marie and Pierre Curie. She won two Nobel prizes.

1923	Robert Millikan (American)
1924	Karl Siegbahn (Swedish)
1925	James Franck and Gustav Hertz (German)
1926	Jean Perrin (French)
1927	Arthur Compton (American) and Charles T. R. Wilson (British)
1928	Owen Richardson (British)
1929	Prince Louis Victor de Broglie (French)
1930	Sir Chandrasekhara Raman (Indian)

358

1931 *No award*
1932 Werner Heisenberg (German)
1933 Erwin Schrödinger (Austrian) and Paul Dirac (British)
1934 *No award*
1935 Sir James Chadwick (British)
1936 Victor Hess (Austrian) and Carl Anderson (American)
1937 Clinton Davisson (American) and George Thomson (British)
1938 Enrico Fermi (Italian)
1939 Ernest O. Lawrence (American)
1940–42 *No award*
1943 Otto Stern (American)
1944 Isidor Isaac Rabi (American)
1945 Wolfgang Pauli (Austrian)
1946 Percy Bridgman (American)
1947 Sir Edward Appleton (British)
1948 Patrick M. S. Blackett (British)
1949 Hideki Yukawa (Japanese)
1950 Cecil Frank Powell (British)
1951 Sir John Cockcroft (British) and Ernest Walton (Irish)
1952 Edward Purcell and Felix Bloch (American)
1953 Frits Zernike (Dutch)
1954 Max Born (German/British) and Walther Bothe (German)
1955 Polykarp Kusch and Willis Lamb, Jr. (American)
1956 William Shockley, Walter Brattain and John Bardeen (American)
1957 Tsung Dao Lee and Chen Ning Yang (Chinese/American)
1958 Pavel Cherenkov, Ilya Frank and Igor Tamm (Russian)
1959 Emilio Segrè and Owen Chamberlain (American)
1960 Donald Glaser (American)
1961 Robert Hofstadter (American) and Rudolf Mossbauer (German)
1962 Lev Landau (Russian)
1963 Eugene Wigner (American), Maria Goeppert-Mayer (German/American) and Hans Jensen (German)
1964 Charles Townes (American) and Nikolai Basov and Alexandr Prokhorov (Russian)
1965 Richard Feynman and Julian Schwinger (American) and Sin-itiro Tomonaga (Japanese)
1966 Alfred Kastler (French)
1967 Hans Bethe (American)
1968 Luis Alvarez (American)
1969 Murray Gell-Mann (American)

△ Italian physicist Enrico Fermi. He produced the first nuclear chain reaction during World War II.

1970 Hannes Allfven (Swedish) and Louis Néel (French)
1971 Dennis Gabor (British)
1972 John Bardeen, Leon Cooper and John Schrieffer (American)
1973 Ivar Giaever (American), Leo Esaki (Japanese) and Brian Josephson (British)
1974 Sir Martin Ryle and Antony Hewish (British)
1975 James Rainwater (American), Aage Bohr and Benjamin Mottelson (Danish)
1976 Burton Richter (American) and Samuel Ting (American)
1977 Sir Nevill Mott (British), John Van Vleck (American) and Philip Anderson (American)
1978 Peter J. Kapitsa (Russian), Arno Penzias (American) and Robert W. Wilson (American)
1979 Sheldon Glashow (American), Abdus Salam (Pakistan) and Steven Weinberg (American)
1980 James Cronin and Val Fitch (American)
1981 Kai Siegbahn (Swedish), Nicolaas Bloembergen and Arthur Schawlow (American)
1982 Kenneth G. Wilson (American)
1983 Subrahmanyan Chandrasekhar and William Fowler (American)
1984 Carlo Rubbia (Italian) and Simon van der Meer
1985 Klaus von Klitzing (West Germany)

1986	Ernst Ruska and Gerd Binnig (West German) and Heinrich Rohrer (Swiss)
1987	Karl Müller (Swiss) and Johannes Bednorz (West German)
1988	Leon Lederman, Melvin Schwartz and Jack Steinberger (American)
1989	Norman Ramsey (American) and Hans Dehmelt (American) and Wolfgang Paul (West German)

Chemistry

1901	Jacobus van't Hoff (Dutch)
1902	Emil Fischer (German)
1903	Svante Arrhenius (Swedish)
1904	Sir William Ramsay (British)
1905	Adolf von Baeyer (German)
1906	Henri Moissan (French)
1907	Eduard Buchner (German)
1908	Ernest Rutherford (New Zealand/ British)
1909	Wilhelm Ostwald (German)
1910	Otto Wallach (German)
1911	Marie Curie (French)
1912	Victor Grignard and Paul Sabatier (French)
1913	Alfred Werner (Swiss)
1914	Theodore Richards (American)
1915	Richard Willstätter (German)
1916–17	No award
1918	Fritz Haber (German)
1919	No award
1920	Walther Nernst (German)
1921	Frederick Soddy (British)
1922	Francis Aston (British)
1923	Fritz Pregl (Austrian)
1924	No award
1925	Richard Zsigmondy (German)
1926	Theodor Svedberg (Swedish)
1927	Heinrich Wieland (German)
1928	Adolf Windaus (German)
1929	Sir Arthur Harden (British) and Hans von Euler-Chelpin (German/ Swedish)
1930	Hans Fischer (German)
1931	Carl Bosch and Friedrich Bergius (German)
1932	Irving Langmuir (American)
1933	No award
1934	Harold Urey (American)
1935	Frédéric and Irène Joliot-Curie (French)
1936	Peter Debye (Dutch)

1937	Sir Walter Haworth (British) and Paul Karrer (Swiss)
1938	Richard Kühn (German)
1939	Adolf Butenandt (German) and Leopold Ružička (Swiss)
1940–42	No award
1943	Georg von Hevesy (Hungarian/ Swedish)
1944	Otto Hahn (German)
1945	Artturi Virtanen (Finnish)
1946	James Sumner, John Northrop and Wendell Stanley (American)
1947	Sir Robert Robinson (British)
1948	Arne Tiselius (Swedish)
1949	William Giauque (American)
1950	Otto Diels and Kurt Alder (German)
1951	Glenn Seaborg and Edwin McMillan (American)
1952	Archer Martin and Richard Synge (British)
1953	Hermann Staudinger (German)
1954	Linus Pauling (American)
1955	Vincent du Vigneaud (American)
1956	Sir Cyril Hinshelwood (British) and Nikolai Semenov (Russian)
1957	Lord Todd (British)
1958	Frederick Sanger (British)
1959	Jaroslav Heyrovský (Czech)
1960	Willard Libby (American)
1961	Melvin Calvin (American)
1962	Max Perutz and Sir John Kendrew (British)
1963	Karl Ziegler (German) and Giulio Natta (Italian)
1964	Dorothy Hodgkin (British)
1965	Robert Woodward (American)
1966	Robert Mulliken (American)
1967	Ronald Norrish and George Porter (British) and Manfred Eigen (German)
1968	Lars Onsager (American)
1969	Derek Barton (British) and Odd Hassel (Norwegian)
1970	Luis Leloir (Argentinian)
1971	Gerhard Herzberg (Canadian)
1972	Christian Anfinsén, Stanford Moore, and William Stein (American)
1973	Ernst Fischer (West German) and Geoffrey Wilkinson (British)
1974	Paul Flory (American)
1975	John Cornforth (Australian) and Vladimir Prelog (Swiss)
1976	William Lipscomb (American)
1977	Ilya Prigogine (Belgian)
1978	Peter Mitchell (British)

1979	Herbert Brown (American) and George Wittig (German)
1980	Paul Berg, Walter Gilbert (American) and Frederick Sanger (British)
1981	Kenichi Fukui (Japanese) and Roald Hoffman (American)
1982	Aaron Klug (British)
1983	Henry Taube (American)
1984	Bruce Merrifield (American)
1985	Herbert Hauptman and Jerome Karle (American)
1986	Dudley Herschbach and Yuan Lee (American) and John Polyani (Canadian)
1987	Charles Pedersen and Donald Cram (American)
1988	Johann Deisendorfer, Robert Huber and Hartmut Michel (German)
1989	Sidney Altman and Thomas Cech (American)

Physiology and Medicine

1901	Emil von Behring (German)
1902	Sir Ronald Ross (British)
1903	Niels Finsen (Danish)
1904	Ivan Pavlov (Russian)
1905	Robert Koch (German)
1906	Camillo Golgi (Italian) and Santiago Ramón y Cajal (Spanish)
1907	Charles Laveran (French)
1908	Paul Ehrlich (German) and Elie Metchnikoff (Russian/French)
1909	Emil Theodor Kocher (Swiss)
1910	Albrecht Kossel (German)
1911	Allvar Gullstrand (Swedish)
1912	Alexis Carrel (French)
1913	Charles Richet (French)
1914	Robert Bárany (Austrian)
1915–18	*No award*
1919	Jules Bordet (Belgian)
1920	August Krogh (Danish)
1921	*No award*
1922	Archibald Hill (British) and Otto Meyerhof (German)
1923	Sir Frederick Banting (Canadian) and John Macleod (British)
1924	Willem Einthoven (Dutch)
1925	*No award*
1926	Johannes Fibiger (Danish)
1927	Julius Wagner-Jauregg (Austrian)
1928	Charles Nicolle (French)
1929	Christiaan Eijkman (Dutch) and Sir Frederick Hopkins (British)
1930	Karl Landsteiner (American)

△ Sir Alexander Fleming, discoverer of penicillin.

1931	Otto Warburg (German)
1932	Edgar Adrian and Sir Charles Sherrington (British)
1933	Thomas H. Morgan (American)
1934	George Minot, William P. Murphy and George Whipple (American)
1935	Hans Spemann (German)
1936	Sir Henry Dale (British) and Otto Loewi (German/Austrian)
1937	Albert Szent-Györgyi (Hungarian)
1938	Corneille Heymans (Belgian)
1939	Gerhard Domagk (Belgian)
1940–42	*No award*
1943	Henrik Dam (Danish) and Edward Doisy (American)
1944	Joseph Erlanger and Herbert Gasser (American)
1945	Sir Alexander Fleming, Howard Florey and Ernst Chain (British)
1946	Hermann Muller (American)
1947	Carl and Gerty Cori (American) and Bernardo Houssay (Argentinian)
1948	Paul Mueller (Swiss)
1949	Walter Hess (Swiss) and Antônio Moniz (Portuguese)
1950	Philip Hench and Edward Kendall (American) and Tadeus Reichstein (Swiss)
1951	Max Theiler (S. African/American)
1952	Selman Waksman (American)
1953	Fritz Lipmann (German/American) and Hans Krebs (German/British)
1954	John Enders, Thomas Weller and Frederick Robbins (American)
1955	Hugo Theorell (Swedish)
1956	André Cournand and Dickinson Richards, Jr. (American) and Werner Forssmann (German)

△ Crick and Watson researched the structure of DNA.

1957	Daniel Bovet (Italian)
1958	George Beadle, Edward Tatum and Joshua Lederberg (American)
1959	Severo Ochoa and Arthur Kornberg (American)
1960	Sir Macfarlane Burnet (Australian) and Peter Medawar (British)
1961	Georg von Békésy (Hungarian/American)
1962	Francis Crick and Maurice Wilkins (British) and James Watson (American)
1963	Alan Hodgkin and Andrew Huxley (British) and Sir John Eccles (Australian)
1964	Konrad Bloch (German/American) and Feodor Lynen (German)
1965	Francois Jacob, André Lwoff and Jacques Monod (French)
1966	Charles Huggins and Francis Peyton Rous (American)
1967	Ragnar Granit (Swedish) and H. Keffer Hartline and George Wald (American)
1968	Robert Holley, Har Gobind Khorana and Marshall Nirenberg (American)
1969	Max Delbrück, Alfred Hershey and Salvador Luria (American)
1970	Sir Bernard Katz (British), Ulf von Euler (Swedish) and Julius Axelrod (American)
1971	Earl Sutherland, Jr. (American)
1972	Rodney Porter (British) and Gerald Edelman (American)
1973	Karl von Frisch and Konrad Lorenz (Austrian) and Nikolaas Tinbergen (Dutch)
1974	Albert Claude and Christian de Duve (Belgian) and George Palade (Romanian/American)
1975	David Baltimore and Howard Temin (American) and Renato Dulbecco (Italian)
1976	Baruch Blumberg and Carleton Gajdusek (American)
1977	Rosalyn Yalow, Roger Guillemin and Andrew Schally (American)
1978	Werner Arber (Swiss), Daniel Nathans and Hamilton Smith (American)
1979	Godfrey Hounsfield (British) and Allan McLeod Cormack (American)
1980	George Snell (American), Jean Dausset (French) and Baruj Benacerraf (Venezuelan)
1981	David Hubel and Roger Sperry (American) and Torsten Wiesel (Swedish)
1982	Sune Bergstrom and Bengt Samuelsson (Swedish) and John Vane (British)
1983	Barbara McClintock (American)
1984	César Milstein (British), Georges Köhler (West German) and Niels Jerne (Danish)

362

1985	Michael Brown and Joseph Goldstein (American)
1986	Rita Levi-Montalcini (American/Italian) and Stanley Cohen (American)
1987	Susumu Tonegawa (Japanese)
1988	Sir James Black (British) and Gertrude Elion and George Hitchings (American)
1989	J. Michael Bishop and Harold E. Varmus (American)

Literature

1901	René Sully-Prudhomme (French)
1902	Theodor Mommsen (German)
1903	Björnstjerne Björnson (Norwegian)
1904	Frédéric Mistral (French) and José Echegaray (Spanish)
1905	Henryk Sienkiewicz (Polish)
1906	Giosuè Carducci (Italian)
1907	Rudyard Kipling (British)
1908	Rudolf Eucken (German)
1909	Selma Lagerlöf (Swedish)
1910	Paul von Heyse (German)
1911	Maurice Maeterlinck (Belgian)
1912	Gerhart Hauptmann (German)
1913	Sir Rabindranath Tagore (Indian)
1914	*No award*
1915	Romain Rolland (French)
1916	Verner von Heidenstam (Swedish)
1917	Karl Gjellerup and Henrik Pontoppidan (Danish)
1918	*No award*
1919	Carl Spitteler (Swiss)
1920	Knut Hamsun (Norwegian)
1921	Anatole France (French)
1922	Jacinto Benavente (Spanish)
1923	William Butler Yeats (Irish)
1924	Wladyslaw Reymont (Polish)
1925	George Bernard Shaw (Irish)
1926	Grazia Deledda (Italian)
1927	Henri Bergson (French)
1928	Sigrid Undset (Norwegian)
1929	Thomas Mann (German)
1930	Sinclair Lewis (American)
1931	Erik Karlfeldt (Swedish)
1932	John Galsworthy (English)
1933	Ivan Bunin (Russian)
1934	Luigi Pirandello (Italian)
1935	*No award*
1936	Eugene O'Neill (American)
1937	Roger Martin du Gard (French)
1938	Pearl S. Buck (American)
1939	Frans Eemil Sillanpää (Finnish)

1940–43	*No award*
1944	Johannes V. Jensen (Danish)
1945	Gabriela Mistral (Chilean)
1946	Hermann Hesse (Swiss)
1947	André Gide (French)
1948	Thomas Stearns Eliot (Anglo-American)
1949	William Faulkner (American)
1950	Bertrand Russell (British)
1951	Pär Lagerkvist (Swedish)
1952	François Mauriac (French)
1953	Sir Winston Churchill (British)
1954	Ernest Hemingway (American)
1955	Halldór Laxness (Icelandic)
1956	Juan Ramón Jiménez (Spanish)
1957	Albert Camus (French)
1958	Boris Pasternak (Russian)–declined
1959	Salvatore Quasimodo (Italian)
1960	Saint-John Perse (Alexis Saint-Léger) (French)
1961	Ivo Andrić (Yugoslavian)
1962	John Steinbeck (American)
1963	George Seferis (Giorgios Seferiades) (Greek)
1964	Jean-Paul Sartre (French)–declined
1965	Mikhail Sholokhov (Russian)
1966	Shmuel Yosef Agnon (Israeli) and Nelly Sachs (Swedish)
1967	Miguel Angel Asturias (Guatemalan)
1968	Yasunari Kawabata (Japanese)
1969	Samuel Beckett (Irish)

▽ Ernest Hemingway, journalist, adventurer, and novelist.

△ Soviet writer Alexander Solzhenitsyn was forced into exile for his dissident views.

1970	Alexander Solzhenitsyn (Russian)
1971	Pablo Neruda (Chilean)
1972	Heinrich Böll (West German)
1973	Patrick White (Australian)
1974	Eyvind Johnson and Harry Edmund Martinson (Swedish)
1975	Eugenio Montale (Italian)
1976	Saul Bellow (American)
1977	Vicente Aleixandre (Spanish)
1978	Isaac Bashevis Singer (American)
1979	Odysseus Alepoudhelis (Greek)– known as Odysseus Elytis
1980	Czeslaw Milosz (Lithuanian/ American)
1981	Elias Canetti (Bulgarian)
1982	Gabriel García Márquez (Colombian)
1983	William Golding (British)
1984	Jaroslav Seifert (Czechoslovakian)
1985	Claude Simon (French)
1986	Wole Soyinka (Nigerian)
1987	Joseph Brodsky (Russian)
1988	Naguib Mahfouz (Egyptian)
1989	Camilo José Cela (Spanish)

Peace

1901	Henri Dunant (Swiss) and Frédéric Passy (French)
1902	Elie Ducommun and Albert Gobat (Swiss)
1903	Sir William Cremer (British)
1904	Institute of International Law
1905	Baroness Bertha von Suttner (Austrian)
1906	Theodore Roosevelt (American)
1907	Ernesto Moneta (Italian) and Louis Renault (French)
1908	Klas Arnoldson (Swedish) and Fredrik Bajer (Danish)
1909	Auguste Beernaert (Belgian) and Paul d'Estournelles (French)
1910	International Peace Bureau
1911	Tobias Asser (Dutch) and Alfred Fried (Austrian)
1912	Elihu Root (American)
1913	Henri Lafontaine (Belgian)
1914–16	*No award*
1917	International Red Cross
1918	*No award*
1919	Woodrow Wilson (American)
1920	Léon Bourgeois (French)
1921	Karl Branting (Swedish) and Christian Lange (Norwegian)
1922	Fridtjof Nansen (Norwegian)
1923–24	*No award*
1925	Sir Austen Chamberlain (British) and Charles Dawes (American)
1926	Aristide Briand (French) and Gustav Stresemann (German)
1927	Ferdinand Buisson (French) and Ludwig Quidde (German)
1928	*No award*
1929	Frank Kellog (American)
1930	Nathan Söderblom (Swedish)
1931	Jane Addams and Nicholas Butler (American)
1932	*No award*
1933	Sir Norman Angell (British)
1934	Arthur Henderson (British)
1935	Carl von Ossietzky (German)
1936	Carlos de Saavedra Lamas (Argentinian)
1937	Viscount Cecil of Chelwood (British)
1938	International Office for Refugees
1939–43	*No award*
1944	International Red Cross
1945	Cordell Hull (American)
1946	Emily Balch and John Mott (American)
1947	Friends Service Council (British) and American Friends Service Committee
1948	*No award*
1949	Lord Boyd Orr (British)
1950	Ralph Bunche (American)

Year		Year	
1951	Léon Jouhaux (French)	1974	Sean MacBride (Irish) and Eisaku Sato (Japanese)
1952	Albert Schweitzer (Alsatian)	1975	Andrei Sakharov (Russian)
1953	George C. Marshall (American)	1976	Betty Williams and Mairead Corrigan (British)
1954	Office of the U.N. High Commissioner for Refugees	1977	Amnesty International
1955–56	No award	1978	Mohammed Anwar El Sadat (Egyptian) and Menachem Begin (Israeli)
1957	Lester Pearson (Canadian)	1979	Mother Teresa (Albanian/Indian)
1958	Dominique Georges Pire (Belgian)	1980	Adolfo Pérez Esquivel (Argentinian)
1959	Philip Noel-Baker (British)	1981	Office of the U.N. High Commissioner for Refugees
1960	Albert Luthuli (South African)	1982	Alva Myrdal (Swedish) and Alfonso Robles (Mexican)
1961	Dag Hammarskjöld (Swedish)	1983	Lech Walesa (Polish)
1962	Linus Pauling (American)	1984	Bishop Desmond Tutu (South African)
1963	International Red Cross and League of Red Cross Societies	1985	International Physicians for the Prevention of Nuclear War
1964	Martin Luther King, Jr. (American)	1986	Elie Wiesel (Romanian/American)
1965	UNICEF (U.N. Children's Fund)	1987	Oscar Arias Sánchez (Costa Rican)
1966–67	No award	1988	United Nations peace keeping forces
1968	René Cassin (French)	1989	The Dalai Lama (Tibetan)
1969	International Labor Organization		
1970	Norman Borlaug (American)		
1971	Willy Brandt (West German)		
1972	No award		
1973	Henry Kissinger (American); Le Duc Tho (North Vietnamese)—declined		

▽ Archbishop Desmond Tutu called for international action to end apartheid in South Africa.

Economics (since 1969)

1969	Ragnar Frisch (Norwegian) and Jan Tinbergen (Dutch)
1970	Paul Samuelson (American)
1971	Simon Kuznets (American)
1972	Kenneth Arrow (American) and Sir John Hicks (British)
1973	Wassily Leontief (American)
1974	Gunnar Myrdal (Swedish) and Friedrich von Hayek (Austrian)
1975	Leonid Kantorovich (Russian) and Tjalling Koopmans (Dutch)
1976	Milton Friedman (American)
1977	James E. Meade (British) and Bertil Ohlin (Swedish)
1978	Herbert Simon (American)
1979	Theodore Schultz (American) and Sir Arthur Lewis (British)
1980	Lawrence Klein (American)
1981	James Tobin (American)
1982	George Stigler (American)
1983	Gerard Debreu (American)
1984	Sir Richard Stone (British)
1985	Franco Modigliani (American)
1986	James Buchanan (American)
1987	Robert Solow (American)
1988	Maurice Allais (French)
1989	Trygve Haavelmo (Norwegian)

Pulitzer Prizes

The Pulitzer Prizes in Journalism, Letters, and Music were established under the will of Joseph Pulitzer, a Hungarian-born journalist who became one of America's greatest newspaper publishers.

When he died in 1911, Pulitzer left $2,000,000 to Columbia University to set up a school of journalism and award prizes for achievement in the fields of drama, journalism, literature, and music. Winners are chosen by an advisory board.

The prizes were first awarded in 1917. We give those for the past 12 years; for a full list see *The World Almanac and Book of Facts*.

PRIZEWINNERS, 1978–1989

Meritorious Public Services

1978	Philadelphia Inquirer.
1979	Point Reyes (Cal.) Light.
1980	Gannett News Service.
1981	Charlotte (N.C.) Observer
1982	Detroit News
1983	Jackson (Miss.) Clarion-Ledger.
1984	Los Angeles Times.
1985	Ft. Worth (Tex.) Star-Telegram.
1986	Denver Post.
1987	Pittsburgh Press.
1988	Charlotte Observer.
1989	Anchorage Daily News.

General News Reporting

1978 (1) Richard Whitt, Louisville Courier-Journal; (2) Anthony R. Dolan, Stamford (Conn.) Advocate.

1979 (1) San Diego (Cal.) Evening Tribune; (2) Gilbert M. Gaul, Elliot G. Jaspin, Pottsville (Pa.) Republican.

1980 (1) Philadelphia Inquirer; (2) Stephen A. Kurkijan, Alexander B. Hawes Jr., Nils Bruzelius, Joan Vennochi, Robert M. Porterfield, Boston Globe.

1981 (1) Longview (Wash.) Daily News staff; (2) Clark Hallas and Robert B. Lowe, Arizona Daily Star.

1982 (1) Kansas City Star, Kansas City Times; (2) Paul Henderson, Seattle Times.

1983 (1) Fort Wayne (Ind.) News-Sentinel;
(2) Loretta Tofani, Washington Post.

1984 (1) Newsday (N.Y.); (2) Boston Globe.

1985 (1) Thomas Turcol, Virginian-Pilot and
Ledger-Star, Norfolk, Va. (2) William
K. Marimow, Philadelphia Inquirer.

1986 (1) Edna Buchanan, Miami Herald;
(2) Jeffrey A. Marx and Michael M.
York, Lexington (Ky.) Herald-Leader.

1987 (1) Akron Beacon Journal; (2) Daniel R.
Biddle, H.G. Bissinger, Fredric N.
Tulsky, Philadelphia Inquirer; John
Woestendiek, Philadelphia Inquirer.

1988 (1) Alabama Journal; Lawrence (Mass.)
Eagle-Tribune; (2) Walt Bogdanich,
Wall Street Journal.

1989 (1) Louisville Courier-Journal; (2) Bill
Dedman, Atlanta Journal and
Constitution.

National Reporting

1978 Gayford D. Shaw, Los Angeles Times.

1979 James Risser, Des Moines Register.

1980 Charles Stafford, Bette Swenson Orsini,
St. Petersburg (Fla.) Times.

1981 John M. Crewdson, New York Times.

1982 Rick Atkinson, Kansas City Times.

1983 Boston Globe.

1984 John Noble Wilford, New York Times.

1985 Thomas J. Knudson, Des Moines (Ia.)
Register.

1986 Craig Flournoy and George Rodrigue,
Dallas Morning News; Arthur Howe,
Philadelphia Inquirer.

1987 Miami Herald; and New York Times.

1988 Tim Weiner, Philadelphia Inquirer.

1989 Donald L. Barlett and James B. Steele,
Philadelphia Inquirer.

International Reporting

1979 Richard Ben Cramer, Philadelphia
Inquirer.

1980 Joel Brinkley, Jay Mather, Louisville (Ky.)
Courier-Journal.

1981 Shirley Christian, Miami Herald.

1982 John Darnton, New York Times.

1983 Thomas L. Friedman, New York Times;
Loren Jenkins, Washington Post.

1984 Karen Elliot House, Wall St. Journal.

1985 Josh Friedman, Dennis Bell, Ozler
Muhammad, Newsday (N.Y.).

1986 Lewis M. Simons, Pete Carey, Katherine
Ellison, San Jose (Calif.) Mercury News.

1987 Michael Parks, Los Angeles Times.

1988 Thomas L. Friedman, N.Y. Times.

1989 Glenn Frankel, Washington Post; Bill
Keller, New York Times.

Editorial Writing

1978 Meg Greenfield, Washington Post.

1979 Edwin M. Yoder, Washington Star.

1980 Robert L. Bartley, Wall Street Journal.

1982 Jack Rosenthal, New York Times.

1983 Editorial board, Miami Herald.

1984 Albert Scardino, Georgia Gazette.

1985 Richard Aregood, Philadelphia Daily
News.

1986 Jack Fuller, Chicago Tribune.

1987 Jonathan Freedman, The Tribune (San
Diego).

1988 Jane Healy, Orlando Sentinel.

1989 Lois Wille, Chicago Tribune.

Criticism or Commentary

1978 (1) Walter Kerr, New York Times;
(2) William Safire, New York Times.

1979 (1) Paul Gapp, Chicago Tribune;
(2) Russell Baker, New York Times.

1980 (1) William A. Henry III, Boston Globe;
(2) Ellen Goodman, Boston Globe.

1981 (1) Jonathan Yardley, Washington Star;
(2) Dave Anderson, New York Times.

1982 (1) Martin Bernheimer, Los Angeles
Times; (2) Art Buchwald, Los Angeles
Times Syndicate.

1983 (1) Manuela Hoelterhoff, Wall St.
Journal; (2) Claude Sitton, Raleigh
(N.C.) News & Observer.

1984 (1) Paul Goldberger, New York Times;
(2) Vermont Royster, Wall St.
Journal.

1985 (1) Howard Rosenberg, Los Angeles
Times; (2) Murray Kempton,
Newsday (N.Y.)

1986 (1) Donal J. Henahan, New York Times;
(2) Jimmy Breslin, N.Y. Daily News.

1987 (1) Richard Eder, Los Angeles Times;
(2) Charles Krauthammen,
Washington Post.

1988 (1) Tom Shales, Washington Post;
(2) Dave Barry, Miami Herald.

1989 (1) Michael Skube, News and Observer,
Raleigh, N.C. (2) Clarence Page,
Chicago Tribune.

Special Citation
1978 Richard Lee Strout, Christian Science Monitor and New Republic; E.B. White, New Yorker.
1984 Theodore Geisel ("Dr. Seuss").
1985 William Schuman, composer, educational leader.
1987 Joseph Pulitzer, Jr.

Spot News Photography
1978 John H. Blair, UPI.
1979 Thomas J. Kelly III, Pottstown (Pa.) Mercury.
1980 UPI.
1981 Larry C. Price, Ft. Worth (Tex.) Star-Telegram.
1982 Ron Edmonds, Associated Press.
1983 Bill Foley, AP.
1984 Stan Grossfeld, Boston Globe.
1985 The Register, Santa Ana, Calif.
1986 Carol Guzy and Michel duCille, Miami Herald.
1987 Kim Komenich, San Francisco Examiner.
1988 Scott Shaw, Odessa (Tex.) American.
1989 Ron Olshwanger, St Louis Post-Dispatch.

Feature Photography
1978 J. Ross Baughman, AP.
1979 Staff Photographers, Boston Herald American.
1980 Erwin H. Hagler, Dallas Times-Herald.
1981 Taro M. Yamasaki, Detroit Free Press.
1982 John H. White, Chicago Sun-Times.
1983 James B. Dickman, Dallas Times-Herald.
1984 Anthony Suad, Denver Post.
1985 Stan Grossfeld, Boston Globe; Larry C. Price, Philadelphia Inquirer.
1986 Tom Gralish, Philadelphia Inquirer.
1987 David Peterson, Des Moines Register.
1988 Michel duCille, Miami Herald.
1989 Manny Crisostomo, Detroit Free Press.

Editorial Cartooning
1978 Jeffrey K. MacNelly, Richmond News Leader.
1979 Herbert L. Block, Washington Post.
1980 Don Wright, Miami (Fla.) News.
1981 Mike Peters, Dayton (Oh.) Daily News.
1982 Ben Sargent, Austin American-Statesman.
1983 Richard Lochner, Chicago Tribune.
1984 Paul Conrad, Los Angeles Times.
1985 Jeffrey K. MacNelly, Chicago Tribune.
1986 Jules Feiffer, Village Voice (N.Y. City)
1987 Berke Breathed, Washington Post.
1988 Doug Mariette, Atlanta Constitution, Charlotte Observer.
1989 Jack Higgins, Chicago Sun-Times.

Feature Writing
1979 Jon D. Franklin, Baltimore Evening Sun.
1980 Madeleine Blais, Miami Herald Tropic Magazine. Janet Cooke, Washington Post.
1981 Teresa Carpenter, Village Voice, New York City.
1982 Saul Pett, Associated Press.
1984 Peter M. Rinearson, Seattle Times.
1985 Alice Steinbach, Baltimore Sun.
1986 John Camp, St. Paul Pioneer Press and Dispatch.
1987 Steve Twomey, Philadelphia Inquirer.
1988 Jacqui Banaszynski, St. Paul Pioneer Press Dispatch.
1989 David Zucchino, Philadelphia Inquirer.

Explanatory Journalism
1985 John Franklin, Baltimore Evening Sun.
1986 New York Times Staff.
1987 Jeff Lyon and Peter Gorner, Chicago Tribune.
1988 Daniel Hertzberg, James B. Stewart, Wall Street Journal.
1989 David Hanners, William Snyder, Karen Blessen, Dallas Morning News.

Specialized Reporting
1985 Randall Savage, Jackie Crosby, Macon (Ga.) Telegraph and News.
1986 Andrew Schneider and Mary Pat Flaherty, Pittsburgh Press.
1987 Alex S. Jones, New York Times.
1988 Dean Baquet, William Gaines, Ann Marie Lipinski, Chicago Tribune.
1989 Edward Humes, Orange County (Calif.) Register.

368

Fiction

1978 James Alan McPherson, Elbow Room.
1979 John Cheever, The Stories of John Cheever.
1980 Norman Mailer, The Executioner's Song.
1981 John Kennedy Toole, A Confederacy of Dunces.
1982 John Updike, Rabbit is Rich.
1983 Alice Walker, The Color Purple.
1984 William Kennedy, Ironweed.
1985 Alison Lurie, Foreign Affairs.
1986 Larry McMurty, Lonesome Dove.
1987 Peter Taylor, A Summons to Memphis.
1988 Toni Morrison, Beloved.
1989 Anne Tyler, Breathing Lessons.

Drama

1978 Donald L. Coburn, The Gin Game.
1979 Sam Shepard, Buried Child.
1980 Lanford Wilson, Talley's Folly.
1981 Beth Henley, Crimes of the Heart.
1982 Charles Fuller, A Soldier's Play.
1983 Marsha Norman, 'night, Mother.
1984 David Mamet, Glengarry Glen Ross.
1985 Stephen Sondheim, James Lapine, Sunday in the Park with George.
1987 August Wilson, Fences.
1988 Alfred Uhry, Driving Miss Daisy.
1989 Wendy Wasserstein, The Heidi Chronicles.

History

1978 Alfred D. Chandler, Jr., The Visible Hand: The Managerial Revolution in American Business.
1979 Don E. Fehrenbacher, The Dred Scott Case: Its Significance in American Law and Politics.
1980 Leon F. Litwack, Been in the Storm So Long.
1981 Lawrence A. Cremin, American Education: The National Experience, 1783–1876.
1982 C. Vann Woodward, ed., Mary Chestnut's Civil War.
1983 Rhys L. Isaac, The Transformation of Virginia, 1740–1790.
1985 Thomas K. McCraw, Prophets of Regulation.
1986 Walter A. McDougall, ... The Heavens and the Earth.
1987 Bernard Bailyn, Voyagers to the West.
1988 Robert V. Bruce, The Launching of Modern American Science 1846–1876.

1989 Taylor Branch, Parting the Waters: America in the King Years, 1954–63; and James M. McPherson, Battle Cry of Freedom: The Civil War Era.

Biography or Autobiography

1978 Walter Jackson Bate, Samuel Johnson.
1979 Leonard Baker, Days of Sorrow and Pain: Leo Baeck and the Berlin Jews.
1980 Edmund Morris, The Rise of Theodore Roosevelt.
1981 Robert K. Massie, Peter the Great: His Life and World.
1982 William S. McFeely, Grant: A Biography.
1983 Russell Baker, Growing Up.
1984 Louis R. Hartan, Booker T. Washington.
1985 Kenneth Silverman. The Life and Times of Cotton Mather.
1986 Elizabeth Frank, Louise Brogan: A Portrait.
1987 David J. Garrow, Bearing the Cross: Martin Luther King, Jr. and the Southern Christian Leadership Conference.
1988 David Herbert Donald, Look Homeward: A Life of Thomas Wolfe.
1989 Richard Ellmann, Oscar Wilde.

Poetry

1978 Howard Nemerov, Collected Poems.
1979 Robert Penn Warren, Now and Then: Poems 1976–1978.
1980 Donald Justice: Selected Poems.
1981 James Schuyler, The Morning of the Poem.
1982 Sylvia Plath, The Collected Poems.
1983 Galway Kinnell, Selected Poems.
1984 Mary Oliver, American Primitive.
1985 Carolyn Kizer, Yin.
1986 Henry Taylor, The Flying Change.
1987 Rita Dove, Thomas and Beulah.
1988 William Meredith, Partial Accounts: New and Selected Poems.
1989 Richard Wilbur, New and Collected Poems.

General Nonfiction

1978 Carl Sagan, The Dragons of Eden.
1979 Edward O. Wilson, On Human Nature.
1980 Douglas R. Hofstadter, Gödel, Escher, Bach: An Eternal Golden Braid.

1981 Carl E. Schorske, Fin-de-Siecle Vienna: Politics and Culture.
1982 Tracy Kidder, The Soul of a New Machine.
1983 Susan Sheehan, Is There No Place on Earth for Me?
1984 Paul Starr, Social Transformation of American Medicine.
1985 Studs Terkel, The Good War.
1986 Joseph Lelyveld, Move Your Shadow; J. Anthony Lukas, Common Ground.
1987 David K. Shipler, Arab and Jew.
1988 Richard Rhodes, The Making of the Atomic Bomb.
1989 Neil Sheehan, A Bright Shining Lie: John Paul Vann and America in Vietnam.

Music
1977 Richard Wernick, Visions of Terror and Wonder.
1978 Michael Colgrass, Deja Vu for Percussion and Orchestra.
1979 Joseph Schwantner, Aftertones of Infinity.
1980 David Del Tredici, In Memory of a Summer Day.
1982 Roger Sessions, Concerto For Orchestra. (Special Citation) Milton Babbit.
1983 Ellen T. Zwilich, Three Movements for Orchestra.
1984 Bernard Rands, Canti del Sole.
1985 Stephen Albert, Symphony, RiverRun.
1986 George Perle, Wind Quintet IV.
1987 John Harbison, The Flight into Egypt.
1988 William Bolcom, 12 New Etudes for Piano.
1989 Roger Reynolds, Whispers out of Time.

British English

Over the years the American and British versions of the English language have changed, and today there are many words and phrases that have different meanings, depending on where you are. Here are some common British words with their American meanings.

aubergine eggplant
biro ballpoint pen
biscuit cracker or cookie
bonnet hood of a car
boot trunk of a car
braces suspenders
catapult slingshot
chemist's drugstore
chips french fries
clingfilm plastic wrap
cloakroom lavatory; or checkroom
crisps potato chips
courgettes zucchini
cupboard closet
diversion road detour
draughts checkers
drawing pin thumbtack
dressing gown bathrobe
dual carriageway divided highway
dustbin trashcan
flat apartment
flex electrical cord
ground floor first floor (first floor = second floor, etc.)
haberdashery notions

helping police with their enquiries being questioned
hoarding billboard
ice lolly popsicle
interval intermission
ironmonger's hardware store
juggernaut heavy truck
jumper sweater
lift elevator
loo toilet
lorry truck
lucky dip grab bag
motor car automobile
nappy diaper
pavement sidewalk
petrol gas
plain chocolate dark chocolate
plimsoll gym shoe
pram baby carriage
queue line (of people)
reel of cotton spool of thread
return ticket round-trip ticket

ring up call on phone
roundabout traffic circle; carousel
scone biscuit
semi-detached house duplex house
shoelace string
silencer muffler
single ticket one-way ticket
skipping rope jumprope
squash a light drink made of fruit juice or syrup diluted with water
stalls orchestra seats
subway underpass
sweets candy
terrace house row house
tights pantyhose
tower block high-rise building
tram streetcar
underground subway
van pickup truck
vest undershirt
waistcoat vest
windscreen windshield

International Abbreviations

Abbreviations – usually just the initial letters of words – are a quick and easy of writing long or complicated names. Here are some common abbreviations that are used and understood wherever English is read or spoken.

AAA American Automobile Association
A.B. or **B.A.** Bachelor of Arts
A.C. Alternating current
A.D. *Anno Domini*, in the Year of Our Lord.
adj. Adjective
Adm. Admiral
adv. Adverb
AEC Atomic Energy Commission
AFL-C10 American Federation of Labor and Congress of Industrial Organizations
AID Agency for International Development
a.k.a. Also known as
a.m. *Ante meridiem*, before noon
AM Amplitude modulaton
anon. Anonymous
Apr. April
assn., assoc. Association
Aug. August
Ave. Avenue
a.w.o.l. Absent without official leave

b. Born
B.C. Before Christ
Blvd. boulevard
BSc Bachelor of Science

c. *Circa*, about; *centum*, one hundred; cent
C Celsius, Centigrade
cap. Capital; capital letter
Capt. Captain
CARE Cooperative for American Remittances to Everywhere, Inc.
ch., chap. Chapter
CIA Central Intelligence Agency
cf. *Confer*, compare
cm Centimeter
co. Company; county
c/o Care of
CO Commanding officer

c.o.d. Cash (or collect) on delivery
Col. Colonel
coll., colloq. Colloquial
Con. Conservative
conj. Conjunction
cont., cont'd. Continued
corp. Corporation
Cpl. Corporal
C.S.A. Confederate States of America

d. Died
DAR Daughters of the American Revolution
DC Direct current
D.C. District of Columbia
D.D.S. Doctor of Dental Surgery
dec. Deceased
Dec. December
Dem. Democrat
dept. Department
Dr. Doctor

E East
EC European Community
ed. Edition; edited; editor
EEOC Equal Employment Opportunity Commission
e.g. *Exempli gratia*, for example
eq. Equal; equation
esp. Especially
E.S.T. eastern standard time
et al. *Et alii*, and others
etc. *Et cetera*, and so forth

F Fahrenheit
FBI Federal Bureau of Investigation
FCC Federal Communications Commission
FDA Food and Drug Administration
FDIC Federal Deposit Insurance Corporation
Feb. February
ff. Following [pages]

fig. Figure
FM Frequency modulation
Fri. Friday
ft. Foot

g Gram
GB Great Britain
gen. general
G.M.T. Greenwich Mean Time
GNP Gross national product
govt. Government

h Hour
ha Hectare
hi-fi High fidelity
HMS Her (or His) Majesty's Ship
Hon. Honorable
hp Horsepower
HQ Headquarters
hr. Hour
ht. Height
Hz Hertz

I. Island
ICBM Intercontinental ballistic missile
ibid. *Ibidem*, in the same place
i.e. *Id est*, that is
ill. Illustrated
IMF International Monetary Fund (U.N.)
inc. Incorporated, including
I O U I owe you
IQ Intelligence quotient
IRA Irish Republic Army
Is. island(s)
ISBN International Standard Book Number

Jan. January
Jr. Junior

kg Kilogram
kHz Kilohertz
km Kilometer
km/h Kilometers per hour

KW Kilowatt

£ *Libra*, pound (money)
l Liter
Lab. Labor
lat. Latitude
lb *Libra*, pound (weight)
Lib., L. Liberal
Lieut., Lt. Lieutenant
log. Logarithm
long. Longitude
Ltd. Limited

m Meter
M. Monsieur
Maj. Major
Mar. March
max. Maximum
M.D. Doctor of Medicine
mg Milligram
MHz Megahertz
min. Minute; minimum
misc. Miscellaneous
ml Milliliter
Mlle. Mademoiselle
mm Millimeter
Mme. Madame
Mon. Monday
MP Member of Parliament
mph Miles per hour
Mr. Mister
Mrs. Mistress
Ms. Miss or Mrs.
MS Manuscript
Mt. Mount

n. noun
N North
NASA National Aeronautics and Space Administration
NATO North Atlantic Treaty Organization
N.B. *Nota bene*, note well
NCO Non-commissioned officer
no. *Numéro*, number
Nov. November
N.T. New Testament

ob. *Obiit*, died
Oct. October
OK, O.K. Correct
op. *Opus*, work
op. cit. *Opere citato*, in the work cited

O.T. Old Testament

p. Page
pen. Peninsula
per cent., % *Per centum*, by the hundred
pfc. private, first class
Ph.D. Doctor of Philosophy
pl. Plural
PLO Palestine Liberation Organization
p.m. *Post meridiem*, afternoon
P.O. Post office
pop. Population
POW Prisoner of war
pp. Pages
P.S. *Post scriptum*, postscript
PTA parent-teachers' association
P.T.O. Please turn over
Pvt. Private (rank)
PX post exchange

Q.E.D. *Quod erat demonstrandum*, which was to be shown
q.v. *Quod vide*, which see

R *Rex*, king; *regina*, queen; river
rd. Road
ref. Reference
Rep. Republican
Rev. Reverend
RIP *Requiescat in pace*, rest in peace
rpm Revolutions per minute
R.S.V.P. *Répondez, s'il vous plaît* (Fr.) Reply, if you please

s Second
S South
s.a.e. Stamped addressed envelope
Sat. Saturday
sec. Second
SEC Securities and Exchange Commission
Sept. September
sing. Singular
soc. Society
Soc. Socialist
sp. Species; spelling
sq. Square
Sr. Senior

SS steamship
St. Saint; strait; street
Sun. Sunday
syn. Synonym

temp. Temperature
Thur. Thursday
TNT Trinitrotoluene
tr. Transpose; translation
Tues. Tuesday

UFO Unidentified flying object
U.K. United Kingdom of Great Britain and Northern Ireland
U.N. United Nations
UNESCO United Nations Educational, Scientific, and Cultural Organization
UNICEF United Nations Children's Fund
univ. University
U.S.A. United States of America
U.S.S.R. Union of Soviet Socialist Republics

v. Verb
v., vid. *Vide*, see
v., vs. Versus
V Volt
VHF Very high frequency
VIP Very Important Person
viz. *Videlicet*, namely
vol. Volume

W West
W Watt
Wed. Wednesday
WHO World Health Organization (U.N.)
wt Weight

Xmas Christmas

YHA Youth Hostels Association
YMCA Young Men's Christian Association
YWCA Young Women's Christian Association

zool. Zoology

Index

In this index the figures in *italics* denote illustrations in the book. In a work of this kind it is not possible to index every entry; otherwise the index would be almost as long as the book itself. For entries not found in the index, look in the relevant charts and alphabetically arranged glossaries.

A

abacus *236*
abbreviations, international *370–371*
abstract art 298
Abyssinian cat 190
Academy awards *328*
accumulator battery 224
Acquired Immune Deficiency Syndrome *see* AIDS
Actinides 226
adder *180*
Afghan hounds 188
Africa 48, *48*, 49, 111, *145*
  countries of *105–106*
  exploration and discovery 116
  population growth 47
African elephant 195
AIDS (Acquired Immune Deficiency Syndrome) 166, *169*
aircraft *144–145*, 272, *272–279*, *276*
  disasters *278–279*
airship *278–279*
albatross 182, *183*
albatrosses 182
Alcock and Brown 273
Aldrin, Edwin *16*, *22*
Alexander the Great 110, *110*
Alexandria, Pharos of *149*
algae 219
Allen, Bryan 272
alliances 50
alligators 180
alpha-particles 226
alphabets 49, 282, *283*
Alpine ski racing 355, *355*
amateur radio, licensed 292
Amazonian rainforest 210, *218*
American colonies *138*

amphibians and reptiles 180, *180–181*
Andersen, Hans Christian *311*
Andromeda galaxy *12*
angiosperms 214
angles *237*
Angora cats 190
Anguilla 46
animals 170–206
  classifying *172*, 203, *203*
  in danger 205, *205–206*
  life spans *199*
  miscellany 192–197, *192–197*
  names and homes 198, *198–199*
annelids 174
antelopes 186, 194
ants 176, *176*
apartheid *364*
aphids 176
Apollo missions *16*, 22, *22*
apterygote insects 176
Arab League, the 54, *54*
Arabic alphabet 49
Arabic number system 236, *237*
arch 306, *307*
arch dam 247
archeologists 296
Archimedes 223
architecture 296, 306, *306–309*
Arctic tern *173*
area *238*
Aristotle 222
arm muscles *157*
Armstrong, Neil *16*, 22
Artemis, Temple of *149*, *307*
arteries 159, *159*
arts and entertainment 296–332
Asia *104*, 111, *116*
  countries *104*
  exploration and discovery 116

Asian elephant 195
assassinations 125, *125–127*
associated states 46
asteroids 8, *8*
astronauts *16*
  see also space exploration
astronomy 8, 9, *20–21*, 223, *223*
athletics *38*, 151, 334–336, *337–338*
Atlantic Ocean 28
atmosphere 39, *39*
atmosphere, the 28, 39, *39*
atomic bomb 113
atoms 226, *226*
  atomic numbers 228–229
Aurorae, the *21*
Austen, Jane *311*
Austerlitz, battle of *111*
Australasia 117
Australia 46, *56–57*
  exploration and discovery 117
  states and territories 107
Australian territories 46
Australopithecus 150
automobiles 258–259, *258–260*, 262–263
  auto racing 336, 339, *339*, *340*
autumn (Fall) 20
avocet, wading *184*
Avogadro's Law 230

B

babies, human 153, 162, *162–163*
Babylonians *149*, 222
Bach, Johann Sebastian 314, *314*, *317*
backbone 154, *161*
badminton 341
Baird, John Logie 292–293, *293*

Baird's television 249
ball and socket joint 154
ballet 300, 319, 319
ballooning 272, 272
baseball 335, 341, 341
basketball 342
bats 186, 192, 192
battery
  dry 250
  lead-acid 224
battles, major 114–115
Bayeux Tapestry, the 111
beagles 188
beam bridge 244
bears 193, 193
Beatles, The 125, 320,
    321
Beaufort scale 39
beaver's dam 198
Becker, Boris 351
Becket, Thomas à 127
bees 176, 202
Beethoven Ludwig van
    317
beetle, great diving 177
Bell's first telephone 249
Benz, Karl 258, 260
Bermuda 46
berries 214
beta particle 226
biathlon 355
Bible, the 136
bicycles 255
Big Bang', the 6, 9
billiards 342, 342
binary code 236
birds 171, 182–183,
    182–185, 198, 200
birth 162
bison, American 205
black bears 193
black holes 6, 7
blackbird 184
bladderwrack (seaweed)
    219
Blanchard and Jeffries
    272
bleeper 294
blood, human 153,
    158–159, 158–159
bloodhounds 188
blue tit 184
bobsled 356
body, human 150–169,
    150–169
Boer War, the 143
Bolivar, Simon 142
bomber aircraft 145, 274,
    275
Bonaparte, Napoleon
    110, 111
bone marrow 154

bones see skeleton,
    human
bony fishes 178
books 282, 284
Boston, Ralph 336
Bourgeois Gentilhomme,
  Le (Molière) 325
bowls (flat green) 342
boxing 333, 335, 342,
    343
Boyle's Law 230
brain, human 160–161,
    160–161
Brancusi, Constantin 303
Brando, Marlon 329
breathing 158–159,
    158–159
bridges 244, 246
bristlecone pine 210
Britain see UK
British Empire 46, 46, 47,
    50, 51
British English 369
broadleaved trees 217
bromeliads, S. American
    218
bronchioles 158
bronchus 158
bronze (alloy) 250
brown bear 193, 193
Brownie (camera) 286
Budapest 145
buildings, tallest 247
bulk freight carriers 256
bumblebee, white-tailed
    176
Burmese cat 190
Bush, George 118
Bushnell, David 255
business communications
    294–295, 294–295
butterflies 176
butterfly 176
buttress dam 247
Byzantine Empire 135

C
Cabaret (movie) 331
cable television 203, 324
cacti 211
caddis fly 177
caecilians 180
Caesar, Julius 130
camels 255
cameras
  photographic 286,
    286–287
  polaroid 249
  video 297
Canada 61–62, 107

provinces and
    territories 107
canals 256
Canidae 188
Canterbury Tales
  (Chaucer) 311
capacity 239
cape dogs, wild 189
capital (architecture) 306
Caproni Ca-60 (seaplane)
    277
caracal (cat) 190, 190
cardiac muscle 156
carrack (ship) 268
carrier pigeons 288
cart champions 340
Carthaginians 129
cartilaginous fishes 178
cartography see map
    making
cat family, the 190–191,
    190–191
cattle 194
cave paintings 281, 282,
    298
cedar 217
cells 150, 219
Central America 102
ceramics see pottery
cerebrum 160–161
Ceres 18
Cervantes, Miguel de
    310–311
Ceylon see Sri Lanka
Chain Pier, Brighton
  (Constable) 301
chameleon 181
Chaplin, Charlie 327
Chappé's semaphore 290,
    291
Charlemagne 132
Charles I beheaded 138
Charles's Law 230
Chateau Wood 115
Chaucer, Geoffrey 310,
    311
cheetahs 190
chemical engineering 244
chemistry 225–229,
    226–227
  Nobel prizes 359–360
  oil-based chemicals
    244, 244
chess 334, 343, 343
chicken 182, 182
chimeras 178
chimpanzees 186
China
  clay 304, 304
  dynasties 304
Chinese language 49, 280
Chiroptera 192

chlamydomonas *219*
chlorophyll 208, *220*
Chordates 174
Christmas Island 46
Churchill, Winston *118, 119*
circulatory system 153, 158–159, *158–159*
civil engineering 244, *245*
climate 22, 34, 39, *39–41*
clouds *40*
cockchafer *200*
cockroaches 176
Cocos Islands 46
coelenterates 174
collies 188
Collins, Michael 22
colonies 46
Colossus of Rhodes *149*
Columbus, Christopher *136, 271*
COMECON (Council for Mutual Economic Assistance) 54
comets 8–9, *9, 18, 20*
command module 22
'Common Market' *see* EC
Commonwealth, the 51, *51, 54*
communications 280–295
satellites 22–23, *24*
communist theory *142*
composers, great *317*
compound eyes 176
computers 233, *233–235*
see also business communications
conical projection 42, *42*
conifers 217
Constable, John *300, 301*
Constantine, Arch of *307*
Constantinople (Istanbul) *135*
constellations, star 8, 9–11
listed *10–11*
container ship *266*
continental shelf 34
continents *103–106*
continental drift 28–29, 38, *38*
contour feathers *182*
convection currents 38
Cook, Captain James *117*
core, Earth's *45*
corn *212*
corona *15*
Cortés, Hernando *117*
cortex *160*
cotton 243
cougars *see* pumas

Council for Mutual Economic Assistance *see* COMECON
countries of the World 46–109
gazetteer *55–101*
statistics *102–109*
coyote 188
Crab Nebula 7
Cresta run 356
Crick, Francis *361*
crocodiles 180
Cromwell, Oliver *110*
croquet 343, *343*
Cruikshank, George *310*
Crusaders (routes to the Holy Land) *133*
crust, Earth's 32, *34*, 38, 45
cubism 298
cud-chewing animals 194, *194*
Cugnot's steam carriage 257, *258*
cuneiform writing *222, 282*
Curie, Marie and Pierre *357*
curling 356
customary system (measurements) 238
cycling 344
cylindrical projection 42, *42*
Cyrillic script 49

D

da Gama, Vasco *271, 272, 298*
da Vinci, Leonardo *255*
Daedalus *272*
Daguerrotype camera *286*
Daimler, Gottlieb 258, *259–261*
daisywheel printer *233*
Dalton's chart of elements *228*
dams 247
Dante, Alighieri *312*
Darius the Great 288
Dark Ages 334
Darwin, Charles *171, 225*
day 43, *43*
deciduous trees 217, *217*
decimal numbers 236, *237*
defense agreements 50
Degas, Edgar *300*
deoxyrybonucleic acid *see* DNA

dependencies 46
depression (cyclone) *41*
desert, plants *211*
deserts *37*
diaphragm 156, *158*
diatoms 219
Dickens, Charles *310, 312*
dicotyledon plants *207*, 208, *214–215*, 220
digestive system, human 152, 164, *164*
dingo 188
dinosaurs 204, *204*
Diplodocus 204
disc jockeys *324*
discovery *see* exploration and discovery
discus-throwing 333
dish, radio telescope *292*
Divine Comedy (Dante) *312*
diving *see* swimming and diving
diving beetle *177*
DNA (DeoxyryboNucleic Acid) 153, 225, *361*, 362
dodo 205, *206*
dogs 188, *188–189*
Don Quixote (Cervantes) *310*
dragonflies 176
drugs, dangers of 125, 165–166, *165–166*
addictive *165*
drums *316*
drupes 214
duck *183*
Dürer, Albrecht *300*
Dust Bowl, the 209–210
dwarf stars 6

E

eagle 182, *183, 184*
earth embankment dam 247
Earth, Planet 8, 18, *19*, 28–45
geology 28–33, *30–3. 36–38, 36–38, 45*
map making 42, *42, 4.*
time zones 43, *43*
and weather 34, 39–41, *39–41*
earthquakes 32, *32–33*
earwig 176
Easter Island statues *302*
Eastern Orthodox Chur 122

EC (European
    Community) 54, *54*
echidnas 186
echo-location (bats) *192*
eclipse *15,* 16, *17*
economics prizes, Nobel
    365
Edison, Thomas A. 297,
    327
    phonograph *249*
egg cell *see* ovum
Egypt
    boats *254, 268*
    geometry and surgery
        222
    pyramids *149*
    tomb paintings *298*
Einstein, Albert 229
El Alamein *145*
electrical engineering 244
electricity and electronics
    232, *232,* 251
    see also business
        communications;
        engineering; radio
        and television
electromagnetic waves
    292
Electronic Numeral
    Integrator and
    Calculator *see*
    ENIAC
elements 228, *228–229*
elephants *187, 195, 195*
empires, former *46,* 47,
    50, 51, 110–111,
    110–111, 135
endopterygote insects 176
energy *see* electricity;
    physics
engineering 244,
    244–249
English language
    British words *369*
    international
        abbreviations
        370–371
ENIAC (Electronic
    Numeral Integrator
    and Calculator) 233
Enola Gay bomber *113*
Entente Cordiale 50
entertainment *see* arts and
    entertainment
equestrian sports *335,*
    344
    see also horse racing
equinoxes 20
Ericsson, Leif 111
erosion *37,* 209–210, *210*
Æthelred the Unready 111
Europe 29, *103*

European Community
    54, *54*
    European empires 46,
        46, 47
Everest, Mount 36, *36,*
    146
evergreen plants 217
evolution *171*
exopterygote insects 176
explorers
    space 22–23, *22–27,*
        225
    World 116, *116–117,*
        271
extinct animals

F

F-111 (combat airplane)
    275
facial muscles *157*
Fall, the 20
Fardier (horseless
    carriage) *258*
Felidae 190
fencing 344, *344*
fennecs 188
Ferdinand, Archduke
    Franz 125
Fermi, Enrico *358*
fern, life cycle of a *211*
FIFA (Fédération
    Internationale de
    Fooball Association)
    348
fire salamander *181*
fish 178, *178–179*
    flatfish *179*
Fleming, Sir Alexander
    360
flies 176
flowering plants 214,
    214–216
Flying Fortress (bomber)
    274
'Flying Mattress'
    (airplane) *277*
Fokker D.VIII (airplane)
    274
fold mountain *45*
food chains 207
football 334, 335–336,
    344, *344–345*
Ford Model T *259*
forest destruction 205,
    210, *210,* 213
fossils *170, 221*
fox, red *188*
French Empire *46,* 47
French Guiana 46
French language 49

frog *180*
fruit 214
fruit bats 192
fungi 208, 219
    edible *219*
fusion 14, *14,* 226

G

Gagarin, Yuri *147*
galaxies 8, 12–13, *12–13*
Gale, Leonard D. 290
game birds 182
Gandhi, Mahatma *127*
gasoline engine 258–259,
    258–259, 263
Gaudí, Antoni *308*
gentoo penguin *185*
geese 182
'General Sherman' (tree)
    210
geology 28–29, *30–33,*
    36, *36–38,* 38, *45*
    geological periods
        30–31
geometry 222
German shepherd dogs
    188
Ghana, Empire of 111
Giacometti, Alberto 297
giant stars 6
giraffe *194*
Giselle (ballet) 319
glacials *see* Ice Ages
glaciers 29
Globe Theater, London
    325
glue sniffing 165, *166*
gluttons (wolverines) 197
Godwinsson, Harold *111*
golf 346, *346*
Gone with the Wind
    (movie) 327
Gossamer Albatross
    (man-powered flight)
    272
Graf, Steffi *352*
Grand National
    champions (Nascar)
    340
grasshoppers 176
gravity 6, *17*
gravity dam *247*
Great Britain *see* UK
Great Fire (of London)
    139
Great Lakes, the *35*
great ram's horn *173*
Great Western (ship) *270*
Greece, ancient 222–223,
    222–223

Greek alphabet 49, 222, *283*
Greek architecture 306, *306–307*
Greek hoplite *112*
Greek pottery *304*
'green revolution' 212
Greenwich meridian 43
greyhounds *189*
grizzly bears 193
Guernica (Picasso) *298*
guillotine, the French *141*
gulls 182
Gutenberg's printing press *248*
Guyane Française 46
gymnastics 346, *346*

H

Hadrian's Wall 111
hagfishes *178*
Halicarnassus, Mausoleum of *149*
Halley's comet 9
Handel, George Frideric *317*
Hanging Gardens of Babylon *149*
Hannibal *129*
hares *187*
Hargreaves's spinning jenny *248*
Harrier (warplane) *275, 276*
hawks 182
Haydn, Franz Joseph 314
Haydon, Benjamin *313*
heart, human 158–159, *158–159*
Hebrew alphabet *283*
hedgehogs 196
helium 12, 14, *14*
Hemingway, Ernest *362*
Henry VIII, King of England *120*
Henry the Navigator *116*
Hepburn, Katherine *329*
heredity *153*
Hermann's tortoise *181*
heron *184*
herring 178
Hertz, Heinrich 292
Herzogin Cecilie (ship) *269*
Hillary, Edmund *146*
Himalaya mountains 29, *36, 38*
Himalayan bears 193
Hindenburg (airship) *278–279*

Hindi 49
history, World 110–149
  assassinations 125, *125–127*
  chronology *128–148*
  explorers 116, *116–117*
  historical measures 239
  leaders 118–124, *118–124*
  major wars *111,* 112, *112–115*
  'Seven Wonders of' *149*
Hitler, Adolf *145,* 260
hockey
  field 347, *347*
  ice 354, *354*
Holbein, Hans *120*
Hollywood 327
Holy Family, Temple of, Barcelona *308*
Holy Roman Empire *132*
Homo erectus 151
Homo habilis 150
Honda VFR 750F *261*
hood ornaments *260*
hoplite *112*
hornet's nest *198*
horse 186, *255*
horse chestnut *217*
horse racing 334, *347*
horse-shoe bat *186*
hospitals 242
housefly *177*
hovercraft *267*
human species 48, 111, *150*
hummingbird nest *198*
Hungarian uprising *146*
hurles *338*
hydrogen 12, 14, *14,* 226
hyenas 196, *196*
hyrax *195*

I

Icarus 272
ice *37*
Ice Ages 29
ice hockey 354, *354*
ice skating 354
Iliad (Homer) 280
illuminated manuscripts *282*
imperial system (measurements) 238
Impressionism 298
India 71–72, *124, 127*
Indian elephants 195
Industrial Revolution 242, 255–256

infrared rays 292
insect-eaters 196, *196*
insects 176, *176–177, 200*
internal combustion engine *see* gasoline engine
International Date Line 43
international identification letters
  airplanes 276–277
  automobiles 262
international organizations 50–51, *50–54*
  the Commonwealth 51, *51, 54*
  other groups 54, *54*
  the UN 50–51 *50, 52–53*
inventions *248–249*
invertebrates 170, 174, *174–175*
ions 227
'Iron Duke', the *see* Wellington
islands, largest *37*
Ivan the Great *135*

J

jackals 188
jaguars 190, *191*
Jansky, Karl 292
jawless fishes 178
jazz 320, *320–321*
Jefferson, Thomas *118*
John, King *134*
jousting *334*
Jupiter 8, 18, *19, 23*

K

Kanawa, Kiri Te *318*
kangaroos 186, *197*
Keats, John *313*
Kennedy, President John F. 125
Kennedy, Robert *127*
keratin 182
Kfr (Israeli airplane) *275*
kidneys, human *152*
King, Martin Luther 125
kingfisher *185*
Kiss, The (Brancusi) *303*
koala bears *197*
Kodiak bears 193, *193*
Kublai Khan *116*

L

acrosse 347, *347*
Laika (dog) 24, *189*
akes, largest 35
ampreys *178*
anguages of the World
    48–50, *49*
Lanthanides 226
arch 217
asers 252
Last Emperor, The
    (movie) *332*
Latin American
    Integration
    Association 54
atitude and longitude 42,
    42, 44
aughing hyena 196, *196*
ava 32, *32–33, 36–37*
eaders, modern 124,
    124–125
eitz camera *286*
enin, Nikolai *144*
ennon, John 125
eonardo *see* da Vinci,
    Leonardo
eopards 190, *190*
tterpress printing *284*
ver and pulley 252
cense plate *262*
chen *219*
ghtning *40*
incoln, Abraham *142*
innaeus *see* Linné, Karl
    von
nné, Karl von *203*
notype composing
    machine *285*
erature 310, *310–313*
    Nobel prizes *362–363*
hography, offset *284*
ve Aid concert (1985)
    148
ards 180, *181*
oyd's of London *309*
ocomotion No 1 *264*
comotives 264, *264*
ng jumpers 333, *336*
ouis XIV of France *121,
    319*
ge tobogganing, 356,
    356
amière, Auguste and
    Louis 327
ngs 158–159, *158–159*
ce 296
ther, Martin *136*
nxes 190

M

Madonna in Majesty, The
    (Giotto) *300*
Magellan, Ferdinand *271*
Magna Carta (King
    John's seal) *134*
magnetic radiation 14
mail *see* postal services
mailbox, U.S. *289*
Malay bears 193
mammals 186, *186–187*
Mandarin (Chinese
    language) 48
Mandela, Nelson *321*
mantle, Earth's 38, *45*
manuscripts, illuminated
    282
Manx cat 190
map making 42, *42, 44*
marathon races *334*
Marco Polo *116*
Marconi, Guglielmo *249,
    292, 292*
Marianas Trench 34, 36
Mars 8, 18, *19*, 23
marsupials *see* pouched
    animals
marten *197*
martial arts *335*
Marx, Karl *142*
M*A*S*H *323*
mathematics 236,
    236–241, 238
matter, states of *253*
Maximilian I, Emperor
    314
Maxwell, James Clerk
    292
May bug *200*
Maya, the 111, 223
mayflies 176
measurements *see* weights
    and measures
mechanical engineering
    244
Mendeleyev, Dmitri *228*
Mercator, Gerhardus 42
Mercury 8, 18, *19*
Mercury space capsule *25*
meridian 43
Messerschmitt (airplane)
    274
metallurgy 244
meteor tracks *21*
meteorology *see* weather
'Methuselah' (tree) 210
metric system
    (measurement) 238,
    238–239

Mickey Mouse *323*
microscope *224*
Middle Ages 298, 306,
    334, *334*
migration
    animal 171, *173*
    people 111
military aircraft
    274–275, 276
Milky Way, the 7, 8, 12,
    12
mining engineering 244
MIR (Soviet space
    station) *26*
miscellany *357–371*
moas *205*
moles 196, *196*
Molière, Jean Baptiste
    325
molluscs 174
Mollweide projection *42*
monarchs, European 120,
    120–121
Monera 219
Monet, Claude 298
monocotyledon plants
    *207, 208, 214–215,
    221*
monotremes 186, *187*
Montgolfier brothers *272*
Moon, the 8, *15*, 16,
    16–17, 22
    landings *16*, 22
moose *194*
Morse, Samuel 290,
    290–291
    Morse code *290*
moths 176
motorcycles 261, *261*
    sport 336, 348, 349,
    349
mountain lions *see* puma
mountains, highest *36*
movies 297, 327,
    327–332
Mozart, Wolfgang
    Amadeus *317*, 318
multi-racial society 48
Munch, Edvard *299*
muscles, human 156,
    156–157
mushrooms 208, *219*
music 314, *314–322*
    ballet 319, *319*
    opera 318, *318*
    popular 320, *320–322*
Mustiladae (weasels) 197
My Fair Lady (movie) *330*
Mycota 219

N

Napoleon *see* Bonaparte,
  Napoleon
NATO (North Atlantic
  Treaty Organization)
  54, *54*
Neanderthal man *151*
Nehru, Jawaharlal *124*
Neptune *19*
nervous system 150, 153,
  160–161
nests *198–199*
New Orleans, battle of
  281
newspaper press *284*
Newton, Sir Isaac *230*
nictitating membrane *191*
Nijinsky, Vaslav *319*
Nobel, Alfred *357*
  prizes 357, *357–365*
'noble gases' 226
Nordic ski competition
  355, *355*
Norgay, Tenzing *146*
North America 29
  countries of *102*
  exploration and
    discovery *117*
North Atlantic Treaty
  Organization *see*
  NATO
Northern and Southern
  Lights *21*
Northrop's Flying Wing
  277
nuclear fusion 14, *14*, 226
nuclear submarine *257*
numbats *197*
numeration 236, *236–237*

O

ocean liner *256*
ocean trench 34, 36
Oceania *106*
ocelots 190, 191
Odyssey (Homer) 281
oil-based chemicals *244*
Olds, Eli Ransom *259*
Oldsmobiles *259*
Oliver Cromwell 110, *110*
Oliver Twist (Dickens)
  310
Olympia *149*
Olympics *333*, 335, *338*,
  356
Open University *293*
opera 318, *318*

Opera House, Paris *318*
optical fibers *281, 291*
optical telescopes *223*
orbital space station *26*
Organization of American
  States *54*
ostrich *183*
ovaries
  human *162–163*
  plant *221*
oven bird nest *198*
ovum 162, *163*
owls *182*
oxygen 28, 158, 170, 209
ozone layer *243*

P

paddle steamers *268, 269*
painting 298, *298–301*
Palladio, Andrea *309*
panda, giant *206*
Pangaea 28
paper sizes *240*
Paris Opera House *318*
Parkes Observatory *8*
partridges *182*
passenger liners 256, *256*
passenger pigeon *205*
peace prizes, Nobel
  363–364
Peary, Robert *117*
pelican *185*
pencil, graphite *282*
penguin, gentoo *185*
penguins *182*
pens *283*
penumbra *17*
Perceval, Spencer *125*
periodic table 228,
  228–229
Persian cats *190*
Peter the Great *139*
Pharos of Alexandria *149*
Philadelphia Story, The
  (movie) *329*
phonograph *249, 297*
photocopiers 295, *295*
photography 286,
  286–287
photosynthesis *207, 221*
phototypesetting *285*
physics 224, 230,
  230–231
  Nobel prizes *357–359*
physiology and medicine
  (Nobel prizes)
  360–362
Picasso, Pablo *298*
pigeons *205, 288*
Pioneer spacecraft *25*

piranha, S. American *178*
plaice *179*
planets 8, 18–19, *19*
  Earth 28–45
plants 207–221,
  207–221
  flowering 214,
    214–216
  and people 212–213,
    212–213
  protists 219, *219*
  trees and shrubs 210,
    217, *217–218*
plates, Earth's 29, 32, 38
  38
platypuses *186*
Pluto 8, *19*
Polar bears 193, *193*
polaroid camera *249*
pole vaulters *336*
pond skater, common *17*
poodle, toy *189*
popes, Roman Catholic
  122, *122–123*
poppy *209*
popular music 320,
  320–322
population, World
  47–48, *47–48*
porcelain *see* pottery and
  porcelain
postal services 288,
  288–289
pottery and porcelain
  304, *304–305*
pouched animals 186,
  187, 197, *197*
Praying Hands (Dürer)
  300
presidents, American 11
  118, *118, 142*
Presley, Elvis *320*
pressure cooker *248*
prickly juniper *216*
prime ministers, British
  119, *119*
printing 284, *284–285*
  Gutenberg's press *248*
  paper sizes *240*
Prodigal Son, The (Rodi
  303
projections, map makin
  42, *42, 44*
prothallus *211*
Protista 219
protons 226, *226*
Proxima Centauri 9
Przewalski's horse *206*
Puccini, Giacomo *318*
Puerto Rico 46
  Trench 34
puff adder *180*

Pulitzer, Joseph 365
  prizes 365, 365–369
pulley 252
pulsars 7, 7
pumas 190, 191
pygmy shrew 196
pyramids of Egypt 149

Q

quasars 6, 6, 7
Queen Elizabeth II 51, 51,
  124

R

rabbits 187
race 48
racism 48
radiation 226, 226
radio telescope 8, 292
radio waves 7
radio and television
  292–293, 292–293
  entertainment
  323–324, 323–324
  see also business
  communications
radiolarians 219
raft, log 257
rail travel 257, 264,
  264–265
rainforest, Amazonian
  210, 212–213, 218
Ramapithecus 150
Reagan, Ronald 118
red shift 12, 21
reflex cameras 287
Reformation, the 122
refraction (of light) 231
relativity 229
Rembrandt van Rijn 298,
  301
Renaissance, the 223,
  298, 299, 302
Renoir, Pierre Auguste
  298
reproductive system,
  human 153, 162,
  162–163
reptiles 180, 180–181
respiratory system 153,
  158–159, 158–159
Rhodes, Colossus of 149
Ring of Fire' (volcanoes)
  32
rivers, longest 35
road transportation
  258–259, 258–263,
  261

robots 232
Rock and Roll stars 322
Rocket, Stephenson's
  264, 264
Rockies, the 29
Rodin, Auguste 303
Rogers, Richard 309
Roman theater 296
Rome ancient 239, 306,
  307
Romulus and Remus 128
Roosevelt, F.D. 118
Rosendahl, Heide 338
rubber 213
rugby 335–336
ruminants see cud-
  chewing animals
Russia see USSR
Russian language 48, 283
Russian Revolution 144
Rutan, Richard 273

S

saber tooth cat 191
Sabre, F-86 (warplane)
  274
Sadat, President Anwer El
  125
Safety (airplane) 276
saguaro cactus 211
Sahara desert 34
sailing ships 268–269
St Bartholomew's Day
  massacre 137
St Paul's Cathedral,
  London 308
salamander, fire 181
salamanders 180
San Andreas fault 29
San Francisco earthquake
  33
Santa Maria (ship) 271
satellites 22–23, 24, 41
Saturn 19, 27
Saturn rocket launcher 22
schooner 269
science and technology
  222–253
  mathematics 236,
  236–241, 238
  technology 242–244,
  242–249
Scotch pine 217
scramble racing 348
Scream, The (Munch) 299
sculpture 302, 302–303
sea horse (fish) 178
sea planes 277
sea travel 254, 266,
  266–271, 270

semaphore 290, 291
sense organs 153,
  160–161, 160–161
sequoia 217
Sequoia National Park,
  California 210, 210
servals 190
'Seven Wonders of the
  World' 149
shaggy ink cap 219
Shakespeare, William
  310, 325, 325
shark's teeth 201
sheep 202
ships 254, 266, 266–271,
  270
shrews 196, 196
Siamese cat 190
signaling, long distance
  290, 290–291
  see also business
  communications;
  radio and television
silicon chip 235
silverfish 176
single-celled animals 219
Sirius (ship) 270
skeleton, the human 152,
  154, 154–155
ski-bob racing 355
ski sports 355
skunk 197
Skylab 27
Sleeping Beauty (ballet)
  319
sloth bears 193
slow worm (lizard) 181
Smilodon (extinct cat)
  191
Smith, Captain John 138
snakes 180
snooker 342
snowflake 251
soccer 335, 348, 348
social sciences 224
Solar system, the 8–9,
  14–19
  the Moon 16–17,
  16–17
  the planets 8, 18–19,
  19
  the Sun 14–15, 14–15
  aurorae 20, 21
Solzhenitsyn, Alexander
  363
Sopwith Camel (airplane)
  274
sorting machine, mail 288
South Africa 89, 107,
  116, 143
South America
  countries of 102

exploration and discovery 117
population growth 47
Soviets, the *see* USSR
space exploration 22–23, 22–27
Spanish Empire 47
Spanish language 48
sparrow *185*
spectacled bears 193
Spectre de la Rose (ballet) *319*
speedway 349, *349*
sperm *162*
spider fossil *170*
spirogyra 219
Spitfire, Supermarine *274*
sport 333–356
sports cars *340*
spotted hyena 196, *196*
spring (season) *20*
Sputnik 1 22, *24*
squirrel, red *187*
Stalin, Joseph *118*
stamps *289*
Standing Woman, Figure of (sculpture) *297*
stars 6–15, *7, 12, 12–15, 14*
States of the Union *108*
steam
   engine *242*
   locomotives 257, 264, *264–265*
   ships *256, 268*
Stephenson, George 264
stereoscopic camera *286*
sternwheeler *269*
stingrays *179*
stomach *164*
Stone Age 296, 302
Stonehenge 223
storms *40*
streetcars, electric 258, *259*
string instruments *314*
submarines 255, *257*
subways *265*
Suez Canal *143*
sugar beets *212*
Sumerian clay tablet *282*
summer *20*
sun animals 219
Sun, the 6, 14–15, *14–15, 18–21*
   aurorae *20, 21*
sunflower *207*
superkart *339*
supertanker *266*
surgery 222
Swahili 49
swallows' nests *199*

Swan Lake (ballet) 319
swans 182
swifts *173, 183*
swimming and diving 350, *350*

T

table tennis 350, *350*
T'ang dynasty *304*
tea-pickers *213*
technology *see* science and technology
telegraphy 290, *290–291*
telephone 249, 281, 291, *294*
telescopes 223, 292
teletext machine *294*
television *see* radio and television
Telstar satellite *24*
tennis 351, *351–352*
tenpins 334
tenrecs *196*
termites 176
terrapins 180
terriers 188
terriers, West highland *189*
Thatcher, Margaret *119*
theater 325, *325–326*
thermodynamics, laws of 231
Thrust Measuring Rig (aircraft) 276, *276*
tides *34*
tigers 190
timber *212*
time zones 43, *43*
'Tin Lizzie' *259*
tire treads *251*
toad, midwife *181*
tonic Sol-Fa *316*
tornado 40
tortoise *173,* 180, *181*
transportation 254–279
   travel by air 272, *272–279, 276*
   travel by rail 264, *264–265*
   travel by road 258–259, *258–263, 261*
   travel by sea 266, *266–271, 270*
transuranium elements 226
tree creeper *184*
trees and shrubs 210, *210, 213,* 217, *217–218*

cutting down of 212–213, *212*
   section through a tree *216*
Trevithick, Richard 264
Triceratops 204
trilobite (fossil) *170*
Triple Entente 50
tuataras (reptiles) 180
tuba *316*
tundra 211
tunnels *245–246*
Tupolev TU-28 (Soviet airplane) *275*
turkeys 182
Turtle (submarine) *255*
turtles 180
Tutu, Archbishop Desmond 364
Tyrannosaurus 204

U

UK (United Kingdom of Great Britain and Northern Ireland) 46, 47, *96–97, 103*
   British Empire 46, *46, 50,* 51
   the Commonwealth 51, *51, 54*
   prime ministers 119, *119*
ultraviolet light *see* UV
umbra *17*
UN (United Nations) 50–51, *50,* 288
   Assembly/Security Council 51
Union of Soviet Socialist Republics *see* USSR
United States (of America) 46, *97–98,* 102
   map *109*
   population growth 47
   presidents 111, 118, *118, 142*
   States of the Union *108*
Universal Postal Union 288
Universe, the 6–27
uranium 226
Uranus *19*
Urdu 49
urinary system, human 152, *152*
USSR (Union of Soviet Socialist Republics) *95–96, 115, 146*
   cosmonauts *24, 147*
   language 48, *283*

republics *107*
Revolution *144*
tsars *135, 139*
UV (Ultraviolet Light)
253

V

Vail, Alfred 290
van Gogh, Vincent *301*
VCR (Video Cassette
Recorder) *292, 297*
Venus 8, *19*
Verdi, Giuseppe 318
Vermeer, Jan 298
vertebrates 170, 174, 178
Victoria, Queen *121*
video camera 297
Video Cassette Recorder
see VCR
videotext 295
Viking longship *267*
Vinland 111
volcanoes 32, *32–33,
36–37*
volleyball 353, *353*
volume 239
Vostock spacecraft *24*
Voyager (aircraft) *273*
Voyager (spacecraft) 27
voyages and disasters
270, *270–271*
voyages, famous *271*
vultures 182

W

Wagner, Richard 318
warplanes *274–275*
wars, major *111*, 112,
112–115
Warsaw Pact, the 54, *54*
Washington, George 111,
118, 140
wasp *177*
water 28, 34, *34–35*
water polo 353, *353*
waterfalls *36–37*
Waterfront, On the
(movie) 329
Watson, James 361
Watt, James 242
wave power *243*
weasel family, the 197,
197
weather 22, 34, 39,
39–41
satellites 22, *41*
WMO 53
weightlifting 354, *354*
weights and measures
238, *238–241*
Wellesley, Arthur *see*
Wellington
Wellington, Duke of *141*
white dwarf stars 7
Whitney, Eli 243
William of Normandy
111
Wimbledon champions
352
windjammer *269*

winter *20*
winter sports 354–356,
354–356
wolves *188, 203*
wombats 186
Wordsworth, William
313
World, the 46–109
gazetteer *55–101*
'Seven Wonders of' *149*
statistics *102–109*
time zones 43, *43*
see also Earth; history
World Wars I and II
50–51, *113–115,
144–145*
Wren, Sir Christopher
306, *308–309*
Wright brothers'
airplanes *144, 272*
writing 282, *282–283*

X

X-rays 7, *155*, 286

Y

yaks 194
Yeager, Jeana *273*
yellow dwarf 14

Z

zero 236, 237
Zeus, Statue of *149*

Acknowledgements

The publishers wish to thank the following for supplying photographs for this book:

Page 24 Novosti; 35 Camera Press; 49 ZEFA; 51 Hulton Picture Company; 110 Mansell Collection; 118 Camera Press; 122 Camera Press; 132 Ancient Art & Architecture Collection; 142 Novosti; 143 Mary Evans Picture Library; 146 Camera Press; 147 Novosti; 148 Camera Press; 151 Camera Press; 184 Camera Press; 210 Camera Press; 213 Camera Press; 223 Camera Press; 234 Camera Press; 259 Toyota; 270 Mary Evans Picture Library; 273 Popperfoto; 278 + 9 Mansell Collection; 284 Camera Press; 290 Mary Evans Picture Library; 293 Hulton Picture Company; 298 Ancient Art & Architecture Collection; 300 Mansell Collection (top), Visual Arts Library (middle); 301 Visual Arts Library; 302 Camera Press; 304 Michael Holford; 308 Camera Press; 309 Mansell Collection (top), Camera Press (bottom); 311 Mansell Collection; 312 Mansell Collection; 318 Camera Press (top), Mansell Collection (bottom); 321 Camera Press; 323 Kobal Collection; 324 Hulton Picture Company; 325 Mary Evans Picture Library (left), Mansell Collection (right); 327 Kobal Collection; 329 Kobal Collection; 330 Kobal Collection; 331 Kobal Collection; 332 Kobal Collection; 333 Camera Press; 334 Camera Press; 335 Camera Press; 336 Camera Press; 338 Camera Press; 347 Camera Press; 348 Camera Press; 349 Camera Press; 351 Camera Press; 352 Camera Press; 357 Hulton Picture Company; 358 Camera Press; 361 Camera Press; 362 Camera Press; 363 Camera Press; 364 Camera Press.

f you've enjoyed INFOPEDIA, you'll love

THE KIDS' WORLD ALMANAC® SERIES

With more than a million copies in print, *The Kids' World Almanac* books are ideal for students ages 8 to 14. Filled with facts, charts and illustrations, these books are an ideal introduction to reference books, research, and the joys of "looking it up."

All books are 288 pages and fully illustrated.

Please send me . . . . .

_____ KIDS' WORLD ALMANAC OF RECORDS & FACTS @ $6.95 ea.   _____

_____ SECOND KIDS' WORLD ALMANAC OF RECORDS & FACTS @ $6.95 ea.   _____

_____ KIDS' WORLD ALMANAC OF ANIMALS & PETS @ $6.95 ea.   _____

_____ KIDS' WORLD ALMANAC OF BASEBALL @ $6.95   _____

_____ KIDS' WORLD ALMANAC OF THE UNITED STATES @ $6.95   _____

Subtotal _____

Plus $1.00 per book shipping _____

Total _____

Name _____

Address _____

City _____ State _____ Zip _____

Please enclose a check or money order payable to PHAROS BOOKS for the total amount and return to: Sales Dept., Pharos Books, 200 Park Avenue, New York, NY 10166.

Prices subject to change. Offer expires 1/1/92.

Why Wait?

Order your 1991 WORLD ALMANAC® AND BOOK OF FACTS today!

Available December 1990

Enjoy the convenience of having the 1991 WORLD ALMANAC AND BOOK OF FACTS delivered to your home. Why wait? Order your WORLD ALMANAC today.